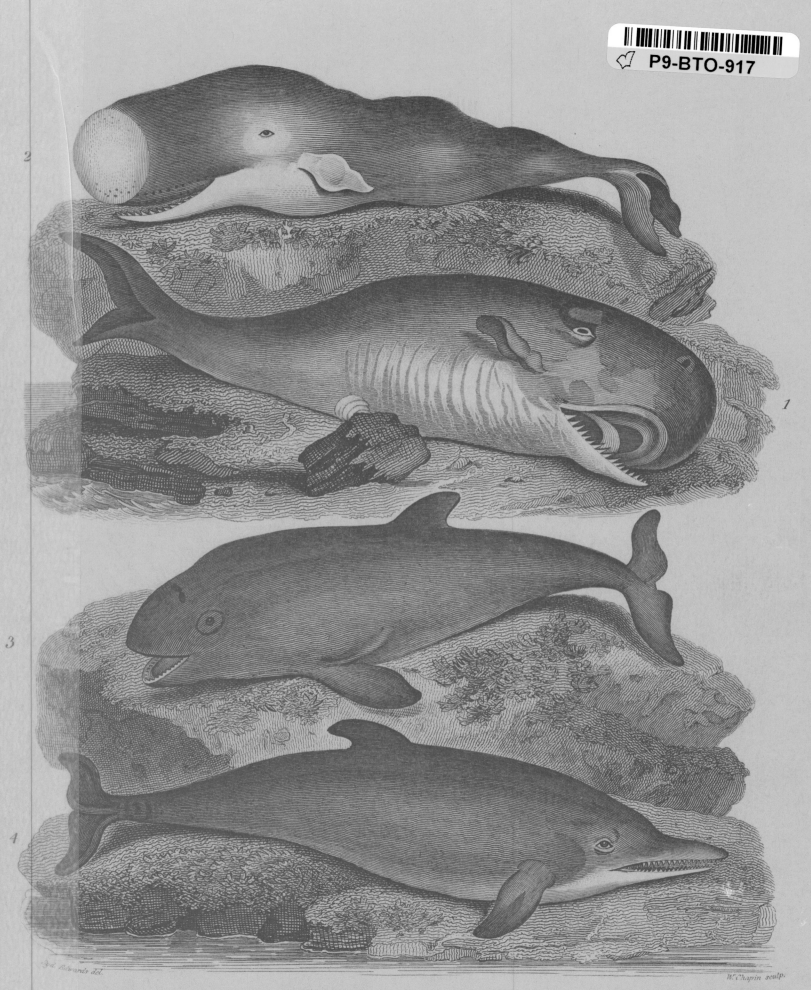

Fd. Edwards del.

W.Chapin sculp.

1.P. Macrocephalus. Blunt headed C. — 2. var P. Gibbosus Shreb. Gibbous C. — 3. D. Phocæna Porpoise. — 4. D.Delphis Dolphin.

THE BOOK OF

WHALES

THE BOOK OF

WHALES

WRITTEN AND ILLUSTRATED BY

RICHARD ELLIS

ALFRED·A·KNOPF NEW YORK
1981

THIS IS A BORZOI BOOK
PUBLISHED BY ALFRED A. KNOPF, INC.

Published in the United States by Alfred A. Knopf, Inc.,
New York, and simultaneously in Canada by Random
House of Canada Limited, Toronto. Distributed by
Random House, Inc., New York.

Library of Congress Cataloging in Publication Data
Ellis, Richard, [date]
   The book of whales.

   Bibliography: p.
   Includes index.
   1. Whales. 2. Whaling. I. Title
QL737.C4E25   599.5   80-7640
ISBN 0-394-50966-8

Manufactured in the United States of America
Published November 18, 1980
Second Printing November 1981

For T.A.

Already we are boldly launched upon the deep; but soon we shall be lost in its unshored, harborless immensities. Ere that come to pass; ere the Pequod's weedy hull rolls side by side with the barnacled hulls of the Leviathan; at the outset it is but well to attend to a matter almost indispensable to a thorough appreciative understanding of the more special leviathanic revelations and allusions of all sorts which are to follow.

It is some systematized exhibition of the whale in his broad genera, that I would now fain put before you. Yet is it no easy task. The classification of the constituents of a chaos, nothing less is here essayed.

HERMAN MELVILLE
Moby-Dick

For all these reasons, then, any way you may look at it, you must needs conclude that the great Leviathan is that one creature in the world which must remain unpainted to the last. True, one portrait may hit the mark much nearer than another, but none can hit it with any very considerable degree of exactness. So there is no earthly way of finding out precisely what the whale really looks like. And the only mode in which you can derive even a tolerable idea of his living contour is by going a whaling yourself; but by so doing, you run no small risk of being eternally stove and sunk by him. Wherefore, it seems to me you had best not be too fastidious in your curiosity touching this Leviathan.

Moby-Dick

CONTENTS

Color illustrations follow page 140.

PREFACE

In its formative stages this book was intended to be a field guide to the whales, dolphins, and porpoises of the world. It was to have contained a few brief paragraphs and an illustration for each species. One could easily have stuffed this book into the pocket of a slicker or taken it aboard ship. If an unknown black and white cetacean appeared in the distance off the ship's bow, one could flip open the book to "small black-and-white porpoises" and, noting the color pattern and behavior of that animal, quickly make the identification. I suppose that it is still possible to use the book in this manner, but the "few brief paragraphs" have metamorphosed into full-scale essays with profuse bibliographic references and footnotes.

As originally written, the book contained all the cetaceans of the world, but the metamorphosis from field guide to comprehensive survey has necessitated yet another change: I have divided the work into two volumes, the first on the whales and the second on the porpoises and dolphins. This separation was made along some obvious and some not so obvious lines. The great baleen whales and the sperm whale are here because there is no question about whether or not they are actually whales, and some of their smaller relatives, such as the pygmy right whale and the pygmy sperm whale, are also included in this volume because whatever else they may be, they are certainly not dolphins. The beaked whales are also included here because they, too, are not dolphins or porpoises. A number of cetaceans that are known in English as "whales" of one sort or another, such as the killer whale or the pilot whale, have not been included in this book, not because I would identify them as dolphins, but rather because they share more of the characteristics of the dolphins than of the whales. English names for cetaceans are most confusing. For this reason I regret my inability to include all the cetaceans in one volume, but to do so would make this book so unwieldy as to nullify the advantages of inclusion.

When I began the research that ultimately led to the illustrations and text of this volume, I innocently assumed that most of the necessary information would be available to the diligent researcher and that it would be only a matter of time and organization before the species accounts and anatomically correct illustrations would take shape. In a few cases this did happen, for there are some species that have been extensively studied, measured, and photographed.

However, most species of cetaceans were not so easy to capture, either literally or figuratively. When you see a bird or a terrestrial mammal, you can often be assured of seeing most of the animal, even if it is flying away or concealed in the underbrush. With whales, however, quite the opposite is true. Even if you are in the right place at the right time—which often involves being on the open sea or in an inhospitable location such as Tierra del Fuego or the Canadian Arctic—the best you can hope to see of a living whale is a small portion of the animal as it swims by. You cannot go to a museum to study the actual shape of the whales, either, because their very size makes it impossible to keep them in collections; therefore, models or drawings are the only sources available to research at this level. There is actually one species of whale that has never been seen alive, its existence being documented only by scattered skeletal remains that have washed ashore on remote beaches. (Since I could not illustrate this animal, photographs of the skull are used in place of the species illustration. The photographs of the beaked whale *Indopacetus pacificus* allow the reader to see virtually all the known evidence of this "unseen" whale.)

Although some of the other beaked whales have been observed in the flesh, these occasions are so infrequent that the discovery of a single specimen is reason enough for the publication of a scientific paper. No sooner had I written the account of Shepherd's beaked whale, an animal long believed to be restricted to New Zealand waters, than one was reported from Península Valdés, Argentina, in 1975. During the following year another specimen was discovered in the Juan Fernández Islands off the coast of Chile.

The status of the world's whales is constantly in a state of flux. No discussion of the great whales would be complete without the history of human predations on them, but this predation has been cyclical and variable, changing according to the dictates of technology, the availability of whales, and various international agreements. At the 1978 meeting of the International Whaling Commission (IWC) in London, the status of the California gray whale was changed from a "protected" stock to a "management" stock, thereby creating the possibility of limited hunting of this previously protected species. New quotas were imposed on the Eskimos for the taking of bowhead whales—which quotas, they said, they intend to ignore. Because no method has been found to estimate accurately the world population of sperm whales, no quotas were set at all. At the 1979 IWC meeting, in a stunning reversal of traditional policy, all pelagic (open-ocean) whaling was banned, effectively protecting the sperm whale, since this was the species hunted by the great Soviet and Japanese fleets. Now only the minke whale can be hunted by these fleets, which will hunt them in the Antarctic. Between the writing and the actual publication of this book, the 1980 IWC meeting will be held, but unless we intend to restrain publication until there are no more whales—or no more IWC—some cutoff date has to be selected. This book, therefore, is not a "completed" work, but rather a way station along the road to a better and fuller understanding of cetaceans. It is the nature of the book, as it is the nature of its subjects, to present as many questions as answers.

Living in New York City, I am regularly asked why, as a painter and student of whales, sharks, and other marine life, I do not reside in a more suitable maritime environment, such as Florida, California, Hawaii, or even New Bedford. I do travel in search of my subjects, but I live here because of the research facilities available in New York. In the library of the American Museum of Natural History, one of the world's great institutions of its kind, I can obtain virtually any scientific paper, from any year, from any country. When I wanted to see Titian Peale's original drawings of cetaceans, published in Philadelphia in 1858, all I had to do was fill out the call slip with the appropriate number. I needed a 1725 document that was critical to the (still unresolved) problem of the "scrag whale" on the coast of New England, and it was quickly before me. The same is true for papers published in Buenos Aires in 1911, New Zealand in 1940, Oslo in 1960, or Tokyo in 1978. Nothing is more frustrating to a researcher than the inability to obtain a given paper or to verify a certain citation. Conversely, one of the great pleasures of bibliographic research is knowing that almost everything you require is at hand and can be made available in the time it takes to check the card catalogue and fill out the call slip.

I have, on occasion, traveled afield to look for whales, but by and large the libraries have been my field trips, my laboratories, my research vessels. I am more than grateful to the people who were so helpful to me in these institutions; without them I would have wandered through the stacks darkly. In the American Museum, I was guided by Sandy Jones, Mildred Bobrovich, and Pam Haas; at the New Bedford Whaling Museum, Richard C. Kugler opened its files to me; and at the National Audubon Society, I was ably assisted by librarians Michelle Epstein and Nancy Turell.

Nancy died before the book was completed, and I dedicate the research aspect of this work to her memory. At *Audubon* magazine Les Line gave me the encouragement to research and produce the portfolio of whale paintings that appeared in the January 1975 issue and essentially marked the beginning of my career as a whale painter. Anita Finlayson and David Hill of the Rare Animal Relief Effort provided much in the way of assistance and materials.

I cannot begin to thank all those others who provided much-needed help, guidance, and advice, but some people extended themselves far beyond my expectations, and I want to single them out: William Aron of the National Oceanic and Atmospheric Administration (NOAA), Washington, D.C.; Ed Asper of Sea World, Orlando; Peter Beamish of Ocean Contact, Newfoundland; David and Melba Caldwell of the University of Florida at Saint Augustine; William C. Cummings of Oceanographic Consultants, San Diego; Edwin J. Gould, former Deputy Director of the U.S. Delegation to the IWC; Ashbel Green and Nancy Clements at Knopf; J. H. W. Hain of the Sea Education Association, Woods Hole; C. Scott Johnson, Don Ljungblad, and F. G. Wood of the Naval Oceans Systems Center, San Diego; David A. Henderson of California State University at Northridge; Age Jonsgard of the University of Oslo; William C. Kardash and Kate Bouvé of the Center for Environmental Education; John McCosker of the Steinhart Aquarium, San Francisco; James Mead and Charles Potter of the Smithsonian Institution; Daniel Odell of the University of Miami; Hideo Omura and Masaharu Nishiwaki of the Whales Research Institute, Tokyo; Roger Payne of the New York Zoological Society; William F. Perrin of the National Marine Fisheries Service (NMFS), La Jolla; Karen W. Pryor; Dale W. Rice of the NMFS, Seattle; Graham J. B. Ross of the Port Elizabeth Museum, South Africa; George Ruggieri of the New York Aquarium, Coney Island; David Sergeant of the Arctic Biological Station, Quebec; Leighton R. Taylor of the Waikiki Aquarium, University of Hawaii; Einar Vangstein, International Whaling Statistics, Sandefjord, Norway; William A. Watkins and William E. Schevill of the Woods Hole Oceanographic Institution; Victor B. Scheffer; Craig Van Note of the Monitor Consortium, Washington, D.C.; and Bernd and Melany Würsig of the University of California at Santa Cruz.

During my actual field trips I was aided and abetted by Juan Bremer and Mario Rueda at Scammon's and Guerrero Negro Lagoons in Baja California, Mexico; by Jim Hudnall, Sylvia Earle, Al Giddings, and Chuck

Nicklin at Maui; by Milt Shedd, Frank Todd, Frank Powell, and Bill Evans at Sea World, San Diego; and in Quebec by T. Walker Lloyd, Russ Kinne, and Elver Lassen. In Newfoundland I worked with Peter Beamish and the intrepid staff of "Ocean Contact," and Ken Balcomb was kind enough to introduce me to the famous "J-pod" of killer whales in Puget Sound. Without the competence of Ricardo Mandojana, I would have been completely lost in the topographic and linguistic wilds of Patagonia. I am also deeply indebted to the whales, without whom none of this would have been possible—or necessary. I hope that I have served them well.

Richard Ellis
New York, New York
January 1980

GLOSSARY

ALBINISM. Absence of pigmentation in animals that are normally pigmented.

ALLOPATRIC. Having separate and mutually exclusive areas of geographical distribution. *See also* SYMPATRIC.

AMPHIPOD. An order of small crustaceans that are laterally compressed. Includes whale food, *Ampelisca,* and whale lice, *Cyamus.*

ANTARCTIC CONVERGENCE. The circumpolar line of demarcation in the Southern Hemisphere that marks the meeting of the cold Antarctic waters with the warmer, more northerly currents. Also known as the Polar Front.

BALEEN. The fibrous plates attached to the upper jaw of certain whales and used to filter small food organisms from the water. Also known as WHALEBONE or BONE.

BARNACLE. One of an order (Cirripedia) of crustaceans that are enclosed in a calcareous shell. Of two types: acorn and stalked barnacles.

BARREL. A unit of measurement for whale oil, equaling approximately 35 gallons.

BENTHIC. Pertaining to the sea bottom or to organisms that live on the sea bottom.

BRIT. Minute marine organisms, such as crustaceans of the genus *Calanus.* A major food source for certain species of whalebone whales.

CAUDAL FIN. The tail fin of a marine vertebrate. Applicable to cetaceans as well as fishes.

CAUDAL KEEL. The ridges on the top and bottom of the tail stock. Vertical in cross section in cetaceans; horizontal in some sharks and fishes.

CEPHALIC. Pertaining to the head.

CETACEAN. A marine mammal of the order Cetacea, which includes whales, dolphins, and porpoises.

CLASSIFICATION. The systematic grouping of organisms into categories based on shared characteristics or traits; taxonomy.

CONSPECIFIC. Of the same species. Usually employed when two species that were previously differentiated are found to be the same.

COPEPOD. Minute, shrimplike crustaceans of the order Copepoda, occurring in high concentrations near the surface.

CRUSTACEAN. Of the class Crustacea. Breathes through gills, or branchiae, and has a body commonly covered by a hard shell. Includes barnacles, crabs, shrimps, lobsters.

DECAPOD. Of the order (Decapoda) of crustaceans that includes shrimps, lobsters, crabs. Of crustaceans, with 5 pairs of legs; of cephalopods, with 10 arms.

DEEP SCATTERING LAYER (DSL). Stratified populations of organisms in most oceanic waters that scatter sound. Generally found during the day at depths of 200 to 800 meters and may be found in layers 50 to 200 thick.

DIATOM. Any of various minute, one-celled or colonial algae of the class Bacillariophyceae, often parasitic on the skin of cetaceans.

DOLPHIN. *See* PORPOISE. (Also refers to the fish known as *Coryphaena hippurus.*)

DORSAL. Of, toward, on, in, or near the back.

DORSAL FIN. The back fin in marine vertebrates. Present in most cetaceans and fishes.

ECHOLOCATION. To orient or navigate by means of reflected sounds; to range by acoustical echo analysis. Used by bats and odontocete cetaceans.

EUPHAUSIID. Of an order of shrimplike crustaceans, widely distributed in oceanic waters. The Antarctic species *Euphausia superba* forms the principal food of many of the baleen whales. *See* KRILL.

FALCATE. Curved and tapering; sickle-shaped.

FAMILY. A taxonomic category ranking below an order and above a genus.

FATHOM. The common unit of depth in the English system. Equals 6 feet (1.83 meters).

FLENSE. To strip the blubber from a dead whale. Instruments used in this activity are known as "blubber hooks" or "flensing knives."

FLIPPERS. The pectoral limbs or forelimbs of marine mammals, including cetaceans and pinnipeds.

FLUKES. The horizontally oriented tail fin of cetaceans, containing no skeletal structure.

FUSIFORM. Spindle-shaped; tapering gradually at both ends.

GENUS. A group of closely related species. In taxonomy, a category ranking below a family and above a species. In scientific nomenclature it is followed by the name of the species to form the binomial.

KNOT. A speed unit of 1 nautical mile (6,076.12 feet) per hour. (Note: "Knots per hour" is a meaningless expression, because knots refer to speed, not distance.)

KRILL. Norwegian term, now in general use for euphausiids. Whale food.

LOB-TAILING. The behavior in cetaceans that involves raising the tail flukes out of the water and slapping them on the surface.

MAMMAL. A vertebrate animal characterized by self-regulatory body temperature (warm-bloodedness), hair, and milk-producing mammary glands in the females.

MANDIBLE. The jaw; in cetaceans, the lower jaw or jawbone.

MAXILLA. The upper jaw.

MAXILLARY. Pertaining to the upper jaw; or, the bones of the upper jaw.

MELON. The bulbous forehead of certain odontocete cetaceans (not including the sperm whale and pygmy sperm whale), which contains oil and is thought to be involved in sound production.

METER. The basic unit of length in the metric system. Equals 3.2804 feet.

MORPHOLOGY. The structure and form of an organism. Distinct from a consideration of function.

MYSTICETI. The order of baleen or whalebone whales. From the Greek *mystax* ("moustache") and *cetus* ("whale").

NEKTON. Pelagic animals that are active swimmers, such as most of the adult squids, the fishes, and the marine mammals.

NERITIC. Pertaining to the waters of a shoreline.

ODONTOCETI. Toothed whales. From the Greek *odous* ("tooth") and *cetus* ("whale").

ONTOGENY. The history of the development of an individual organism.

ORDER. A group of closely allied organisms. Ranks between a family and a class.

OSTEOLOGY. That part of zoology dealing with the structure, nature, and development of bones. Therefore, OSTEOLOGICAL: pertaining to bone structure and development.

PEDUNCLE. A stalk. In cetaceans, the tail stock between the anus and the insertion of the flukes.

PELAGIC. Of, pertaining to, or living in open oceans, rather than in waters adjacent to land or in inland waters.

PLANKTON. The passively drifting or weak-swimming organisms in the upper layers of the sea.

PORPOISE. *See* DOLPHIN.

PREMAXILLARY. Anterior to (in front of) the upper jaw. Most cetaceans have elongated premaxillary bones, which account for the elongated profile.

PROGNATHOUS. Having jaws that project forward to a considerable degree.

RORQUAL. Any of several baleen whales of the genus *Balaenoptera* having numerous longitudinal grooves on the throat.

ROSTRUM. A beak or beaklike projection. In cetaceans, the upper jaw.

SPECIES. 1. The fundamental category of taxonomic classification, ranking after a genus and defining a group of interbreeding individuals. 2. An organism belonging to such a category. Represented in binomial nomenclature by the epithet following the genus name.

SPY-HOPPING. The behavior in cetaceans that involves raising the head vertically out of the water, presumably to enable the animal to see above the surface.

STENOPHAGOUS. Feeding on a single kind or limited range of food.

SYMPATRIC. Occupying the same or overlapping geographical areas without interbreeding. *See also* ALLOPATRIC.

SYNONYMY. 1. The quality of being synonymous. 2. A chronological list or record of the scientific names that have been applied to a species and its subdivisions.

SYNONYM. A taxonomic name of an organism that is equivalent to or has been superseded by another designation.

TAXONOMY. 1. The science, laws, or principles of classification. 2. The theory, principles, and process of classifying organisms in established order.

TRY WORKS. The iron pots set in brickwork aboard whaling ships. The process of boiling down the blubber was known as "trying out."

TYPE SPECIMEN. The actual specimen described as the original of a new genus or species.

VENTRAL. Pertaining to or situated on or close to the belly; abdominal; on the lower surface of the body.

VENTRAL PLEATS. The longitudinal grooves on the undersurface of certain species of baleen whales.

THE BOOK OF

WHALES

INTRODUCTION

In not a single country of the globe where shore whaling is being carried on today are there intelligent laws to insure for the future an industry which is yielding millions of dollars every year, or to save from extermination the animals which, of all others on the land or in the sea, have taken the most important place in the history of the world.

> Roy Chapman Andrews
> *Whale Hunting with Gun and Camera*

The earliest known cetaceans are the archaeocetes from the Eocene period, some fifty million years ago. These porpoise-sized creatures, known as *Prozeuglodon,* had well-developed teeth, and their nostrils were located about halfway between the tip of the snout and their present location on top of the head. By the upper Eocene, ten million years later, the ancestral whales had truly begun their remarkable specialization, for we now find the 70-foot *Basilosaurus,* also known as *Zeuglodon.* From its fossilized skeletal remains, paleontologists have concluded that *Basilosaurus* looked more like a sea serpent than a whale, for it was long and slim and had a relatively small skull. The archaeocetes gave rise to the squalodonts, so named for their sharklike teeth, which are believed to be ancestral to the porpoises, such as *Phocoena.* The two living forms of whales, mysticetes and odontocetes, developed from the early archaeocetes, but the derivation of the earlier whales is completely unknown. At some point the ancestors of these primitive cetaceans were transitional between terrestrial and marine mammals—perhaps like the seals of today—but the record shows only fully aquatic protocetaceans and none of the intermediate forms. It is as if some primitive land mammal suddenly leaped into the sea and immediately produced the profound modifications necessary for an aquatic existence.

All living cetaceans are divided into two general groups: the odontocetes (toothed whales) and the mysticetes (baleen whales). The dentition of odontocetes is widely varied. Some species of dolphins have over 200 teeth; killer whales and other large dolphins* have large, interlocking, peglike teeth; and one species, the narwhal, has only 1 tooth, a long spiral tusk that may reach a length of 8 feet. (Only the male narwhal has this tusk; females have no visible teeth at all.) In the beaked whales of the genera *Mesoplodon, Ziphius,* and *Hyperoodon,* only the males have erupted teeth, and most of them have only two. Some of these teeth are most peculiar in shape, and in the strap-toothed whale, *Mesoplodon layardii,* the teeth curve up over the upper jaw until the animal is barely able to open its mouth. Female beaked whales have no visible teeth at all. The sperm whale and its little cousins, the pygmy and dwarf sperm whales, have teeth only in the undershot lower jaw, and the teeth of a big bull sperm whale may be 10 inches long. (These are the teeth that were made into scrimshaw.)

With the exception of the pygmy right whale, which does not get much longer than 20 feet, the baleen whales are large creatures that feed on relatively small organisms. Hanging from the upper jaw in all mysticetes is a series of horny plates that overlap and are fringed on the inner margin with hairlike bristles. Those species with long baleen, such as the bowhead whale (in which the largest plates may be 14 feet in length), feed by slowly swimming with their mouths open through swarms of food organisms, taking in huge mouthfuls, and then expelling the water by raising their huge tongues. The rorquals, which are characterized by multiple throat grooves, gulp mouthfuls

*The semantic problem concerning the usage of the terms "porpoise" and "dolphin" will not be resolved here, because there does not seem to be a solution. Some animals are known unequivocally as porpoises, and others are known only as dolphins, but there are a number of species for which either appellation is acceptable. Size is not a criterion; neither is the presence or absence of a beak. The controversy is an excellent justification for the continuing use of scientific nomenclature.

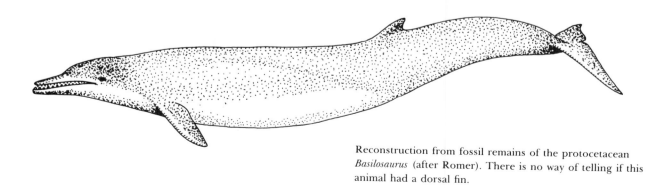

Reconstruction from fossil remains of the protocetacean *Basilosaurus* (after Romer). There is no way of telling if this animal had a dorsal fin.

of food and water and then force the water out through the baleen plates. The throat grooves expand when the whale ingests its watery meal and contract when the water is expelled. Observations of rorquals feeding have shown that theirs is a very energetic operation, with much splashing and rolling in the water. One baleen whale, the gray, is a bottom feeder, sucking up quantities of amphipod crustaceans from the bottom and forcing out the muddy water through its short, coarse baleen plates. Most species of baleen whales are migratory and feed primarily in specific areas, only at a given time of the year. The blue, fin, sei, and humpback feed in the high northern and southern latitudes during the summer season and move off the feeding grounds to breed and deliver their young. The gray whale feeds for approximately four months in the area of the Bering Sea and then makes a five-thousand-mile migration to the protected lagoons of Baja California, Mexico, the longest such journey of any mammal.

All cetaceans are carnivorous, though only one, the killer whale, regularly eats warm-blooded animals such as porpoises, seals, penguins, and even larger whales. The other species eat animal food, ranging in size from small amphipods and euphausiids through various fishes and invertebrates, up to the giant squid, the occasional food of the sperm whale. Many species of cetaceans are specialized feeders, preferring one type of food. The blue whale eats almost nothing but krill, *Euphausia superba;* pilot whales in certain areas eat only the squid *Illex illecebrosus;* but other cetaceans are less selective and will consume whatever food is available. There are no vegetarian cetaceans.

Every living whale is classified according to the presence of teeth or baleen. The largest group is the odontocetes, or toothed whales, which includes all the porpoises and dolphins, the killer whale, the sperm whale, and the pygmy sperm whales. A much smaller group is the mysticetes, the whalebone or baleen whales, composed of only five genera: the rorquals, the gray whale, the humpback, the right whales, and the pygmy right whale. There is no accepted sequence for the classification of cetaceans, nor is there total agreement on the names or status of all the species. I have chosen to follow the 1977 *List of the Marine Mammals of the World* by D. W. Rice for sequence and nomenclature, with some variations. Those animals marked with an asterisk are included in this volume.

ORDER MYSTICETI (BALEEN WHALES)

Family Eschrichtiidae
Genus Eschrichtius
Eschrichtius robustus (Gray whale)

Family Balaenopteridae
Genus Balaenoptera
Balaenoptera acutorostrata (Minke whale)
Balaenoptera edeni (Bryde's whale)
Balaenoptera borealis (Sei whale)
Balaenoptera physalus (Fin whale)
Balaenoptera musculus (Blue whale)
Genus Megaptera
Megaptera novaeangliae (Humpback whale)

Family Balaenidae
Genus Balaena
Balaena glacialis (Right whale; black right whale)
Balaena mysticetus (Bowhead whale; Greenland right whale)
Genus Caperea
Caperea marginata (Pygmy right whale)

ORDER ODONTOCETI (TOOTHED WHALES)

Family Platanistidae
Genus Inia
Inia geoffrensis (Bouto; Amazon dolphin)
Genus Lipotes
Lipotes vexillifer (Whitefin dolphin; Chinese lake dolphin)

Genus Pontoporia
Pontoporia blainvillei (Franciscana; La Plata dolphin)
Genus Platanista
Platanista gangetica (Ganges River dolphin; susu)
Platanista indi (Indus River dolphin; susu)

Family Delphinidae
Genus Steno
Steno bredanensis (Rough-toothed dolphin)
Genus Sousa
Sousa chinensis (Indo-Pacific humpbacked dolphin)
Sousa teuszii (Atlantic humpbacked dolphin)
Genus Sotalia
Sotalia fluviatilis (Tucuxi)
Genus Tursiops
Tursiops truncatus (Bottlenose dolphin)
Genus Stenella
Stenella longirostris (Spinner dolphin)
Stenella clymene (Short-snouted spinner dolphin)†
Stenella attenuata (Pacific spotted dolphin)
Stenella plagiodon (Atlantic spotted dolphin)
Stenella coeruleoalba (Striped dolphin)
Genus Delphinus
Delphinus delphis (Common dolphin; saddleback dolphin)

†This species is not included in Rice's list, since it was identified and described only after Rice's publication appeared. See Perrin et al. 1977.

Genus Lagenodelphis
Lagenodelphis hosei (Fraser's dolphin; Sarawak dolphin)
Genus Lagenorhynchus
Lagenorhynchus albirostris (Whitebeak dolphin)
Lagenorhynchus acutus (Atlantic white-sided dolphin)
Lagenorhynchus obliquidens (Pacific white-sided dolphin)
Lagenorhynchus obscurus (Dusky dolphin)
Lagenorhynchus australis (Peale's dolphin)
Lagenorhynchus cruciger (Hourglass dolphin)
Genus Cephalorhynchus
Cephalorhynchus commersonii (Commerson's dolphin)
Cephalorhynchus eutropia (Black dolphin)
Cephalorhynchus heavisidii (Heaviside's dolphin)
Cephalorhynchus hectori (Little pied dolphin)
Genus Lissodelphis
Lissodelphis peronii (Southern right whale dolphin)
Lissodelphis borealis (Northern right whale dolphin)
Genus Grampus
Grampus griseus (Risso's dolphin; gray grampus)
Genus Peponocephala
Peponocephala electra (Melon-headed whale)
Genus Feresa
Feresa attenuata (Pygmy killer whale)
Genus Pseudorca
Pseudorca crassidens (False killer whale)
Genus Globicephala
Globicephala melaena (Longfin pilot whale)
Globicephala macrorhynchus (Shortfin pilot whale)
Genus Orcinus
Orcinus orca (Killer whale)
Genus Orcaella
Orcaella brevirostris (Irawaddy River dolphin)
Genus Phocoena
Phocoena phocoena (Harbor porpoise)
Phocoena sinus (Vaquita, Gulf of California porpoise)
Phocoena dioptrica (Spectacled porpoise)
Phocoena spinipinnis (Burmeister's porpoise; black porpoise)
Genus Neophocoena
Neophocaena phocaenoides (Finless porpoise)
Genus Phocoenoides
Phocoenoides dallii (Dall porpoise)

Family Monodontidae
Genus Delphinapterus
**Delphinapterus leucas* (White whale; beluga)

Genus Monodon
**Monodon monoceros* (Narwhal)

Family Physeteridae
Genus Physeter
**Physeter macrocephalus* (Sperm whale)
Genus Kogia
*Kogia breviceps (Pygmy sperm whale)
*Kogia simus (Dwarf sperm whale)

Family Ziphiidae
Genus Berardius
**Berardius arnuxii* (Southern giant bottlenose whale)
**Berardius bairdii* (Baird's beaked whale)
Genus Ziphius
**Ziphius cavirostris* (Goosebeak whale; Cuvier's beaked whale)
Genus Tasmacetus
**Tasmacetus shepherdi* (Shepherd's beaked whale; Tasman whale)
Genus Indopacetus
**Indopacetus pacificus* (Indo-Pacific beaked whale; Longman's beaked whale)
Genus Hyperoodon
**Hyperoodon ampullatus* (North Atlantic bottlenose whale)
**Hyperoodon planifrons* (Southern bottlenose whale; flathead whale)
Genus Mesoplodon
**Mesoplodon hectori* (Hector's beaked whale)
*Mesoplodon mirus (True's beaked whale)
**Mesoplodon europaeus* (Gulf Stream beaked whale; Antillean beaked whale; Gervais' beaked whale)
**Mesoplodon ginkgodens* (Ginkgo-toothed whale)
*Mesoplodon grayi (Scamperdown whale; Gray's beaked whale)
**Mesoplodon carlhubbsi* (Arch-beaked whale; Hubbs' beaked whale)
**Mesoplodon bowdoini* (Deep-crested whale; Andrews' beaked whale)
**Mesoplodon stejnegeri* (Saber-toothed whale)
**Mesoplodon bidens* (Sowerby's beaked whale; North Sea beaked whale)
**Mesoplodon layardii* (Strap-toothed whale; Layard's beaked whale)
**Mesoplodon densirostris* (Dense-beaked whale; Blainville's beaked whale)

Although it is not always possible to make a clear distinction between porpoises and dolphins, some species are now and have always been known as whales. All the filter feeders, or baleen whales, are included in this category, as are the sperm whale and its small relatives, the pygmy and the dwarf sperm whales. The two members of the family Monodon-

tidae, the beluga and the narwhal, are certainly not dolphins, nor are the various species of beaked whales. There may be some confusion in the exclusion of some species whose common name includes the word *whale*—such as the pilot whale, killer whale, or melon-headed whale—but these animals are probably closer in their affinities to the dolphins. It might be said that calling an animal a whale does not necessarily make it one.

Cetaceans are found in all the oceans of the world, from deep within the polar ice to the tropics. There are freshwater dolphins, restricted to certain rivers; and one species, the whitefin dolphin, is found only in Tung Ting Lake and its adjacent waters in China. The killer whale is probably the most widely distributed of all cetaceans, found in polar, temperate, and tropical oceans all over the world. Many species are migratory, moving from one area to another in clearly defined routes, whereas in other species the movements and distribution are poorly known. In recent years certain species have turned up in unexpected locations; for example, Fraser's dolphin, *Lagenodelphis hosei,* which was previously known only from a skeleton found on a beach in Borneo, has now appeared in the eastern tropical Pacific, off Taiwan, off Australia, and in the Caribbean.

There is even the possibility of still-undiscovered cetaceans. Some of the beaked whales are known only from single skeletons, and there may be *Mesoplodons* whose remains have not yet washed ashore and been discovered by knowledgeable cetologists. On a remote beach in Tierra del Fuego, R. N. P. Goodall (1978) discovered the collected remains of some fourteen species of cetaceans and added substantially to our knowledge of the range, habits, and osteology of many of them. In 1964, during a whale-marking and observation cruise off the coast of Chile, a number of cetologists saw and photographed many of the expected species, including blue, fin, sei, sperm, and smaller cetaceans. (As whalers will attest, the west coast of South America is a particularly productive area for their efforts.) On November 24 and 27, however, "there were eight sightings . . . of small whales which we could not identify" (Clarke et al. 1978). The investigators chased and photographed these odontocete, single-blowhole, beakless whales, which had light-colored heads and dark bodies, were in a school of fifteen to twenty animals, and were about 20 feet (6.0 meters) long. (Only Risso's dolphin, *Grampus griseus,* fits this general description, but it is not known to exceed a length of 13 feet.) To demonstrate the exciting state of basic cetological research, I quote the observer's concluding paragraph in full:

We can only conclude that these whales seen off Chile in 1964 may be a new species, possibly of the genus *Pseudorca* or *Grampus.* It is clearly important to obtain specimens as soon as opportunity affords. The animal agrees well with the "undescribed whale" reported and figured by Wilson (1905, p. 472; 1907, p. 4 and Whales Plate I) as 20–30 feet long, black above but with some white around the mouth or chin, and characterized by a high dorsal fin "erect, pointed and sabre-shaped"; several were seen in the Ross Sea during the British National Antarctic Expedition (1901–1904), but they have never been reported since.

In 1967 a sport-fishing boat captain saw eighteen to twenty small cetaceans near the island of Tobago in the northeastern Caribbean. He described them in this way: "The heads back to the dorsal fin and abdomens were white, and the backs brownish gray. On the larger ones, the dorsal fin was close to ca. 0.6m (2 feet) high and hooked slightly backward" (Erdman et al. 1973). These whales, which were about 16 to 18 feet (4.9 to 5.5 meters) long, might very well be the same kind of mysterious animal observed by Clarke off Chile.

Some species exist in uncountable numbers, roaming the open oceans far offshore, but others, closer to human habitation, shipping, and industry, are all too easily counted—and killed. The California gray whale, which was known in historical times from the western Pacific and the eastern Atlantic, exists now as a relict population of some 15,000 animals that pass close to the shoreline of western North America. The Indus River susu, *Platanista indi,* another primitive species, is probably the most endangered of all cetaceans, having been reduced to some five hundred-odd animals in the Indus River while hunting continues.

The cetaceans are perhaps the most highly specialized of all mammals. They are more or less fishlike in shape and, like the fishes, have a caudal fin used for propulsion and pectoral fins used for steering. The caudal fin of a cetacean, commonly known as the flukes, functions in an up-and-down movement, whereas the fishes, whose tails lie in the vertical plane, use a side-to-side motion. (In defining the whale, Melville wrote that it "is a spouting fish with a horizontal tail.") Most cetaceans have a dorsal fin, which is believed to help stabilize the animal in the water. Neither the caudal fin nor the dorsal fin has any bony internal support structure, but both are composed solely of connective tissue. Although some species have a number of hairs on the head, for the most part the mammalian hair in cetaceans has been replaced in function by a layer of fat or blubber, which serves to insulate the animal against the cold of its warmth-absorbing habitat. Like all other mammals, whales and dolphins give birth to live young and nurse them by means of mammary glands. They are warm-blooded; that is, they maintain a constant body temperature, regardless of ambient water conditions. Even though the ancients confused cetaceans with fishes, one further difference separates them unequivocally: all whales breathe air and must do so regularly. For fishes the life-sustaining oxygen is extracted from the water by means of gills.

The smallest whales (to use the term in a general and inclusive sense) are 5 to 6 feet in length and weigh perhaps 85 pounds. (Because of individual and geographic variations, records for the smallest mature specimens are rarely kept; nevertheless, the common porpoise, *Phocoena phocoena,* and the Franciscana, *Pontoporia blainvillei,* are usually considered to be the smallest of all cetaceans.) The largest of all whales are the blue whales, long considered the largest animals ever to have lived on earth; they can reach a length of 100 feet and a weight of 150 tons.* The largest cetacean, therefore, is over 3,500 times heavier than the smallest. The great whales have reached their colossal proportions because the restraints of gravity do not apply to them as they do to other vertebrates. They are supported not by legs, but by the buoyancy of water, and because they are not bound to the land or by the structural limitations of bone, they have become "the ultimate extreme of giantism in the evolution of mammals" (Colbert 1955).

Whales cannot breathe through their mouths, but they do feed and swallow underwater, so they must be able to open their mouths without having water enter the trachea and then the lungs. Most species of cetaceans have a single breathing orifice located on the top of the head; this facilitates breathing while the greater part of the animal remains submerged. (The baleen whales have a bipartite blowhole, and the sperm whale, *Physeter,* and the pygmy sperm whale, *Kogia,* have a single blowhole located at the anterior end of the snout.) In all other species the single blowhole is located above the eyes and is accompanied by a series of powerful muscles that tightly close the opening when the animal dives.

In addition to the structural adaptations to the aquatic habitat, whales have concurrently developed sensory capabilities that are well suited to this environment. The nature of water makes for poor visibility, and vision, therefore, is considered only a short-range sensory receptor in marine mammals. (From the position of the eyes it is assumed also that many species do not have binocular vision; the sperm whale, for example, probably cannot see at all in front of its nose.) Water is an excellent conductor of sound, and the speed of sound in water is approximately five times greater than in air. Thus, it is to be expected that hearing would be the dominant sense in whales. All species produce sounds of one sort or another, and many odontocetes rely on echoes for food-finding, navigation, and communication—their auditory system is very highly developed. The external ear of a cetacean is visible only as a small opening behind the eye. This opening leads to the auditory canal (meatus), which transmits sound to the middle ear (tympanic cavity) and thence to the inner ear, where the sounds are transmitted to the brain. (Baleen whales have a hard, waxy plug that conducts sound in the auditory canal, and its annual laminations allow accurate estimates of the age of these whales.) Because sound is so important to those species that echolocate, they must be able to use it effectively, and they have developed remarkably efficient directional hearing capabilities. The ear opening itself is not an effective sound collector, and it is believed that porpoises—at least *Tursiops,* on which most experimentation has been conducted—can hear through the lower jaw, which has a pocket of sound-conducting fat connected to the inner ear. Each side of the jaw receives and transmits separate auditory signals, resulting in precise directional hearing.

Sound reception in mysticete whales is poorly understood, but it has been demonstrated that the ear plug is a good conductor of sound. Too, the low-frequency sounds that they emit travel much farther in water than the high-frequency clicks and whistles common to the odontocetes. The low moaning calls of the baleen whales may be used for long-range communication. Other senses of taste, smell, touch, and so on are known to exist in varying degrees in certain cetaceans, but the definitive study on these ancillary senses has yet to be done.

The lungs of whales are not particularly large. Their ability to remain underwater for extended lengths of time and to dive deeply is a function of efficient oxygen utilization more than of oxygen quantity. The muscles of whales are rich in myoglobin, an oxygen-bonding pigment that accounts for the almost black color of the meat in some species, but, more significantly, allows for a much higher oxygen accumulation

---

*The title of "largest animal ever to have lived" may be disputed. In a recent article Ostrom (1978) discussed a dinosaur, discovered in Colorado and nicknamed "supersaurus," that seems to be considerably larger than any previously known species. If it proves to be as large as it seems from the bones that have been unearthed, the dinosaur may have measured over 100 feet long and weighed over 100 tons.

in the muscle tissue. Whales also renew 85–90 percent of the contents of their lungs with each breath, as compared to a 10–15 percent turnover for humans (Slijper 1962).

Under normal conditions most cetaceans breathe regularly at the surface, submerging between breaths. When feeding, mating, escaping from predators, or acting under some form of stress, cetaceans can remain below the surface for extended periods of time, and some of them can dive to extraordinary depths. Shallow-water species, like freshwater dolphins, obviously never have the opportunity to dive very deeply, but some of the odontocetes are the deep-diving champions of the mammalian world. A bottlenose dolphin was trained to dive to 1,000 feet (300 meters) and a pilot whale to 1,654 feet (500 meters);* and sperm whales have been found entangled in telegraph cables at depths in excess of 3,000 feet (1,000 meters). Bottlenose dolphins can remain submerged for seven minutes and sperm whales for ninety; and some of the bottlenose whales have also been known to remain submerged for close to two hours.

During deep dives certain anatomical adjustments are made, including the collapse of the thoracic cavity, which reduces the lung volume as the pressure increases, and a significant slowing down of the heartbeat, which means that the oxygen is not used up as rapidly. Whales are also able to shut down the nonessential circulation of blood to those areas where it is not needed and to rely on the oxygen retained in the myoglobin of the muscles. Human divers are susceptible to the bends, which results when nitrogen bubbles in the bloodstream are not allowed to return to solution and block blood vessels. However, this condition comes from breathing compressed air; and since the air that the whale takes into its lungs before a dive compresses and expands as a function of the depth of the dive, there is no problem of nitrogen bubbles. Prior to deep dives Tuffy was observed to hyperventilate, and at the conclusion of their long dives sperm whales lie at the surface and pant, taking approximately one short breath for every minute spent below.

In most animals breathing is an automatic action that does not have to be planned in advance. Since whales cannot breathe underwater, they must be able to get to the surface or they will die. This raises the closely related questions of sleep and anesthesia. If whales sleep, then they must not lose consciousness to the extent that they are unable to rise to the surface and breathe regularly. (There is evidence that some species sleep, but it is far from conclusive. On their three-month journey from Alaska to Baja California the gray whales appear not to sleep at all.) In captivity certain species have been observed to doze and to make a minimal effort to raise the blowhole above the surface at regular intervals. Similarly, if a captive porpoise or whale is anesthetized, care must be taken not to overdose the animal so that it cannot breathe.

It is believed that all living species of cetaceans are descended from a common ancestor, but the paleontological record is dim. All known fossil whales seem to be fully developed aquatic mammals; we do not know the steps that led to their return to the sea. There seems to be no question that the ancestors of whales and dolphins were land-dwelling creatures; the evolutionary development of whales as we know it clearly points to this conclusion. The forelimbs of whales, now reduced to paddlelike appendages, contain the bones of a mammalian arm and hand; the pelvis is present in some species, but represented only by a rudimentary bone embedded in the muscle below the spine; the buds of hind limbs are visible in the embryos of cetaceans; and on rare occasions a whale or dolphin is found with unformed, protruding hind limbs. At some time in their lives, usually in the prenatal stages, most whales show evidence of hair, a uniquely mammalian trait.

All those appendages that would otherwise interfere with smooth passage through the water—legs, ears, genitalia, and the like—have been incorporated into the fusiform body, leaving the cetaceans as hydrodynamically well designed as any creatures in the sea. (Not all whales are swift and graceful in the water. The huge bowhead is a ponderous and slow-moving beast; and some of the primitive freshwater dolphins, the Platanistidae, are ungainly, blind animals, inhabiting muddy rivers and swimming on their backs or sides.) For the most part, cetaceans are superbly designed for the job they have to do. Their skin is smooth, and they move through the water with scarcely a ripple. One reason for this smooth flow is that in some species the skin actually ripples. Known as "laminar flow," this process permits the animal to reduce drag to such an extent that it swims faster than its energy output would seem to allow.

Not all cetaceans have been rated for speed; but of those that have, the fastest seems to be the gigantic blue whale, which has been recorded at speeds over 30

*Tuffy, the bottlenose dolphin, was trained to switch off a sonic beacon, and Morgan, the pilot whale, retrieved objects from the bottom at known depths. Both series of experiments were conducted at the U.S. Navy facility at Point Mugu, California.

miles per hour (48 kilometers per hour) (Lockyer 1976). Other speedsters are the fin whale, the sei whale, the killer whale, and some of the smaller cetaceans, such as the Dall porpoise and the spotted dolphin, *Stenella attenuata.* Many of the smaller cetaceans leap out of the water at high speed, a behavior known as "porpoising," and the larger whales also jump, but not while rapidly swimming. In the larger whales, such as rights, sperms, humpbacks, and grays, these leaps from the water are called "breaching," and the whale usually lands on its back or side with a tremendous splash. In captivity some species of smaller cetaceans have been trained to make extraordinary leaps, as much as twenty feet out of the water. The bottlenose dolphin, the most familiar species in captivity, readily demonstrates its leaping ability in oceanarium shows. These animals are extremely flexible and can also be trained to "scull," which involves lifting the upper body out of the water and rapidly beating the flukes underwater to produce a fast backward motion (in porpoise shows this is known as "tail-walking"); they can do forward and backward somersaults; and the neck is flexible enough to allow this species to throw a ball by holding it between its lower jaw and chest. Wild dolphins perform many stunts as well. Some are natural acrobats, like the dusky dolphins, which naturally perform exuberant somersaults, and the spinner dolphins, named for their habit of leaping from the water and making as many as seven full rotations on the long axis before reentry.

Some species, such as killer whales, pilot whales, gray whales, and sperm whales, poke their heads out of the water, apparently to look around; this behavior is known as "spy-hopping" or "spying out." Other whales slap their tails on the surface, lie on their sides, wave their flippers in the air, or leap out of the water altogether. Many cetaceans are recognizable by their specialized behavior. Blue whales breathe three to five times at the surface, then raise their flukes in the air before a prolonged dive. Gray whales and humpbacks also "throw their flukes" before a dive, but fin whales almost never do. The swift little Dall porpoise does not ride bow waves, but zigzags in front of a fast-moving vessel, often raising a "roostertail" of spray as it swims at the surface. The "blows" of whales are distinctive, although not clearly understood. Some authorities maintain that mucus and foam are contained in the spout,* but others hold that the heated, com-

pressed air from the lungs vaporizes on contact with the outside air, thereby producing the characteristic spout. It is most visible in the larger whales, although sometimes a small, misty cloud can be seen over the head of a swimming porpoise. The rorquals have a tall plume of a spout, which can be thirty feet high in a blue whale and will be visible for miles on a good day. The blow of the right whales resembles an inverted cone and is often seen as two distinct jets, and the sperm whale, whose blowhole is located at the tip of the snout, shoots a tall spout obliquely forward, at a 45-degree angle.

In the open ocean, other types of behavior have been observed, many of which seem to serve no useful function and might very well be interpreted as play. For years it was believed that porpoises and dolphins riding the bow wave of a fast-moving vessel were simply swimming faster than the boat, but numerous tests on different species showed that they were not capable of such speeds on their own and that, therefore, they must be using the speed of the vessel to enhance their own. Dolphins have been observed to ride the bow wave with no apparent motion save the occasional planing of their flippers or flukes to correct their position in the water, and it is now believed that the animals are taking advantage of a pressure wave created by the forward motion of the boat. Bottlenose dolphins, common dolphins, spinners, and various other species will intercept a ship and joyfully ride the constant wave. A Risso's dolphin named Pelorus Jack was a celebrity in New Zealand waters at the turn of the century, as he regularly accompanied steamers across the Cook Strait, leaping and splashing before the boats. In the wild, porpoises are also known to ride the pressure wave of some of the larger whales, a behavior that is thought to have led to bow riding. Other activities that can be described as play include surfing in breaking waves near shore and playing with floating objects in the water. Captive bottlenose dolphins play with feathers, bits of shell or cloth, rubber balls, or any small objects, carrying them around the tank by snout or flipper for hours, and even the great sperm whale has been observed toying with a floating plank in the North Pacific (Nishiwaki 1962).

There are significant differences in the social structure of whale groups, from the solitary humpbacks to

---

*In Seattle in 1979 the anatomist Joseph Fanning presented a paper that offered a demonstrably plausible explanation. In terrestrial mammals the laryngotracheal junction contains cilia that effectively

remove mucus from the breathing apparatus. Since this apparatus in cetaceans contains no cilia, these secretions must therefore be removed "by the violent, cough-like, expiratory movements of the blow to form part of the visible plume." In other words, every exhalation of a whale is a cough.

the small family groups of fin whales, the larger pods of killer whales, the harem and bachelor schools of sperm whales, and, finally, the massed thousands of the Delphinid genera *Stenella* and *Delphinus.* Most species have a definite breeding season, and it is believed that certain areas are designated for breeding and calving. The best-known examples of this breeding segregation are the gray whales, which regularly arrive in the lagoons of Baja California, where the females deliver the young of the year, nurse them for a couple of months, and then begin the long swim back to the northern feeding areas. Other large whales behave in a similar fashion—the bays of Península Valdés, Argentina, are nursery areas for southern right whales—and it is assumed that the rorquals move off the Antarctic feeding grounds in the spring to mate and calve, although their breeding destinations have not been discovered.

The gestation period for most cetaceans is about a year, but there are the expected variations. Sperm whales, for example, take sixteen months to deliver a calf, while the gestation period for the harbor porpoise is ten to eleven months. The newborn calves are proportional in size to their parents and are born fully capable of functioning in their aquatic environment. Most species seem to deliver in a caudal (tailfirst) presentation, but not necessarily to prevent the baby from drowning if there is trouble with the delivery, since reflexive breathing does not occur until the blowhole hits the air. Another apocryphal behavior seems to be the mother's pushing the newborn to the surface for its first breath. In numerous observed births of captive bottlenose dolphins this behavior was observed only in the case of stillborn calves. (The terminology of cattle—"bull" and "cow"—is sometimes applied to the larger whales, particularly sperm and gray whales, but these terms are not used as frequently with reference to the smaller cetaceans, for which "male" and "female" are preferred. Baby cetaceans of all species are usually called "calves," although "juveniles" is sometimes used.)

Unlike the fishes, whales have not developed bright colors, but they do exhibit great variations on the theme of black and white. There are all-white cetaceans, all-black varieties, and some spectacular combinations. (Some cetaceans do show other colors: the white-sided dolphin *Lagenorhynchus acutus* has a yellowish flash on the flank; the common dolphin *Delphinus* is characterized by a tan thoracic patch; and the blue whale is bluish gray. But by and large, most cetaceans are black, white, black and white, or gray.) Most

whales (with the obvious exception of the all-white beluga) are dark above and lighter below, a condition known as countershading. This serves to neutralize and camouflage the whale's appearance in the water as the light strikes it from above, casting a shadow on its lighter undersides.

Less easy to explain is the profusion of light patches, streaks, stripes, and chevrons in the various species. Most of the rorquals are dark above and lighter below, but the northern minke whale has a broad white band on each flipper, and the fin whale, the world's only asymmetrically colored mammal, is white on the right side of the lower jaw, black on the left. The genus *Lagenorhynchus* consists of six species, all of which display an intricate pigmentation pattern that is diagnostic of the species. Many of the porpoises show pronounced white markings on a black ground, and the beaked whales, usually nondescript in color, are often crisscrossed with white streaks, made either by the suckers of squid on which they feed or by the teeth of other beaked whales. Perhaps the most spectacularly colored of all cetaceans is the killer whale, whose deep black color is set off by flashes, lenses, and swoops of snow white and by a grayish saddle behind the dorsal fin. A number of records document albino or semialbino whales, one of which was a snow-white sperm whale caught off Japan in 1957. The color of its eyes was not noted. Carolina Snowball was a white bottlenose dolphin captured off South Carolina in 1962 and exhibited for over three years at the Miami Seaquarium. Other species in which albinism is known to occur are the right, gray, killer, fin, bowhead, and pilot whales. Moby-Dick, created by Herman Melville in *Moby-Dick or, The Whale,* was not an albino; only his forehead and hump were white.

Perhaps the most important information gained from the observation of captive cetaceans concerns their extraordinary ability to echolocate, to locate objects by emitting high-pitched sounds that are reflected back as they bounce off the objects. This ability was first discovered in Florida in 1946 when Arthur McBride, an early researcher of dolphins, noticed that porpoises were able to avoid his nets, even though it was night and the animals could not possibly see them. It soon became apparent to investigators that the bottlenose dolphins were emitting clicking noises, and further experiments showed conclusively that they were listening to the echoes of their own sounds. By the use of this sonar the dolphins are able to locate objects in the water, differentiate objects by size and density, avoid submerged artifacts, and find food.

Most other toothed whales have been shown to produce the clicking sounds required for echolocation, and further analysis of odontocete sounds (especially those of bottlenose dolphins, Pacific white-sided dolphins, and sperm whales), has demonstrated that these animals also use certain phonations for purposes of communication. Bottlenoses have individual "signature whistles," and sperm whales emit click sequences (called "codas") that identify each whale. Other odontocete cetaceans, such as the beluga, have been recorded producing squeaks, squeals, barks, chirps, whistles, and moans. (Nineteenth-century whalers christened the beluga the "sea-canary" because of the variety and volume of its vocalizations.) When the recorded "screams" of killer whales are broadcast in the vicinity of belugas or gray whales, both evince a definite fright or avoidance reaction. Although not all toothed whales have been investigated, it is believed that most of them have an echolocating capability. The means by which the sounds are broadcast and received are not clearly understood, but the clicks apparently originate in the bulbous forehead, known as the "melon," and are received in the lower jaw. The whistling sounds, which can be produced simultaneously with the clicks, are thought to emanate from the blowhole and the larynx, but the mechanics of sound production are not known. Cetaceans have no vocal cords.

The sperm whale, unique in so many respects, represents a singular puzzle with regard to sound production. Its greatly elongated snout, filled with clear liquid wax and equipped with a complicated arrangement of tubes, valves, and air sacs, may be instrumental in the production of the knocks, bangs, and clicks that have been recorded from this animal. Some of these sounds may be used for navigation or for the location of prey species, but, to date, only the communication function of these sounds has been satisfactorily established (Watkins and Schevill 1977).

The baleen whales can also produce sounds, but these are mostly low-frequency noises described as moans, sighs, or belchlike utterances. The gray whale is suspected of making some brief clicking sounds, and a captive gray whale named Gigi was recorded as producing growls, moans, grunts, rumbles, and clicks. When a humpback was trapped in a net in Newfoundland, a series of experiments was devised to determine if the whale could navigate blindfolded through a maze of hanging poles. The whale showed no evidence of an ability to navigate by echolocation (Beamish 1978). The humpback is the most celebrated of all

cetacean singers, having two phonograph records to its credit. The males sing repeated, recognizable songs throughout the warm-water mating grounds of Hawaii, the Caribbean, and Bermuda. Of these songs Peter Matthiessen (1971) wrote, "No word conveys the eeriness of the whale song, tuned by the ages to a purity beyond refining, a sound that man should hear each morning to remind him of the morning of the world."

One of the most puzzling aspects of cetacean behavior is their occasional predisposition to beach themselves and die in shoal water or on the beach. There are recorded instances when they were able to turn around and yet refused to do so; and at other times well-meaning observers have tried to shove or tow them to the safety of the sea, only to have the whales return to the beach and certain death. Many species of odontocetes are given to this curious phenomenon; and in a few animals such as the pilot whales, *Globicephala,* and the false killer whale, *Pseudorca crassidens,* the behavior is so common as to be diagnostic. The circumstances and the species vary from stranding to stranding, so it is difficult—if not impossible—to discover the reasons or causes of this behavior. It has been assumed that the stranding animals somehow become disoriented or lost, perhaps because of a dysfunction of their echolocating or navigating mechanisms.

Among the suggested causes of mass strandings are beaches that slope too gradually for efficient reflection of broadcast signals; mass parasitic infestations of the inner ear, which would render the hearing or receiving faculties inoperative; underwater sounds that confuse the animals; unusual weather conditions; predator harassment; or even a "death wish," which makes their behavior tantamount to suicide.* Any or all of these may contribute to the mass stranding of cetaceans, but no one of the explanations seems entirely satisfactory. Some acousticians believe that the sonar capabilities of whales are far too sophisticated for them to become confused by gently sloping beaches. While parasites certainly can and do infest the inner ear of cetaceans, it seems unlikely that the critical moment of infestation would occur simultaneously in as many as two hundred animals. There are too many underwater

*Almost all cetaceans have been recorded to strand individually, but the discussion here concerns those instances in which many animals —sometimes as many as two hundred—come ashore at once. A further distinction is made between animals that come ashore alive and those that die at sea and are washed ashore. However, this distinction is obviously difficult to sustain, since most stranded animals are discovered dead, and their condition immediately before coming ashore is not known.

sounds nowadays—far more than there were in the days before steam and diesel power, not to mention subsurface drilling operations—and whales stranded long before the Industrial Revolution. Predators lurking offshore might be responsible for chasing some species into shallow water, but how are we to explain the strandings of killer or sperm whales, two apex predators with no natural enemies? Unusual weather conditions appear to be insignificant in some cases and inapplicable in others. F. G. Wood (1978) of the Naval Oceans Systems Center in San Diego has suggested a new hypothesis to explain the phenomenon of mass strandings: "cetaceans still retain, from their amphibious ancestors, a subcortically induced incentive to seek safety on shore when severely stressed— a 'blind' (but not directionless) emotional response." As Wood himself admitted, such a behavior would be maladaptive; that is, it would be genetically self-destructive and should long ago have been eliminated from the behavioral repertoire of the cetaceans.

Without resorting to such arcane theories, however, it is possible to assign a simple recovery function to the stranding of single animals. Rather than a self-destructive act, the animal may be trying to save its own life. Since cetaceans must surface in order to breathe, difficulties in remaining afloat—as a result of parasitic infestations, external or internal injuries, stress, or whatever—might cause the animal to seek the shallows, where it could breathe without having to swim. This action often proves to be destructive, because the whale is trapped by retreating tides or adversely affected by the heat of the sun, but we assume the whale could not predict this. In any event, self-preservation seems a much more useful and practical explanation than self-destruction.

Faced with an animal so literally out of its element, Good Samaritans have often tried to refloat the whale, assuming that as a creature of the water, it belonged there and not on dry land. Most efforts of this kind have been marked by the whale's refusal to return to the sea and what has often been interpreted as a repeated "suicidal" desire to beach itself again, even after it has been towed out to sea. Those who would save the whale by returning it to the water were possibly doing exactly the wrong thing.

In *A Whale for the Killing,* a fin whale trapped in a pond in Newfoundland was shot hundreds of times by the townspeople, apparently because they could not resist such a huge target. In this case, therefore, there is no question about the whale's injuries—it eventually died from the multiple wounds—and *in extremis,* the whale repeatedly came out of the water. Farley Mowat, the Canadian author/biologist who chronicled this unfortunate series of events, assumed at first that the injured whale should be in the water, but then realized that perhaps the opposite was true:

The scales were off my eyes and now I saw the truth. She had not grounded by accident, neither had she been beached by the malice of men. She had *deliberately* gone ashore because she was too sick to keep herself afloat any longer. I had misread the evidence, but now it was unmistakable.

It is possible, therefore, to assume that individual whales strand because they are putting themselves in a position where breathing will be easier, or where they will not drown. The problem of mass stranding is probably connected with this phenomenon, at least insofar as one of the whales or the "leader" is concerned, but there are still too many variables in these situations that we do not understand.

From the moment when the first man saw the first whale, their destinies were conjoined. Long before the thought of hunting the whale occurred, we can assume that primitive people watched various species offshore, spouting and blowing. (In New England, before civilization drove the whales away, the bays of Massachusetts and Connecticut were home to large numbers of black right whales, which were quickly eliminated by the colonists.) Whales that washed ashore provided an enormous store of meat and oil, and it probably did not take long for natives in coastal areas to realize that this chance occurrence could be improved upon by actively going after the whale, instead of waiting for the whale to come to them. The earliest-known whalers include the American Indians of the east and west coasts, Eskimos, Basques, and primitive Norwegian villagers.

By about A.D. 1000 the Basques on the French and Spanish coasts were involved in a thriving industry that would eventually reduce the Biscayan right whale to such low numbers that it has never recovered, although it is not extinct. The Greenland right whale, once plentiful enough in the waters of Spitsbergen, Iceland, and Greenland to support a major industry, was so mercilessly slaughtered in the seventeenth, eighteenth, and nineteenth centuries that it has barely survived to this day. There are no Greenland right whales left in the eastern Arctic, and only a limited number remain in the waters of Alaska, where they are protected from all but Eskimo subsistence hunting. The right whales were rich in oil and blubber, and instead of teeth they had long, flexible baleen plates, known as whalebone. The oil was used for illumination and the bone for everything in which strength and flexibility were needed: corset stays, buggy whips, umbrella ribs, skirt hoops, and so on. (It was also useful for disciplining uncooperative schoolchildren; when a whalebone whip was used for this purpose, it was said that the child got a "whaling.") Even the fringes of the baleen were used as stuffing for upholstered furniture. By the mid-eighteenth century the right whales had been so reduced in numbers that the whalers looked further offshore for other species. (The stock of bowheads in the western Arctic was not discovered until the nineteenth century.) They found the sperm whale, a deep-water species whose "case" contained a vast amount—sometimes as much as fifteen barrels—of the valuable spermaceti oil, used in the manufacture of expensive smokeless candles. The history of the sperm whale fishery is too well known to repeat here, but suffice it to say that this whale was responsible for the rise of a major New England industry and for the ascendancy of such whaling ports as New Bedford, Nantucket, Mystic, and Sag Harbor. Fortunes were made and lost in this industry, and the novel that many believe to be the most important in American literary history—*Moby-Dick*—was written by an ex-whaleman, within the framework of a New Bedford whaling voyage.

The discovery of petroleum in Pennsylvania in 1859 postdated the decline of the sperm whale fishery, whose downfall is attributable to rising costs, the difficulty in getting hands to ship out for the two or three years sometimes required for a whaling voyage, and an unaccountable shortage of whales, which made the voyages even longer, as the captains scoured the whaling grounds looking for their catch. (It seems unlikely that the sperm whale population was reduced by the fishery; sperm whales were and are by far the most numerous of the great whales, and even at the peak of the fishery the entire fleet could not have taken more than 10,000 whales per year, a number that was easily covered by the species' normal fecundity.) This fishery slowed and eventually ceased altogether. The *Wanderer,* last of the full-rigged whaling ships, sailed out of New Bedford on August 25, 1924, and was wrecked on Cuttyhunk Island the next day. From 1846 to 1874 some 8,000 gray whales were killed, mostly in the waters of Baja and northern California, and a population that probably never had been much higher than 12,000 animals was drastically reduced.

Of the "great" whales only the rorquals were unmolested by the open-boat whalers; the blue and fin whales were too fast and much too powerful for men who had to row up on them and stab them with a hand lance. In 1867 the Norwegian Svend Foyn invented the grenade harpoon, an exploding missile that penetrated deep into the vitals of the whale. With this invention the most destructive period in the history of whaling had begun. Foyn hunted in the waters of northern Norway, killing blue and fin whales. But it was not until the turn-of-the-century discovery of the Antarctic feeding grounds of the blue, fin, sei, and humpback whales that the industry hit its stride. First the slow-moving humpbacks were decimated and then the giant blues. When there were too few blue whales to hunt, the whalers turned to the next largest species, the fin whale, then to the sei, and finally to the little minke.

Since 1946, whaling has been regulated by the International Whaling Commission,* an organization made up of representative whaling nations and ostensibly dedicated to the preservation of whales in order that they might be harvested efficiently. In practice, however, the whaling nations seemed intent on nothing less than destroying the resource on which their industry depends. But in recent years only the Soviets and the Japanese have continued to conduct pelagic whaling operations, resulting in what seem to be economic as well as political disasters for both countries. Despite massive reductions in stocks and worldwide condemnation, these countries have persisted in hunting the whales.

Only the sperm whale exists today in numbers approximating its previous abundance. The blue, fin, sei, right, bowhead, and humpback are all considered endangered, and IWC signatories are forbidden to kill them. (There are a number of non-IWC nations, including Portugal, Somalia, Chile, South Korea, and China, where whaling is still conducted without regard for protected or endangered species and in violation of the other restrictions enacted by the IWC.) The gray whale, having been brought to a near-extinction level by the end of the nineteenth century and again heavily hunted from factory ships in the 1920s and 1930s, has been fully protected since 1946. The species now seems to have reached its preexploitation level, and it has been removed from the protected category.

*Member nations of the IWC are Argentina, Brazil, Canada, France, Mexico, Panama, Great Britain, New Zealand, the United States, Australia, Denmark, Iceland, Japan, Norway, South Africa, the Netherlands, Peru, Seychelles, Spain, Sweden, and the Soviet Union.

Seen in a contemporaneous perspective, whaling was an integral part of European and American industry and enterprise from the seventeenth to the early twentieth century. It would be pointless to criticize the industry from the vantage point of our current ecological sensitivity, for we must assume that the whalers believed their prey to represent an inexhaustible natural resource. But we must also realize that the whaling industry learned almost nothing from its own experience. One after another, the species of whales were slaughtered into economic extinction, which meant it was no longer worth hunting that particular species. We must consider ourselves fortunate that enough of the great whales escaped the harpoon to enable us to sense the majesty of these creatures, leviathans that still ply the oceans of the world, singing their haunting songs into the abyss. Singing humpbacks, hundred-foot blues, mass-migrating grays: surely they represent a most moving and significant aspect of our natural heritage. Without them we would be diminished by an emotional factor far greater than the tremendous bulk of the whales themselves.

We are now caught up in a period of whale consciousness, as conservation groups the world over campaign to protect the great whales, the killer whales, the dolphins. In aquariums and oceanariums around the world—even in Japan where the people eat porpoises—the bottlenose dolphins, killer whales, belugas, and others are the stars of the show. Cetolo-gists are studying the navigational abilities of whales, their diving abilities, hearing, hydrodynamics, sound production, and anatomy and dozens of other aspects of cetacean biology. We are on the threshold of an understanding of some of the world's most interesting creatures. But the secrets of cetaceans are not readily revealed, and we approach some species as if they were created to be captured and trained for our amusement. This attitude is as misguided as the one holding that whales were put on earth to provide us with cat food, margarine, and lipstick. We should approach the cetaceans—and the other creatures that share our fragile environment—as Henry Beston (1928) would have us do:

We need another and a wiser and perhaps a more mystical concept of animals. Remote from universal nature, and living by complicated artifice, man in civilization surveys the creature through the glass of his knowledge and sees thereby a feather magnified and the whole image in distortion. We patronize them for our incompleteness, for their tragic fate of having taken form so far below ourselves. And therein we err, we greatly err. For the animal shall not be measured by man. In a world older and more complete than ours they move more finished and complete, gifted with extensions of senses we have lost or never attained, living by voices we shall never hear. They are not brethren, they are not underlings; they are other nations, caught with ourselves in the net of life and time, fellow prisoners of the splendour and travail of the earth.

GRAY WHALE

Eschrichtius robustus Lilljeborg 1861

The family Eschrichtiidae contains only this species. Although the gray is a baleen whale, it differs from all the others in numerous respects. It is not closely related to any other species, but its external appearance places it somewhere between the right whales and the rorquals. Like the right whales, the gray has no dorsal fin and a narrow upper jaw, but the head is not as large and the baleen is comparatively short. In place of the dorsal fin, the gray whale has a series of bumps or knuckles, starting about two-thirds of the way down the back and extending to the base of the tail. (Even though it looks as if these bumps ought to be related to the dorsal processes, the number varies from whale to whale, from a minimum of nine to a maximum of fourteen.) The first of these bumps, at the forward end of the series, is the largest, constituting almost a hump.

As is characteristic of other whalebone whales, female gray whales are somewhat larger than males. The

maximum length is reported to be about 50 feet (15.24 meters). Scammon (1874) wrote that "forty-four feet would be regarded as large, although some animals have been taken that were much larger."* Gilmore (1961) reported the weight of a 43.8-foot (13.35-meter) female at 36.4 short tons.

The gray whale's head is proportionally small, only one-fourth or one-fifth of the total body length. The upper jaw extends beyond the lower and is considerably narrower. The gray whale has throat grooves, but of the most rudimentary sort. There are usually two parallel grooves about 15 inches (38 centimeters) apart and about 5 feet (152 centimeters) long, but

*Charles Melville Scammon (1835–1911) was to the gray whale what Scoresby was to the Greenland right whale and what Beale and Bennett were to the sperm whale: an acute observer of the species while actively engaged in its pursuit and capture. Like Scoresby, Scammon was a whaling captain who recorded his observations and experiences (Beale and Bennett were ship surgeons who went on long sperm-whaling voyages). His book, *The Marine Mammals of the Northwestern Coast of North America: Together with an Account of the American Whale-Fishery,* is considered a classic of its kind, and it contains a great deal of firsthand information that would otherwise have been lost. Scammon's Lagoon in Baja California, known to the Spaniards as *Laguna Ojo de Liebre* (Jackrabbit Springs Lagoon), was named for him, and he holds the dubious honor of having the gray whale's louse, *Cyamus scammoni,* named for him as well.

Dorsal view of a gray whale. Notice the position of the blowholes and the narrow upper jaw that extends beyond the lower.

occasionally three grooves or even four are seen. The baleen of the gray whale is short, coarse, and yellowish-white in color, and there are between 140 and 180 plates per side. There are four "fingers" (no thumb is visible) in each flipper, and often the dorsal surface is abraded so that the outline of the bones can be seen. Broad and fan-shaped, the flukes are unique in that the trailing edges, often quite thin in the other whales, are thick and rounded in the gray whale.

The most noticeable and distinguishing attribute of the gray whale is its color. The ground color is dark gray or black, but the animal is so covered with a profusion of spots, scars, patches, and clusters of barnacles that it presents a mottled, grayish appearance. (In the Bering Sea, Goedel and Dalheim [1979] observed a white California gray whale, and although they could not see the entire animal, they saw enough to suggest that the animal "might be an albino.") Many of the scars and scratches are the result of barnacles' coming off, but examination of fetal gray whales has indicated that the species is born with spots and various irregular light markings. Examining a newborn calf stranded at Scammon's Lagoon, Eberhardt and Norris (1964) wrote, "over the undamaged portion of the skin were many light gray flecks and patches, which clearly represented true skin color and not the scarring effect of ectocommensals." Clusters of barnacles are found primarily on the rostrum, on the flippers, between the eye and the flipper, and on the tail peduncle, and they seem to be oriented to the direction in which the water flows over the whale's body when it is swimming (Kasuya and Rice 1970). The species has numerous hairs on the rostrum and lower jaw that are eventually covered with barnacles and, therefore, would appear to serve no tactile function in the whale. Andrews (1914) regarded these hairs, along with the short baleen plates and certain osteological characteristics, as evidence of the "primitive" status of the gray whale. That the species is at least 150,000 to 200,000 years old has been demonstrated by the discovery of a fossil gray whale of this age at San Pedro, California, in 1971 (Daugherty 1972).

This species has been given many names during the short time it has been known. Scammon, who contributed materially to its exposure and its slaughter, listed "hard head," "mussel digger," "devilfish," "gray back," and "rip-sack." Hard head and devilfish are the result of their occasional attacks on boats—usually by females defending their young. Mussel dig-

ger comes from the whale's sometime habit of rising from the bottom "besmeared with mud," and rip-sack originated with the manner of flensing, or cutting off the blubber. According to Andrews (1914), the Japanese know this animal as *Koku-kujira,* which he translated as "devil-fish." Dr. Hideo Omura (1974), the director of the Whales Research Institute of Tokyo, however, gives the name as *Kokujira.*

Until fairly recently, the gray whale was technically known as *Rhachianectes glaucus,* which can be translated as "gray swimmer along rocky shores" (Gilmore 1961). The currently accepted name is *Eschrichtius robustus;* the generic name for D. F. Eschricht, a nineteenth-century German zoologist, and the species name from the Latin for "strong" or "solid."

The gray whale is the only large whale with a heavily mottled appearance and a knobby ridge down the back. There is not much difficulty in identifying this species in life, but its occasional appearance in literature and in locations where it is not expected has caused taxonomists a great deal of trouble. In 1725 a report published by the Royal Society of London contained this description by the Hon. Paul Dudley, Esq.: "The Scrag Whale is near a kin to the Fin-back, but instead of a Fin upon his Back, the Ridge of the Afterpart of his Back is scragged with half a Dozen Knobs; he is nearest the right Whale in Figure and for Quantity of Oil; his bone is white, but will not split." Dudley's account "respects only such whales as are found on the Coast of *New-England,*" and this description does not conveniently apply to any known species from that area. Many authors have tried to turn it into an undernourished right whale, but the baleen of a right whale (referred to in the eighteenth century as "bone" or "whalebone") is black, not white. Dudley's descriptions of the other species are remarkably accurate and leave no room for doubt. Of this report, True (1904) wrote, "all of these are recognizable and have been assigned to their proper places generically, except for the scrag whale, which is, and always has been, a stumbling block to cetology." This early report is the only known reference to what might be a gray whale in the western Atlantic, so it will continue to puzzle cetologists until some other material appears. "We think it not improbable," wrote van Deinse and Junge (1937), "that along the Atlantic coasts of North America in future, skeleton fragments of this species will be found." To date, they have not appeared, and the cetologists who have tried to identify the scrag whale from Dudley's less than explicit description "have always been frustrated by various irreconcilable data, the chief of which is perhaps the utter lack of specimens'' (Schevill 1952).

There are a few records of gray whale remains in the eastern North Atlantic, indicating that this species existed there in A.D. 500 and perhaps as recently as the seventeenth century. The 1937 report of van Deinse and Junge, which was concerned primarily with the description of these remains, is the first publication of the "astonishing conclusion" that the bones were from *Rhachianectes glaucus,* now *Eschrichtius robustus.* (The authors wrote that the name ought to be *Eschrichtius gibbosus,* and they also felt that the presence of the gray whale in the eastern Atlantic demonstrated the possibility of its being found in the western portion of that ocean; therefore, the identification of Dudley's scrag whale was now clear.) A skull and part of a rib were found at Weiringermeer Polder when part of the Zuider Zee was drained in 1930, and another skull fragment was found at IJmuiden, also in Holland. Remains of this species were also found in Cornwall and Devonshire, England, and on the Swedish island of Gräsö. In an examination of a seventeenth-century Icelandic journal, Fraser (1970) suggested that one of the illustrations is probably of the Atlantic gray whale. Rice and Wolman (1971) hypothesized that the whales spent the summer feeding in the Baltic Sea, where the amphipod *Ampelisca macrocephala* is abundant, and that they wintered (and presumably mated and calved) "perhaps along the Mediterranean coast of southwestern Europe or northwestern Africa."

The life history of the gray whale is defined in movement. It makes the longest migration of any mammal, an annual round trip of some 10,000 miles (16,000 kilometers), from the icy waters of the Bering and Chukchi seas in the high western Arctic to the warm lagoons of Baja California, Mexico. Feeding takes place primarily (but not exclusively) in the cold waters of the whales' summer range, and in the winter they move southward, where they will give birth and mate once again. Although they are often observed in concurrent migrations—that is, many whales can be seen in the course of a day or a week or a month—gray whales are not social animals. The migrations are composed of small groups, sometimes single animals or pairs moving together, as opposed to a single herd movement. It might be said that the gray whales all do the same thing at about the same time, but they do not do it together. Gilmore (1961) has calculated that the whales, swimming at about 4–5 knots for twenty hours a day, swim about 60–70 miles (97–113 kilometers) per day, taking two and a half to three months to complete the journey. When migrating, the whales breathe two or three times at ten-second intervals, then throw their flukes in the air, and submerge for three to five minutes.

Pregnant females are the first to arrive at the lagoons, followed by the mature males and then the immatures of both sexes. (Rice and Wolman estimated that gray whales reach sexual maturity at about 8 years, when they are approximately 38.5 feet [11.7 meters] in length.) It appears that the pregnant females give birth shortly after they arrive in the lagoons, though very few descriptions of the actual delivery exist. In an unpublished abstract Storro-Patterson and Kipping (1977) wrote of their observation of the "birth and subsequent behavior and development of a gray whale, *Eschrichtius robustus.*" Storro-Patterson told me that the abstract "is about as much as I have written about that interesting event." I have, therefore, taken the liberty of reproducing the entire abstract, since it would appear to be the most complete description of the birth of a gray whale:

On 13 January 1975, a gray whale birth was observed. A large gray whale cow made a slow 360 roll close to our drifting boat. As her ventral surface came into view, the

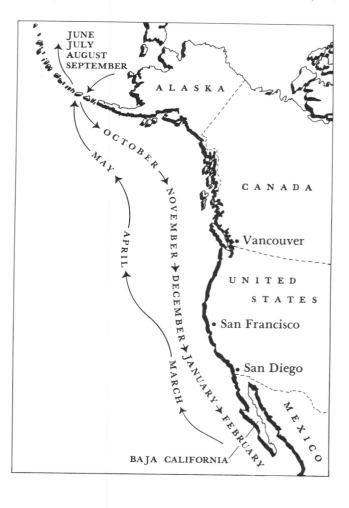

rostrum of the calf in the process of being born was seen protruding from her vagina. Seconds later, the calf was on the surface. The calf took its first three breaths unassisted; the cow then lifted the calf clear of the water. The breathing and swimming of the calf were at first uncoordinated and labored. It would move its caudal peduncle from side to side as well as up and down. The flukes were folded, with the tips pointing forward. It lunged at the surface, and a few times audibly took in water, attempting to breathe just below the surface. After thirty minutes, the calf twice attempted to approach our boat. For the first hour, although it swam constantly, it progressed no further than our drifting boat. During the next half hour, it gradually outdistanced our boat. After 1 1/2 hours it made a steady swim against a strong current, possibly assisted some by its mother. After three hours, its swimming behavior was similar to the other young calves in the lagoon.

Cousteau saw and photographed a cow whale in labor, but "a sudden storm prevented photographer [Philippe] Cousteau . . . from witnessing the moment of birth" (Cousteau and Diole 1972).

Rice and Wolman reported that "all near term fetuses were positioned in the uterus with the tail pointed towards the cervix; this would ensure caudal presentation at birth, as is usual in cetaceans." The average size of a newborn gray whale calf is about 15.5 feet (4.7 meters), although there is a certain amount of variation (Eberhardt and Norris 1964). The new-born whales are dark in color; and although they have no barnacles at birth, even those with the stalk of the umbilical cord still attached are hosts to the omnipresent whale lice. (Since the lice are present in the vaginal area of the female, it is assumed that the transfer takes place during the birth of the baby.) Nichols (1975) reported that newborn whales have "wrinkles on the side and the top of the head." This condition is clearly evident in Cousteau's series of photographs of a baby whale that had stranded (and subsequently died, despite efforts to save it) in Scammon's Lagoon. The stranding and death of newborn calves appears to be a fairly common occurrence; Cousteau wrote, "from the air we could see about ten dead whale calves lying in the lagoon," and various other authors (for example, Gard 1974) have discussed similar circumstances. In many of these cases, infant mortality may be a result of simple stranding as the tide ebbs (Eberhardt and Norris 1964).

Most infants survive, and their behavior has been observed on numerous occasions. The calves remain in almost constant contact with the mother, rolling over on her and splashing about while she remains placid and supportive (Ellis 1977). Nursing has not been positively identified, but Nichols described how "several mothers were seen repeatedly to roll slowly on their sides, belly toward their young with pectoral and fluke protruding from the water. The baby then dove toward the location of the mother's nipples, remaining submerged until the mother rolled back into normal position a minute later." Scientists are understandably reluctant to accept circumstantial evidence, but it would appear that this is an adequate description of the nursing behavior of the gray whale, even if the actual transfer of milk was not observed. (The only aspect of the behavior that is lacking an explanation is the way in which an animal with an inflexible upper lip grasps the nipple. Alternatively, it has been suggested that the milk is squirted into the mouth of the calf.)

Much of our knowledge of the habits and biology of young gray whales was acquired at Sea World, San Diego, from March 13, 1971, to March 13, 1972. Here, for the first time in history, a baleen whale was successfully maintained in captivity.* The whale was a female gray, captured in Scammon's Lagoon at an age estimated at about 2 months. Named Gigi, she arrived at Sea World measuring 18 feet 2 inches in length and weighing 4,150 pounds (1,867 kilograms). (Actually, she was Gigi II; the first Gigi died after two months of an infection from the harpoon used to capture her. Gigi II was captured with a tail rope.) Her first home was a 55,000-gallon tank, where she was fed on a formula of whipping cream, ground squid and bonito, cod liver oil, brewer's yeast, vitamins, corn oil, and water through a tube inserted into her throat. Gray whales are normally weaned at about 7 months of age, so she was gradually converted to a diet of frozen squid, served in twenty-pound (nine-kilogram) blocks, which gradually thawed and melted.

It has always been known that the growth of baleen whales is prodigious during their first year, but this was the first time that regular measurements could be taken. By May 29, 1971, she was 19 feet 10 inches long and weighed 5,525 pounds. By mid-November, Gigi was close to 25 feet long and was weighed at 7,600 pounds. She had been transferred to a 1-million-gallon tank and was eating over 1,000 pounds of squid per day. When she was released, she weighed nearly 14,000 pounds (6,350 kilograms) and was 26.7 feet

*In 1956 a minke whale was kept in a pool that was part of the Mito Aquarium in Japan. It had been trapped in a net and was towed to the aquarium. After a month of slow, counterclockwise swimming, it escaped. This whale would better be described as having been temporarily incarcerated, not "maintained in captivity" (Kimura and Nemoto 1956).

(8.15 meters) in length. (For her year in captivity her average weight gain was about 27 pounds per day, or a little over 1 pound per hour.)

Because the opportunity was unique, scientists descended on Sea World to examine Gigi. She was tested for respiration and metabolism, mechanical function of her heart, blubber thickness, and blood coagulation. Her chromosomes were examined, her feeding was observed, and she was fitted out with a telemetry device. She was weighed and measured regularly, and her every move was recorded. When she was released off Point Loma, San Diego, it was hoped that she would join the ongoing northward migration, and she was equipped with a radio pack to enable scientists to track her movements. Contact was maintained from March 13, 1972, to May 5, when the signal ceased. The last transmissions indicated that she was just south of San Francisco, obviously moving north (Evans 1974). Gigi was also cryogenically (low-temperature) "branded," with a two-foot- (sixty-centimeter-) square mark just behind the blowhole, to make her recognizable even after she had lost the radio pack. She has been sighted a number of times since her release, indicating that she successfully survived her captivity and seems to have adapted to life in the wild. In late 1979 Gigi was positively identified in San Ignacio Lagoon, Baja California. She was accompanied by a newborn calf, indicating that she had made a completely successful readjustment.

After spending approximately two months on the breeding grounds, the whales swim northward until they reach the waters of the Bering and Chukchi seas, arriving around May or June. En route, they stay fairly close to shore (but not as close as they stay on the southward migration) until they reach Vancouver Island, which seems to be a staging area for the crossing of the open waters of the Gulf of Alaska. This part of the migration remains a mystery, for the whales are not sighted again until they appear in the far northern waters. The path from Vancouver to Siberia is not known. Gilmore (1960) believed that they follow the prevailing currents, particularly the Alaska Gyral, and pass west of the Aleutian chain, whereas Ichihara (1958) thought that they pass through the Aleutians, fanning out in the western Bering Sea, until they arrive at Navarin and Anadyr on the east coast of Siberia. The question of the actual route is still unresolved, but Rugh and Braham (1979) were able to identify accurately the location at which the southbound whales passed through the Aleutian Islands. From Cape Sarichef, a promontory on Unimak Island, they were able

to watch and count the whales migrating through Unimak Pass. They were able to estimate that some 11,179 whales passed, and allowing for those that made their way through Unimak Pass before or after the survey dates (November 20 to December 9, 1977), they then calculated the total gray whale population at 15,000.

We now know slightly more about where the whales go, but there are still major questions regarding how they navigate for this incredible journey. They do occasionally emit pulses that are interpreted by some as echolocation clicks (Asa-Dorian and Perkins 1967), but other researchers have written that "there is no evidence that they navigate by echolocation" (Cummings and Thompson 1971). So they do emit sounds, but we do not know the function of these sounds. In a 1968 discussion, in which some 60,000 feet of magnetic tape recordings were analyzed, Poulter stated that gray whales are quite vocal, their repertoire including clicks, rasps, and the "bong of a huge Chinese gong."* Most sounds were made by mother-calf combinations. Poulter concluded that "the gray whale is among the more vocal of the whales" and that the confusion in the past was due to the background noise of snapping shrimp, which almost completely masked the whale's vocalizations.

It is also likely that navigation is accomplished by memory and vision (Daugherty 1972). Vision underwater might be useful in shallow coastal areas, but these whales are often observed lifting their heads vertically out of the water, exhibiting a type of behavior known to the whalers as "spy-hopping," or "spying out." It is believed that this allows the whale to get its bearings by sighting out of the water.

When the gray whales arrive in the Bering Sea, they begin a four-month feeding period. It is not known if the whales eat at any other time, but a number of observations of apparent feeding behavior have been made in locations other than the Arctic waters. For example, Gilmore (1961) reported "criss-crossing through a dense school of small fish, like anchovies, off San Diego"; Sund (1975) saw three or four whales "rising through bait fish with their mouths agape" off Monterey; and Sprague et al. (1978) observed "what appeared to be feeding activities" in a small group of

*In this study, conducted at Scammon's Lagoon in 1967, the author noted that the clicks were most often heard in conjunction with the passage overhead of a plane or helicopter, indicating a particular sensitivity by the whales to this type of noise: "It was not uncommon for the whale to appear to strike at the helicopter with its flukes as it dived very close; on one occasion the whale threw enough water on the helicopter to kill the motor. Fortunately, it was close enough to the beach so it was able to land there instead of on the water."

young whales in Laguna San Quintin, Baja California.* It may be that the gray whales feed for four months and fast for the rest of the year (that, after all, is what the rorquals do, though they migrate away from their food source), but since the gray whales are almost always in the vicinity of some food organisms, they are likely to eat sporadically on the migrations or in the lagoons. Even if some whales feed elsewhere, the overwhelming majority seem to feed only in the north. Of his experiences in Baja, Scammon wrote, "little or no food has been found in the animals' stomach." Andrews (1916), having examined numerous specimens in Korea, remarked, "Although the stomachs of a great many gray whales were carefully examined, I could never discover what constitutes their food, and no one else seems to have had much better success." Both of these observers examined specimens that had been caught at the southern end of their migration, where breeding and calving, rather than feeding, seem to be the predominant activities. After summarizing the available data, Rice and Wolman wrote that "the stomachs of migrating whales are almost invariably empty."

Observing the whales in Magdalena Bay, Norris and Würsig (1979) saw apparent feeding behavior in the fast-flowing tidal rip at the bay's entrance, where the food organisms are stirred up by the turbulent water. In this same paper (unpublished as of this writing, but presented at the Third Biennial Conference of the Biology of Marine Mammals at Seattle in October 1979), they also observed the segregation of the males and females in the lagoons. Calving and nursing females remained deep within the protected waters of the lagoons, while the males stationed themselves at the entrance. Courtship activities were also observed, with much attendant splashing and thrashing, which the authors suggest might drive some nursing calves away from their mothers and result in some of the otherwise unexplained stranding of young calves.

In the north the gray whales consume gammaridean amphipods (known also as water fleas), which are small crustaceans that live on or in the bottom sediments. Rice and Wolman examined a female that had been killed by Eskimos off Saint Lawrence Island, Alaska, and found that the most common food organism was the 1-inch (25-millimeter) amphipod, Ampelisca macrocephalus. Other, similar benthic organisms were also found. If we accept the idea that gray whales are bottom feeders, we must then ask the question of how this mode of feeding, unique among the whalebone whales, is accomplished. Wilke and Fiscus (1961) observed gray whales in the Chukchi Sea in about twenty-four fathoms of water, "making a large muddy blotch in the water as they came to the surface to blow. It seems apparent that in feeding along the bottom the whales gathered mud along with food and were expelling through their baleen as they rose to the surface." After examining the baleen plates of thirty-three gray whales, Kasuya and Rice (1970) found that thirty-one of them had worn the plates down on the right side (and also scraped off barnacles on that side), indicating that they fed on their sides and, curiously, that they were predominantly "right-sided."

When the blocks of frozen squid would thaw in Gigi's tank, she would swim along so that her cheek was nearly parallel to the bottom. "As she swam over the squid, she left a clean swath 30–50 cm wide. It was apparent that the squid were being sucked up in sort of a pulsation, as some squid briefly reappeared after their first disappearance into her mouth," claimed Ray and Schevill (1974). (Squid are not the natural food of gray whales, but the authors pointed out that "her bottom sweeping habit we suppose to be natural since it appears appropriate for catching the animals that comprise the recorded natural food of this species of whale.") Ray and Schevill suggested that the food is brought into the mouth by some sort of suction, probably having to do with the action of the tongue. While she was feeding, Gigi's throat grooves were seen to expand, possibly in relation to a movement or flexion of her tongue.

After about four months on the Arctic feeding grounds (around September), the gray whales again turn toward the south. They begin to appear off Oregon in mid-November and stay close to the shore from that point on, the first ones arriving in Baja in early January. In 1960, Gilmore estimated a total gray whale population of about 5,000, which were distributed as follows in the various lagoons and bays of Baja: Scammon's Lagoon and Vizcaino Bay, 2,500 whales; Ballenas Bay and San Ignacio Lagoon, 500; Magdalena Bay, 1,500; various smaller bays, 500.* This distribu-

*This is a particularly interesting observation, because it not only locates the whales in a lagoon where they were known infrequently in the past, but also identifies a possible food item. Barnard (1964) found the amphipod Ampelisca compressa to be extremely abundant in Laguna San Quintin.

*There are also records of gray whales swimming entirely around Cabo San Lucas and into the Gulf of California. They have been observed at Yavaros in Sonora and at Bahia Reforma in Sinaloa,

tion is more or less consistent (although the total number has risen since 1960), and there is no reason to suppose that the whales do not return to the same lagoons every year. In San Ignacio Lagoon, Swartz and Cummings (1978) identified numerous individuals in consecutive years, indicating that at least some whales return annually to the same lagoons.

In order to make the 5,000-mile journey in the allotted time, the whales must keep moving almost twenty-four hours a day, a requirement that leaves hardly any time for sleep. Gilmore (1961) believed they rest very little during the migrations and sleep when they arrive at the lagoons. (Although it is something of an oversimplification, we may say that these mammals neither eat nor sleep for eight consecutive months out of every year.) At Matancitas, Cousteau crept up on the whales unnoticed: "Undoubtedly the whales had been sleeping; but then they awoke with a start, one after another, and, in a great uproar of splashing and spray and gigantic tails smashing about in the water, they disappeared beneath the surface." When migrating or feeding, gray whales breathe every ten or fifteen seconds before making a protracted dive, but while sleeping, "they lie quietly at the surface, barely awash, head and flukes hanging limply, raising slightly every 8–10 minutes for a slow breath" (Gilmore 1961).

The lagoons of Baja are tidal and often shallow, and the whales are sometimes seen in water that is barely deep enough to float them. Scammon wrote,

as the season approaches for the whales to bring forth their young . . . they formerly collected at the most remote extremities of the lagoons, and huddled together so thickly

mainland Mexico (Gilmore and Ewing 1954). It is possible that these refuges, far from their known breeding grounds, saved at least some of the whales during the periods of heavy whaling.

that it was difficult for a boat to cross the waters without coming into contact with them. Repeated instances have been known of their getting aground and lying for several hours in but two or three feet of water, without apparent injury from resting heavily on the sandy bottom, until the rising tide floated them.

Since the gestation period of the gray whale is approximately twelve months, mating and parturition occur in the same location, the lagoons, each winter. There have been numerous observations of the mating behavior of gray whales, more perhaps than of any other species, because the animals are so highly visible in the accessible waters of Baja California. Almost all calves are born within a five-to-six-week period, from late December to early February; this is a result of the long migration route and the restricted calving grounds (Rice and Wolman 1971). The gray whale is believed to give birth every other year, so half the females are nursing and, therefore, not receptive to the advances of the males. This situation leads to an abundance of males, roughly two males to every non-nursing female. Gilmore refers to this unbalanced arrangement as a *ménage à trois,* since two males are often attendant on a single female. Mystery writer Erle Stanley Gardner, who went to Scammon's Lagoon in 1960 to "hunt the desert whale" (using only a camera, not a harpoon), was witness to the mating activities:

Gray whale bottom-feeding.

Three bull whales and an acquiescent, amorous female of the species were engaged in a series of maneuvers which apparently included a battle among the bulls and coy encouragement on the part of the cow. . . .

By this time it became very apparent even to a casual observer that the whales were in that condition which can best be described as "emotionally aroused. . . ."

Apparently one of the males would get in complete readiness to consummate his conquest of the acquiescent cow, when another bull, getting under him and charging with all of his might, would throw the first bull out of the way and up into the air. The displaced bull, quite apparently all in readiness for what was to have been an amorous interlude, found himself pushed high into the air and rolled over on his back. He would therefore return in angry indignation to find that the bull who supplanted him was in turn being shouldered out by a third bull.

The anthropomorphic references to "angry indignation" might be better suited to one of Gardner's Perry Mason stories, but his descriptions are nonetheless interesting, for they demonstrate at least some degree of intraspecies aggression, which Gilmore (1961) said does not exist. ("They are in fact, timid animals, more ready to flee than fight.") At Magdalena Bay in 1974 a group of scientists witnessed the mating behavior of the grays. One of them, Nichols, wrote,

Whales in groups of three, four and sometimes more were found at the surface headed up tide and all rolling over each other in such close physical contact it was difficult to see where one began and the other ended. Pectorals seem to be used to pat, rub and even clasp the partner. While actual intromission could not be seen, belly to belly contact seemed to be frequent and on two occasions a pair of whales was seen to rise from the water in the spy-out position locked together in this attitude.

In one situation the gray whale is far from timid: when the calf is threatened. The cows demonstrate an extraordinary inclination to protect their young; Caldwell and Caldwell (1966) wrote, "the maternal defense of the young is perhaps as highly developed in this species as in any other animal." Scammon's account of the whale fishery is replete with observations of injuries inflicted on whalemen by enraged females: "Hardly a day passes but there is upsetting or staving of boats, the crews receiving bruises, cuts, and, in many instances having limbs broken; and repeated accidents have happened in which men have been instantly killed, or received mortal injury." With other whales, such as the bowhead or the humpback, the calves were often struck because their predicament would bring the adult females close enough to be harpooned. The situation with the grays was often entirely different, and great care was taken not to harm the calves, for fear of the mother's wrath. If the calf is injured, claimed Scammon, "the parent animal, in her frenzy, will chase the boats, and, overtaking them, will overturn them with her head, or dash them to pieces with a stroke of her ponderous flukes." In some instances the whalers would escape by rowing themselves into water too shallow for the whales to follow; Scammon recounted an obviously apocryphal tale in which an enraged cow whale chased the whalemen onto shore, where they were advised to climb trees. (There are no trees at Scammon's Lagoon; even if the story were true, climbing on the roots of mangroves would afford little sanctuary.) When Dr. Paul Dudley White was at Scammon's trying, unsuccessfully, to obtain an EKG of a gray whale, one of the boats of Expedition Heartbeat was holed by a female protecting her calf (White and Matthews 1956). And Walker (1949) reported an instance in which a mother attempted to shield her calf from an observation helicopter.

The gray whale is the most heavily parasitized of all cetaceans. The barnacle *Cryptolepas rhachianecti* adheres to the skin in quantities, often forming solid white areas. (Their profusion and solidity, particularly on the rostrum, led Andrews [1914] to the erroneous conclusion that the gray whale had a cornified area on the snout, "similar to the 'bonnet' of the Right Whale.") Gilmore (1961) doubted the idea that the whale's breaching is an attempt to rid itself of barnacles, because "they are so deeply imbedded they cannot be pulled off with a hook." In and around the barnacles—but not limited to them—are found whale lice of three species, *Cyamus scammoni*, *C. ceti*, and *C.*

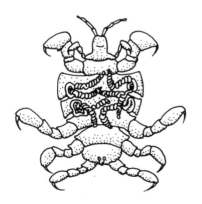

Cyamus scammoni. Host: gray whale.

kessleri. The first of these is the largest of the whale lice, measuring up to 1.06 inches (27 millimeters) and having corkscrew gills and an uneven purple coloration (Leung 1976). The lice (which are crustaceans, not insects) are most abundant on the flippers and flukes, in the umbilicus, and sometimes in the genital groove. They congregate quickly in open wounds or scars, and Leung (1965) reported a single whale from which over one hundred thousand *C. scammoni* were collected.

Although stories tell of sharks attacking gray whales, they are not very numerous, and the animal's traditional enemy is the killer whale, *Orcinus orca.* Because he had never witnessed an attack, Gilmore (1961) wrote "that the gray whale has been able to adopt its inshore habitat largely through success in remaining unseen and unheard by the killer-whale, and that the killer-whale has been so unaware of the gray whale it has never learned to include it on the menu." For the sake of the gray whale we would wish that this were true. Scammon described an attack by three killers on a cow and her calf in 1858, and although the calf was "grown to three times the bulk of the largest killers," the orcas prevailed, killing the calf and driving off the mother. Of the thirty-five whales that Andrews (1916) saw at the Korean whaling station of Ulsan, seven of them had part of the tongue torn away.* Often the grays will escape (see Morejohn 1968), but there are also reports of gray whales so paralyzed with fright that they turn over on their backs in the presence of killers and do not even struggle. (Andrews [1914] reported one of these incidents. Faced with a gray whale on its back, Captain Johnson, an intrepid whaler, "shot it in the breast.") When acousticians played the recorded underwater sounds of killer whales in the vicinity of gray whales, the grays "immediately swirled around and headed directly away from the killer whale sounds" (Cummings and Thompson 1971). Migrating gray whales (which were recorded producing "low-frequency moaning sounds"), spied out when looking for killer whales. Cummings and Thompson concluded that the grays "recognize the voice of the killer whale, that they can easily localize the sounds under water, and that they

flee killer whale phonations probably as a sign of potential danger."*

Gray whales often breach, throwing themselves almost completely out of the water and usually landing on their back or side. The reasons for this spectacular behavior are unknown, but Nichols suggested that it relates to male courtship or display. Other observers have referred the behavior to the need to loosen parasites. Many of the great whales breach, and we do not know what it signifies for any of them. (Payne [1976] believes that right whales are communicating their positions to other right whales by their resounding splash-landings.) Smaller cetaceans also leap from the water, but this is usually accomplished while in rapid forward motion; gray and right whales leap from more or less stationary starts, since they are not capable of rapid swimming. We do not know why the porpoises leap, either; perhaps they all jump for sheer exuberance, as a demonstration of their mastery of the interface between air and water, an area that only the cetaceans dominate.

Of all the great whales the distribution of the California gray whale is by far the best understood. From the waters of the Bering and Chukchi seas to the lagoons of Baja California, these whales can be located at virtually any time of the year as they make their annual migrations.

But there were other gray whales. We have already discussed the extinct Atlantic population, of which the only evidence is a few scattered bones on the coast of western Europe. When Roy Chapman Andrews was in Japan in 1910, he believed that the gray whale was extinct on both sides of the Pacific. Hearing that a type of whale known as *Koku-kujira* was being hunted from Korean whaling stations, he returned to the Orient to see if this could be the gray whale. On his arrival at the whaling station of Ulsan, Andrews (1916) saw a catcher boat coming in with a whale in tow:

We had hardly left the shore, when the siren whistle of a whale ship sounded far down the bay and soon the vessel swept around the point into view. At the port bow hung the dark flukes of a whale, the sight of which made me breathe hard with excitement, for one of two things must happen—

---

*In recent years the reputation of the killer whale has been changing from that of a bloodthirsty murderer to that of a bumbling black-and-white buffoon in oceanarium shows. While *O. orca* is undoubtedly intelligent and responsive to training in captivity, it is still the largest living predator on warm-blooded prey. (The sperm whale is larger, but feeds mostly on invertebrates, such as squid.) There are numerous records of killers attacking large whales and demonstrating a particular preference for the tongue and lips. In the wild they also eat whole seals, sea lions, and porpoises.

*In a 1971 *National Geographic* article, Walker wrote that gray whales assume a vertical position for swallowing, that they breach to make "course corrections," and that they navigate by echolocation. Cummings and Thompson took issue with Walker's curious theories and wrote that "there is no evidence that whales swallow this way or that they navigate by echolocation." The idea that a whale breaches to check on its location before landing on its back is a most unlikely suggestion.

either I was to find that here was an entirely new species, or else was to rediscover one which had been lost to science for thirty years.

It was not a new species, but it was *Eschrichtius robustus* (known to Andrews as *Rhachianectes glaucus*), the gray whale of the western Pacific. From the high Arctic the whales moved southward in two distinct populations: one coming down the North American coast to Baja and the other traveling from the Sea of Okhotsk, past Kamchatka and Sakhalin, past the northern islands of Japan, and finally stopping at the southern tip of the Korean peninsula, an area marked by numerous small islands and bays.

The western population of gray whales was hunted by the Japanese in the eighteenth century, first with harpoons and later with nets (Omura 1974). When the whales were sighted from shore, a fleet of boats would set out to drive them into shallow water, where they would be entangled in nets and stabbed with harpoons, spears, and even swords. (A Kuniyoshi print of about 1850 shows Miyamoto Nusashi, a famous samurai, astride a curiously speckled whale, which he is killing with his sword [Brewington and Brewington 1969].) The Japanese net fishery did not last very long; the whales seemed to disappear from Japanese coastal waters, and by the latter part of the nineteenth century, the Japanese were participating in modern whaling, using steel-hulled catcher boats and harpoon guns (Terry 1951). The gray whale was not seen again in Japanese waters. According to Omura (1974), it probably was driven away by industrial development and joined the Korean stock. Instead of migrating along the eastern coast of Japan (possibly to calve in the protected waters of the Suo Gulf and Seto Sea), the whales stayed far to the west, in order to rendezvous in the waters of southern Korea. Here, however, they were in even more trouble. The Japanese, who annexed Korea in 1910 and controlled it until the end of World War II, had numerous whaling stations in their colonies, one of which was Ulsan, where Andrews "rediscovered" the gray whale in 1912. From these Korean shore stations, Norwegian captains with Japanese crews and Korean shore workers methodically eliminated the so-called Korean gray whale. Mizue (1951) reported that the last of this species was taken in 1933, and none has been seen there since. In later years biologists have searched the country for some record of recent sightings, but the results have been negative. Bowen (1974) went through Korea "in taxis, on foot, in boats," but could find no record of the gray whale and so reported it extinct.* An occasional gray whale wanders down the western side of the Pacific, but these are believed to be strays from the Bering Sea (Nishiwaki and Kasuya 1970). The fact that the Korean stock has not reappeared since 1933 indicates that the eastern and western stocks were separate and probably did not intermingle.

Gray whales were probably hunted for hundreds—perhaps thousands—of years by various aboriginal populations that inhabited the western shores of the North American continent. Almost everywhere along their migration route they were vulnerable to shore whaling. The gray whale was an easy species to kill, and since the calves are born off the uninhabited coast of Baja California and mature as they head north, the aborigines did not encounter the problem of enraged females defending their calves. In the Arctic, gray whales were hunted by Siberian and Alaskan Eskimos. Scammon describes the eight-man boats used by the "Esquimaux," their lances, knives, floats, and other equipment, and their manner of killing and dividing up the whale:

The choice pieces for a dainty repast, with them, are the flukes, lips, and fins. The oil is a great article of trade with the interior tribes of "reindeer-men:" it is sold in skins of fifteen gallons each, a skin of oil being the price of a reindeer. The entrails are made into a kind of souse, by pickling them in a liquid extracted from a root that imparts an acrid taste: this preparation is a savory dish, as well as a preventative of the scurvy. The lean flesh supplies food for their dogs, the whole troop of the village gathering about the carcass, fighting, feasting, and howling, as only sledge-dogs can.

After crossing the relatively safe Gulf of Alaska (during the southward migration), the whales are met by the Indians of the northwest coast; "like enemies in ambush, these glide in canoes from island, bluff, or bay, rushing upon their prey with whoop and yell, launching their instruments of torture, and like hounds, worrying the last life-blood from their vitals" (Scammon). Less romantic descriptions of the techniques of the northwest coastal Indians (for example, Drucker 1951) have produced a less hysterical picture of this enterprise, in which the Nootka of Vancouver

*In a 1977 paper Brownell and Chun disputed Bowen's findings, reporting "at least 67 gray whales" taken in South Korean waters between 1948 and 1966. Because North and South Korea, as well as the People's Republic of China, are not members of the IWC, the authors stated their belief that the "western Pacific stock of gray whales will become extinct in the near future unless meaningful international protection is achieved."

Island would perform elaborate rituals before setting out after a whale, presumably hunting it with few or no war whoops. The natives of the Aleutian Islands (known as Aleuts) may have hunted the gray whale, but the literature is not explicit on the species they sought. They did hunt whales using spears with the points dipped in aconite, a poison that was probably effective in killing even a large whale (Heizer 1943).

Before the mid-nineteenth-century discovery of the breeding grounds of the gray whales, offshore whalers probably had some contact with these animals, but because their main object was the sperm whale, they probably ignored the strange, mottled creature with the sharp nose and the knobby back. (In his "Distribution of Certain Whales as shown by Logbook Records of American Whaleships," Townsend [1935] listed 557 California grays, but did not identify the locations at which they were taken. Furthermore, he had access only to the records of New England whaleships, and San Francisco whalers such as Scammon—whose logbooks exist—were not included.) Sperm whales are deep-water creatures, and the sperm whalers would not ordinarily encounter gray whales except perhaps on their Bay of Alaska crossing. Known to the New England sperm whalers as the Kodiak Ground, this area was a particularly productive area in the summer, just when the gray whales would be making their passage (Gilmore 1959).

West coast whalers discovered the Lower California whaling grounds as early as 1846, and by 1848 some fifty-odd vessels had gone to Magdalena Bay for "between the seasons" whaling (Henderson 1972). In 1856, Captain Scammon made a whaling voyage to Magdalena Bay, and in the following year, commanding the brig *Boston,* he "made a whaling discovery which stands as one of the most important episodes in the story of the gray whale fishery" (Henderson 1972). In 1858 he crossed the barrier bar into the lagoon that now bears his name and came upon the greatest single concentration of gray whales in the world. Scammon did not try to keep his discovery a secret from other whalers; in fact, he went there as the captain of a whaling fleet in 1858/59. (The season for "lagoon whaling" began in December and extended to the following April, so the dates are expressed in combined years.) During that season eighteen vessels came to Scammon's, including the ill-fated bark *Black Warrior.* Lost against the shore while leaving what was then known as Middle Lagoon, this ship gained immortality in translation, for the lagoon was known from that time onward as Guerrero Negro. Scammon made

three more voyages to Baja to hunt the devilfish, but by 1862/63 he noticed that the whales were becoming scarce in the lagoons, and the whalers patrolled the coastal migration routes rather than waiting for them in the protected estuaries. Different techniques were employed at this time, including "kelp whaling," which consisted of hunting the whales in the offshore kelp beds; "sailing them down," or coming upon them from upwind to dispatch the whales with harpoons; the self-explanatory "whaling among the breakers"; and, in the 1860s, shooting them with "Greener's Harpoon Gun," a swivel-mounted weapon that took a great deal of the danger out of gray whaling, even though it was still conducted from small boats. (Scammon, p. 249, provides a good illustration of this technique.)

The most intensive whaling took place at Baja from 1855 to 1865, after which time the population was severely depleted. For the period 1853–56, Scammon figured that there were "probably not over 30,000" gray whales, and he estimated the "total number which have been captured or destroyed since the bay-whaling commenced in 1846, would not exceed 10,800." He wrote that the number remaining in 1874 was between 8,000 and 10,000. Subsequent studies have shown that all his figures were on the high side. In a detailed study of the logbook records and shipping reports of the period Henderson (1972) found that the maximum number of gray whales killed between 1846 and 1865 was 6,039, allowing for an additional 10 percent that were mortally wounded, but not captured. Rice (1975) reevaluated the earlier data on population size and concluded that "prior to exploitation . . . the California stock of the gray whale numbered no more than 15,000."

If one had to devise a method whereby a population would be severely depleted in a short period of time, it would be hard to improve on the approach used by the nineteenth-century California gray whalers. Since the females were in the shallowest water and were, therefore, the easiest to take, the whalemen killed mainly animals of that sex, most of which were either pregnant or nursing. This virtually guaranteed the inability of the population to regenerate, even if the whaling itself became less intensive. In addition, this particular population was particularly susceptible to decimation, for the entire stock appeared regularly in the same locations and then went into shallow water where the whalers could wait for them or take them as they passed into the lagoons. Shallow-water whaling, while dangerous to the whalers, was far more dangerous to the whales. The whales could neither hide nor escape, and if the whalers missed a given whale in one season, that animal would return to the same spot the following year to give the hunters another chance.

Those whales that were not killed in the lagoons were taken at shore stations along the California coast, which had been established primarily for humpback whaling, but if an occasional gray appeared, it, too, would be killed. From 1866 to 1874 another 2,000 gray whales were killed (Henderson 1972). By the time Scammon's book was published in 1874, the devilfish was extremely scarce in the eastern Pacific; and prior to his "rediscovery" of the western, or Korean, gray whale, Andrews (1916) wrote that "the species had been lost to science and naturalists believed it to be extinct."

The scientists and the whalers were unable to find the gray whales, but because of their extremely restricted breeding grounds, the whales could find each other. Somehow—perhaps by migrating farther offshore or by forsaking the lagoons of western Baja for the undiscovered bays on the Mexican mainland— they began a renaissance. The population grew virtually unmolested until around 1914, when Norwegian factory ships arrived off Magdalena Bay. Again the gray whales were killed en route to their breeding grounds, and again their numbers began to plummet. In the 1920s, Soviet, Japanese, Norwegian, and American whaleships plied the waters of western North America and took the gray whales in the Bering and Chukchi seas as well. The killing continued unchecked until the end of World War II, when the International Convention for the Regulation of Whaling was signed by the various whaling nations. A total of 683 gray whales were killed between 1933 and 1946, even though the species had ostensibly been given full protection as early as 1937. The Soviet Union and Japan did not recognize the 1937 agreement and continued gray whaling in the Arctic until 1946. Between 1938 and 1947 the Soviet factory ship *Aleut* is reported to have taken 471 gray whales, and the Japanese *Tonan Maru*, also operating along the Siberian coast, took 58 gray whales in 1940 (Henderson 1972).

By 1946 the gray whale was fully protected, although there did not seem to be many whales to protect. The Soviets continued to take the species in the Arctic under a provision of the International Convention that permits contracting governments to kill whales if the meat is used for the feeding of aborigines. For the years 1965–73, Rice (1975) reported that the Soviets captured 1,418 gray whales for Siberian

aborigines. At the 1978 IWC meeting the species was removed from the "protected species" category and placed into a "sustained management stock," a category used for species that have "remained at a stable level for a considerable period under a regime of approximately constant catches" (IWC 1978). The noncommercial quota for 1978 was 179 whales, roughly the same number that the Soviets had been taking each year since 1965, according to Rice (1975). (The Soviets, however, have adamantly refused to provide the documentation for their assertion that 179 gray whales are needed for Siberian Eskimo consumption, and there is some suspicion that the meat may be used to feed nonaboriginal peoples, or even fur animals.)

Because of its restricted range and shore-bound habitat, the gray whale is the only species of cetacean that can be counted with a fair degree of accuracy. Various observers have conducted censuses of the population (Gilmore 1960, Rice 1961, Hubbs and Hubbs 1967, and others), and it is now estimated that the population is about 15,000 (Rugh and Braham 1979). The number has thus more than doubled in twenty years, but the figure would appear to be relatively stable, indicating a leveling off of the increase. In 1961, Rice wrote, "the rate of increase in wild mammalian populations tends to decrease as the carrying capacity is approached."

It is this same proximity to shore that makes the migration of the gray whales one of the great natural spectacles of our time. Hundreds of thousands of visitors each year visit the Cabrillo National Monument at Point Loma, San Diego, to watch the majestic passage of the whales, and many more observe from other vantage points along the California and Oregon coasts. Whale-watching cruises have become a major tourist attraction in southern California, and certain boats will take tourists all the way down to San Ignacio Lagoon. (Scammon's Lagoon has been declared a whale sanctuary by the Mexican government, and it is off-limits to tourists.) The heavy tourist traffic may represent another threat to this beleaguered species, since it has been shown that too much activity will cause the whales to move from one breeding area to another. (When salt was being loaded at Guerrero Negro from 1957 to 1967, the whales were not seen there, but when the loading facilities were switched to Scammon's, the whales returned to Guerrero Negro.)* This relict population of what Andrews

---

*According to Wolman and Rice (1979), "there is no evidence that San Diego Bay, California, was ever a calving area."

called "living fossils" is further threatened by technology: the Mexican government is drilling for oil in the Vizcaino Desert, south of Scammon's Lagoon, and if oil should be found there, the natural place to load and ship it would be from the protected entrances to the lagoons. Recent suggestions in the press also seem unfavorable to the species: the gray whale, having "returned" to previous population levels, should be taken off the Endangered Species List, and perhaps Soviet and Japanese whalers should even be permitted to "harvest" some from the California herd, according to an article in the *New York Times* (1978).

Undoubtedly because of the increased boat traffic in the lagoons, the whales have begun to interact with the boats—and in some cases, the people in the boats—in a way that is unique for baleen whales. In the past, visitors in small boats could approach within ten to twenty feet of the whales in the lagoons. But recently certain animals, known as "curious whales," have come up to the boats, rubbed them with their rostrums, and even permitted themselves to be petted and stroked. During the 1976–77 season, Swartz and Cummings recorded no less than twenty-five occurrences of this "friendly whale" behavior, involving fifteen cetaceans. One encounter lasted for well over two hours, although others took an hour or less. In all these instances, it was the whale that initiated the encounter, approaching the boat and then performing the various actions that have so excited the whale watchers of Baja in recent winters.

The gray whale has barely survived two catastrophic assaults on its numbers, although it was probably never as depleted as the blue, fin, or humpback populations. Another effort, that of the Japanese and Soviet pelagic whalers, would probably deprive the world of this unique animal once and for all. Its very existence, in spite of the massive efforts to eliminate it, should assure it a permanent place among our dwindling natural resources.

THE RORQUALS

The order Mysteceti gets its name from the Greek *mystax* ("moustache") and *ketos* ("whale"), referring, of course, to the baleen plates in the whale's mouth. In this order there are three families: the Eschrichtiidae (gray whale); Balaenidae (right whales); and the Balaenopteridae, which includes all genera with baleen plates, a dorsal fin, and throat grooves. The genus name *Balaenoptera* is derived from the words for "whale" and "wing" and refers to the dorsal fin. The larger right whales, Balaenidae, have no dorsal fin, but the curious and rare pygmy right whale has a dorsal fin as well as the long, flexible baleen of its larger relatives. Five of the six species of balaenopterids (the blue, fin, sei, Bryde's, and minke whales) are known as rorquals and are similar in overall morphology, whereas the sixth, the humpback, is placed in its own monotypical genus.

The word "rorqual" comes from the Norwegian and means "tube" (or "furrow") whale, *rör hval,* referring to the multitude of pleats on the throats of these animals. Many possibilities have been mentioned for the function of these grooves, and it is likely that they serve more than one purpose. They surely allow for the expansion of the whale's throat when it is taking in huge quantities of water and the small crustaceans or fish that make up its diet, but why, then, do the grooves in some species extend as far back as the navel? Other suggestions are that the grooves enable the whale to increase its speed in the water by reducing drag or that "they may act like bilge keels on a ship's bottom and have a stabilizing function" (Ommanney 1971).

Ever since mankind's earliest exposure to whales, their name has been a synonym for great size. The leviathan of the Bible is probably a whale, as is the "great fish" that swallowed Jonah. Since the earliest visible whales probably were dead and washed ashore, it is not surprising that those who depicted them drew them as obese and expanded creatures, often inflated by the gases of their decomposition. The throat muscles, tensed in life, had relaxed when the whale died, and the bulging sac of the whale's distended throat contributed to the erroneous picture of the whale. So, too, did the whales that people saw first; the right whales, with their huge heads, down-curved mouths, and slow swimming habits, are hardly the epitome of grace.

The rorquals, which can attain a known weight of 136 tons (Budker 1959) and even higher estimated weights, present another matter altogether.* That some of them attain colossal size is unequivocally correct, but they are not fat and awkward at all. They are, in fact, graceful and powerful swimmers, integrated into their environment in a way that humans can only dream of. Their overall proportions represent the quintessence of speed. The rorquals, especially the blue, fin, and sei whales (the largest of the genus), are probably the fastest of all whales, and when pressed or injured (exhibiting what Lockyer [1976] called "maximum speed when alarmed"), they very well might be the fastest animals in the sea.† With their mouths agape and their throats expanded, these great whales are probably less than graceful, but when moving at speed with their mouths closed, they are hydrodynamic perfection. Biologist G. R. Williamson, who has

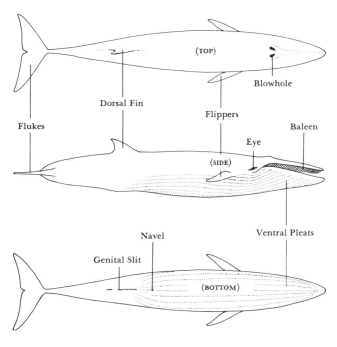

TOPOGRAPHY OF A RORQUAL

*The 136-ton figure was given by Budker for a blue whale that was 89 feet (27.1 meters) long. The maximum size for blue whales is discussed in the species account that follows. Authenticated records report blue whales from 93 to 98 feet long (28.35–29.88 meters) and the possibility of even larger specimens.

†This sort of statement can engender endless argument, and definite answers are hard to come by. There are those who claim the title for various scombroid fishes, like the tuna; others who choose the wahoo or the sailfish; and still others who claim the title for the mako shark, which feeds on many of the fishes mentioned above. Still other schools hold their speed champions to be various smaller cetaceans, such as the Dall porpoise or the killer whale. The assumption of great speed in the larger rorquals is based on actual observation and on prodigious displays of power that these animals have shown. They can tow hundred-ton catcher boats for hours, and they can, in rare instances, hurl their own weight completely out of the water, an astounding accomplishment for an animal that may weigh eighty tons or more.

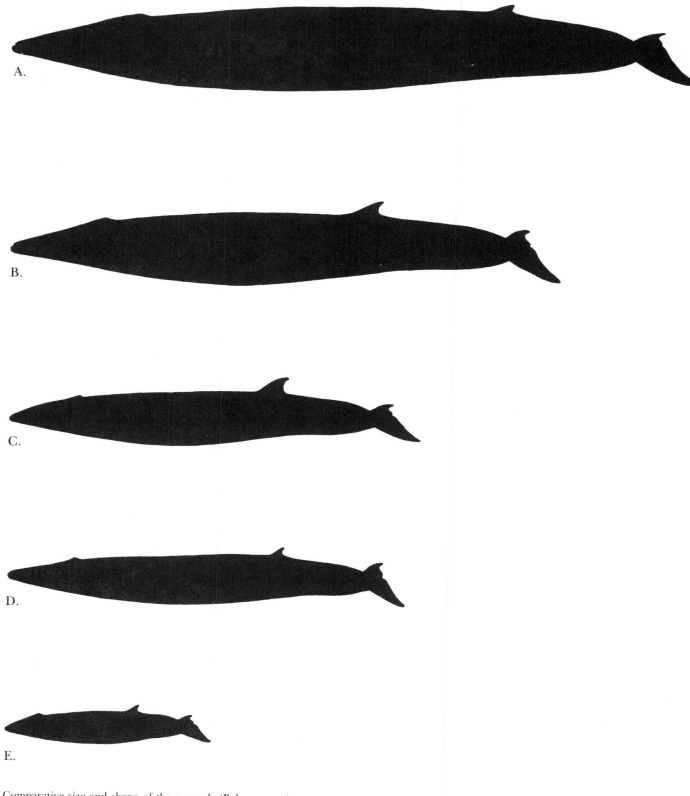

Comparative size and shape of the rorquals (Balaenoptera):
A. Blue whale (*B. muscalus*)
B. Fin whale (*B. physalus*)
C. Sei whale (*B. borealis*)
D. Bryde's whale (*B. edeni*)
E. Minke whale (*B. acutorostrata*)
Note particularly the position and size of the dorsal fin in the
different species and the "Roman nose" of the sei whale.

made a particular study of the shape of rorquals, has written a number of technical and popular papers on the subject and has photographed live minke and sei whales underwater. In 1974 he described them thus: "both the minke and the sei whales had a highly streamlined silhouette. The throat region was nearly flat, and the ventral grooves were held into the body. . . . This streamlining is in keeping with their ability to swim fast, and undoubtedly other rorqual species are equally sleek."

The baleen plates of the balaenopterids are short compared with those of the right whales, and most of the species are classified as "swallowers," as opposed to "skimmers" (Nemoto 1959). Only the sei whale, which has finely meshed baleen fringes, feeds on copepods and other tiny crustaceans by "skimming," which is slowly swimming through swarms of food organisms with the mouth partially open. The other rorquals swallow huge mouthfuls of food, often turning on their sides during the process and splashing energetically. After ingesting a huge quantity of food organisms and water, the whale forces the water out with its tongue (perhaps it also contracts the throat muscles —another possible function of the pleats), while the food remains trapped in the hairy fringes of the baleen. The water is often ejected so forcibly that it squirts out of the whale's closing mouth (Andrews 1916). The tongue of the rorqual is not as mobile as that of the right whales; it is more an extension of the floor of the mouth, used to force the water out before the food is swallowed. Pivorunas (1979) has calculated that an adult blue whale may "engulf" as much as seventy tons of water with each mouthful.

Although they are known to eat a variety of food organisms, the predominant item in the diet of the rorquals is krill. This is a general term that simply means "whale food" in Norwegian (Matthews 1932),

but it is usually applied to an Antarctic crustacean, *Euphausia superba.* This shrimplike crustacean is found only south of the Antarctic Convergence, which is also called the Polar Front, in vast swarms or rafts. These congregations may be miles in extent, sometimes coloring the sea red, but they are not found at depth. J. W. S. Marr, in a 1956 study of *E. superba,* wrote that "the adolescent and adult forms of krill upon which the whales mainly subsist are concentrated in the Antarctic surface layer, the vast majority in fact being crowded into an even narrower surface zone." (The surface habitat of the rorquals' food is a good—but hardly definitive—argument for the whales' surface existence. Under duress, blue and fin whales have been known to descend to great depths [Scholander 1940], but unless they are harpooned, they seem to have no reason to dive deeply.)

The list of organisms consumed by the five species of rorquals is surprisingly long and varied, although it remains fairly narrow in range. In the Antarctic the staple food of the blue, fin, and minke whales is *E. superba,* but other euphausiids are eaten in southern waters, such as *E. vallentini,* which seems to be the food preference of the pygmy blue whale (a subspecies of the great blue whale) in the Antarctic and subantarctic waters of the southern Indian Ocean. In northern waters where *E. superba* does not occur, the rorquals eat a variety of small food items, from copepods and other small crustaceans (such as *Calanus finmarchius,* which is known as "brit" in the North Atlantic) to small fishes. In some areas fin whales eat a predominantly fish diet, whereas in other areas they eat crustaceans almost exclusively (Jonsgard 1966, Mitchell 1974). Bryde's whale, with its coarse baleen fringes, is a fish eater.

Specific distribution of the stocks of rorquals is discussed in some detail in the accounts of the species,

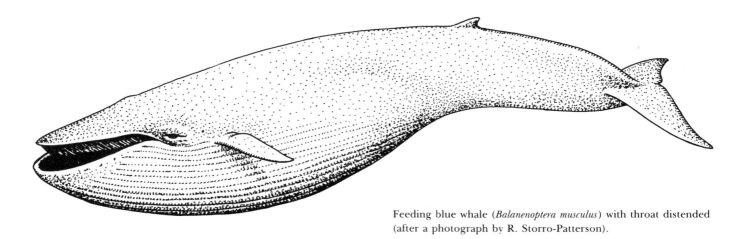

Feeding blue whale (*Balanenoptera musculus*) with throat distended (after a photograph by R. Storro-Patterson).

but they share some common characteristics. They are all migratory animals, with the possible exception of the pygmy blue whale, but many of their movements are not fully understood. The blue and fin whales of the Southern Hemisphere, for example, move south to the edge of the pack ice in the southern summer (December to April) to feed, but their whereabouts for the remainder of the year are unknown. Bryde's whale inhabits temperate and subtropical waters, but the other species are found in the colder waters of the world, usually moving toward the poles to feed. The rorquals bring forth their young in warmer waters, and it is assumed that they breed there as well. The gestation period for these large whales is eleven to twelve months, so that parturition takes place in that phase of the migratory cycle when the whales are in the warmer portion of their range.

The history of each species with regard to the whaling industry is virtually the same: each animal was exploited ruthlessly until it became impractical to search for that particular species; then the whalers would move on to the next smallest type of rorqual. Until the invention of the grenade harpoon, the rorquals were safe from the rapacious whalers. The whales were too fast and too strong, and their Antarctic concentrations were all but unknown. When the technology coincided with the discovery of the whale's southern feeding grounds, the carnage that ensued was unprecedented. From the dominance of sperm whaling in our historical record, it might be assumed that Yankee whalers were successful in terms of total numbers of animals taken, as indeed some of them were. However, there is no comparison between their success and that of twentieth-century whalers. It was not the mid-nineteenth century, the heyday of New England whaling, that saw the peak catches recorded, nor was it the early twentieth century, when the various whaling nations began to exploit the southern stocks of whales. According to the *International Whaling Statistics,* the greatest number of rorquals taken in one season in the Antarctic was 39,572, for the season of 1930/31.* In this season 29,410 blue whales were killed, 10,017 fins, and 145 seis. (By the following year the price of oil had fallen so sharply that the Norwe-

gians did not go south, and only 6,488 blues were taken. By the season of 1932/33, however, the number of blue whales killed in the Antarctic was 18,891.) The season of 1961/62 was close to 1930/31, with a total of 35,607 rorquals captured.*

After more than half a century of unmitigated greed and wanton destruction, the whaling industry has finally reached a level of diminishing returns that has greatly restricted its activities. The humpback and the gray whales are protected, and the bowhead and the right whale are so rare as to be considered commercially extinct. All the rorquals have been so reduced in numbers that they are protected almost throughout their range; of the great whales only the minke is still being hunted extensively. Because the IWC has banned whaling for sperm whales, the minke is left as the sole target for the Soviet and Japanese whaling fleets. In the Antarctic the catch limit for 1977/78 was 5,690 animals, and for the Northern Hemisphere the quota allowed for another 2,955 minkes to be killed.† At the 1979 IWC meeting in London the quota for minke whales was set at over 12,000 animals. The total quotas for the other hunted rorquals were as follows: 604 fin whales, 100 sei whales, and 743 Bryde's whales. The blue whale is totally protected throughout the world, and no nation may legally kill one. The relatively small size of the minke makes it uneconomical to hunt it with exploding harpoons—too much of the meat might be destroyed—so it is likely that "cold" harpoons will be employed. When these instruments are used, the whale does not die instantly, but pulls against the ship until it tires and dies. The whaling industry would appear to be succumbing to the combined pressures of adverse world opinion and economic disaster, but the whaling nations persist, making one more attempt to wring the final yen or ruble from the last of the great whales.

*These totals are for blue, fin, and sei whales only. Bryde's whale was included in the sei statistics, and minke whales were not hunted at all. If humpback and sperm whales are added to the totals, the early 1960s become the years of the greatest whale slaughter in history. In 1960/61 a total of 65,658 whales were killed throughout the world's oceans; in 1961/62 the total was 66,326. For comparison, Townsend (1935) estimated that the number of whales killed in any one year by the great American whaling fleet in the nineteenth century never exceeded 10,000 animals.
†The figures in this section are quoted from the April 1979 *Schedule,* the document issued by the International Whaling Commission that contains the catch quotas agreed on at the previous year's meeting. The figures for the 1979 meeting were obtained from numerous published reports of the proceedings.

*Since whaling seasons in the Antarctic began in December and did not end until the following April, they are always expressed in terms of two years.

MINKE WHALE

Balaenoptera acutorostrata Lacépède 1809

The smallest of the rorquals, the minke whale is a very large animal by any standards other than those used for baleen whales. It has been called "tiny" (Hill 1975), but for an animal that can reach a length of 33.5 feet (10.2 meters) and a weight of over 11 tons (10,000 kilograms) "tiny" seems an inappropriate adjective. (Of all the animals now alive, only the other whales and two fishes—the whale shark and the basking shark—are larger than a full-grown minke.) *Acutus* means "sharp" in Latin, so the trivial portion of its scientific name describes the minke as a sharp-snouted whale.

In this species the rostrum is markedly triangular and proportionately shorter than that of any other rorqual. It has a single ridge on the rostrum, and the double blowhole is forward of the eye. Unlike the larger baleen whales, the minke cannot easily be identified by its blow, since the exhalation is small and not often seen. The baleen plates, which number about 300 on each side of the upper jaw, are yellowish-white, a diagnostic character of the species. The minke is dark gray to black above and white below, with considerable variation in the integration of the two colors. Various stocks show streaks of lighter color in the vicinity of the flipper or the ear, and some sport chevrons on the back, similar to those seen on fin whales. The ventral surface of the flukes is white, bordered with gray. The dorsal fin is high and prominently falcate, and this species has 60–70 ventral grooves that do not reach the navel, but end just beyond the point of the flippers. The most prominent and recognizable field mark is the broad white band on the dorsal surface of the flipper, a characteristic that can often be seen when the animal is in the water and that occurs in no other cetacean.

This species has been known by various other names, including "lesser rorqual," "little piked whale," and "sharp-headed finner," but the name minke (pronounced "minky") has ousted all the others from popular usage. Its origins are somewhat uncertain, since the other names have been used concurrently until fairly recently. Allen (1916) refers to the name "minkie" and quotes Millais's 1906 account of the derivation. Age Jonsgard wrote to me that Meincke was a German laborer working for Svend Foyn, inventor of the grenade harpoon. Meincke "one day mistook a school of this whale species for blue whales. . . . most probably he made this mistake during Foyn's whaling operations in the Varanger Fjord be-

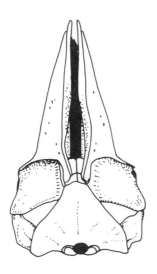

Dorsal view of the skull of the minke whale, *Balaenoptera acutorostrata* (after Allen).

tween 1868 and 1885." The name has been in use since Meincke made his mistake, but it did not gain wide currency until other nations began to follow the Norwegian example in hunting this species.* Jonsgard's 1951 paper in *Norsk Hvalfangst-tidende* (Norwegian Whaling Gazette) was entitled "Studies on the little piked whale or minke whale," and its publication probably marked the beginning of the general acceptance of the term "minke" (at least among whalers) and the gradual elimination of the other names.

The only other similarly sized whale with which the minke might be confused is the bottlenose whale, *Hyperoodon,* but the latter, which can reach a length of perhaps 30 feet (9.15 meters), has a small, triangular dorsal fin, unlike the high, curved fin of the minke. The bottlenose whales also have a pronounced beak and forehead, which are lacking in the minke. There is the remote possibility of confusing the pygmy right whale, *Caperea marginata,* with the minke in the Southern Hemisphere, but this species is rarely seen at sea.

When the population of a given species is heavily exploited (for example, the blue whale or the various species of *Stenella* that were involved in the American tuna fishery in the Pacific), one of the side effects can be the increased study of the animals caught and, therefore, new information on their habits, biology, and stocks. When the fishery for the minke whale was concentrated in the North Atlantic and Japanese waters, all the whales taken looked more or less alike, and it was naturally assumed that there was a single worldwide species. (Some faint suggestions of differentiation were made in the late nineteenth century by

*The Norwegians were by far the most accomplished hunters of the minke whale in the years preceding 1971, when the exploitation of the Antarctic stocks began. It is likely that the Norwegian whalers passed along their vernacular name, in addition to other information, to those who were to hunt the minke when the stocks of the larger rorquals fell too low to be profitably hunted. The ultimate acknowledgment of Meincke's unfortunate error can be found in the current Japanese name for this species: it used to be *Koiwashi-kujira* ("lesser sei whale"), but it is now *minku.*

Burmeister, Scammon, and others, but for the most part the animals they described were ignored. By the middle of this century, however, reports of strangely marked (actually, strangely unmarked) minke whales began to emanate from the Southern Hemisphere. In 1867, H. C. Burmeister, director of the museum at Buenos Aires, described a minke whale that was found in Argentina and differed in numerous osteological aspects from *B. acutorostrata.* Significantly, Burmeister did not describe the color of the whale, particularly the flippers, because he was sick for two weeks before he could get to examine the animal, and by then, "putrefaction had already destroyed the whale's external appearance." Burmeister named the "new" species *Balaenoptera bonaërensis* (for Buenos Aires), and it remained in the background of minke whale research— such as it was—because this whale was simply not large enough to be commercially investigated.

As the stocks of the larger whales declined, the minke came more and more under the eye of the harpoon gunner, and more of them were taken. It soon became apparent that there was in fact a difference between northern and southern minkes: whereas all the northern animals had a white band on the flipper, a significant proportion of the southern animals did not. In addition, the other feature supposedly present in all (and only) minke whales—cream-white baleen plates—was also seen to be modified in the southern whales. Some of the southern minkes had no flipper stripe and had baleen that was white at the front of the mouth, but grayish-brown toward the rear (Williamson 1961). In the Antarctic whaling season of 1963/64, Japanese whalers captured ninety-six minke-type whales, all of which had uniformly colored flippers and bicolored baleen (Kasuya and Ichihara 1965). *B. bonaërensis* may be specifically distinct (Nishiwaki [1972] listed it as the "New Zealand piked whale"), but most cetologists recognize the various forms only at the subspecies level: *B. acutorostrata acuto-*

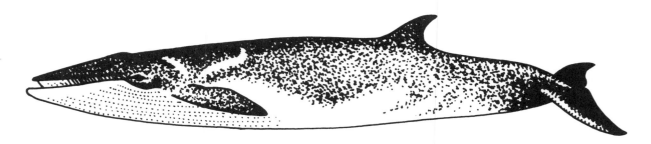

Minke whale, *Balaenoptera acutorostrata* var. *bonaërensis.* Notice the stripeless flipper and the dark baleen at the rear of the mouth.

rostrata from the North Atlantic; *B. a. bonaërensis* from the Southern Hemisphere; and *B. a. davidsoni* from the North Pacific. (The last was described by Scammon [1874] and differentiated by cranial dimensions.) If *bonaërensis* proves to be a valid species, it will be unique among the rorquals, for it is the only one found exclusively in the Southern Hemisphere. Omura and Kasuya (1976) have shown that there are measurable osteological differences between the northern and southern populations, and Doroshenko (1979) has demonstrated that there are no less than seven distinct populations in the Southern Hemisphere, which can be differentiated by "a whole series of morpho-physiological features characteristic of it alone but within the general genetic pool of the species." Doroshenko identifies each population according to its winter habitat: "In the South Atlantic there are the Brazilian, African and the lesser part of the Madagascan populations; in the South Pacific sector of the Antarctic there are the New Zealand, Pacific and Chilean-Peruvian populations; and in the Indian Ocean, the Indian population and the greater part of the Madagascan population are to be found." (In 1963, Deraniyagala named *B. a. thalmaha,* a subspecies of what was obviously Doroshenko's "Indian population," but this was not recognized by the scientific community as a valid distinction.)

The minke whale feeds on a variety of organisms, depending on its location and the availability of prey species. In the North Atlantic its major food item is the capelin, followed in importance by cod, herring, salmon, squid, and shrimp (Sergeant 1963). In the North Pacific they eat sardines, anchovies, herring, and copepods (Omura and Sakiura 1956), and in the Southern Ocean, they feed on krill almost exclusively. The minke is a highly migratory species, and some of its movements seem to be dictated by food concentrations, though others are apparently a function of sexual segregation. In the Northern Hemisphere the whales move northward in the spring and early summer and southward in the autumn. Opposite movements are observed in the Antarctic. Of all baleen whales, minkes are found closest to the edge of the polar ice, sometimes entering the ice fields. There have been instances in which minkes became trapped in the ice; when the openings are too small for the animals to breathe in the normal rolling manner, they may poke their heads vertically until the blowhole is exposed (Taylor 1957).

Not a schooling species, minkes are usually seen alone or in groups of two to four animals. They have been recorded to segregate by sex, the females being found closer to shore and the males most often being taken farther out to sea (Jonsgard 1951). Like all rorquals, the minke is a fast swimmer; but unlike the others, it has a frequently fatal inclination to approach ships. The ships so innocently approached might very well be whaling vessels. Sergeant (1975) reported that minkes are "tame to stopped ships" and might follow draggers for the discards. Scammon, who knew the species as the "sharp-headed finner whale" and noted that the whalers often called it a "young Finback" or a "Finback's calf," wrote that the species "frequently gambols about vessels when under way, darting from one side to the other beneath their bottoms." South of Newfoundland, Beamish and Mitchell (1973) tape-recorded and photographed a minke whale that circled their vessel, dived under it, and surfaced alongside. They wrote, "The minke . . . commonly approaches ships, and will remain within a few tens of meters of a quiet vessel." On the shores of Britain minke whales strand more often than any other species of whale. In fact, Fraser (1974) ranked this species fourth in the number of overall cetacean strandings—only the harbor porpoise, common dolphin, and pilot whale strand more frequently in England. The minke is also known from the beaches of the European mainland, Asia, and both coasts of North America. Sullivan and Houck (1979) recorded three specimens that have stranded in California since 1965, and in Little Compton, Rhode Island, I observed minkes washed ashore in the summers of 1976 and 1977.

For many years, investigators were puzzled by low-frequency underwater noises, which they called "A-train" sounds. It was not known if these were the sounds of a submarine or perhaps some unknown object. Now called "thump trains," these low-frequency sounds (between 100 and 200 Hz) are now believed to be made by minke whales and were first recorded in the Antarctic by Schevill and Watkins (1972). Other minke whale noises have since been identified, including "various ping sounds and clicks produced irregularly in short trains" (Winn and Perkins 1976). Since it is believed that mysticetes do not echolocate—that is, send out clicks and analyze the returning echoes—these sounds must serve some other function. They may be signals to another whale, perhaps transmitting information about the sender's location, sex, or inclinations.

On the average, female minkes are larger than males. Females reach sexual maturity at about 24 feet (7.3 meters) and males at about 22 feet (7 meters), and this occurs at about 2 years of age (Omura and Sakiura, 1957). After a gestation period of nine and a half to ten months, an 8–9-foot (2.5–2.7-meter) calf is born and nurses for about six months.

In 1956 a 20-foot (6.10-meter) specimen of undetermined gender was kept at the Mito Aquarium, Japan, in a large pool that was closed off from the sea by a net barrier. It did not eat, did not appear to sleep, and swam slowly in a counterclockwise direction for thirty-seven days before it escaped through the nets into the sea (Kimura and Nemoto 1956). This was the first baleen whale captured for observation, but its escape precluded any prolonged studies.

There are at least three distinct populations of minke whales, which are sometimes assigned subspecific status. In the western North Atlantic this mammal occurs from Baffin Bay south to Newfoundland and the Gulf of Saint Lawrence, to Chesapeake Bay, and to northeast Florida and the Bahamas in the winter. It is found in the eastern Atlantic from the Barents Sea to Norway, Iceland, and Greenland, sometimes stranding as far south as England. In the eastern North Pacific the population ranges from the Chukchi Sea to northern Baja California in the summer and from central California to the Revillagigedo Islands in the winter. It is a fairly common species in the coastal waters of Japan, the Bering Strait, and Kamchatka. There is a large population in the Southern Ocean, ranging northward into the South Atlantic, Indian, and South Pacific oceans. The minke is not as coastal an animal as the gray whale, but it is rarely seen as far as 100 miles (160 kilometers) from shore (Omura and Sakiura 1957).

Since the Middle Ages, Norwegians have hunted the minke whale for food. The earliest records show that the whales were trapped in fjords and then shot with poisoned arrows (Jonsgard and Long 1959). By the nineteenth century the bows and arrows had been replaced by rifles in the fjord hunting. Concurrently, the most famous of the Norwegian whalers, Svend Foyn, had invented the grenade harpoon, and the age of efficient, mechanized whaling had begun. Although the Norwegians roamed the world in search of the larger, more profitable species, their small-whale fishery (for minkes, belugas, pilot whales, and bottlenose whales) was conducted in their own front yard. In the waters of northern Scandinavia, Iceland, Spitsbergen, and the Barents Sea they hunted in vessels of up to eighty feet, and a prosperous industry was developed by the 1930s. In the years that followed, Norwegian whalers took some 3,000 minkes annually, a

figure that affected the North Atlantic population to some degree (Jonsgard 1974), but the last Norwegian whaling station was shut down after the 1971 season.

Across the Atlantic the Canadians also hunted the minke, particularly in Newfoundland waters, where they were taken along with pilot whales for use as mink food and for human consumption as well. A similar small-whale fishery was conducted off Japan, and this species has been killed in various numbers by whalers from Brazil, South Africa, and Korea. None of these efforts, however, seriously threatened the numerous minkes in the world's oceans. (Most accounts prior to 1970 considered the minke not worth taking; in 1938, Norman and Fraser wrote, "lesser rorquals have no commercial value.")

During the Antarctic whaling season the Japanese and the Soviets took 3,054 minkes in 1971/72, 5,745 in 1972/73, and 7,713 in 1973/74 (Gambell 1975). This small whale, once of "no commercial value," had achieved the dubious distinction of becoming the most intensively hunted baleen whale in the world. Estimates of the total population of Antarctic minkes range from 200,000 to 300,000 animals, and the maximum sustainable yield (MSY) has been calculated at about 5,000 animals per season. Even though the MSY figure was produced within the International Whaling Commission, catch quotas are far in excess of this number. For 1975/76 the catch quota was set at 9,360 minkes, and for 1976/77 the figure was an incredible 11,924 animals, more than twice the figure that the IWC had determined the population could sustain. (For comparison, IWC quotas for the three other rorquals still hunted—fin, sei, and Bryde's whales—for the 1976/77 season totaled 3,339 whales.) In other words, having driven the great whales to the brink of extinction, the whalers were beginning to work on the less great.

At the 1979 IWC meeting in London some significant advances in the conservation of whales were made. The entire Indian Ocean was declared a sanctuary for whales, and despite bitter opposition a resolution banning factory-ship whaling was passed. This prohibition was directed specifically at the Soviet Union and Japan, the only nations actively engaged in offshore whaling with factory ships and catcher boats. Japan asked for—and received—an exception to hunt minke whales with its flotilla of whaleships. The highly recognizable and symbolic sperm whale is protected by the new rulings, so the only whale now being hunted on a large scale will be the minke. The quotas

were raised from 10,173 for 1978 to an all-time high of 12,006. Having been defeated in their desires to continue pelagic whaling, the factory-ship whalers now seem ready to take their vengeance out on the minke, the smallest and most available of the baleen whales.

BRYDE'S WHALE

Balaenoptera edeni Anderson 1878

This species is slightly smaller than the sei whale, to which it bears a considerable resemblance. It is the least known of all the large whales, so the data are likely to be somewhat confusing, if not actually contradictory. For instance, Norman and Fraser (1938) gave the maximum size for this species at "just over 49 feet" (14.9 meters), whereas Leatherwood and associates (1972) recorded "the maximum length of approximately 45 ft." (13.7 meters). In 1958, three mature specimens, two females and a male, were taken at a whaling station in Western Australia (Chittleborough 1959), and they ranged in length from 34.75 feet to 38.5 feet (10.6–11.74 meters). It is likely that throughout the world there are various populations that Best (1975) called "more morphologically distinct than any so far described for a balaenopterid (with the possible exception of the minke whale)." These populations differ primarily in size, but variations in color and baleen plates are also seen. In some cases the differences are significant enough for taxonomists (for example, Soot-Ryen 1961) to suggest that more than one species of the animal is commonly known as Bryde's whale, but the most recent opinions hold that only a single species exists.

In a 1976 study of Bryde's whale in the North Pacific, Kawamura and Satake described two populations that appeared to differ in number of ventral grooves, size of the dorsal fin, and structure of the filtering apparatus. Kawamura (1978) has written that the "South Pacific animals are smallest in the filter area of any animals examined," but this would appear to be a geographical variation, not a taxonomic differentiation.

Bryde's whale was originally described by Anderson in 1878 from a specimen that stranded about twenty miles up Thayboo Choung, a creek in Burma, in 1871. He named the species *edeni* after "the Hon'ble Ashley Eden, having been the means of saving this Whale to Science." According to Anderson's account, the whale "exhausted itself by its furious struggles, during which

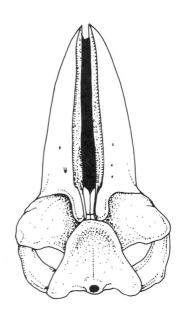

Dorsal view of the skull of Bryde's whale *Balaenoptera edeni* (after Omura).

36

it is said to have roared like an elephant and so loud as to be heard a long way off; it died the same night or in the morning of the following day.''

The species remained a mystery until Olsen (1913) described a "new species," *Balaenoptera brydei,* from South Africa. Olsen named his discovery after Johann Bryde, the Norwegian consul to South Africa, who was instrumental in establishing the whaling operations in South Africa and who arranged for Professor Olsen to come from Norway to examine the whales.* He examined only the exterior features of the animals and was, therefore, unable to make the necessary comparisons with Anderson's specimen, of which just the skeleton remained.

Bryde's whale is unique among the rorquals for the presence of lateral ridges on either side of the central ridge of the rostrum, a character that can be used for field identification, but only when the animal is quite close. It is dark blue-gray in color and lighter below; sometimes, but not always, the undersides have a yellowish cast. The dorsal fin is extremely falcate and is often ragged on the trailing edge, for unknown reasons. The baleen plates are relatively short and are "of very strong construction" (Norman and Fraser). Most descriptions refer to the white (or whitish) anterior plates of this species, but an occasional reference will not mention this character (for example, Omura 1959). The author may have been referring to a population in which the white plates are absent, or the omission may have been an oversight. It is probably safe to say that Bryde's whale has whitish plates in the front of the mouth and darker ones in the rear. The inner bristles, which correspond in color to the outer surface, are coarse and thick. The plates number about 300 on a side, although the number varies with individuals, and there is often a pronounced gap at the front of the mouth between the right and left baleen series. There are about forty-five ventral pleats, which extend as far back as the umbilicus. Very little is known about gestation or birth in this species, but from examination of near-term fetuses and from extrapolation from data on other balaenopterids it is believed that calves are about 11 feet (3.35 meters) at birth.

Even though there are distinct differences between the sei whale and the Bryde's whale, their overall similarity is such that one author wrote: "the primary differences between these two species are very subtle ones. . . . they will often be impossible for the layman to tell apart" (Leatherwood et al. 1972). This confusion is not only a problem for whale watchers, but also a cause for concern among the whalers. The differences are as follows: the sei whale, *B. borealis,* is the larger of the species, averaging four to five feet longer than Bryde's. The dorsal fin of the sei is larger (in fact, it is the largest dorsal fin of all the rorquals), and the ventral pleats of the sei stop before the umbilicus; those of Bryde's whale (and all other Balaenopteridae) extend to or beyond the navel. Bryde's is the only baleen whale with a central and two flanking ridges on the rostrum; all other rorquals have a single ridge. Its baleen is whitish at the front of the mouth and darker

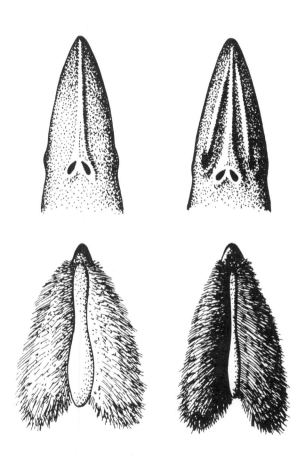

Left: Sei whale. Top: Rostrum, showing single median ridge. Bottom: Baleen and wide palate. Right: Bryde's whale. Top: Rostrum, showing triple median ridge. Bottom: Baleen and narrow palate.

*Olsen's proposed name, *B. brydei,* has been preempted by Anderson's earlier name, since the two were shown to be conspecific, but Johann Bryde's name is permanently associated with this species in the vernacular, not only in English (in which the name is pronounced "breeda"), but in other languages as well. In French the species is called *Baleine de bryde;* in Dutch, *Bryde vinvisch;* in Spanish, *Ballena brydea;* and in Norwegian, *Brydehval.* The name proposed in Japanese by Omura (1959) is *Nitari-kujira,* which can be roughly translated as "sei whale like a fin whale," from the word *nitari,* which means "resemble" (Omura, personal communication).

toward the rear, with coarse, dark bristles on the inside edges, whereas the baleen of the sei is dark outside, with a white, fleecy mat on the inside surface.* In addition, the baleen plates of Bryde's are much shorter than those of the sei, "the longest blades of a Bryde's whale being about 19 inches, whereas in a sei whale of the same length they are about 27 inches long" (Norman and Fraser). The palate in the upper jaw that separates the two "sides" of baleen differs in proportions; in the sei whale it is wider and heavier than it is in the Bryde's whale. "This character is deemed a very essential character beside other[s] such as the baleen plate[s] and the ventral grooves" (Omura and Fujino 1954). There are some additional osteological differences, particularly in the rostrum, that are too technical for this account. It would also be possible for the amateur to confuse a Bryde's whale with a young fin or blue whale, but the differences are quite substantial. Further, the latter animals are barely weaned by the time they reach the size of a full-grown Bryde's whale.

Bryde's whale is what Nemoto (1959) termed a "swallower"; that is, it feeds by ingesting great amounts of water and food organisms, expelling the water through the baleen plates, and swallowing huge mouthfuls of food. It is given to occasional deep dives in search of food, but does not throw its flukes into the air as it dives. In contrast to the crustacean- and krill-feeding sei whale, this species is known primarily as a fish eater, but the population on the coast of Japan feeds on crustaceans, in proportions sometimes approaching 50 percent of the stomach contents (Omura 1966). For the 225 specimens taken in the 1976/77 season in the South Pacific and Indian oceans (under special permit), the stomachs contained *only* euphausiids, including *Euphausia diomedea, E. recurva,* and *Thysanoessa gregaria* (Kawamura 1977). Off Australia it feeds on anchovies (Chittleborough), and in other locations the species has been recorded as consuming various small, schooling fishes, such as herring, pilchards, sardines, and mackerel. In 1913, Olsen recorded

some curious stomach contents of Bryde's whales examined at South African whaling stations, including "no less than 15 penguins, and a malagass" (the Cape gannet, *Sula capensis*). He also noted that the whales "were seen hunting among large crowds of small sharks," a statement that has often been modified to read that the species eats sharks (Mörzer Bruyns 1971, Nishiwaki 1972, and others). Even though Olsen said that his *Balaenoptera brydei* is "a very voracious species, more so than any other species of its genus," he conceded that birds are not normal fare for a baleen whale and "probably dived down into the open mouth of the whale endeavoring to catch fish in that abundant hunting ground."

Bryde's whales have not been sighted at sea very often—or if they were, the identification was not certain—but Nishiwaki has written that "they often form a very dense school, with tens of whales or sometimes over a hundred being observed at one sighting." Gaskin (1972) reported that schools of fifteen have been sighted from the air in New Zealand waters. Although the data are far from conclusive, Bryde's whale is assumed to be a nonmigratory species, making relatively short journeys in search of food and apparently returning to the area whence it came.

A careful reading of the literature on Bryde's whale could easily—and erroneously—lead to the conclusion that the species has substantially increased its range since its identification by Anderson in 1878. Increased awareness of the species and its subsequent differentiation from similar species (especially the sei whale) have resulted in a remarkable extension of its range. At first, Bryde's whale was thought to be restricted to the waters of southeastern Asia (Anderson 1878). Then specimens began to turn up in South Africa (Olsen 1913), Baja California (Kellogg 1931), Singapore (Junge 1950), Australia (Chittleborough 1959), the Caribbean (Soot-Ryen 1961), Brazil (Omura 1962a), and Japan (Omura 1962b). These scattered reports, as well as other less detailed accounts, have led to the conclusion that Bryde's whale is virtually worldwide in distribution in the temperate and subtropical warmer waters of the world, between 40° N and 40° S. (It had been assumed that this species did not penetrate to the Antarctic, but Best reported that five animals were taken south of 40° S, though "it is possible that these animals were still north of the subtropical convergence.") In his 1975 discussion of this species Best reviewed the known populations of Bryde's whale throughout the world, tentatively classifying them into different stocks that may be discrete

---

*Despite the differences in baleen, sei whales and Bryde's whales have been feeding more or less successfully for thousands of years, but recently there have been arguments claiming that neither species does a very good job of feeding itself. Symons (1955) suggested that the "poor straining mechanism" of *B. edeni* was a deterrent to its moving into the Antarctic, where it would have to eat euphausiids and where its "comparatively poor mat" would prove unequal to the task. Kawamura (1974), on the other hand, wrote that the sei whale's filtering apparatus, with its dense mat of fleecy baleen hairs, was not very efficient, either. Therefore, the whale could never get enough to eat. These arguments seem reminiscent of the discussions of the aerodynamic inefficiency of the bee: it should not be able to fly, but, being unable to read the engineers' conclusions, it flies anyway.

and, in some cases, may be morphologically distinguishable by minor features, such as size or length of baleen plates. There appear to be two habitats occupied by Bryde's whales: coastal stocks include populations of Baja California, Brazil, the Gulf of Mexico, the west coast of South Africa, and New Zealand. The pelagic stocks include those off eastern Japan, including the Bonin Islands; in the waters of Chile; in the South Atlantic (South Africa to Brazil); off the east coast of South Africa; and off Western Australia. Were it not for the long-lasting confusion between this species and the sei whale, the movements and habits of Bryde's whale might be much better understood.

This species is now known to be an inhabitant of the vast reaches of the North Pacific, maintaining two—or possibly even three—discrete populations (Privalikhin and Berzin 1978). After the IWC differentiation of sei and Bryde's whales in catch statistics, it was assumed that the two species occupied different habitats, Bryde's being the warmer-water species. Soviet biologists tagged two sei whales and one Bryde's whale at the same location in the eastern Central Pacific, indicating that the ranges occasionally overlap (Privalikhin and Berzin 1978). D. W. Rice was also aboard the Soviet catcher boat *Vnushitel'nyi,* a participating vessel in the 1975 Soviet-American Cooperative Cetacean Research Cruise, and he made the following observations in 1979: Bryde's whales are seen mostly as single animals, but infrequently as pairs. When surfacing, the head of the Bryde's whale breaks the surface first, and the dorsal fin does not emerge until the head is below the surface. He saw two breaches for this species: "They rose clear of the surface in a long, smooth arc, and fell into the water with a tremendous splash as minke whales often do. In the course of hundreds of encounters, I have never seen a sei whale breach, and have seen a fin whale do so only once."

It is difficult to imagine an animal forty-five feet long that remained unknown to science until 1913. (In 1916, Andrews called this "a very doubtfully established species.") It was known from skeletal remains from Burma, Singapore, Curaçao, and other exotic ports of call and from infrequent specimens in the flesh from South Africa. (Norman and Fraser, writing in 1938, said, "Bryde's whale is commonest on the coast of Cape Colony, occurs also off Natal and Angola, and has been reported at Granada in the West Indies.") Because of its anatomical differences from the sei whale, it was accepted as a valid species as early as 1913, but no attempts were made by the whaling industry (the only people who saw enough of them to

record their separate identities) to report Bryde's whales in their catch statistics. Kellogg wrote in a footnote that 34 Bryde's whales were taken off Baja California. He continued, "assuming that this identification is correct, it is likely that some of those listed as sei whales in the reports furnished by stations located elsewhere along the Pacific coast have been misidentified." This has been the story of Bryde's whale throughout its contact with humans, and throughout its range.

Its only salvation was its avoidance of the Antarctic, where the most intensive whaling in history took place between 1925 and 1972. In other areas, however, Bryde's whale was not as fortunate, even though the whalers were not sure (or, more likely, did not care) which species they were taking. In South African waters from 1917 to 1967, 1,564 Bryde's whales were taken from Cape Province whaling stations (Best 1974), although the author warned that "these statistics, especially for the early years, must be viewed with caution, as the species may not have been distinguished from the sei whale in some of the returns."

Writing of the Bryde's whale in the eastern North Pacific, Rice (1974) suggested that all the "sei" whales taken off Baja California may have been Bryde's whales, "because sei whales are scarce in this area whereas Bryde's whales are common." In offshore Japanese waters the story is much the same. Sei whales have been hunted in the western North Pacific since 1899, the year of the first steel whale catcher that was armed with a modern harpoon gun (Terry 1951). North Pacific whaling has been conducted mostly off the Japanese coasts, the adjacent Asian mainland (including Korea), and around the Bonin Islands, some 520 miles (837 kilometers) southwest of Honshu. (In pre–World War II days the Bonin region accounted for about 15 percent of all Japanese North Pacific whaling, according to the 1947 calculations by Shimada.) In 1954, Omura and Fujino examined 411 "sei" whales that had been killed off Bonin in May and June of 1952. They noticed the narrow palate, the short, dark baleen, and the length of the ventral grooves. It was apparent that these were, in fact, Bryde's whales, and therefore statistics for this area (and for all other locations except the Antarctic) required reexamination for the possibility that the catch of sei whales was made up, at least in part, of Bryde's whales.

With the decline of baleen whale stocks in the Antarctic, Bryde's whale—now that it was known not to be a sei whale and, therefore, was not affected by restrictions on sei whale hunting—has fallen increasingly under the eye of the harpooners. After 1971, Soviet and Japanese whalers directed their attention to the western North Pacific and the South Atlantic, where record numbers of Bryde's whales have been taken in recent years. (These are also the major sperm whale grounds, and since the sperm has always been a heavily hunted species, the whalers are likely to be in these areas, anyway.) In 1971, 1,287 Bryde's whales were killed; in 1972, 352; and in 1973, 1,541 (Best 1975). Although the IWC catch quotas for Bryde's whales are not particularly high (1,363 for 1975/76, 1,500 for 1976/77), the figures have been calculated on an absolute minimum of information. Best (1975) wrote: "Very few estimates of population size for Bryde's whale are available. . . . up to 1973 Japanese scouting vessels had made no distinction between the two species [sei and Bryde's] so that direct sighting estimates were not available for Bryde's whales." We simply have no idea how many Bryde's whales there are, although Scheffer, in a 1976 article, gave the following statistics: "Numbers before commercial whaling—100,000?; Estimated numbers today—40,000?; Percentage remaining today—?" In the *Report to the Secretary of Commerce of the Administration of the Marine Mammal Protection Act of 1972* for 1974 it was calculated that 5,000–18,000 Bryde's whales inhabit the western North Pacific, but "estimates of populations elsewhere in the world have not been made."

Little known at the turn of the century, Bryde's whales may be in trouble today, even though we have not learned enough about the species to know if it migrates. The "outlaw" or "pirate" whaling nations, those that take whales but do not belong to the IWC,* are at liberty to kill whatever whales they can get, and there is no reason to assume that Bryde's whales are exempt from their predations. The *Sierra,* which is the most infamous of the "pirate whalers" and has variously flown the convenience flags of the Bahamas, Somalia, and Cyprus, was reported to be taking Bryde's whales and selling the meat to Japan.† In 1976, Japan unilaterally issued itself a collecting per-

mit for scientific study of a previously unreported stock of Bryde's whales in the South Pacific. (Under certain provisions of the International Conventions, scientific collecting can be permitted, even though the species is protected or the particular area has been closed to commercial whaling.) The Japanese took 225 Bryde's whales at this time (120 in the South Pacific and the Coral Sea and 105 from the Indian Ocean) and then analyzed the stomach contents and the baleen plates. Enough variations were found in the filter area of the baleen plates for Kawamura (1978) to conclude that Bryde's whales from the South Pacific were clearly different from those forms taken in the North Pacific and in Japanese waters.

SEI WHALE

Balaenoptera borealis Lesson 1828

The vernacular name of this animal, pronounced "say," is derived from the Norwegian word *seje,* the name for the pollack or coalfish, *Pollachius virens.* The whale was named for the fish because the two used to arrive off the coast of Norway at the same time of year. Although the sei whale is not primarily a fish eater, it has been named for a fish by the two nations who hunted it most: *sejhval* by the Norwegians, and *Iwashi-kujira,* "sardine whale," by the Japanese. The sei whale

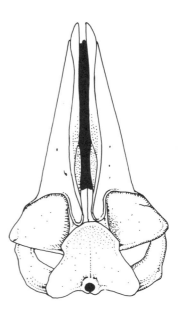

Dorsal view of the skull of sei whale, *Balaenoptera borealis.*

---

*Somalia, Chile, Portugal, South Korea, and China.
†On July 15, 1979, the *Sierra* was rammed by a ship registered to the Fund for Animals, a conservationist group. Off Oporto, Portugal, Paul Watson sailed the *Sea Shepherd,* which had been outfitted with concrete in her bows for duty as an icebreaker, directly into the *Sierra,* first forward to destroy the harpoon gun and then amidships to wreck the cargo holds. The *Sierra* was repaired, and early in 1980 she set out again, presumably to resume her nefarious activities. She was never to kill whales again, for on February 6 a series of internal explosions—of undetermined origin—sank her in Lisbon harbor, where she lies as of this writing.

was originally known as "Rudolphi's rorqual," after Professor Karl Asmund Rudolphi of Berlin, who first described it, but the anglicized version of the Norwegian name is now the accepted appellation. The name *borealis* was applied because the species was originally described as *"rorqual du nord"* (Cuvier 1836), from a specimen taken off Germany.

The sei whale is dark bluish-gray above (although Nishiwaki [1972] described it as "dark chocolate colored"), with irregular white markings on the ventral surface. One of them, an anchor-shaped patch on the chest, is diagnostic. This species is almost always seen with a random pattern of oval whitish spots that were originally believed to be part of the whale's normal coloration, but may be scars left by the parasitic worm *Penella antarctica* (Andrews 1916a) or by lampreys. These skin parasites are rarely observed in situ, and it is assumed that they are acquired in temperate waters and fall off by the time the whales arrive in the Antarctic (Matthews 1938). Two Soviet scientists, Ivashin and Golubovsky (1978), actually saw "the parasites falling and the wounds appearing" on Bryde's whales captured off Madagascar. They observed that the oval white scars were the work of *Penella,* perhaps a new and undescribed species, since the parasites did not fit the description of the known species, such as *Penella balaenoptera.* Others suggest that the white scars are the product of the "attacks" of a small shark, *Isistius brasiliensis* (Jones 1971). In order to calculate the migration patterns of Antarctic sei whales, Shevchenko (1977) examined the scars on the skin of the whales and concluded that the whales passed through a "vulnerable zone" of warm water where the sharks, known to be warm-water inhabitants, would inflict these wounds. On the basis of the relative number of these scars, Shevchenko was able to differentiate the whales of the West African population from those of the western part of the Indian Ocean. While this explanation for the scars seems simple and the results seem clear, there is still no empirical evidence that would directly implicate the little sharks in the formation of the wounds.

The underside of the flukes and flippers is gray, and the flippers are relatively small, perhaps 9–10 percent of the whale's total body length. In profile its rostrum is somewhat arched, giving it a slightly "Roman-nosed" appearance, but like all other balaenopterids—except the Bryde's whale—it has a single median ridge on the rostrum, running from tip to blowhole. The dorsal fin of the sei is high and curved, propor-

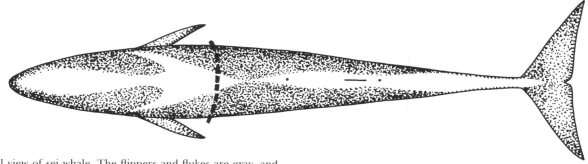

Ventral view of sei whale. The flippers and flukes are gray, and the characteristic anchor-shaped patch is seen on the chest. The ventral pleats end at the dotted line.

tionally larger than that of any other rorqual.* The ventral pleats in the sei whale number about forty to sixty, averaging forty-seven (Matthews 1938), and are shorter than those of any other member of the genus. They end about midway between the tip of the flipper and the navel, whereas in other species the pleats extend to or beyond the umbilicus.

The baleen plates number between 300 and 380 per side and are dark in color, having finely matted, whitish inner bristles that have been compared in texture to wool (Allen 1916) or even to silk (Matthews 1938). In his monograph on the sei whale Andrews (1916a) described the unique iridescent nature of the baleen: "When held in the sun in one position the blade is blue, and at another angle the color changes to light green. This is a distinctive character of the baleen of *Balaenoptera borealis,* for it does not appear in the whalebone of related species." Seis are occasionally found with some white baleen plates, usually in conjunction with a white spot on the right upper jaw, "which may be a tendency towards the asymmetry found in the fin whale" (Matthews 1938). Although smaller at maturity than the blue or fin whale, the sei is still a large whale; the largest specimen, a female, was measured at 65.6 feet (20 meters) in length (Nishiwaki 1972), although most recent specimens are smaller, somewhere between 40 and 50 feet (12.20–15.24 meters).

It is possible to confuse the sei whale with any of the large rorquals—only the minke is easily distinguished from its huge relatives since they are all very large whales that are basically gray in color, Andrews (1916a) noted that for many years the sei whale was probably thought to be a young fin or blue whale. The sei most closely resembles the blue whale, as both are bluish-gray and have a pattern of whitish spots. (The spots on the blue whales, however, are more plentiful, giving the whale a mottled appearance. The sei has a random, sparse pattern of spots or scars.) The fin whale has a white lower jaw on the right and particolored baleen. The animal most likely to be mistaken for a sei, and vice versa, is the Bryde's whale. The two are so similar that whalers did not distinguish them; "the separation of one from the other requires a fuller

examination than the whalers usually had time to make" (Budker 1959). Bryde's whale is somewhat smaller, has dark baleen with coarse black interior fringes, and has three rostral ridges where the other rorquals have one. Although Bryde's whale is known to occur off Japan (Omura 1966), early whaling statistics for the western North Pacific recorded any rorqual that was not a fin or a blue as a sei. The IWC kept no separate records of Bryde's whale statistics until 1970; both species were combined in the "sei" category.

Although the other rorquals are characterized as "swallowers," the sei whale has been grouped with the right, bowhead, and California gray whales as a "skimmer" (Nemoto 1959). Not as restricted in its diet as the blue whale, which eats only euphausiids, the sei is a specialized feeder, and the baleen plates seem to have evolved in response to its feeding habits. The fine, fleecy bristles on the plates appear to be designed for feeding on organisms smaller than those consumed by the other rorquals, and indeed this is the case. Sei whales feed on copepods such as *Calanus finmarchius* (known collectively as "brit" or *"aate"* in the North Atlantic). These minute crustaceans congregate in huge rafts, through which the whale swims as it feeds, "skimming" the concentrated organisms. (The "swallowers" take in great mouthfuls of water and eject it forcibly through the plates, often turning on their sides and splashing about.) In the North Pacific the predominant food organism is the copepod *Calanus pacificus,* but other copepods, euphausiids, fish, and squid are also eaten (Kawamura 1973). The sei whale is an opportunistic feeder, and in other locations it will feed on other crustaceans, including *Euphausia inermis,* which Andrews (1916b) described as "the little red shrimp . . . which is about three-quarters of an inch long." In Antarctic waters the sei will eat the "large" (2.5 inches, or 63.5 centimeters, in length) crustacean *Euphausia superba,* which is known as krill and is "the main diet of all the southern Balaenopterids" (Marr 1956). Matthews (1932) suggested that the yellowish color of the blubber of sei whales taken off Mexico was a result of their consuming the "red crab," *Pleuroncodes planipes.* Because of the thin, yellowish quality of the sei whale's blubber, old whalers often referred to it as the "oilcloth whale" (Norris 1978). Off Patagonia the sei whale feeds almost exclusively on the crustacean *Munida gregaria* and its larval stage, which is known as "lobster krill" (Matthews 1938). Sei whales also feed on fish such as sand lancers, herrings, cod, sauries, and sardines (Nishiwaki 1972).

In an interesting series of experiments and observa-

*Scammon did not specifically mention the sei whale, but he did refer to a finback with a dorsal fin that was "strikingly larger than in most southern Finbacks," and since the sei whale is known to occur off the coasts of California and Oregon, he may have been describing it. His illustration shows an animal with an extremely large dorsal, much too large for a fin whale. When describing the baleen, Scammon made no mention of the bicolored plates characteristic of the fin whale, so it is possible that his "Finback" was, in fact, a sei.

tions Kawamura (1974) concluded that sei whales could not get enough to eat from the small copepods and that the filtering apparatus of this species was not very effective. Therefore, the sei whale was always hungry. Commenting on these findings, Lockyer (1976) wrote: "This statement may be well founded for certain areas where sei whales have been caught and examined, but the fact remains that many sei do penetrate far south to the Antarctic where they certainly feed to capacity on euphausiids and amphipods." Of all the rorquals only the sei appears to skim through the dense patches of crustaceans in the manner of right whales and also to gulp mouthfuls of water and food organisms, as do the other swallowers, the blue, fin, Bryde's, and minke whales.

The catholic tastes of the sei whale may in some way account for its irregular travels; it will appear in great numbers in a given area and then disappear from that region for many years. In the summer of 1885, thousands of seis appeared off the coast of northern Scandinavia—of which 722 were taken by Norwegian whalers—and they have not returned. Since 1948 only 3 have been caught in these waters (Jonsgard 1974). Except for these unusual large congregations, sei whales are most often seen in small groups of two to five animals. Since they are not thought to dive deeply, they surface to breathe at a shallow angle, rolling slowly in the water and blowing a spout of about 15 feet (4.6 meters). Because they feed on small fish and crustaceans at the surface, seis can often be seen surrounded by numbers of seabirds that are feeding on the same organisms. The flukes are not raised out of the water during a dive. The sei is one the swiftest of the large whales. Andrews (1916b) likened the sei whale to the cheetah, because it is fast for short sprints, but "does not have the strength and staying power of its larger relatives," and Nishiwaki (1972) recorded "a maximum swimming velocity of 30 knots (or 50 km/hr) for a short time."

After a twelve-month gestation period, a 15-foot (4.6-meter) calf is born. It nurses for about six months, by which time it has reached a length of about 28 feet (4.6 meters). Like the blue and fin whales, the sei moves toward the higher latitudes to feed in the summer and into warmer temperate waters for breeding when the ice begins to form. (However, the northern and southern populations move at different times, since the northern summer is the southern winter and vice versa.) Of all the great whales, the sei has penetrated least into the Antarctic, but there is evidence now that the reduction in numbers of the fin and blue whales has brought the seis into areas where the other species have been depleted (Chapman 1974). The possibility also exists that the seis are moving farther south to take advantage of the food supply that is flourishing with the reduction in numbers of its primary predators.

From specimens collected at California whaling stations in 1956–66 a most curious phenomenon was observed. Some 7 percent of the sei whales taken were infected with an unidentifiable disease that caused the degeneration of the baleen plates. One would naturally assume that these whales, deprived of their feeding apparatus, would have difficulty in obtaining food, but none of the diseased animals was emaciated, and most had anchovies, sauries, or jack mackerel in their stomachs. None had euphausiids or copepods, "because filter feeding would be impossible" (Rice 1961). This condition has not been reported in sei whales anywhere else in the world.

There are probably three separate stocks of sei whales: the North Pacific, from the Gulf of Siam north to Japan, Korea, and eastern Siberia, and down the North American coast from Alaska to Mexico; the North Atlantic, from Spitsbergen, Novaya Zemlya, and the Greenland and Barents seas to Norway and south to Spain; and the western North Atlantic, from the Davis Straits, Labrador, and New England. Mead (1977) mentioned strandings from Louisiana, the Dominican Republic, and Mexico. In the Southern Hemisphere the sei whale summers in all oceans, but it is not usually found as close to the ice pack as the blue and fin whales. During the southern winter, seis are north of 40° S, but their migratory patterns are poorly known, "perhaps because they spend the winter in far offshore waters" (Rice 1974). On the whole, the movements of sei whales are not as well documented as those of the other rorquals. As Mackintosh wrote in 1942, "sei whales are referred to here and there, but they are of less importance and the data referring to this species are less important." This assessment was to change dramatically in a few decades, and the data were to become vital.

The stocks of the different species of great whales, although they do not integrate, are inextricably bound together by human predations. The story of whaling, particularly in the Antarctic, is one of ruthless slaughter on a leviathan scale, overlaid by a thin (and all too recent) veneer of scientific terminology and pretense. Although the situation has changed for the better over the last few years with the defection of some of the major nations from the ranks of the whalers, the tragic truth of the industry's short and inglorious history still obtains: one species after another was hunted until it became economically unfeasible to continue; then that species was declared "protected," and the whalers moved on to the next available victim.

Nowhere has this approach been more evident than in the case of the blue whale, which is now considered economically extinct—and is, therefore, fully protected. The sei whale, a smaller version of the blue, has had a similar history, compressed into a much shorter period of time. First the humpbacks were hunted in the Antarctic: they were the slowest swimmers, they were rich in oil, and they floated, conveniently, when they were killed. Then came the great blues and fins; for "catch-per-unit-effort" they were much more profitable than any other species. The story of the decimation of the blue and fin whale populations is told elsewhere, but it bears directly on the chronicle of the sei, for it was only when the larger species had been reduced in numbers that the whalers turned their attention to it. At first, the sei was treated as a poor relation; its blubber was thin, and only in large numbers could it be considered a worthwhile whale to kill. (The IWC assigned a value of six sei whales to equal one "blue whale unit," the index of productivity in the whaling industry.)

The sei whale also arrived too late in the Antarctic. First came "a wave of blue whales passing southwards, succeeded by a wave of fin whales following at about a month's interval" (Matthews 1938). In the halcyon days of southern whaling, by the time the seis arrived, most of the whalers were ready to head north with their cargo of oil. Up to 1960, sei whales were taken in relatively insignificant quantities, but by the 1965/66 season they accounted for an astonishing 71.9 percent of the total catch in the Antarctic (Kawamura 1974). Over 20,000 sei whales were killed in that season, as the fin whale catch dropped from a high of 28,761 in 1960/61, to 7,811 in 1964/65, and to 2,536 in 1965/66 (McHugh 1974). As an indication of the decline of the fin and blue whale populations, Nasu (1973) reported on a 1966/67 Antarctic whaling voyage during which 5 blues, 22 fins, and 1,137 sei whales were sighted. It has been estimated that a total of 106,886 sei whales were killed in the Antarctic from 1959 to 1971 (Chapman 1974). (While this massive carnage was going on, sei whales were being killed elsewhere, but not on such a large scale. For example, in 1965 another 5,074 animals were killed in areas other than the Southern Ocean.) The original Antarctic population has been estimated at 150,000 ani-

mals, and the latest figures indicate that there are some 50,000–80,000 sei whales left in the Antarctic (Gambell 1975). The IWC catch quota for the 1976/77 season was 1,995 sei whales; for 1977/78 it was 855; and for 1978/79 it was 84. It seems that the end of the slaughter is at hand, but it has been a long struggle during which hundreds of thousands of sei whales died. As early as 1938, Matthews predicted this debacle:

The sei whale has not yet been of much economic importance on most of the world's whaling grounds, particularly in the Antarctic. But it is suggested that when the serious diminution of numbers of the larger and more profitable species, which appears to be imminent, arrives, this species will suffer considerably and will be in danger of being reduced to a very small remnant in a short time.

Because the history of whaling is such that investigations of the population and biology of a given species take place only when that species is threatened, it was not until 1974 that the stocks of Southern Hemisphere sei whales were examined. A special IWC meeting was convened in La Jolla that year, and the resulting papers were published in 1977 (IWC 1978). Most of the papers presented at this meeting concerned population biology and "management," since the pelagic whaling fleets were still engaged in factory-ship whaling and had to have some figures to justify their endeavors.* Some of the papers presented at this meeting are listed in the bibliography, but many of them are excluded since they involve the arcane formulas for estimating populations and are understandable only to a biologist trained in that specialty. In one paper Kawamura (1978) wrote that "it is reasonable to suppose that the sei whale had actually been free from competition for food since the great depletion of Southern right whales from the mid-19th century onward, and this perhaps led to the probable growth of the sei whale population which had been relatively untouched for half a century."

In 1976, Gambell observed that the pregnancy rate of sei whales had been rising since 1946: approximately twice as many pregnant whales were taken after 1946 as in the years before the war. Since sei whales were not hunted intensively until the 1960s, the increase in the pregnancy rate is believed to be an evolutionary response, either to the destruction of the competitive blues and fins or, later, to the threat to the sei

*At the 1979 IWC meeting, factory-ship whaling was banned. Further, certain nations may still hunt the sei whale from shore stations, but the Soviet and Japanese catcher boats will no longer chase the sei whale in Antarctic waters.

whale population itself. It is clear, however, that despite the learned papers and complicated formulas, our knowledge of the natural history of the great whales is still minimal, and most of our analyses of the behavior and biology of these great creatures are little more than fancy guesswork.

FIN WHALE

Balaenoptera physalus Linnaeus 1758

Because of its sleek lines, the fin whale has been called the "greyhound of the sea." In 1916, Roy Chapman Andrews wrote that "it well deserves the name, for its slender body is built like a racing yacht and the animal can surpass the speed of the fastest ocean steamship." Second in size only to the blue, the fin whale is an enormous animal, with a maximum recorded length of 82 feet (25 meters); however, most animals have been measured in the 65–75-foot (20–23-meter) range. Large fin whales can weigh over 50 tons (45,000 kilograms), but since they are considerably slimmer than blue whales, a fin will weigh much less than a blue of the same length. Also known as the "common rorqual," "finback," "finner," or "razorback" (the last

because of the prominent keels on the dorsal and ventral aspects of the caudal peduncle), this species is one of the fastest of the great whales. It is reported to be able to reach and sustain a speed of 20 knots; "no other species of whale can swim for such long periods

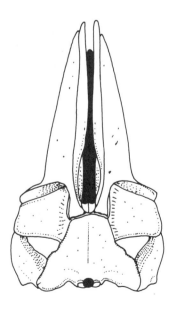

Dorsal view of the skull of the fin whale, *Balaenoptera physalus* (after Allen).

of time at such high speeds'' (Nishiwaki 1972). When a fin whale is not racing, its movements are more leisurely. Its "blow" is high (fifteen to twenty-five feet), and it breathes about every two minutes before making a deep dive that may last as long as fifteen minutes, but is usually somewhat shorter. The fin whale rarely, if ever, brings its flukes out of the water when diving, even if it is being chased or has been harpooned.

Perhaps the most unusual aspect of the fin whale is its strikingly asymmetrical coloring. The lower jaw is white on the right side and black on the left. This arrangement is reversed inside the mouth and on the tongue, where it is the right side that is pigmented and the left that is light. The baleen plates in the forward one-third of the mouth on the starboard side are whitish; and the rear two-thirds, as well as all the plates on the left side, are dark grayish-blue. The transition from light to dark is by no means regular: the dark coloring on the left side seems to flow from a black band that begins behind the right eye and arches over the whale's right shoulder behind the blowhole, until it blends with the uniform dark gray coloring on the animal's left side. There are also some pale streaks, one of which emanates from the ear hole, and a more or less symmetrical V-shaped mark on the back, sometimes known as a "chevron." The underside of the whale, including the ventral surfaces of the flippers and flukes, is white.* There have been a few recorded instances of sei whales or minke whales with asymmetrical coloring or bicolored baleen plates, but the fin whale is the only mammal in the world that is consistently asymmetrical in its pigmentation.

The rostrum of this species is sharply pointed, and there is a single ridge on the upper surface. The baleen plates number between 350 and 400 per side, and the number of white plates on the right side is about 150. The fin whale, like the other large rorquals, is not completely hairless; there is a varied pattern of sparse hairs on the upper and lower jaws, and Nishiwaki (1972) referred to "a distinct clump of hairs at the tip of the lower jaws." The ventral pleats end evenly at the navel, and the average number of grooves is about eighty-five, although the number varies widely. Flukes are about 25 percent of the body length, and the dor-

*The reasons for the finner's unique coloring can only be guessed at; there have been a number of well-reasoned explanations, but the answer remains hidden in the realm of teleological speculation. Mitchell (1974a) contended that the whale is countershaded, with the colors being rotated 90° on the animal. Therefore, as the whale circles its prey counterclockwise, it is effectively camouflaged and the fish do not see it clearly. Using the same information to arrive at the diameterically opposite conclusion, Mowat (1972) suggested that the species circles a herring school clockwise, showing its white belly to the schooling fish in an effort to frighten them with the great expanse of white and thus packing them more tightly together to facilitate feeding. Watkins and Schevill (1979) "noted no apparent preference" as they observed fin whales feeding; they "turned on their right or left side."

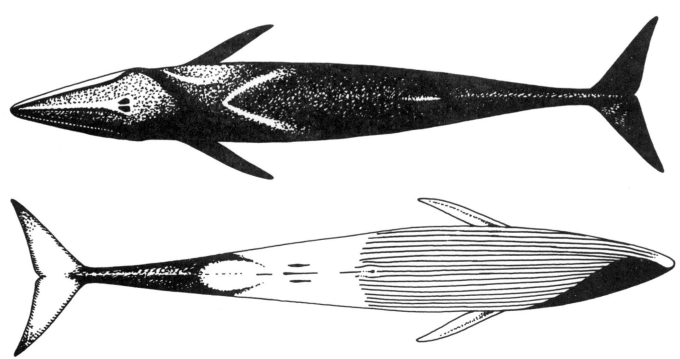

Dorsal view of fin whale, showing asymmetrical coloring and white chevron. Ventral view of fin whale. Notice black coloring on chin and white ventral surface of flukes.

sal fin, which gives the animal its common name, is relatively tall (up to 24 inches) and falcate. The name *physalus* is probably a derivative of the Greek word *physa* ("bellows"), a reference to the pleated, expandable throat of this species and other rorquals. The Japanese call the fin whale *Nagasu-kujira,* from *nagai* ("long") and *su* ("furrow").

Only close relatives of the fin whale could possibly be mistaken for it, since this family comprises the largest animals that ever lived. Within this family, however, a certain amount of confusion is possible. Not surprisingly, the blue whale looks blue in the water, whereas the fin whale is definitely gray. Sei and Bryde's whales are somewhat smaller; Bryde's whale has three ridges on the rostrum; and only the minke whale has all-white baleen and a white flipper stripe. There are additional differences in the diving behavior, coloring, spouts, and dorsal fins. Since the southern populations of the fin whale are geographically separate from the stocks in the Northern Hemisphere, some regard it as a subspecies, with the name *Balaenoptera physalus quoyi* having precedence (Hershkovitz 1966; Red Data Book 1976).

At birth a fin whale calf is considerably larger than most other animals—except, of course, its fellow rorquals. No fin whale birth has ever been observed, but examination of nearly full-term fetuses has enabled us to ascertain their size at birth. (There are infrequent records of twin fetuses, and even triplets, quadruplets, and quintuplets have been observed. Jonsgard [1953] reported one instance of a "litter" of six, but the odds against these multiple embryos surviving are very high.) A fin whale is probably 21.3 feet (6.5 meters) in length at birth, and it weighs about 2 tons (1,800 kilograms). It is thought that they nurse for about six months, by which time they will be about 40 feet (12.2 meters) long, almost twice their size at birth. They reach sexual maturity somewhere between the ages of 6 and 10 years,* and they continue growing, but at a much slower rate, until they are mature: males at about 64 feet (19.5 meters) and females at 65.5 feet (20 meters) (Mackintosh and Wheeler 1929). As in all the rorquals, females grow larger than males, and the very largest specimens have been females. A curious statistic that has emerged from the voluminous literature on this species is the undeniable predominance of females over males. The average figures are 55 percent females to 45 percent males (Mackintosh and Wheeler 1929), although in some circumstances the percentage of females has been as high as 65 percent (Mitchell 1974a).

In 1962, Nemoto identified a secondary sexual characteristic in fin whales: the tip of the snout in mature males is swollen "like a goose neck." As shown in the photographs accompanying Nemoto's description, the tip of the rostrum is considerably enlarged in mature males, but not in younger males or in females of any age. Age determination has been of great importance in analyzing the stocks of whales and their potential for exploitation. Of particular value is the accurate identification of sexual maturity, which enables scientists to identify those age levels at which a whale is able to reproduce and, thus, replenish the population. From the examination of the reproductive organs the whale's degree of sexual maturity was determined; then the scientists directed their studies toward the problem of how old the whale was when it was captured.

The earliest determinations of age depended on the obvious criterion of size—the bigger whales were probably older than the smaller ones—but more accurate methods were required. Among the techniques used have been the counting of scars, examining of the ovaries of females, measuring of ridges and furrows in the baleen plates, ascertaining of the amount of darkening of the eye's crystalline lens, and analyzing of ear plugs. For years, scientists had known of these horny, laminated plugs, but it was assumed that they were merely waxy secretions in the auditory canal (meatus) of the baleen whales. In 1955, Purves discovered that they were excellent conductors of sound and postulated that these plugs, rather than being secretions of wax that interfered with the whale's hearing, were, in fact, an important part of its auditory apparatus. Measuring about 7 inches (178 millimeters) in length in mature fin whales, the plugs are composed of alternate dark and light layers, one dark and one light per year in juveniles; however, their production seems to slow down as the whale matures (Roe 1967). (There has been much internecine discussion about the true nature of the ear plug laminations, and the interpretation of the data has not been settled.)

Fin whales are believed to reach a maximum age of 50 years, but one Japanese study (Ohsumi et al. 1958)

---

*Sexual maturity in males is determined by the presence of seminal fluid in the testes; in females the presence of a corpus luteum indicates that ovulation has taken place. After the ovarian follicle has produced an egg, the corpus luteum produces hormones during pregnancy. Eventually, the corpus luteum shrivels into a white mass of connective tissue, then known as the corpus albicans. If the egg is not fertilized, this process takes only a few days. The number of corpora albicantia is useful in determining the age of mature females.

stated that "the physically mature fin whales (more than 24 years old) are very rare in the Northern Pacific." Fin whales are thought to be monogamous and are most often seen in pairs, although some larger aggregations have been recorded. A possible observation of a mated pair was discussed in Farley Mowat's book, *A Whale for the Killing* (1972), in which a fin whale thought to be a male remained just outside the bay in which a female was trapped and did not leave until she died.*

Fin whales have been recorded to make low-frequency moans and grunts, which may be audible to other whales for great distances underwater. In addition, the fin whale was the first baleen whale recorded to make "communication signals," consisting of "chirps and whistles" (Perkins 1966), and other variable sounds, including "a long train of high-frequency pulses as two fin whales approached within 50 yd of a ship during an encounter off Nova Scotia in September 1971" (Thompson et al. 1979). The purpose of these sounds is not known, but there is some evidence that these whales may announce the availability of food to other whales (Beamish, personal communication). If this is so, it would be a very rare occurrence, indeed; no other mammal is known to indicate a food source to other members of the same species unless they belong to some integrated group. Perhaps the great whales, unique in the animal kingdom and not threatened by predators, can afford to notify their fellows of a food supply. Under other circumstances, any animal that sent such a signal would not only attract potential competitors for the food, but would also announce its location to those who would prey on it. Watkins and Schevill (1979) observed fin whales coming from a distance to other feeding whales; although it is possible that the approaching whales may have been attracted by sounds associated with feeding, the authors speculated "that the calls of the finback, sometimes heard during feeding, may have alerted these

*To me this is the most moving and tragic story of a single whale that has ever been recorded. After becoming trapped in a small bay in southwest Newfoundland, a pregnant whale was murdered by the local "sportsmen," who shot hundreds of soft-nosed and steel-jacketed bullets into her as she swam around the enclosed bay. Farley Mowat, himself a resident of the town of Burgeo on the stormy south coast of Newfoundland, became obsessed with saving the whale; his story is a strange counterpoint to Ahab's mission of vengeful destruction. Mowat was not able to save the whale, but in his failure he greatly enriched the limited literature that concerns the interactions of whales and human beings. Sitting in a dory on the pond, Mowat watched as the wounded whale passed directly beneath his boat. He wrote: "It was then that I heard the voice of the Fin Whale for the third time. It was a long, low, sonorous moan, with unearthly overtones in a higher pitch. It was unbelievably weird and bore no affinity with any sound that I have heard from any other living thing. It was a voice not of the world we know."

whales to the presence of a concentration of feeding whales."

The fin whale is a deep-ocean species, seldom found in waters of less than 656 feet (200 meters). In its almost cosmopolitan habitat the fin whale's diet varies with the availability of food organisms; but since the whales of different stocks are thought not to integrate, the diet of a given population is more or less predictable. Demonstrating this food-specific character, fin whales in Nova Scotia have been found to eat krill, whereas those examined from Newfoundland stations had mainly capelin in their stomachs (Mitchell 1974b). Herring, capelin, and euphausiids are all available as food in the Gulf of Saint Lawrence (Sergeant 1976). In the North Pacific, fin whales consume small pelagic fishes such as herring, capelin, and pollack and crustaceans such as *Euphausia* and *Thysanoessa* (Nemoto 1959). Antarctic fin whales feed almost exclusively on krill. When eating, the fin whale has been observed to turn on its side, rolling on the surface. Aerial observations of feeding fin whales have shown that the throat becomes greatly distended as the animal takes in a mouthful of water and food organisms. In some instances the "amount of throat enlargement . . . nearly doubled the diameter of the whale" (Watkins and Schevill 1979). Andrews wrote: "I could see with the glass that always when taking a mouthful of shrimps, they turned on their sides, letting the great under jaws close over the upper, the water spurting out in streams from between the plates of baleen."

The krill, which makes up a large proportion of the fin whale's diet in many parts of its range, is a creature of the surface layer, not found below 330 feet (100 meters) (Marr 1956), but there are references to fin whales' diving to incredible depths. Leatherwood and colleagues (1976) cited a figure of "at least 755 ft" (230 meters), and Kooyman and Andersen (1969) recorded two instances of harpooned fin whales: one "collided with bottom" at 1,640 feet (500 meters); and another, harpooned with a depth manometer attached, reached 1,164 feet (355 meters). These are, of course, abnormal circumstances, but fins are well known for their strength and speed in the water. Andrews recorded a four-hour struggle with a harpooned finner that took place in Alaskan waters. (In the same chapter of *Whale Hunting with Gun and Camera*, Andrews described the killing of a female attended by a calf and the subsequent killing of the calf: "the harpoon crashed into his side, going almost through him.")

The fin whale is a highly migratory species, moving

regularly toward cold-water feeding areas in the higher latitudes during the spring and early summer and toward temperate waters for breeding and calving during the fall and winter. (They feed very little, if at all, in the lower latitudes.) The gestation period is about eleven months, and the birth occurs in the warmer waters. After about six months of nursing, the 40-foot calf and the 60-plus-foot mother begin their journey to the cold-water feeding grounds.

Fin whales are found throughout the offshore waters of the world. In the North Atlantic, the North Pacific, and the Southern oceans, separate stocks of fin whales have been identified. There are at least six distinct populations in the North Atlantic: the Arctic, eastern North Atlantic, and northern Norway; eastern Greenland and western Iceland; the west coast of Norway and the Faeroes; Scotland south to Spain and Portugal; western Greenland; and Canada. (The Canadian population may be divided again into two more stocks, the Newfoundland-Labrador whales and the Nova Scotia–Gulf of Saint Lawrence group.) Sergeant (1976) has described the distribution of fin whales in the North Atlantic as "a patchy continuum with relatively small movements necessitated mainly by the search for food." In the North Pacific there are probably two major stocks, Asian and American, with another smaller population in the East China Sea and perhaps a small but distinct population in the Gulf of California. The largest remaining group of fin whales is in the Antarctic, where as many as eight separate stocks have been identified. Although there is a certain amount of movement between areas, the stocks have been isolated on the basis of marking, blood typing, and other characteristics. In the Southern Hemisphere the stocks winter in these areas: Chilean-Peruvian, west of northern Chile and Peru; South Georgian, east of Brazil; West African, west of South Africa, Angola, and the Congo; East African, off eastern Africa and Madagascar; Crozet-Kerguelen, east of Madagascar; East Australian, in the Coral Sea; and New Zealand, in the Fiji Sea and the adjacent waters eastward (Chapman 1974).*

Fin whales strand more frequently than any other

*This breakdown is found in D. G. Chapman's paper entitled "Status of Antarctic Rorqual Stocks," which is based on an unpublished manuscript prepared by M. V. Ivashin for a special IWC meeting held in Honolulu in 1970, the sole subject of which was the Antarctic fin whale. The importance of the fin whale to the whaling community is demonstrated by the convening of this meeting and by the subsequent publishing of a book entitled *The Whale Problem* (Schevill 1974). It reproduces papers concerning some other species of whales, but, by and large, it is devoted to the fin whale.

species of rorqual except the minke. In the records kept by the British Museum, Fraser (1974) reported a total of 34 fin whales found on the coasts of the British Isles from 1913 to 1966. (During the same period 106 minke whale strandings were noted.) Whaling operations in the North Atlantic or the North Sea may have been responsible for some of these occurrences, either when whales that had been wounded beached themselves or when dead whales washed ashore. Budker and du Buit (1968) recorded a recently born fin whale calf, 22.3 feet in length, that stranded alive at Le Pouldu on the Brittany coast of France. It struggled for two hours, "moaning and groaning," before it died. No large whale was seen in the vicinity of the stranding, so it was assumed that the calf "went astray on his own and came ashore to die there." There are numerous records of fin whales stranding on the coasts of New England.

For countless centuries the fin whale swam the world's oceans, virtually unknown and unmolested. In *Moby-Dick*, Melville wrote: "Of a retiring nature, he eludes both hunters and philosophers. Though no coward, he has never yet shown any part of him but his back, which rises in a long sharp ridge. Let him go. I know little more of him, nor does anybody else." The sparse information on this species came mostly from beached specimens and was, therefore, directed toward the animal's not unimpressive size and external appearance. From 1868, when the Norwegian Svend Foyn perfected and employed his grenade harpoon, to the turn of the twentieth century, such fin whaling as there was took place in the North Atlantic and was conducted primarily by Norwegians. In 1904, Carl Anton Larsen, another Norwegian, founded the first shore-whaling station in the Antarctic, located at Grytviken, South Georgia. (A shore station was one where the whales had to be brought ashore to be processed; this technique quickly became obsolete.) By 1910 there were six more shore stations in the various islands in the whale-rich South Atlantic, and close to fifty catcher boats prowled the Antarctic, returning with their catch—humpbacks, blues, and fins—to the factory ships that were anchored in the protected bays of the islands of the South Shetlands, the South Orkneys, South Georgia, and the Falklands. In 1925 the floating factory ship *Lancing* arrived in the Antarctic; she had a slipway for hauling whales up to the cutting deck, an innovation that freed the whalers from their dependency on the lifelines of shore. They could now go anywhere the whales could go, kill the whales, and process them on the spot. It was unquestionably the beginning of the most intensive period of whaling in history.*

At first the blue whale was the predominant object of the southern fishery, but the stocks were soon depleted and the attention of the whalers turned to the abundant fin whales. It was in 1937/38 that fin whale catches in the Antarctic surpassed the blue whale statistics: 14,381 fins to 14,304 blues. By the following season the fin whale catch was 28,009, as opposed to 14,923 blues. Blue whale catches took a precipitous drop after that season, but the number of fin whales killed from then until the 1960s (with time out for fighting World War II and refitting the ships when the war had ended) was well over 15,000 per annum and often closer to 30,000 (McHugh 1974). From 1938 to 1964, fin whales were the mainstay of the whaling industry in the Antarctic, and a "virgin" population estimated to have been about 400,000 animals was reduced to some 80,000 whales (Gambell 1975). In the Pacific and the Atlantic similar depletions were taking place. The original Pacific stocks were thought to number perhaps 45,000 fin whales; by 1975 there were probably between 14,000 and 19,000. The primeval North Atlantic populations have been estimated at between 30,000 and 50,000 whales (Sergeant 1976), and projections of the number remaining range from 7,000 to 30,000.

Although most fin whaling has ceased (Canada and Norway have completely given up pelagic whaling, and only the nations that are not members of the IWC take fin whales outside certain restricted areas), it will take many years—perhaps as long as a century—for the fin whale population to reach anything like its preexploitation levels. Scheffer (1976) estimated that only 22 percent of the original population of fin whales remain throughout the world, and even with the protective measures now imposed, the fin whale was declared "vulnerable" by the Red Data Book. The whales themselves seem to be compensating for their reduced numbers. In studies of ear plug laminations of whales caught between 1910 and 1951, it was noticed that the age at sexual maturity seems to be getting lower and the reproduction rate has risen sharply (Gambell 1976). Whereas 65 percent of the females taken during the period 1925–31 were pregnant, that figure rose to 80 percent during 1932–41 (Mackintosh 1942). These changes are thought to be "density dependent" (Gambell 1976); this suggests that as their numbers are reduced, the whales reproduce faster and more frequently in an unconscious racial attempt to stave off extinction.

BLUE WHALE
Balaenoptera musculus Linnaeus 1758

The blue whale is probably the largest animal that has ever lived on earth,* but its maximum dimensions are open to question. Various authorities have produced different records for the known maximum length, usually around 100 feet (30.5 meters), and then have suggested that the really huge specimens of 110–120 feet were taken before scientists were concerned about comparative size. Nishiwaki (1972) said that "the largest ever recorded was a 31 m [101.68-foot] female taken from the Antarctic Ocean," but the method of measurement was not mentioned. This is critical, since the usual points between which the overall length is computed are the tip of the rostrum and the notch of the flukes. In their comprehensive study of blue whales in the Antarctic, Mackintosh and Wheeler (1929) found that the largest specimen was 93.5 feet (28.5 meters). However, they wrote, "if measurements were taken from the projection of the lower jaw to the tips of the flukes beyond the notch, 100 feet is not an improbable length for a blue whale."

The weight of these giants has only been estimated, because very few full-grown blue whales have been weighed, for obvious reasons. To do so, one must weigh the animal in parts, total the various components, and add a percentage for body fluids lost in the cutting process. Blue whales taken in the Antarctic include an 82-foot female weighing 219,838 pounds (Nishiwaki and Oye 1951) and an 83-foot male weighing 242,397 pounds (Ohno and Fujino 1952). After feeding in the Antarctic for a full season, a 100-foot blue whale might weigh as much as 200 tons. In order to give a realistic impression of the size of this animal,

---

*In 1935, C. H. Townsend published the results of his analysis of the logbooks of whaleships that had sailed from American ports in the nineteenth and early twentieth centuries. From 744 vessels making a total of 1,665 whaling voyages during this period, the total number of whales killed was 58,877. In just two seasons, 1931/32 and 1932/33, a total of 71,706 whales were killed in the Antarctic (McHugh 1974).

*According to Romer (1974), the largest known dinosaur was *Diplodocus,* reaching a known length of 87 feet (26.5 meters). In 1979 an 8-foot (2.44-meter) fossilized shoulder blade was discovered in Dry Mesa, Colorado, belonging to a dinosaur that seems to be considerably larger than any previously known species (Ostrom 1978). This animal was nicknamed "supersaurus," but in 1979 an even larger dinosaur, named "ultrasaurus," was discovered at the same site. It now appears that the largest dinosaurs may have been almost as long—but not nearly as heavy—as the blue whale.

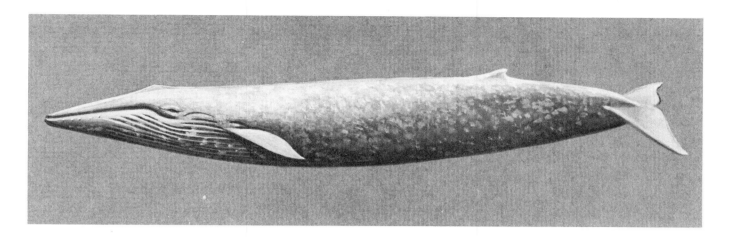

comparisons to objects of known size are usually made: it weighs as much as thirty elephants or 1,600 people, and it is as long as three railroad cars. However, the only way to understand fully the size of this creature is to see one. In the water "it does not give the impression of ungainly bulk or superfluous size. It is only when it is dead and hauled out on to dry land that any proper conception of its immensity can be obtained" (Norman and Fraser 1938).

The blue whale is blue, a slate- or grayish-blue whose intensity is accentuated when the animal is seen in the water. It is mottled with lighter spots, which are concentrated most heavily on the back and shoulders and rarely appear on the head, flippers, or flukes. The underside of the whale is usually the same color as the dorsal surface and is sometimes marked with lighter spots, small ones on the pleated throat and occasional white "splashes" in the genital area. The underside of the flukes is dark, but the flippers are sometimes light or even white below, and often the tip of the flipper is unpigmented. In the northern North Pacific and the Antarctic, blue whales often acquire a patina of yellowish microorganisms on the underside; this accounts for the name "sulphur-bottom," which is often encountered in the literature.* Since some blue whales are taken before the diatom film has formed, not all captured blues have this distinctive yellowish-brown film, often visible to the naked eye. Omura (1950) wrote that the "infection" of the diatom *Cocconeis ceticola* forms only after the whales have been in the Antarctic for a month. One scientist, unaware of this chronology, remarked peevishly: "the Newfoundland

and American whalemen call this animal "sulphur bottom," a most inappropriate name, for there is no suggestion of yellow on its body" (Andrews 1916). Melville, who probably never saw the bottom of a blue whale, described it as a "brimstone belly, doubtless got by scraping along the Tartarian tiles in some of his profounder divings."

Blue whales are not particularly susceptible to infestations of whale lice *(Cyamidae)*, but, in addition to diatoms, various "passengers" attach themselves to this species. Rice (1972) reported the presence of the barnacle *Xenobalaena globicipitis*, usually found on the hind margin of the flukes. Too, the whalesucker, *Remora australis*, a fish related to the more familiar sharksucker, will be seen clinging to the sides of the whale. This remora is harmless to the whale, just

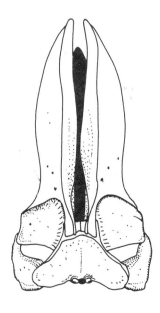

Dorsal view of the skull of the blue whale, *Balaenoptera musculus* (after Allen).

*Scammon knew the species as *Sibbaldius sulfureus.* Other descriptive binomials have been *Balaenoptera gigas, Rorqualus major,* and *Sibbaldius antarcticus.* Sir Robert Sibbald was a Scot who described a specimen that stranded in the Firth of Forth in 1692, and his name is often associated with the species.

going along for the ride, but lampreys, which take bites from the whale's blubber, are often seen.

The baleen of the blue whale is black, and there are some 300–400 plates on each side of the upper jaw. At the front of the mouth the plates are about 20 inches (50 centimeters) in length, and at the rear they are about 40 inches (100 centimeters). The skull is less sharply pointed than that of any other rorqual; the upper jawbones are flared and wide, whereas those of the other members of the genus are narrow, producing a V-shaped skull. This wide, flat upper jaw is one of the diagnostic features of the blue whale and led to its early names of "flathead" and "broad-nosed whale" (Dewhurst 1834). There is a single ridge on the rostrum, extending from the nostrils almost to the tip. For an animal of this size the fins are quite small; the dorsal fin, situated far back on the tail stock, is only 1–2 feet (25–50 centimeters) high in an adult specimen, and the flippers measure about 12 percent of the total length of the animal. (In an 85-foot whale the flippers would be a little over 10 feet long.) The ventral grooves reach the navel and number about ninety, but, as in all balaenopterids, the number will vary from individual to individual. The blue whale has about twenty to forty hairs on the lower jaw and two more rows of hairs on the dorsal surface of the rostrum.*

Seen from a distance, the blue whale can be identified by its size and color, by the size and shape of its "blow" (which is as much as 30 feet [9.1 meters] high and is narrow, rather than diffuse), and by the way it rolls in the water when it breathes. First the blowhole is exposed, then the long expanse of the back, and finally the small dorsal fin. The blue whale will often show its blowhole and dorsal fin simultaneously, which few other whales do. After a series of short breaths at the surface, the whale will lift its flukes out of the water before making a longer (ten-to-fifteen-minute) and probably deeper dive.

Balaenoptera comes from the Greek words for "whale" and "wing" and refers to the dorsal fin; this differentiates it from the genus *Balaena*, which has no dorsal. The word *musculus* is Latin for "muscle," an extremely appropriate name for this powerful creature.† The name in Japanese is *Shironagasu-kujira*,

which means "white fin whale," since it appears much lighter in color than the dark gray fin whale.

At sea it is possible to confuse the fin whale or perhaps the sei whale with the blue. The white undersides, asymmetrical coloration, and definite gray color will identify the fin whale, the only other species that even approaches the size of an adult blue whale. The sei whale is smaller, with a slightly Roman nose and a high, falcate dorsal fin. The blue whale "throws its flukes" before a long dive, but the other species rarely show theirs. Viewed from above, the wide, curved upper jaw of the blue whale is diagnostic; Leatherwood and associates (1976) likened it to a "gothic arch, slightly flattened at the top."

Within the depleted ranks of the blue whale population there exists a probable subspecies, the pygmy blue whale. In 1960, Japanese scientists, working aboard whaleships in the vicinity of Kerguelen Island in the southern Indian Ocean, noticed that some of the whales they examined were different from the majority, and the differences seemed to be consistent. In the first season of the discovery of this aberrant population (1959/60), the Japanese took 311 of these unusual blues. In 1960/61 they took 1,127; in 1961/62, 381; and in 1962/63, 714. The total for these seasons, 2,533, represents the entire known catch of pygmy blues, since there have been virtually no commercial catches of blue whales since 1964 (Gulland 1976). The pygmy blue whale, which has been given the name *Balaenoptera musculus brevicauda* ("short tail"), varies from the ordinary blue whale in several characteristics:* the most significant difference is in the length of the tail from the dorsal fin aft. The subspecies is somewhat smaller, reaching a known maximum length of 80 feet (24.39 meters), but it is not what one would call a "pygmy" in the true sense of the word. These whales achieve sexual maturity (determined from examination of reproductive organs) at a much shorter length than the great blues; both males and females reach puberty at about 63 feet (19.2 me-

---

*It is a natural assumption that these hairs are vestigial structures, a reminder of the rorqual's distant land ancestors. According to Japanese investigators, however, it is possible that these hairs "possess sensitive tactility like the whiskers of a cat" and might be used "to feel the currents of water upon their heads" (Nakai and Shida 1948).

†George Small, in his book entitled *The Blue Whale* (1971), wrote that "the second half of this name is a false cognate. *Musculus* in Latin is the diminutive form of *mouse,* meaning therefore 'little

mouse,' and has nothing to do with muscle." This appears to be an unnecessary complication of a simple etymological situation. Small further confused the matter when he speculated that "Linnaeus must have been in a jocular mood at the time." I think we are better off assuming that Linnaeus was serious and that he meant "muscle" when he selected *musculus.*

*The use of the word "pygmy" has created an unusual problem in the vernacular nomenclature: if one form is a pygmy, what is the other? Among the modifiers frequently used are "ordinary," "true," and "giant," none of which is particularly successful. A 150-ton animal that is 87 feet long is hardly "ordinary"; "true blue whale" is a very odd-sounding name; and "giant blue whale" seems redundant. Perhaps "great blue whale" is the answer.

ters), which is some ten feet shorter than the size at sexual maturity for the larger form. The baleen plates of the pygmy blue are proportionally shorter and wider than those of the blue whale, and the subspecies seems to exist in a restricted habitat in the area north of 54° S, and from 80° E to 0°, the area in the southern Indian Ocean that lies north of the Antarctic Convergence. It was taken mostly in the vicinity of the Kerguelen, Crozet, and Heard islands. There have been reports of pygmy blue whales at Durban (Gambell 1964), and Aguayo (1974) reported that 10 pygmies were taken off the coast of Chile between 1965 and 1967. In his original description Ichihara (1961) noted that "whalers in the Antarctic speak of *Mrybjønner* as a distinct race of blue whales . . . small whales that seem to be distinguished by a large quantity of pale spots on the dorsal surface."* Berzin (1978) described them as "noticeably smaller than ordinary blue whales, and [they] had relatively short, broad tails."

Under ordinary circumstances the discovery of a subspecies of one of the great whales would be an interesting, but not particularly exciting, event. But in this case, because the discovery took place when so many people were concerned with the fate of the whales, this otherwise minor event has led to a bitter, multinational imbroglio that is not settled even today. Tadayoshi Ichihara first described the differences between the whales with the shorter tails and the regular blue whales from specimens caught in the season of 1959/60. Subsequently he published a number of papers that culminated in a comprehensive description of the "new subspecies," which was presented in 1963, but not published until 1966. Between the presentation and the publication, two Soviet researchers, Zemsky and Boronin, wrote an article on the taxonomy of the pygmy blue whale that was published in *Norsk Hvalfangst-tidende* in 1964. Since Ichihara did not propose the name *brevicauda* until 1966, the Soviet scientists, who "published the denomination *brevicauda* without calling it a subspecies" (Ichihara 1975), appear to have been the first to describe the species. Under the rules of zoological nomenclature the full name of the animal would be *Balaenoptera musculus brevicauda* Zemsky and Boronin 1964. The prob-

lem still is not settled, for in the 1977 edition of the *List of the Marine Mammals of the World*, D. W. Rice referred to the Soviet name as a *nomen nudum* (unusable) and said that the first valid publication of the name was by Ichihara in 1966.

If this confusion were not enough for the pygmy blue whale, yet another dispute developed, leading to considerable name-calling and questions of integrity. George Small, a professor of geography at the City University of New York, published a book called *The Blue Whale* in 1971. A popular treatment that displayed a strong antiwhaling bias, it has contributed substantially to the popular misinformation about the world population of blue whales. On the subject of the pygmy blue whale Small was vehement. He referred to it only as the *"pygmy"* blue whale, or the *"so-called pygmy blues,"* contending that the Japanese had invented the subspecies as a way of circumventing IWC regulations on ordinary blue whales. He wrote: "In my opinion the pygmy blue whale was a fraud used as an excuse to continue killing blue whales in a portion of the Antarctic where a few could still be found." (Ichihara responded in 1975 by calling Small's book "slanderous" and accusing him of having "very poor knowledge on the biology of whales.") In 1972, Small's book won the prestigious National Book Award, so it was widely publicized and attracted more readers. His opinions on the pygmy blue and other areas of blue whale biology gained currency, a benefit usually denied to such esoteric titles as "A Note on the Abundance of Antarctic Blue Whales" (Gulland 1976), or "Blue Whales in the Waters Around Kerguelen Island" (Ichihara 1961). Both of these papers, as well as numerous others, refute Small's accusations, but the only people who read the scientific papers are the scientists. There is no question that the Japanese have contributed mightily to the decline of the blue whale, but this is not a valid reason to accuse the Japanese scientists of fraud. The pygmy blue whale appears to be a good subspecies, despite its inopportune discovery; and even the unbiased, but admittedly conservation-oriented, Red Data Book of the International Union for the Conservation of Nature (IUCN), based in Switzerland, recognizes the pygmy blue whale. The population was originally estimated at 10,000 whales in the southern Indian Ocean (Ichihara and Doi 1964) and was reduced by Antarctic whalers and the Japanese during 1959–63 to perhaps 2,000–3,000 by 1964 (Red Data Book 1972). But it may again be approaching its earlier numbers after eighteen years of full protection.

*In his earlier papers on the pygmy blue whale Ichihara referred to a difference in color as a distinguishing characteristic; the pygmies, he wrote (1963), were "silvery gray, rather than the steel blue of the ordinary blue whale." Later he conceded (1975) that "the body color is not a definite criterion . . . since its expression varies from observer to observer." The Norwegian word *myrbjønner*, the name of a small white flower, is thought to refer to the proliferation of white spots on the back of the subspecies.

From the day of its birth, the life history of the blue whale is couched in superlatives. After an eleven-month gestation period, a 24-foot (7.3-meter) calf is born, weighing perhaps 2.5–3 tons (2,250–2,700 kilograms). Feeding on the fat-rich milk of the mother for about eight months, the calf gains about 200 pounds (90 kilograms) per day—8.33 pounds per hour—until it is weaned. At that time it will begin to feed on the small, shrimplike crustaceans known as euphausiids that constitute the diet of the blue whale almost exclusively.*

The actual amount of food required to feed an adult blue whale is astounding. Rice (1972) gave the following analysis of its food consumption:

An average blue whale weighing 75 or 80 tons probably requires about 1.5 million calories per day. Since it fasts for much of the winter, it must consume about twice this amount—or three million calories a day—during the summer months. One pound of *Euphausia pacifica* supplies about 400 calories. This means that it must consume about four tons of krill every day. Its stomach holds about a ton, so it eats four *full* meals a day. Each individual of *Euphausia pacifica* weighs only one-tenth of a gram, so it takes about 40 million of these krill to sustain one blue whale for one day.

When the calf is weaned, it may be almost 50 feet long (15 meters), and it will add as much as 88 pounds per day, "which is remarkable when we consider that its diet consists of tiny crustaceans" (Ruud 1956a).

Sexual maturity is achieved somewhere between 23 and 30 years (Nishiwaki 1972), a figure that has been moved higher and higher with the passage of time. (It was once thought to occur at the age of 2 [Norman and Fraser], then at 8–10, and finally, with the more sophisticated analysis of ear plugs and reproductive organs, at the present figure.) Females reach sexual maturity at 76-plus feet (23-plus meters); males, at 74-plus feet (22-plus meters). (These figures were particularly important during the period when the blue whales were being killed in such great numbers; the

whales were supposed to be protected at least until they had a chance to reproduce.) Like all balaenopterids, female blue whales grow larger than males. Nishiwaki (1972) suggested that blue whales "live to about ninety years and rarely over one hundred years," but the time during which this species was being caught and examined coincided with its decimation, so it is unlikely that many individuals reached old age.

With the obvious exception of the four or five months that the southern blue whales spend in the high latitudes of the Antarctic, the movements of this animal, the largest on earth, are poorly known. From December to April the whales arrive in great numbers in the Antarctic, but for the remainder of the year their travels are a mystery. They were obviously not in the Antarctic, so it was logical to assume that they moved north into the warmer temperate waters to breed and give birth. In 1966, Mackintosh wrote: "The reason for their migrating so far toward the equator for breeding is not quite certain, but it is thought that the newborn calf needs warmer and calmer waters than are found in the polar feeding grounds." These warmer waters are poor in plankton and the crustaceans that blue whales eat, so their feeding takes place in the icy waters of the polar regions. Therefore, they are thought to fast for the remainder of the year, living off the accumulated fat reserves of the previous summer.* Whales taken as soon as they arrived in the Antarctic were invariably thinner than those taken at the end of the season (Laurie 1933). Because of the alternating cycle of the seasons in the Northern and Southern Hemispheres, all the world's blue whales are moving in the same direction at roughly the same time. This explains why "whales of the two hemispheres do not converge at the equator at the same

---

*Although the blue whale is stenophagous (feeding on a narrow range of food), it has been known to eat organisms other than the large euphausiid of the Antarctic, *E. superba.* Among the other small crustaceans that have been found in the stomachs of blue whales are *E. vallentini* from the southern Indian Ocean (the preferred food of the pygmy blue whales); and in the North Atlantic and North Pacific, where *E. superba* does not occur, the blue whale feeds on *Thysanoessa longipes* and other tiny crustaceans. Scammon (1874) noted that large numbers of blue whales were attracted to the waters of Baja California "by the swarms of sardines and prawns with which the waters were enlivened," and Rice (1974) described blue whales off Baja that were "among—and possibly feeding on—shoals of pelagic red crabs, *Pleuroncodes planipes,* which are often abundant in the inshore waters."

---

*It sounds incredible that a warm-blooded animal the size of a blue whale can go for seven or eight months without eating, but the data bear out this unlikely conclusion. Whales taken at subtropical land stations were usually thin, and their stomachs were nearly always empty (Mackintosh 1966). A whale is heavily insulated and does not have to expend a lot of energy to keep itself warm. And since it is virtually weightless in the water, it does not require huge energy outputs to move.

Euphausia superba.

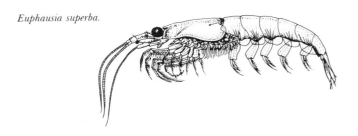

time" (Mackintosh 1966). In the northern summer, April to September, the southern populations leave the Antarctic for the warmer waters farther north; at the same time the northern blue whales are heading for the northern ice fields. In the northern winter, October to March, the pattern is reversed, and all the whales move in a southerly direction—the northern populations to their breeding grounds, and the southern stocks to their feeding grounds in the Antarctic. It is easy to determine why the whales move into the polar waters in the warmer months: that is when their food is plentiful, and they will not get trapped in the closing ice. But why they have to swim thousands of miles to breed and give birth is what Mackintosh (1966) called "the largest unresolved problem concerning their distribution." All we can be sure about their movements after they leave the Antarctic is that they head for the vast reaches of the temperate and subtropical waters, but we do not know if they concentrate in one area or disperse over the millions of square miles of the open southern oceans.

How—or even if—whales communicate over these vast distances is unknown. It has been speculated that low-frequency moans are employed as signals over hundreds or even thousands of miles, "making it possible for the deep-voiced whales to keep in touch with each other across entire ocean basins" (Payne 1977). Nowadays the seas resound with the low-frequency vibrations of the screws of powerful ships, and this ambient noise undoubtedly interferes with the whales' ability to communicate. The voice of the blue whale has been infrequently heard and even more infrequently recorded. Off the coast of Chile, Cummings and Thompson (1971) recorded the "low-frequency moans or pulses" of blue whales and described the sounds as "the most powerful sustained utterances known from whales or any other living source." Beamish and Mitchell (1971), working in the North Atlantic, recorded "sounds principally between 21 and 31 kHz in the presence of a blue whale presumed to be feeding 100–800m from a silent ship."* Blue whale phonations have been described as "not constant tones, but slowly descending moans of intriguing complexity" (Thompson et al. 1979). In 1974 a 72-foot (22-meter) blue whale became trapped in the ice off Cape Ray, Newfoundland. Investigators recorded "seven sequences of short, repetitive pulses" (Beamish 1979).

*The phrase "in the presence of" is often used in connection with a recording of whale sounds in the wild, because the particular individual responsible for the recorded sounds can rarely be unequivocally identified.

In this instance there was no question about the identification of the whale making the sounds, for it was grounded in eight feet of water and immobilized by the closing ice. The hydrophones were within thirty-five feet of the whale, and the animal was visible during the entire experiment, which concluded when increasing wind velocity opened the ice and enabled the whale to escape.

On the feeding grounds, blue whales are usually seen in pairs, which suggests that monogamy is the norm or that calves stay with their mothers for some time. Since approximately half the females examined were pregnant when caught, it is assumed that most females bear a calf every other year (Ruud 1956a).

There is no question that the blue whale is a fast and powerful swimmer. In *A Book of Whales* (1900), Beddard wrote: "Its speed too, when going rapidly is great. Something like twelve miles an hour are accomplished by a *Balaenoptera sibbaldii* when putting its best foot forward." In a later analysis Lockyer (1976) assigned to the blue whale the highest speed ("maximum when alarmed") of any cetacean: 48 kilometers per hour—almost 30 miles per hour. (It should be noted that the maximum speed for the fin whale is 41 kilometers per hour, and the sei whale, the other rorqual thought to be a speedster, has not been timed.) The blue whale's normal pattern of swimming consists of three or four shallow breaths, followed by a dive of ten to fifteen minutes' duration. It is not known if this deep dive has a purpose—in fact, it is not known if it is really a deep dive—since the food that provides the blue whale's diet is found in the upper 330 feet (100 meters). When harpooned, however, the blue is capable of prodigious feats of strength and tremendous dives.

Andrews witnessed a Japanese blue whale hunt in which the whale "was down for ten minutes and came to the surface with a rush which threw half his eighty feet of body into the air. . . . three quarters of a mile of line was out before the animal finally slowed down enough so that the winch would hold. Even then, with the engine at full speed astern, the ship was being dragged ahead at nearly six knots an hour." The same whale also dived straight down to a depth of three hundred fathoms. Whaling literature is replete with stories of blue whales' dragging ships to which they have become fatally attached. Early whalers had little to do with the blue whale; they did not know of its Antarctic migrations (by far the largest concentration of these animals), and the blue was too big and too fast for the kind of open-boat whaling that preceded the steam and diesel catcher boats with the exploding grenade harpoons. In 1818, Scoresby "ordered a general chase" of the whale that he referred to (1820) as "the physalis," which must be the blue whale from the measurements he gave. "One of these whales was shot and the other struck. The former dived with such impetuosity, that the line was broken by the resistance of the buoy as soon as it was thrown into the water. Another physalis . . . dived obliquely with such velocity, that 480 fathoms of line were withdrawn from the boat in about a minute of time. This whale was also lost by the breaking of the line."

It is not possible to assign specific territories to the larger rorquals because "blue and fin whales are great travelers; a study of their distribution is largely a study of their migrations and other movements" (Mackintosh 1966). Nevertheless, it is possible to divide the world's blue whale population into three major geographical groups, which are treated by some authorities as discrete subspecies. The blue whale of the North Atlantic and North Pacific is known as *Balaenoptera musculus musculus;* the whale of the southern latitudes is known as *B. m. intermedia;* and there is also *B. m. brevicauda,* the pygmy blue whale of the southern Indian Ocean.

Apparently the North Atlantic stock was never very plentiful; it has been estimated at a maximum of 1,100 animals (Allen 1970), distributed sparsely around the limits of the northern pack ice in the summer and moving south in the winter. The blue whale has been recorded from the Davis Straits and Greenland, Iceland, Spitsbergen, and the Barents Sea (Jonsgard 1966). Its southerly migrations are known only from random sightings and strandings from as far south as New Jersey (Allen 1916) in the western North Atlantic and the Cape Verde Islands in the eastern sector. There is a small population that can be seen in the Saint Lawrence River in the fall, and one anomalous report told of a single blue whale that entered the harbor in Cristobal in the Panama Canal Zone in 1922 (Harmer 1923).* Little is known about the current population, like the other stocks of blue whales, and the extent of our knowledge was summed up by Rørvik and Jonsgard (1975): "It may be concluded that blue whales on each side of the North Atlantic seem to be composed of several stocks and that migration may take place between the eastern and western side in high north latitudes."

In the western North Pacific, blue whales are scattered in small populations, having an estimated total of 5,000 (Omura and Ohsumi 1974). Since there has been no commercial whaling in this area since 1966, estimates of current numbers are vague. In 1972 a report was published giving the figure at 1,500 (National Marine Fisheries Service 1973). The eastern North Pacific supports "one of the world's last remaining sizable stocks of blue whales," which has been calculated at about 6,000 animals by Rice (1974). The whales can be seen off Baja California from January to April,* but "their whereabouts during the remainder of the year and their relation to populations on the whaling grounds farther north is problematical" (Rice 1974). The current population is unknown, but Rice did not believe that the number has been much decreased.

Because the pygmy blue whale inhabits a zone that is "subantarctic," it is distinguished from the Southern Hemisphere blue whale populations. It is found north of 54° S in the area of the Kerguelen, Crozet, and Heard islands. Possibly, this subspecies does not migrate, but stays in one area throughout the year (Zemsky and Boronin 1964). But scattered records indicate that it might not be quite so restricted in its range, since some were apparently taken at Antarctic shore stations (Mackintosh and Wheeler 1929), at Durban (Gambell 1964), off Chile (Aguayo 1974), and off western Australia (Ichihara 1966). In 1978, Berzin reported "about 20 individuals" in the eastern Pacific off Costa Rica.

It is in the Southern Ocean that the largest numbers of blue whales are found. In December the whales begin to arrive, and they reach their greatest concentration in February, "when almost the whole southern population is assembled in the Antarctic" (Mackintosh and Brown 1956).

The Antarctic was divided into five areas by the IWC

---

*This is a very unusual record, indeed. Aside from being thousands of miles from its normal range, the animal was "carefully measured . . . as having a length of 98 feet." (It had been killed with machine guns because it was becoming a hazard to shipping at the canal's Gatun Locks.) The account was written by Sir Sidney Harmer, president of the Linnean Society of London. He examined and measured the second and third cervical vertebrae and found them to be "substantial confirmation of the recorded length of 98 feet," based on comparison with the vertebrae of whales of known length. If the figures are accurate, it is certainly the longest specimen recorded for the Northern Hemisphere and one of the longest known anywhere.

*Scammon saw blue whales off Baja in 1858, but it was in the month of July. He wrote, "the sea, as far as the eye could discern was marked with their huge forms and towering spouts." Several attempts were made to take these animals, "but their propensity to sink and also to 'run under water' baffled the skill of the whalers to secure them."

in 1932 and, later, into six areas to cover the entire circle. The areas are as follows:

Area I	120° W–60° W
Area II	60° W–0°
Area III	0°–70° E
Area IV	70° E–130° E
Area V	130° E–170° W
Area VI	170° W–120° W

Under the terms of the original IWC convention, factory ships have not been permitted to operate north of 40° S, so this effectively forms the northern boundary of the southern whaling grounds. Roughly congruent with 50° S is the Antarctic Convergence, which marks the meeting of the cold Antarctic and the warmer subantarctic waters and separates the area into distinct biogeographical zones more effectively than lines of latitude. In any event, the whales feed south of the convergence, at the edge of the pack ice. Areas I and IV were considered sanctuary areas between 1938 and 1955 and were officially closed to whaling. The land stations at South Georgia, South Shetland, and the Orkney and Falkland islands were located in Area II, so early catch statistics favor this area. The surface currents of the Antarctic are complex, and they distribute the krill unequally around the Antarctic continent; the whales regularly follow these concentrations (Marr 1956). Areas II and III have always been the most productive; Areas I and VI, the least (Mackintosh 1966). From examination of recovered whale marks it has been suggested that the whales return every year to the same location, essentially defining separate stocks (Brown 1959). In addition, work has been done on analysis of the iodine content of the oil, indicating again that the separate stocks in the Antarctic do not integrate (Lund 1950). When not feeding in the Antarctic, southern blue whales move northward into the South Pacific, South Atlantic, and Indian oceans, but their distribution and breeding grounds are unknown.

As soon as the techniques were developed to take the huge and powerful blue whales on the Antarctic whaling grounds, the blue whale became the most important object of the southern whale fishery. The species had been killed in the North Pacific and the North Atlantic, but it never existed there in such great concentrations as were found in the Antarctic. The Norwegians developed the means of killing the whales and then went out and found the whales to kill with their newly developed technology. In 1868, Svend

Foyn made his first successful whaling voyage using steam-powered vessels and the grenade harpoon. In the whaleship *Spes et Fides* (Hope and Faith), he went to Varanger Fjord in Norway, where thirty rorquals were taken. Foyn also invented the technique of inflating the dead whales with air from a compressor so that they would not sink after they had been brought alongside. In a short period of time, he completely revolutionized the business of whaling by eliminating the two major problems that had stood between the whalers and the huge, oil-rich rorquals, which had heretofore ignored the men with their puny hand-lances and open boats. Fired from a cannon, the grenade harpoon could hold and kill even the largest whale, and no longer would these pleated giants sink when they were killed. Since rorquals were not particularly plentiful off northern Norway, this population of blue and fin whales was rapidly decimated by the efficient Norwegians, and they began to look elsewhere.

There had been reports of whales in the Antarctic; after James Clark Ross visited the area in 1839–42, he returned to England with stories of plentiful whales as far south as 72° S (Stonehouse 1972). A British expedition went south in 1892, equipped to hunt the slow-moving right and humpback whales, and found themselves surrounded by huge, swift rorquals that they were not prepared to hunt. In 1904, Captain Carl Anton Larsen formed the Compania Argentina de Pesca, a combination of Norwegian expertise and Argentine money that became the first Antarctic whaling company. The first shore station was opened at Grytviken ("pot bay," named for the pots that the sealers had left behind) on the island of South Georgia. Soon, factory ships from Chile, Argentina, England, and Norway were taking the humpbacks, but these stocks were rapidly depleted, and the whalers moved farther afield in search of the giant blues and fins. The ratio of blues and fins to humpbacks was 5,087 to 261 by the 1919/20 season, and this was five years before the great floating factory ships would make their appearance.

In the season of 1925/26 the first ship with a stern slipway arrived in the Antarctic. She was the *Lancing,* under Captain Peter Sørlle of Vestfold, and this innovation freed the ships from their ties to the shore stations. With a ramp in the stern, which allowed the crew to haul whales aboard ship and process them at sea, the ships could roam the Antarctic, hunting those whales that had otherwise been out of range. The numbers of blue whales taken grew almost exponentially; at first it seemed that this resource was unlimited and that the only factor controlling the catch was the size of the ships. In 1923, Captain Larsen, in the factory ship *James Clark Ross,* went into the previously untapped Ross Sea on the far side the Antarctic continent and returned with a cargo of 17,500 barrels of oil. In the two following seasons, these figures escalated to 32,000 and 40,000 barrels, enormous amounts for such short-term operations (Ommanney 1971).

During the five years following the arrival of the *Lancing,* the whaling industry recorded its highest catch figures: 1926/27, 6,545 blue whales; 1927/28, 8,334; 1928/29, 12,847; 1929/30, 17,898. The season of 1930/31 was the most successful in the history of whaling. In that four-to-five-month period, 29,410 blue whales were killed in the Antarctic. It was the high point of the southern whale fishery. After that, both the industry and the whales began a progressive decline that almost resulted in the total eradication of the species and has brought the whaling industry to its present position of near financial collapse.

All sorts of steps were taken to try to preserve the blue whale for continued commercial exploitation. There have been sanctuary areas, closed seasons, prohibition on the killing of undersized whales, and overall limits, but as long as the killing continued, so also did the decline in numbers. The arrival of the Japanese in the season of 1934/35, and the Soviets in 1946/47, was not propitious for the whales. Neither was the establishment of the "blue whale unit" (BWU) as a guide to the relative value of the various species of whales taken commercially. Under this system, one blue whale equaled two fin whales, two and a half humpbacks, or six sei whales. Since the whaling nations could reach their totals of BWUs in any combination of species, it was certainly most profitable to kill one blue whale instead of two fins or six seis. (Even though fin whales approach the blue in overall length, there is no comparison in the amount of oil they yield. The average for a blue whale is seventy to eighty barrels, whereas the fin averaged only thirty to fifty barrels. Sei whales, with their thin blubber, produce much less.) As the number of whales continued to decline, it became more and more impractical to hunt them, and the number of whaling nations also declined. Britain sold its whaling fleet to Japan in 1963, the Dutch did the same in 1964, and Norway ceased pelagic whaling in 1968. Now only Japan and the Soviet Union hunt whales, but the only whales that have survived in significant numbers are the minkes and the sperm whales. All the other great whales are fully protected (except from nations outside the IWC or from "pirate" whaling ships), and most of them are considered endangered species.

How many blue whales are left? We do not know. One of the few advantages of commercial whaling was the increase in knowledge about whales, as the scientists were permitted to measure, examine, and count the animals that the whalers killed. With the total cessation of blue whaling, we can safely assume that the population is rising—at least it is no longer falling precipitously—but we have very little idea of the rate of increase. The original Antarctic stock was estimated at some 200,000 animals (Chapman et al. 1964), and the total number of whales killed in the Antarctic (allowing for "recruitment"—additions to the population by birth) has been counted at 300,000 (McHugh 1974). If we use a conservative estimate of eighty-five tons per whale, over twenty-five million tons of blue whales have been taken in the Antarctic since 1920. Recent popular works have significantly misinformed the public regarding the number of blue whales remaining, offering extremely low numbers and presenting opinions as if they were facts. For example, Small wrote, "in the vast North Pacific, there might be a hundred blue whales left alive," and "today the blue whale population probably numbers between 0 and 200 individuals." Less emotional observers have reported "low hundreds" for the North Atlantic (Mitchell 1974); 6,000 for the North Pacific (Rice 1974); and 8,000 (Gulland 1976) to 13,000 (Scheffer 1976), to "20,000 to 30,000 animals" (Nishiwaki 1972) for the Antarctic population.

The blue whale seems to have escaped extinction—at least for the moment. Even now, however, another threat to its existence looms on the Antarctic horizon: the possibility of a commercial krill fishery (McWhinnie and Denys 1980). The vast swarms of *Euphausia superba* are being contemplated as a potential food source for the world's hungry billions. After all, it is much more efficient to harvest the protein source before it is processed by the whale; ten tons of krill are needed to produce one ton of whale (Murphy 1962). The Soviets are experimenting with the manufacture of "krill cakes," and the Red Data Book reported: "Commercial fishing for krill, *Euphausia superba,* which is the staple food of the blue whale in the Antarctic, could be in operation before the end of the century, i.e., sooner than the whale stocks can recuperate to their optimum level."

HUMPBACK WHALE

Megaptera novaeangliae Borowski 1781

Although the humpback shares many of the characteristics of the Balaenopteridae, including ventral pleats, baleen plates, a dorsal fin, and substantial size, it is different in enough particulars to warrant inclusion in a separate genus, *Megaptera*. Whereas the ventral pleats of the rorquals are numerous and narrow, the grooves of the humpback are more widely spaced and average about twenty-eight in number. (For comparison, the average number of pleats for a blue whale is about ninety.) The pleats reach from just aft of the tip of the lower lip to the umbilicus. The baleen plates, which number about 350 per side, are black with coarse, lighter-colored fringes. In the largest specimens, the baleen is no longer than 2.5 feet (76 centimeters).

Much has been written about the dorsal fin of the humpback. There is, in fact, great variation in the fins of individual whales, ranging from a knobby protuberance of indistinct shape to a falcate fin that would do justice to a sei whale. In most instances there is a "step" anterior to the protrusion itself, which is probably responsible for the name. Numerous post hoc arguments have attempted to explain this appellation worthy of Quasimodo, including references to the exaggerated roll of the whale as it dives, presenting a humplike aspect (Budker 1959). We may safely assume that Herman Melville never saw a humpback whale (or if he did, he saw a very unusual specimen), for he wrote: "He has a great pack on him like a peddler; or you might call him the Elephant and Castle whale."

The humpback is a stocky whale, rarely reaching 50 feet (15.24 meters) in length. Nishiwaki (1972) reported that "the largest animals taken were a 19.0 m [63.32-foot] female, and a 17.5 m [57.40-foot] male," but these records, if correct, are far in excess of current known measurements. Scammon (1874) recorded a specimen that "was adjudged to be seventy-five feet in length," but this, too, is excessive and probably erroneous. For Antarctic specimens, Mackintosh (1942) described the largest female (as in most baleen whales, females are larger than males) at 48.9 feet (14.9 meters) and the largest male at 48.5 feet (14.8 meters). These whales were taken during the heyday of Antarctic whaling, when the whales were so numerous that the gunners could be selective; nowadays the humpbacks are considerably smaller. Like other large whales, humpbacks are not frequently, or easily, weighed, but Mackintosh (1942) calculated the

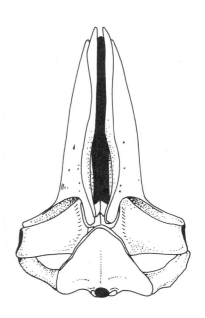

Dorsal view of the skull of the humpback whale, *Megaptera novaeangliae* (after Allen).

weight of a 46.5-foot female at 31.9 tons (32,374 kilograms) not including blood, and Ash (1953), in a study directed specifically to the weight of humpbacks, figured the average weight for a 41.8-foot whale at 29.2 tons, not including blood, intestinal contents, or stomach contents.*

Humpbacks are generally black above and white below. Within this description, however, every possible variation has been seen, resulting in numerous authors' classifying whales by the proportional amounts of black and white (Lillie 1915, Omura 1953, Budker 1959, and others). Although there are apparently groups of whales wherein one pattern is dominant ("white-bellies," "black-bellies," "marble-bellies"), this system has not proved to be reliable. In some whales the white of the undersides extends far up the flanks, but in others the whale is almost entirely black and has only white flippers (Andrews 1909). Some specimens have distinctive white splashes on either side of the chin, which sometimes correspond to white baleen plates. The flippers, which can be as much as one-third the total length of the whale, are almost always white on the ventral surface and mixed black and white on the dorsal surface. The pattern on the upper surface of the flippers is unique to each

*Ash's study was conducted to ascertain the weight gain of whales on the Antarctic feeding grounds. In the season from December to April (the southern summer) humpback whales put on approximately one ton per week, thereby supporting the whalers' recommendation that they be taken as late in the season as possible. Chittleborough (1965) showed that whales arriving on the feeding grounds yielded as much as ten barrels of oil less than those that were beginning their northward migration.

whale, varies little from left to right, and can be used to identify individuals (Hudnall 1978). The flukes, sometimes as much as 18 feet (5.5 meters) across, are always dark on the dorsal surface, and have varying amounts of white on the underside. Since this symmetrical white pattern can often be seen when the animal dives, it has been used as a means of recording and identifying individual whales (Katona et al. 1979).

The flippers or pectoral fins of the humpback are extraordinary appendages. They are longer than those of any other whale: whereas the flippers of a 90-foot blue whale are about 12 feet long, those of a 48-foot (14.6-meter) humpback may be 16 feet (4.88 meters) in length. All cetaceans swim with an up-and-down movement of their tails, so these winglike structures are not used directly for locomotion, but they must give the humpback more maneuverability than the other large whales.* The flippers contain an elongated "hand," consisting of easily recognizable—albeit elongated—finger bones. In 1916, Allen wrote that the "anterior margin of the flipper has a series of eight prominent knobs, corresponding to the carpal joint and the joints of the phalanges of the short first and second bony fingers."

Another distinguishing characteristic of the humpback is the tail. The flukes are gracefully curved and

*In an unusual experiment with a humpback that was temporarily held captive in Newfoundland, Zeitlin (1977) observed that the whale, "after feeling the initial tug on the line [which would have pulled her backward through the maze so she could then swim forward and observers could see if she could negotiate it blindfolded], swam backward, using her flippers." If other large whales can swim backward, the ability has not been often recorded.

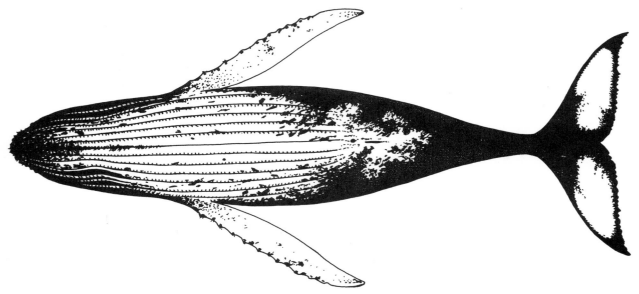

Ventral view of the humpback whale. The pattern on the underside of the flukes varies from whale to whale and can be used to identify individual animals.

provide a haven for barnacles. There is a deep notch on the median line, and the trailing edges are always ragged or scalloped. One might assume that this irregular margin was an acquired characteristic, perhaps related to the barnacles' being pulled off or to another abrasive action, but the peculiar unevenness of the flukes is congenital, since even unborn humpbacks have a ragged tail (Allen 1916). For investigators to determine the migratory movements of whales, they must either mark them and then recover the marks, a procedure that involves killing the whale, or they must be able to recognize individual specimens at sea. In southern right whales the identifying characteristic is the pattern of the callosities on the head (Payne 1976); in bottlenose dolphins the individual variations of the dorsal fin have been used (Würsig 1977). For humpbacks it is the variable pattern of white on the underside of the flukes, visible when the whale dives.

The skin of the humpback whale is covered with scars in addition to the variegated pattern of black and white. Many of these scars have been caused by barnacles, which leave a circular mark when they fall off. A certain amount of scratching probably occurs when two barnacle-encrusted whales come in contact, and this can result in even more scars. There are other scars present in humpbacks and other large whales (and also some smaller cetaceans) that have long been a mystery to cetologists. These are oval marks, some of which look as if the blubber had been scooped out with a spoon. In describing these wounds, Matthews (1938) wrote: "Like other whales, the humpback, while in temperate and tropical waters, is subject to attack by some unknown predator, parasite or disease, which removes semi-ovoid pieces of blubber from the body surface, making oval pits which slowly heal, leav-

ing a white or grey scar." Mackintosh and Wheeler (1929), examining these wounds on blue and fin whales, assumed that they were caused by a microbial infection, but in a 1971 paper E. C. Jones suggested that the wounds are made by a small shark, *Isistius brasiliensis*. The wounds are clean and do not show the ragged edges of lamprey bites (Pike 1951). The shark, which does not get much bigger than 1.5 feet (45 centimeters), is probably the culprit in various "attacks" on tuna, jacks, marlins, and "nearly all of the baleen whales . . . except the right whales" (Jones 1971).*

In addition to displaying scars and barnacles, the humpback is decorated with a series of bumps on the upper jaw and with a fleshy protuberance at the apex of the lower jaw, both of which contain hair follicles from which various bristles grow. The function of these hairs is not known, but they may serve a tactile purpose, enabling the whale to sense the movement of water currents or prey species. The bumps were responsible for one of the humpbacks' earlier trivial names, *nodosa,* from the Latin *nodus* ("knob"). *Megaptera novaeangliae,* the name by which it is currently known, means "big wing of New England" (*mega* = "large" and *pteron* = "wing"), and *novaeangliae* is simply "of New England," from the location of the type specimen, first described by Paul Dudley in 1725 (Allen 1916). In Norwegian the whale is known as *knølhval* ("knob-whale"); in French, *baleine à bosse;* in German, *buckelwal* (*buckel* = "hump"). The Japanese call this species *Zato-kujira. Kujira* means "whale," and *zato* is a name for blind musicians who used to play a

*To demonstrate his theory, Jones took a freshly caught *Isistius* and pushed its teeth into a nectarine. The result was a neat, round crater wound in the fruit and a plug in the shark's mouth, secured by the hooked upper teeth.

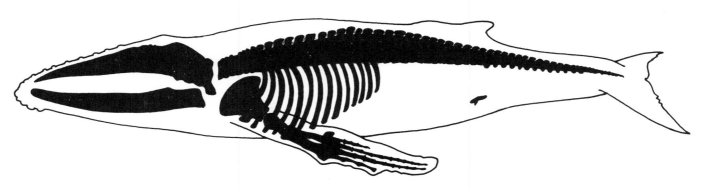

Skeleton and body outline of humpback whale. Notice how the bumps on the leading edge of the pectoral limb coincide with the bones.

string instrument called a *biwa.* The irregular fin and arched back of the whale suggested the *zato,* bent over and carrying the *biwa* on his back (Omura, personal communication).

With its long flippers, scalloped tail, bumps, lumps, and barnacles, the humpback should be difficult to confuse with any other species. From a distance the blow is shorter than that of the rorquals and might be confused with that of a right whale.

Describing the "amorous antics" of humpbacks during the mating season, Scammon wrote,

when lying by the side of each other, the megapteras frequently adminster alternate blows with their long fins, which love pats may, on a still day, be heard at a distance of miles. They also rub against each other with these same huge and flexible arms, rolling occasionally from side to side, and indulging in other gambols which can easier be imagined than described.

Since the whales mate and calve in the same areas each year, it is assumed that the gestation period is about one year. They are thought to breed every two years, but in some populations that have been examined as many as 86 percent of the females were pregnant; this would presume an even higher rate of impregnation (Omura 1953).

One of the known "nursery" areas for humpbacks is Maalea Bay, off the Hawaiian island of Maui. There, on January 21, 1977, James Hudnall (1978) witnessed the birth of a humpback whale:

In ten meters of water . . . at about 12:37 P.M., she began to spend a great deal of time at the surface, mostly on her back, flexing her caudal section repeatedly and slapping her flukes on the water while occasionally waving her pectoral fins in the air. At 1:04 P.M. the first small blow of the calf was seen, and at 1:25 P.M. the cow and calf moved northwest along the coast and out of our range of vision. We were unable to determine the mode of calf presentation (cephalic or breech) due to the white-capped sea surface.

There have been two records of humpback whale births—or almost births—one headfirst and one tailfirst. Dunstan (1957) reported a harpooned female with the tail of a full-term fetus projecting from the vulva, "which shows that tail presentation does occur at birth," but Nickerson (1977) described a stillborn humpback that was presented cephalically.* A newborn humpback is between 12 and 14 feet (3.66–4.27 meters) in length. Although multiple births are rare—of 2,979 cases reviewed by Yablakov and colleagues in 1974, 0.57 percent indicated twin fetuses—Scammon pictured a female suckling twin calves, an illustration that has led many subsequent investigators to assume that this is a common occurrence. In an unusual observation of a humpback nursing its calf in the cold waters off Newfoundland, Williamson (1961) described and illustrated the female on her side with one flipper "waving in the air." In the Hawaiian calving areas the newborn humpbacks are typically seen in the company of two adults, the mother and an "escort" (Herman and Antinoja 1977). Newborn calves are "awkward when born and must practice diving, breath holding, breaching, and many other maneuvers necessary for survival" (Hudnall 1978). Using the examination of ear plugs, baleen ridges, and the corpora lutea of the ovaries, it has been determined that humpbacks reach sexual maturity at about seven, and the maximum age (determined by studying the laminations of ear plugs) of whales in Australian waters was forty-seven years (Chittleborough 1960).

These are acrobatic whales, much given to leaps out of the water, spy-hopping, lob-tailing, fin-flapping, and showing general surface exuberance. (In *Moby-Dick,* Melville said, "He is the most gamesome and

*The question of headfirst or tailfirst presentation in large whales has not been satisfactorily resolved. In 1949, Slijper wrote that most mysticetes' births are probably head presentations, but in 1956 he changed his mind and stated that of twenty-two observed births of cetaceans (of which two were evidently mysticetes), all were tail presentations. Two beluga births have been observed in captivity, and both were cephalic.

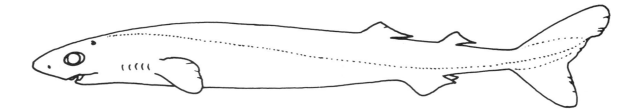

Isistius brasiliensis, the 1.5-foot shark thought to be responsible for the oval bites in the blubber of certain whales and dolphins.

lighthearted of all whales, making more gay foam and white water generally than any other of them.") By far the most spectacular of the humpback's activities is the one known as breaching: the whale throws itself almost completely out of the water, flippers extended, and then lands on its back or side in a thunderous shower of spray. When breaching or swimming underwater (see Hudnall 1977, 1978), this is an extremely graceful animal for its size, but hauled out onto a whaling dock, it collapses into a welter of flabby folds and lumps. At one point, Scammon wrote that the humpback was "decidedly ugly"; but later, discussing the humpback as seen beneath the surface of the water, he said that it moves "gracefully, as a swallow on the wing." When swimming slowly, this species "rolls" in the water, showing its oddly shaped dorsal fin and, just before a prolonged dive, its flukes. In a behavior known as "surface traveling," the whales, usually in pods of three to five, move along the surface, blowing frequently, but not submerging often (Hudnall 1977). It is assumed that this mode of travel is employed when the whales have a particular destination and are not simply loafing along. Estimates of the speed of humpbacks vary from 1–2 miles per hour (2–4 kilometers per hour) to 16 miles per hour (27 kilometers per hour) (Lockyer 1976). It should be remembered that this species was slow enough to be hunted from shore-based open boats by various aborigines, such as the Indians of Massachusetts and the Aleuts, and, nowadays, by the native whalers of Bequia in the West Indies. In the breeding areas, humpbacks are seen in small groups, but in the colder latitudes, where the whales feed, they have been observed in larger congregations. Sergeant (1966) told of herds of 100 to 150 animals observed off Newfoundland's Grand Bank.

Recent observations in Hawaiian waters have shown a complex social arrangement of whales on the breeding and calving grounds. In numerous instances an "escort whale" has been seen accompanying a mother and calf. The role of this escort is not understood, but some observers (Forestell et al. 1979) have identified a protective function, as the escort repeatedly came between the observers and the mother and calf. In a three-year photographic survey of Hawaiian humpbacks,* Glockner and Venus (1979) were able not only to identify many individual whales (usually by color

pattern), but also to make visual determinations of the animals' sex. In the genital region females have a pronounced "hemispherical lobe," which structure is absent in males. Therefore, underwater observation, as well as the analysis of photographs, has provided a means by which the sex of individual whales can be positively known. In bottlenose dolphins the individual that accompanied a mother and calf was always a female (known as an "auntie"), so it was logical to assume that the escorts of humpbacks would be females. Surprisingly, all the escorts positively identified by Glockner and Venus were males. They may, therefore, be "uncles"—or even fathers—demonstrating once again the limitations of our knowledge of whale behavior and the dangers of generalizing the behavior of all cetaceans from our observations of one species.

We do not know if the humpback's jumping is done for reasons of pleasure, communication, or necessity. Roger Payne (1976) believed that right whales breach, especially in rough weather when their vocalizations might not be effectively transmitted, as a means of signaling their location to other right whales. (Slijper [1962] showed a drawing of a humpback doing successive full, backward somersaults, but this behavior seems somewhat fanciful and has not been mentioned by other observers.) If humpbacks jump to loosen parasites, their motivation is excellent, but the method may not be effective. "An adult humpback whale," wrote Sanderson (1956), "is a parasitologist's paradise, and a happy hunting ground for any conchologist, helminthologist, or crustaceologist." The humpback is infested with whale lice and at least three

---

waters of these islands on the part of the whales, but the data can also be read to indicate the same inclination on the part of the researchers.

*At a 1979 Marine Mammal Conference in Seattle a remarkable percentage of the cetacean papers presented (thirteen of sixty-four) concerned the humpback whale population of Hawaii. A statistical analysis of this data strongly suggests a preference for the protected

Cyamus boopis, the parasitic whale louse of the humpback whale (after Leung).

species of barnacles. Different barnacles favor different parts of the whale; there are two varieties of *Coronula,* one that is found on the ventral grooves and the belly *(C. diadema)* and another *(C. reginae)* that occurs on the tail, the lips, and the leading edge of the flippers. The stalked barnacle *Conchoderma auritum* grows only on other barnacles, and not directly on the epidermis of the whale, adding to the whale's festooned appearance, if not to its discomfort. In addition to the ovoid scars mentioned earlier, mature humpbacks also have a profusion of ringlike marks, probably the scars left by the *Coronula* barnacles that have become dislodged or loosened by fresh water. (As any owner of a wooden boat knows, barnacles die in fresh water. It seems that some humpback whales know this, too, because they have been seen at the mouths of rivers such as the Congo, where the barnacles would presumably loosen and fall off.)

Humpbacks are opportunistic in their diet, eating whatever is available in their various feeding grounds, from euphausiids in the Antarctic to other small crustaceans in the Northern Hemisphere and to shoaling fish—capelin, herring, codfish—when available. In 1829 a dead humpback that washed ashore at Berwick, England, contained "six cormorants and another in the throat, so that it may be presumed that this whale had choaked [sic] in an attempt to swallow the bird" (Allen 1916). Humpbacks are "gulpers"; that is, they take in mouthfuls of food organisms and water and then expel the water with much splashing and thrash-

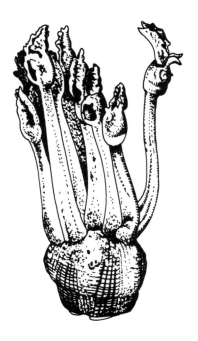

The barnacles of the humpback. *Conchoderma auritum* grows on *Coronula diadema.* Only *Coronula* touches the skin of the whale.

ing: "When feeding, the megaptera opens the mouth and takes in quantities of the floating *Euphausia,* then turn[s] on the side and raise[s] the under jaw, the water rushing out in streams from between the plates of baleen" (Andrews 1909). Watkins and Schevill (1979), who observed a group of humpbacks feeding off Race Point, Cape Cod, Massachusetts, reported that the whales did not seem to cooperate while feeding. Rather, "we have seen apparent competition for food, with as many as seven whales rushing together to the surface . . . pushing and shoving as they went, raising their mouths out of the water together in random orientation, and then falling back onto each other, mouth and throat full (of water at least)." They appeared to be feeding on small schooling fishes, probably herring.

A most unusual feeding behavior has been observed and filmed in Alaskan waters (National Geographic Society 1978). A whale feeding on small fish would dive below the schooling fish and then release a series of bubbles as it spiraled upward. This would effectively create a barrier of bubbles that would concentrate the fish, enabling the whale to burst open-mouthed through the densely packed mass and, thereby, harvest a huge mouthful of fish. This behavior has been called "bubble-net feeding," and no comparable activity is known in any other cetacean. The technique is a complicated and sophisticated achievement, requiring the whale to calculate—or somehow instinctively understand—the relative speed of bursts of bubbles released at successively decreasing depths, so that the net is completed at the moment that the whale reaches the surface. When Watkins and Schevill observed feeding humpbacks, they saw underwater exhalations, "but not in a controlled net of bubbles and apparently not directly related to feeding."

In recent years there has been an increase in cod fishing in Newfoundland waters and, concurrently, more reports of humpbacks trapped in cod nets. The whales appear to blunder into the nets because they do not know the nets are there, not because they are chasing fish. Lien and Merdsoy (1979) have pointed out that they typically "get entangled in the leader, which does not hold fish, indicating that they rub into the gear accidentally." The damage done to the nets —usually by cutting it apart to free the whale—has cost the fishing fleet hundreds of thousands of dollars over the past several years and now represents a new threat to the humpback. The cod fishers have suggested that Canada once again commence whaling (two of the last Canadian whaling stations were located in Newfoundland) in order to remove the troublesome and expensive humpbacks from their fishing grounds.

According to Gaskin (1972), each whale eats about 1.5 tons of krill every day during the summer feeding season in the Antarctic. When migrating, they hardly eat at all. Of 197 whales examined in Australian waters between migrations to the southern feeding grounds, Chittleborough (1965) found food in only five stomachs. On the Grand Bank of Newfoundland, Sergeant (1975) observed humpback and minke whales approaching trawlers to feed on the "incapacitated or dead fish escaping through the nets." Humpbacks are known to approach ships (Mitchell 1974), at least in the North Atlantic, and this behavior may have been generated by their feeding on "discards." During the net hauls, humpbacks were seen "jumping clean out of the water," and one whale, "feeding with the most exaggerated leapings and dives, was totally indifferent to the vessels which crisscrossed its position" (Sergeant 1975). The draggers on these grounds fish for cod, American plaice, and redfish. (The redfish did not attract the humpbacks, wrote Sergeant, "perhaps redfish are too spiny.") When five humpbacks (and a narwhal) were discovered to have been trapped by closing ice in a Newfoundland fjord, attempts were made to feed the whales on dead herring. According to Peter Beamish (personal communication), who tried to free the whales from their entrapment, they definitely ate the herring. (After an unusual warm spell in April 1978, the ice opened up and the whales escaped.)

When a single humpback became entangled in a trap net near Ellison, Newfoundland, in 1976, it seemed an ideal opportunity to test the echolocating ability of this species. (It is known that various species of baleen whales emit short, repetitive clicks in addition to their regular low-frequency moans, but the purpose—if any—of these clicks is unknown. In the smaller odontocetes the clicks are known to be used for echolocating.) Beamish (1978) freed the whale from the net, but kept it captive by fastening a padded harness around the base of the flukes. A maze was set up, and the whale was blindfolded with large neoprene patches affixed with suction cups. (It was under these circumstances that the whale was towed—and later swam—backward.) In thirty-three trials the whale showed no evidence of being able to echolocate, and Beamish suggested "that humpback whales do not echolocate food-sized objects. Clicking sounds pro-duced by the animal were possibly associated with communication (other whales were often in the vicinity) but not made at any of the thirty-three specific times when a biological sonar could have helped the animal to solve a navigation or localization problem."

No aspect of the behavior of humpback whales has received so much attention as their "singing." Although it was widely known that whales made noises, no one suspected the range and repertoire of sounds made by the humpback. (In 1916, Allen wrote, "there seems to be little likelihood that the sound is a conscious vocal utterance, but it may be produced involuntarily through the effort of retaining the breath.") The first humpback recordings were made with a primitive hydrophone in 1952 in Bermuda waters by O. W. Schreiber. Then Frank Watlington recorded the whales in Bermuda from 1953 to 1964, and finally in 1967, Roger Payne, the man who was to make the humpbacks famous, came to Bermuda. He studied and recorded their vocalizations in five successive seasons, from 1967 to 1971. "Upon first hearing humpback vocalizations," he wrote in 1971, "one has the impression of an almost endless variety of sounds." (In addition to the songs, Winn and Perkins [1976] have recorded "moans, belches, yups, snores, screams, grunt-like noises, thumps, knocks, pulses, and high-frequency chirps, cries, whistles and clicks.")

Payne defined a "song" as a "complex repeated pattern of sounds" that occurs in complete sequences. The songs can last anywhere from six to thirty minutes and are, therefore, considerably longer than the song of any bird, most of which run for only a few seconds before the sequence is repeated. Unlike bird songs, the songs of the humpback whales are repeated without any obvious break between the sequences; the pauses between the songs are no longer than the pauses between the notes (Payne 1970).

At first, it was not known which whales were singing, or why, or even how. Concentrated study has begun to reveal some of the answers, but there are still great gaps in our knowledge. The humpback will tell us its musical secrets slowly and gracefully—*largo*, if you will. The whales sing only when they are in their mating areas and not when they occupy the cold-water feeding grounds, thereby defining the singing as a warm-water activity. (There is, however, one anomalous report of a humpback singing in the waters of southeast Alaska, which would indicate that the singing activity is not confined exclusively to the warm-water areas.) Two populations of humpbacks have been studied in some detail: the West Indian (which, through an analysis of songs and the matching of tail patterns, has been shown to be the same as the Bermuda population) and the Hawaiian. Most of the work done on the West Indies–Bermuda stock has been accomplished by Payne and by Howard Winn of the University of Rhode Island. Winn's studies have taken place primarily in the waters northwest of Puerto Rico, in the fairly shallow waters of the Mouchoir, Silver, and Navidad banks. (These West Indian locations, along with some records from Trinidad, Grenada, and the Lesser Antillean Island of Bequia, represent the southern limit of the migration of these whales; in the summer they are found far to the north, perhaps off Newfoundland or Greenland.) Winn and Thompson (1979) presented evidence that the songs of all the humpbacks in the North Pacific are the same, as are those of the whales in the North Atlantic, suggesting that "there is a North Pacific and a North Atlantic dialect." The songs have been carefully analyzed, and detailed sonograms of the sounds and patterns have been reproduced (Payne and McVay 1971, Winn et al. 1971, and others) but the only way to appreciate fully the wild beauty of this submarine music is to listen to it. For those unable to get to Maalea Bay or Silver Bank, there are excellent phonograph records of the whales' songs.*

Payne's research has shown that the Pacific population migrates from Hawaii north to southeast Alaska, and also to the Revillagigedo Islands, south of Baja California. (The exact sequence of this triangular migration is not known, however; the whales may swim north from Hawaii to Alaska and then to the Revillagigedos, or they may go from Hawaii to the Revillagigedos and then north to Alaska.) From recordings made in both places, it has been shown that the songs of the whales in Hawaiian waters and those in the Revillagigedos are exactly the same, and this, with the addition of matching fluke photographs, has shown that these whales can be found in either Pacific location during the breeding season.

The discovery of a whale that sings is extraordinary enough, but when we hear that all the whales in a given population sing the same song, *and then change that song every year,* it becomes one of nature's great mysteries. By comparing sonograms of the songs of the humpbacks—particularly those in Hawaiian waters —researchers began to notice that certain elements of the songs were being phased out annually, as other themes were being added (K. Payne 1979). All the singing whales sing the same song in the breeding areas, and then, after an eight-month period in which they remain almost totally silent—presumably because they are busy eating or migrating—they return to the breeding grounds and begin to sing again. Remarkably, every winter's song is a slightly modified version of the previous year's arrangment, and all the whales seem to have learned the changes and sing the altered version. This annual group modification of behavior is virtually unknown in other animals and suggests a highly developed form of intraspecies communication. In a 1979 discussion of the extraordinary phenomenon that he and his wife discovered, Roger Payne wrote:

The whales don't just sing mechanically; rather, they compose as they go along, incorporating new elements into their old songs. We are aware of no other animal besides man in which this strange and complicated behavior occurs, and we have no idea of the reason behind it. If you listen to songs from two different years you will be astonished to hear how different they are. For example the songs we taped in 1964 and 1969 . . . are as different as Beethoven from the Beatles.

Whales have no vocal cords, so the sounds are not produced in an easily identifiable manner. But they do have a larynx, and Payne speculated that the sounds may be made by the transfer of air from one body cavity to another. Given the variety of sounds and the obvious control of their emissions, humpbacks must have a remarkably sophisticated sound-producing apparatus, but examination of dead whales has not revealed its nature.

Why do the whales sing? Again, we do not know. The sounds may be used to advertise the presence of a breeding male, to warn off potential rivals, or perhaps to establish herd contact with other whales throughout the wide expanse of their breeding grounds. (Water is a much better conductor of sound than air; although the values are affected by the temperature of the medium, sound travels approximately five times faster in water than it does in air. In addition, if there are no obstructions, low-frequency sound can travel for hundreds of miles underwater. The sound of a depth charge fired off Australia was picked up off Bermuda, at a distance of 11,400 miles [19,000 kilometers], or halfway around the world [Hersey

*The first is *Songs of the Humpback Whale,* Capitol Records, ST-620, 1970. Another record, *Deep Voices: The Second Whale Record,* Capitol Records, ST-11598, 1977, includes the sounds of right and blue whales in addition to humpback vocalizations. Judy Collins has recorded a haunting version of an old whaling song, "Farewell to Tarwathie," in which she is accompanied by the recorded sounds of whales (*Whales and Nightingales,* Elektra Records, n.d.).

1977].) According to Payne (1972), the "only singers definitely known in the mammal world are man, the whitelined bat, the bearded seal, and the humpback." The songs of the humpback whale are surely among the most splendid mysteries of the natural world, and they can only add to our respect and admiration for these long-winged leviathans.

Throughout the world the humpback whale makes annual migrations from high-latitude, cold-water feeding grounds to temperate and tropical waters for breeding and calving. The mating areas are generally found along continental coasts or around islands, so this has been a particularly visible species in many areas. The North Atlantic population spends the summer off Greenland, Iceland, and Spitsbergen, moving southward in the fall (August to October) on both sides of the Atlantic. The stock from the western North Atlantic is thought to migrate from the waters of Greenland and Iceland past Newfoundland, the Gulf of Saint Lawrence, and Cape Cod, until it reaches Bermuda, the Caribbean, or even Venezuela. It is not known if the humpbacks that appear in the southeastern Atlantic off Africa and in the vicinity of the Cape Verde and Canary islands are segregated in their northern range from those that mate and calve in the southwestern Atlantic (Mitchell 1974). Recent evidence, however, suggests that the humpbacks that migrate north from the Caribbean and Bermuda to Newfoundland may "cross over" and make a southward migration in the eastern North Atlantic to the waters of Europe and Africa. This would correspond to the triangular migration of the North Pacific humpbacks, some of which travel from Hawaii to southeast Alaska and perhaps to the Revillagigedos before returning to Hawaii.

Intensive hunting of humpbacks in the North Pacific by Soviet and Japanese pelagic whaling fleets has seriously depleted these stocks, making our knowledge of their movements dependent on old records. As in the North Atlantic, discrete populations summer in northern waters to feed and then move southward to breed. From the Bering Sea, Gulf of Alaska, and Chukchi Sea, the whales disperse along the coasts for their fall migrations. One population migrates along the western coast of North America, as far south as Baja and the Sea of Cortez; another follows the coastline of eastern Asia, reaching the Ryukyu, Mariana, and Bonin islands. (The routes are conjectural, and humpbacks do not seem to hug the shoreline the way gray whales do. Nishiwaki [1966] recorded 6 whales that "moved from the east end of the Aleutians to the Ryukyus," but the route is given schematically as a straight line, a somewhat unlikely course.) A single population, variously estimated at 500–800 animals, arrives in Hawaii from northern waters every winter, although their open-water route is still unknown (Herman et al. 1977). Correlation of photographs of fluke coloration patterns (Katona et al. 1979, Darling et al. 1979, and others) has shown that the Hawaiian population consists of the same whales that are seen in the waters of southeast Alaska in the summer months. So even though the actual routes are unknown, the destinations of this particular population are now revealed.

Like the other baleen whales, humpbacks used to congregate in great numbers in the Southern Ocean during the summer months (September–February) to feed on the plentiful krill. Humpbacks in these southern latitudes do not approach the pack ice as closely as do the blue and fin whales, but they are found south of 50°. At least five populations are recognized, each of which migrates northward in the southern winter to a different location. (This segregation of stocks was first noticed by Rayner in 1940, when whales marked in the Antarctic were captured off Australia. He wrote, "the large provinces into which the humpback stock might fall appear to be much more rigid and self contained than those of other species.") There has since been shown to be some intermingling of these southern stocks (Chittleborough 1965), but whale marking, primarily of the Australian and New Zealand stocks, has shown that the populations are quite segregated (Chittleborough 1959b, Dawbin 1956b, and others). Except for their different migratory routes, there is no difference between the humpbacks of one southern population and another; in fact; there is no difference between the whales of the Southern Hemisphere and those of the north. This "bipolarity" of the species "arises from the division of a single unified population into two sections in the not very distant geological past, which have not yet had time to evolve into distinct divergent types" (Ommanney 1971). (Comparison with other rorquals in this same bipolar situation reveals the beginning of an evolutionary divergence in the minke whale, in which the southern form appears to be different enough to classify it as a subspecies, and in the blue whale, in which the size differential between southern and northern stocks has always been evident. Too, a morphologically distinct subspecies, the pygmy blue whale, was identified in 1966.)

From the Antarctic Areas I to VI, the wintering and breeding grounds of southern humpback whales are as follows:

Area I (120° W–60° W): the coasts of Chile, Ecuador, the Galapagos

Area II (60° W–0°): northern Brazil; southwest Africa (Cameroon, Angola, Gabon, Zaire)

Area III (0°–70° E): southwest Africa; east Africa (Mozambique, Tanzania, Kenya, Mozambique Channel, Madagascar)

Area IV (70° E–130° E): western Australia

Area V (130° E–170° W): eastern Australia; New Zealand; Tonga; Fiji

Area VI (170° W–120° W): There are no land masses north of this area except for small island groups in the tropical South Pacific, such as the Cook Islands, where occasional humpbacks have been reported (National Geographic Society 1976).

"Whenever new whaling grounds have been opened up, the humpback whale has always been the predominant species in the catch for the first few years, and then rapidly declines in numbers," claimed Matthews (1938). This has been true throughout the range of the humpback, which now numbers but a fraction of its former abundance. (In his 1976 estimate, Scheffer suggested that the worldwide population of humpbacks is only 7 percent of the number before commercial whaling.) Many factors contributed to the decimation of the humpback: its inshore mating habits made it particularly vulnerable to early shore whaling; it is a slower swimmer than the rorquals; it approaches boats rather than fleeing from them; and in some areas, the Caribbean or the South Pacific, it would cavort and make itself generally visible in warm tropical waters—a positive attraction for the whaler who might otherwise be hunting the bowhead in the icy waters of Greenland or Baffin Bay. The humpback is a docile species, not given to retributive actions toward its attackers, and although it sinks when it is killed (a definite inconvenience), it is still considered an easy whale. (Writing of "humpbacking" in the Friendly Islands [Tonga], Bullen [1899] said that the humpback "had none of the dogged savagery of the cachalot about him, nor did we feel any occasion to beware of his rushes, rather courting them, so as to finish the game as quickly as possible.")

Early records for New England whaling do not differentiate species (although sperm whales were not taken until 1712), so records of "the whale" might be right whales or humpbacks, both of which are known to favor inshore areas for mating and calving. Allen (1942) mentioned records of humpbacks "as early as 1757" off Georges Bank and Nantucket Shoals and wrote that humpbacks were the chief object of the Maine offshore fishery from 1810 to 1840. (There are still humpbacks in the Gulf of Maine; Katona [1975] noted that they are "seen fairly often.") They were hunted from Norway, Iceland, and Newfoundland in the northern part of their range and in Bermuda, Trinidad, Grenada, and the island of Bequia in the Lesser Antilles, where an open-boat fishery for this species continues today, taking a few animals per year (Caldwell et al. 1971). The original population of the northwest Atlantic is unknown, but it has been estimated at about 1,500 animals, with current numbers around 1,000 (Allen 1970). Only the natives of Bequia and the Eskimos of Greenland kill humpback whales in the North Atlantic today; all commercial hunting of this species is prohibited.

The North Pacific populations that feed in the area of the Bering and Chukchi seas were more numerous than their North Atlantic counterparts and were, therefore, more heavily exploited. According to Scammon, "the megapteras are captured by the Indians of the North-western Coast, and the Esquimaux about the shores of the Arctic Ocean," hunting from skin boats and using "toy-like harpoons." In the nineteenth century, Americans sought the humpbacks from Alaska to Baja California; the Japanese hunted in corresponding latitudes in the western Pacific, from the Aleutians south to the Ryukyus, Marianas, Bonin, and Taiwan. Large numbers of humpbacks passed the coasts of British Columbia in the early years of this century; from 1919 to 1929, of 15,323 whales taken off western Canada, 7,301 were humpbacks (Pike 1954). Since the baleen of the humpback is not long enough to be of any value, the whale was hunted for its oil. The quality was not very good, but the abundance of the whales made up for the low-grade oil. In the twentieth century, humpbacks have been almost exterminated in the North Pacific. "During the late 1920's and then again during the early 1960's thousands of North Pacific humpbacks were taken" (Herman 1978). From a population that may have been as high as 15,000 animals, the stock has now been reduced to perhaps 4,000 (Red Data Book 1972) or "5000 to 7500" (Nishiwaki 1966). The last figure seems high for a world population that may not exceed 10,000 animals. (Scheffer estimated 7,000.) In 1974, Rice reported the results of a 1965 coastal survey of the eastern North Pacific, during which he saw "33 groups of humpbacks totaling 102 individuals. . . . Since humpbacks concentrate in coastal waters during the winter, I believe that we saw a fairly large proportion of the population. If so, the entire North Pacific stock now numbers only a few hundred individuals."

The Hawaiian population seems to be a fairly recent phenomenon, since Herman reported no evidence that the humpbacks were there before the arrival of Captain Cook in 1778.* The whales arrive in Hawaii in the winter to breed and give birth, and then they return to their feeding grounds, thought to be in the central North Pacific. Current estimates of this highly visible population are between 500 and 800 animals, and since the breeding grounds of these whales are clearly visible from the islands that border them, this population probably represents the largest assem-

blage of great whales easily visible to the public, with the obvious exception of the migrating gray whales off southern California.*

The humpbacks of the Southern Hemisphere were slaughtered wherever they went. When they came north to the inshore calving grounds of Australia, New Zealand, Africa, and South America, the whalers were waiting for them. In the high southern latitudes near the pack ice of Antarctica, they were killed by the tens of thousands. Only the catch statistics for blue and fin whales exceed those for humpbacks, and the totals are incredible. The following table (taken from Mackintosh 1942) summarizes the catches of whales from the southern whaling centers, 1904–39.

*Negative evidence is bound to be inconclusive since it can show only what did not occur, but the early Hawaiians seemed to have no word for "humpback whale" in their vocabulary, and reports from whalers or missionaries do not mention whales until about 1850. In the records of American whaleships from the nineteenth century, Townsend (1935) showed not a single humpback in Hawaiian wa-

ters, although there were numerous records of whaleships taking sperm whales there.
*There may be more whales immediately off Península Valdés in Argentina, or off the various islands of the Southern Ocean, such as South Georgia or Tristan da Cunha, but Patagonia and Antarctica are not nearly as popular with tourists as the Hawaiian Islands.

TOTAL CATCHES RECORDED AT SOUTHERN WHALING CENTERS 1904–39

Whaling Center	No. of Seasons	Blue	Fin	Humpback	Total
Congo	13	1	22	11,158	11,181
Brazil	4			1,113	1,113
Angola	14	1,106	358	10,127	11,591
East Africa	7			3,218	3,218
Western Australia	12	14	9	15,995	16,018
Madagascar	2	5	24	2,975	3,004
Walvis Bay	11	1,781	374	584	2,739
Natal	31	2,918	9,104	6,081	18,103
Cape Province	24	7,027	7,202	324	14,553
Chile and Peru	26	2,364	2,559	1,726	6,649
Kerguelen Island	3	4	1	118	123
Falkland Islands	6	13	139	179	331
South Georgia	35	39,808	48,301	24,392	112,501
Antarctic	30	206,904	148,595	24,308	379,807
Total		261,945	216,688	102,298	580,931

NOTE: Total number of right whales	755
Total number of sei whales	10,250
Total number of sperm whales	27,433
Total number of "unspecified"	17,157
	55,595
Total number of blue, fin, and humpback	580,931
Total number of whales killed at southern whaling centers, 1904–39	636,526

As an indication of the rapidity with which humpback stocks declined, consider these statistics: in 1910/1911, humpbacks formed 96.8 percent of the catch at South Georgia. In 1916/1917, only 9.3 percent of the catch was humpbacks, the remaining 90.7 percent being blues and fins. This may have been caused by the whalers' desire to take the larger and more profitable rorquals, but if this were so, we should expect the humpback numbers in the Antarctic to rise, which they did not do (Norman and Fraser 1938).

In eastern Australia and New Zealand (data not found in Mackintosh's 1942 table), the humpback was commercially the most important whale species until it became too scarce to hunt. The greatest concentration of humpbacks in the south was in Area IV, the population that migrates north to western Australia (Chittleborough 1959b). This stock numbered between 12,000 and 17,000 whales in its "unfished" state; by 1949 it was at 10,000; and by 1962 there were less than 800 animals in the population. Similarly, the Area V stock (eastern Australia and New Zealand), once numbering 10,000 whales, "is now reduced to about 500 animals" (Chittleborough 1965).

In New Zealand in the 1930s there were two whaling stations in operation, one at Whangamumu and the other at Te-Awaiti. Ommanney (1933) discussed the operation of these stations, both of which were operated in a somewhat less than orthodox manner. At Whangamumu the whales were trapped in a steel net that was stretched from rope cables, and then they were dispatched by lances. After 1910, however, a small steam whaler was employed and the net fishery abandoned. At Te-Awaiti the whales were hunted from fast motor launches and shot with a light harpoon gun. When the whale was made fast, a hollow spear connected to an air compressor was inserted into the whale, and the animal was inflated *while still alive.* "The whale is finally despatched by inserting into the thorax ventrally a long lance with a hollow cast iron head. The head is filled with a pound and a half of gelignite which is exploded within the whale's thorax by means of an electric detonator" (Ommanney 1933). In the long and bloody history of whaling, this surely must be the cruelest method of killing ever devised.

The original Antarctic stock has been calculated at between 90,000 and 100,000 animals. There may now be 1,700 to 2,800 left (Chapman 1974). An estimated 4,000 survive in the North Pacific and another 1,000 in the North Atlantic. Even if we allow for error in the estimating procedures, the total for the world's surviving humpbacks cannot be over 10,000. They are being killed in small numbers in Bequia, Greenland, and Tonga, but otherwise they are totally protected and have been so since 1955 in the North Atlantic, 1964 in the Southern Hemisphere, and 1966 in the North Pacific. Even if such protection continues, it will probably take close to a century for the humpback to reach its preexploitation level. A recent report (Nemoto 1978) seemed to indicate that some populations are already showing signs of recuperation: "The finding of summer feeding schools of humpback whales in shelf waters in the North Pacific is also considered as the indication of the recovery of the number of this species too." In the North Atlantic, however, the humpback population appears to be decreasing. Very few whales have been seen in Bermuda waters in recent years, and Roger Payne (personal communication) has suggested that the combination of humpbacks trapped in the Newfoundland fishermen's nets —perhaps as many as 50 per year—and those taken by the outlaw whalers off Europe and Africa are reducing this already threatened population to a dangerously low level.

RIGHT WHALE
Balaena glacialis Müller 1776

Because it produced plentiful oil and bone, was slow-swimming and easy to kill, and floated when dead, this animal became known in English as the "right" whale.* (The bowhead had the same desirable characteristics and was also the right whale to kill, but when it was differentiated in the vernacular from *Balaena glacialis,* it was called the "Greenland right whale" or the "Arctic right whale.") Among the other names for this species are "black right whale," "Biscayan right whale," "scrag whale" (for thin or undernourished specimens), and various applications of geographical determinants, such as "southern right whale" and "North Pacific right whale."

Roger Payne, a student of this species, called it (1972a) "perhaps the rarest of all wide-ranging mam-

---

*Other whaling countries named it for its physical or geographical characteristics. The Icelanders called it *sletbag* ("smooth back"); in Danish it was known as *svarthval* ("black whale"); in German it is *glattwal* ("smooth whale"), referring to the lack of ventral pleats and dorsal fin; and the Basques called this species *sardaco baleac,* which Allen (1916) translated as "a whale that goes in schools." This appellation, he continued, was rendered into French as *sarde* or *sarda.* The Norwegians call it *nordcaper,* from the North Cape region, where it was hunted in early times. In Spanish the right whale is *Ballena franca,* but the origin of this term is unclear.

mals." Before it was so severely decimated, this species was extremely plentiful and easy to identify. It is shiny black in color, although there are records of albino specimens (Payne 1974), and it bears few of the whitish healed scars that characterize many other large whale species. Like its close relative, the bowhead, this species has neither ventral pleats nor a dorsal fin. (The generic name *Balaena,* which simply means "whale," is used to separate the right whale from the other large whales, the Balaenopteridae, which get their name from the Greek *pteron,* ["wing"], referring to the dorsal fin.) A unique feature of this whale is the presence of numerous callosities, several inches thick, that are more or less symmetrically arranged on the head. The function of these yellowish horny growths is unknown,

but they do serve as a home for the various parasites of the species, including whale lice and barnacles. The most prominent of these callosities occurs on the tip of the upper jaw and is known as the "bonnet." The growths vary from whale to whale and are so distinctive that researchers have been able to identify individual whales from their callosities. (Payne and Dorsey 1979). The growths generally occur in certain locations: on the median line of the upper jaw, in front of the blowhole; on either side of the tip of the lower jaw; in a front-to-back line from the tip of the lower jaw; and above the eye. While these are the usual places for callosities, some whales have them in unusual locations. A female sighted off the coast of Chile in 1964 had a prominent growth on the underside of her chin (Clarke 1965), and other whales have displayed horny growths on the edge of the scalloped lower lip. Hair follicles are present in these callosities, and Payne (1976) has written that "right whales' facial hair grows in the same places that a human's does, and only in these places. The whales appear to have what we call mustaches, as well as eyebrows, beards, and even sideburns."

The right whale is solidly built, reaching a maximum length of 60 feet (18.3 meters). One of the largest known specimens, which beached at Amagansett, Long Island, in 1908, was measured at 56 feet 7 inches (17.26 meters). Most specimens are considerably smaller. It is understandably difficult to weigh an animal of this size, but Japanese scientists weighed the cut-up components of two specimens taken in the North Pacific in 1957. A 38.2-foot (11.65-meter) female weighed 25 tons (22,866 kilograms), and a 40.6-foot (12.4-meter) male weighed 24.5 tons (22,050 kilograms) (Omura 1958). In both cases a percentage of the total was added for blood lost in the cutting

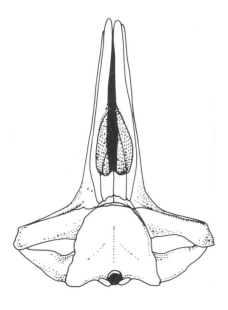

Dorsal view of the skull of the right whale, *Balaena glacialis* (after Allen).

process. The really large specimens have not been weighed, but Omura and colleagues (1969) calculated that a 51-foot (15.5-meter) specimen would weigh 66 tons (59,400 kilograms).* A photograph of a dead right whale taken off Kodiak Island, Alaska, is accompanied by a caption that gives the dimensions as "15 feet high, 22 feet wide, 65 feet long and weighed approximately 250 tons" (Bockstoce 1978). Another photograph of what is apparently the same whale, with the same dimensions given, was reproduced in Morgan's 1978 article on shore-based whaling in Alaska. There is no question that the specimen is immense—the picture in Bockstoce shows thirty-three men standing in front of the whale and a thirty-fourth high above them on the whale's flank—but the weight of 500,000 pounds seems unlikely.

The head of the right whale is large, accounting for almost one-fourth of the total length. The flukes and flippers are also large, and they are often visible: the flukes are raised out of the water when the whale makes a prolonged dive; the flippers, when the whale

*In a curious note, Omura et al. also gave the projected weight of an 83-foot (25.3-meter) right whale—a length it does not even approach—at 185 tons and compared it with the known weight of a similar-sized blue whale (110 tons), thereby demonstrating the bulk of the right whale in comparison to the more slender rorqual. An even more puzzling reference was given by Klumov (1962) when he recorded a weight of "more than 100 tons at the length of 16–17 m." I inquired of Omura about these seeming discrepancies and received a letter telling me that such a weight was not impossible, "because body weight of whales, especially that of baleen whales, can differ greatly according to feeding conditions, days spent at feeding grounds, availability of food, etc."

rolls on its side. Right whales breathe seven to nine times at the surface and then dive for a longer period of time, perhaps as long as fifteen minutes. The "blow" is produced from two widely separated blowholes and is often seen as two distinct jets, which merge into a V-shaped spout. The whale's mouth is a great scooplike affair, having an enormous lower jaw and a comparatively small, narrow upper jaw, from which the baleen plates are suspended. The plates are grayish-black with a fine black fringe, and they number about 250 per side. The hairlike fringes on the baleen plates are particularly dense, numbering from 115 to 140 per inch, commensurate with the small food organisms on which this species normally feeds.

Many specimens have an irregularly shaped white patch on the underside, which has led to these animals' being known as "whitebellies." Collett (1909) found that about one in five whales taken in Norwegian waters was colored this way, but of thirteen whales captured by the Japanese in the North Pacific in 1961–63 (under special permit, since this species is protected worldwide), all but two had some white on their undersides. The basic ground color of the right whale is black, but a number of white juveniles have been observed accompanying normally colored females (Payne 1976). Best (1970) reported that "different individuals viewed from the air varied from a general dark blue-black to a light brown hue dorsally." He also described completely white calves and a "par-

Dorsal view of the right whale, *Balaena glacialis,* showing location of callosities on a typical speciman. Also notice the distinctively shaped flippers and wide flukes.

ticularly large and dun-colored individual." In recent years a number of piebald or spotted whales have been seen in Australian waters. A 1978 magazine article about diving with right whales off Geelong (Australia) contained a photograph of a heavily spotted adult (Stewart 1978), and more recently, in the autumn of 1979, a black female was seen with a "white baby." The photographs of this unusually colored animal show it to be white with an allover, random pattern of black spots (Valerie Taylor, personal communication).

Right whales are slow swimmers, seemingly incapable of speeds over 5 knots, but they are renowned for their leaping ability. Known as "breaching," this activity is mystifying, since we do not know why or how they do it. A whale this slow and heavy should not be able to leap like a sailfish, but, disregarding our limited abilities to analyze its motives and momentum, it breaches anyway.

Only the bowhead could be confused with the right whale at sea; both lack a dorsal fin and ventral pleats, both have a huge head (although the head of the bowhead is proportionally larger), both have long baleen plates, and both are black in color. The callosities are present only in the right whale, and its jaws are less arched. The bowhead is found only in the high northern Arctic, particularly off northern Alaska, whereas the right whale, although rare throughout its range, is found in temperate waters as well as some subpolar locations.

The right whale is found in discrete populations, and it was believed that each of these populations represented a different species. J. A. Allen, whom Rice (1977) called one of the "most notorious 'splitters' in the history of mammalogy," had identified four different species and had resurrected the generic name *Eubalaena* for the right whales. (*Eubalaena* means "true" whale, derived from the Greek *eu* for "good.") It has now been suggested that the bowhead and the right whales belong to the same genus *(Balaena),* but the issue is far from settled. The first name used was *Balaena glacialis,* which Allen pointed out (1916) is "somewhat inappropriate, for this whale frequents northern waters during only a portion of the year." Other forms include the North Pacific right whale, sometimes called *Balaena glacialis japonica,* and the right whale of the Southern Hemisphere, known variously as *Balaena glacialis australis* (Rice 1977) or *Eubalaena australis* (Payne 1976).

Omura and colleagues considered the North Pacific form identical to that of the North Atlantic, but the southern right whale is somewhat more problematical. From eighteenth- and nineteenth-century whaling logbooks Townsend (1935) plotted the location of right-whale catches and sightings in the Northern and Southern Hemispheres and identified a "vacant tropical belt" between 30°N and 30°S. (His research could not identify where all the whales were, but it certainly could identify the areas where the whales were not.) It is apparent, therefore, that the northern and southern stocks of right whales are completely isolated from

Ventral view of a "whitebelly" right whale, showing the irregular white markings (after Collett).

one another and should probably represent at least distinct subspecies, if not full species.*

Right whales are promiscuous; that is, the males will attempt to mate with any available females. The females are not always cooperative, however, and have been seen to avoid the attentions of ardent males cleverly. Payne (1972a) reported that unreceptive females would often swim with their bellies out of the water, or even with their tails and posterior region raised above the surface, in order to make themselves unavailable to the males. (He wrote that the males often waited underwater for as long as twenty-five minutes, until the female had to right herself in order to breathe.) When the male and female are cooperating there is "much stroking and hugging" in conjunction with the act of copulation. After a gestation period of about one year, a single calf is born, approximately 16 feet (5 meters) in length. Right whales are thought to bear calves only once every two, or possibly three, years.

Early researchers believed that the callosities were acquired by the whale's action of rubbing its head against rocks (Beddard 1900), or that these growths were "a kind of corn" (Ridewood 1901). Fetal animals and newborn calves have been observed with the callosities present, so the growths are now known to be congenital and not pathologically acquired (Matthews 1938). Allen (1916) described a harpooned right whale that rose under its tormentor's boat with such an impact that the boat was holed: "the incident shows that the whale manifested some purpose and determination in its action and points to the possible use of the 'bonnet' as sort of a bumper for offensive purposes, akin to the horn of the rhinoceros." Payne (1976) suggested that the callosities on the upper jaw might function as a "splash deflector, preventing water from entering the whale's blowhole," or as abrasive weapons to rub against the flank of a competitor "in aggressive situations."

Whatever their purpose for the whale, the callosities serve as home for the various species of whale lice and other parasites that infest right whales. These amphipod crustaceans, which can be 0.5 inches (12 millimeters) in length, are "host-specific"; this means that certain species infest only right whales, others live only on sperm whales, while still others parasitize only gray whales, and so on. At least three species are known to be parasitic on right whales: *Cyamus erraticus, C. ovalis,* and *C. gracilis* (Leung 1967). Matthews (1938) reported the heaviest infestation in the area of the bonnet, but in the whales he examined at the South Georgia whaling station the cyamids were present all over the bodies of the whales. These lice probably feed on scraps of food or even on the skin of the whale, but they appear to be true parasites, for the advantages are one-sided: if these infestations serve any useful purpose to the whale, we do not know what it is. Kelp gulls *(Larus dominicanus)* and brown-hooded gulls *(L. maculipinnis)* have been observed landing on the exposed backs and heads of whales, presumably to feed on the lice (Cummings et al. 1971).

Other than lice, the right whale's only natural predator seems to be the killer whale. One of the right whales examined by Omura in 1958 had parallel scratches that could have been inflicted by the teeth of a killer whale, and Cummings and associates (1972) recounted an unsuccessful attack by five killer whales on two right whales at Península Valdés, Argentina. (The latter group went to Valdés to record the sounds of right whales, and among other experiments they fabricated floating dorsal fins of killer whales—the large animals ignored the fake fins—and they also played underwater sounds of killer whales to the right whales. The large whales exhibited "no obvious avoidance," but they lifted their heads out of the water—a behavior known as "spy-hopping"—to investigate the sounds.)

Right whales make simple and complex low-frequency noises and a "belch-like utterance" that is their most common sound (Cummings et al. 1972). These low-frequency sounds are characteristic of the baleen whales, and the higher-frequency sounds are more typical of the toothed whales. Payne and McVay (1971) recorded "sounds like grunting, mooing, moaning and sighing," and Scammon (1874), discuss-

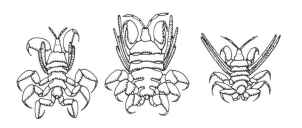

Whale lice of northern and southern right whales.
Cyamus gracilis, Cyamus ovalis, Cyamus erraticus.

*In this account, however, I have combined them, since their biology is similar, if not identical, and since information on one form is applicable to the other. Their histories, similar and tragic though they are, are clearly identified by region and, therefore, by species. Distressing parallels in the northern- and southern-right-whale fisheries brought the populations of both hemispheres to near extinction.

ing harpooned whales, said that they make "a terrific noise called 'bellowing;' this sound is compared to that of a mammoth bull, and adds much to the excitement of the chase and capture." Other out-of-water sounds include "loud high trumpet calls" and a sound like "wind blowing across an open pipe" (Payne 1972b). The governor of Tasmania was kept awake in his residence on the shore of Derwent Inlet by the loud "snoring" of right whales (Sanderson 1956).

In 1969, Dr. Raymond Gilmore, traveling aboard the U.S. Antarctic research vessel *Hero*, discovered the southern right whales that inhabited the protected waters of Península Valdés, Argentina. Since his discovery, this population of whales, numbering perhaps 600, has been subjected to probably the most careful and detailed scrutiny of any population of great whales in history. The whales come close to shore to breed during the months of July to November, and because of the high cliffs that surround some of the beaches, they are easily visible from land. In numerous popular and scientific articles Roger Payne and his associates have revealed fascinating aspects of the daily lives of the right whales of Península Valdés, including observations of mating, feeding, sound producing, and playing. The behavior described by Payne as "play" represents an aspect of the whales' existence that was previously unsuspected. He observed (1976) animals "that are so large, so aloof from the normal torments and buffetings of this world that they are, quite literally, playing with the storm. The same wind that threatens man and his works with destruction is apparently a jovial playmate, a source of boisterous entertainment to the whale." The whales played with Payne's equipment, with seaweed, and with each other. They hurled their forty-ton bodies into the air in exuberant displays that may also have served to signal their location to other whales. They raised their immense flukes in the air and "sailed" downwind, only to swim back to their starting place and do it again and again. (Other animals play with the whales; Payne observed sea lions swimming with "rapid turns, flips and rolls" behind a whale, and he also saw dolphins riding the bow wave of the swimming whales.) Descriptions of the interaction of females and their calves are fascinating and unexpected in the literature of these ponderous leviathans. Here is Payne (1974) on the subject of mother and calf:

The baby will nudge its mother. It will slide off her tail and occasionally wriggle and squirm across her back. A frolicking youngster may slap the water with its flipper or tail,

perform slow rolls or head stands, and rise up vertically, almost out of the water before toppling over with a splash. A calf is able to breach—that is, to jump almost clear of the water—when only a few weeks old.

As the calf grows older, the mother resumes a more active role and begins to play vigorously with her baby. The two of them indulge in joint sessions of breaching, flipper-slapping, and tail-slamming.

For such massive animals, right whales are remarkably flexible. Their seven cervical vertebrae are fused, so there is little head movement, but they can bend their bodies so that the "head nearly touches the flukes" (Collett). Although they swim slowly at the surface when feeding, "their route is erratic, with many quick twists and turns," according to Payne (1974).

Right whales are "skimmers," feeding by swimming through swarms of food organisms, such as copepods, with their mouths open and then closing the mouth and forcing the water out through the baleen strainers; the organisms remain to be swallowed. They feed on the surface with the end of the upper jaw "held well out of the water and the rest of the body submerged" (Watkins and Schevill 1976), and they sometimes feed beneath the surface as well. Of southern right whales feeding on brit ("the minute yellow substance upon which the Right Whale largely feeds"), Melville wrote: "As morning mowers who slowly and seethingly advance their scythes through the long wet grass of marshy meads; even so these monsters swam, making a strange, grassy, cutting sound; and leaving behind them endless swaths of blue upon the yellow sea." Very little is known of the feeding habits of the northern species of right whales, since most of them had been killed before anybody thought to investigate anything other than their location and their oil production. Klumov reported that the main food of right whales in the Northern Hemisphere is Calanoidea (small copepod crustaceans), and Allen (1916) recorded that their diet consists of the small crustaceans known as *Thysanoessa inermis* and *Calanus finnmarchius*. An unusual observation by Clark (1958) concerned a solitary right whale that entered the Cape Cod Canal in Massachusetts in June 1957 and that seemed to be feeding on "tiny fish (spurling, sand eels, etc.)" Watkins and Schevill (1976) described right whales off Massachusetts, feeding on copepods and euphausiids, and in 1979 they published additional remarks on the feeding behavior of this species off Cape Cod, as seen from the air. In addition to eating at the surface, the whales were also seen to feed considerably below the surface: "We have noted right whales feeding, moving back and forth along the same tracks at depths below 10m, where only the light color of the side of baleen in the open mouth of the whale could be seen. Feeding at even greater depths was indicated by acoustical data, which showed that the right whales were feeding on deep, discrete patches of plankton." These whales "bypassed the schooled fish" and fed only on the concentrations of plankton.

In the Southern Ocean, right whales are known to feed on krill and on "shoals of the pelagic *Grimothea,* the post-larval stage of *Munida gregaria* off the coast of Patagonia" (Matthews 1932). In Golfo San José (Península Valdés), Payne (1974) noted that the whales consumed "small crustaceans"—even though they are supposed to eat "only on their summer feeding grounds amidst the abundant breeding swarms of plankton." In the same area, other investigators observed the whales "head-standing" in shallow areas where mussel beds were found, but there is no evidence that right whales eat mussels.

The blow of the right whale, a V-shaped spout that often appears in two distinct jets, is not clearly understood. (The same applies to the spouts of all the great whales, which are more visible and more persistent than the spouts of the smaller cetaceans.) Early observers believed that the whales were spouting water from the blowhole; then it was thought that the whale's warm exhalation was condensing in the cooler air, much as our breath forms a vapor cloud when we exhale on a cold day. (This explanation would seem to be refuted by the existence of a cloud even on the hottest day in the tropics and by the consistent shape of the blows of different species.) Current theories hold that water is trapped in the depression of the blowhole and atomized when the whale breathes out (Payne 1976); or that the air is compressed in the whale's lungs and expands rapidly—and therefore cools—when it is exhaled; or that "a kind of foam containing very fine droplets of oil and mucous . . . could explain the visibility of the blow in tropical regions" (Budker 1959). Some authors remarked that whales have bad breath—that is, the exhalation is foul smelling—but Payne (1976) claimed that this is not usually so: "I have had many whales breathe on me at close range, but only once have I smelled fetid breath." The blows of the great whales are diagnostic. From the tall narrow plumes of the blue and fin whales, to the forward-directed spout of the sperm whale and to the double jet of the rights, what has always seemed so simple—the whale's act of breathing out—has now proved to be yet another conundrum in the wondrous life of the whales.

The distribution of the right whale, like the bowhead, has been greatly reduced by human predations. Since the species is now scarce and has been so for many years, we must turn to the early fishery records to learn of its previous occurrence. The right whale was common off the coasts of Europe (from Spain to northern Norway and Iceland) and in the waters of northeastern North America, where it came into protected waters to breed. Cape Cod Bay, for example, is approximately the same latitude to the north as Península Valdés is to the south, and we might expect to find a historical record of right whales awaiting the first settlers to Plymouth. Starbuck, in his comprehensive history of the American whale fishery (1878), noted that the first settlers to New England found that "large whales of the best kind for oil and bone came daily alongside." In the eastern North Atlantic, the whale fishery predates the first settlements in New England by as much as 600 years. Harmer (1928) recorded the Basques' fishing whales off the Biscay coasts of France and Spain as early as the eleventh century and perhaps even earlier. Right whales were also taken off Iceland and Trömso, Norway, from the thirteenth to the sixteenth centuries. By the year 1700 the right whale was so depleted on the European coasts that the industry ceased, and less than 100 years later the same thing happened across the Atlantic. Townsend's records of American whaling voyages from 1785 to 1913 do not show a single catch or sighting of a right whale in the North Atlantic during the period covered by his extensive study. That the whaleships were there in force can be seen from an examination of the sperm whale catches for this same period, 125 years that spanned the most productive American pelagic whaling. The sperm whalers also hunted in the North Pacific, from the Japan Grounds to the Gulf of Alaska, and they took the oil-rich right whales whenever they could. (Sperm oil was more valuable to the whalers, but the oil from the right whales, known simply as "whale oil," was an important part of the industry.)

With the virtual extirpation of the northern right whales and the corresponding emphasis on the sperm whale fishery, whaleships from England, France, and New England began to roam the oceans in search of whales, the sea's plentiful harvest that required no sowing, only reaping. In 1790 the British brig *Amelia* rounded Cape Horn on her way home with a full cargo of sperm oil and discovered the southern stocks of slow-moving right whales off the eastern coast of South America. In less than fifty years the right whales were hunted—and exterminated—in almost all the coastal areas of the Southern Hemisphere, including Brazil, Peru, the Cape of Good Hope, Australia, Tasmania, New Zealand, and the various southern island groups, such as Tristan da Cunha, South Georgia, Kerguelen, Campbell, Auckland, and Chatham.

From this almost worldwide temperate distribution, the right whales have been reduced to a shadow population. In areas where the whale was once plentiful, records of a single sighting are noteworthy. We have mentioned the whale in the Cape Cod Canal; Chittleborough (1956) recorded two whales off Western Australia, the first such sighting in seventy-five years; R. M. Gilmore (1956) told of a single right whale off the coast of southern California in 1955. A report (Elliot 1953) indicated that right whales were becoming increasingly numerous around Tristan da Cunha in the South Atlantic, but a subsequent study (Best 1974) said that this population "was recently decimated by the operations of a pelagic whaling fleet."

In recent years small numbers of right whales have been sighted in the vicinity of Cape Cod (Watkins and Schevill 1976, 1979) and in the Gulf of Maine (Katona 1975). There have also been infrequent sightings along the eastern coast of North America, from Florida to the Bay of Fundy (Reeves et al. 1978). These sightings have led cetologists to speculate that the right whale may be making a comeback in these western North Atlantic waters, but one study lists no less than eight possible reasons for the stock's "failure to recover more quickly and convincingly" (Reeves et al.). Among these are natural predation, competition for food with other species, accidental entrapment in nets, water turbidity, noise, pollution, and boat collisions. (In 1979 a thirty-foot right whale washed ashore at Easthampton, Long Island, New York. From deep slash wounds on the carcass, it appeared that the whale had been mortally injured by the propeller of a large vessel.) Voicing the concern of cetologists and others who care about the world's whales and other wildlife, Reeves (1979) wrote,

Many people, including myself, believe, perhaps wishfully, that the right whale on this side of the Atlantic is making a painfully slow but steady comeback. There are no good grounds, however, for contesting Dr. Mitchell's [1975] conservative opinion that "the population could number only tens to a few hundred animals. It is apparent that the Northwest Atlantic right whale has not recovered, and there is thus cause for concern regarding its survival as a biological entity."

The first record of a right whale in Hawaiian waters during this century occurred in 1979, when on two separate occasions a single right whale was seen in the company of humpbacks. In this most unusual sighting the right whale was observed once with a single humpback "in frequent contact . . . suggesting courtship" (Baker et al. 1979).

There may be as many as 4,000 right whales left in the world (Scheffer 1976) or no more than 1,000 (Nishiwaki 1972). All right whales have been protected since the 1937 International Whaling Convention, and from that date the North Atlantic and southern populations appear to be increasing very slowly. There does not seem to be a corresponding increase in the North Pacific population, but the reasons for this disparity are unknown.* In their publication of five new records of right whales in the southeastern North Pacific (off the western coast of North America), Rice and Fiscus (1968) wrote, "After more than 30 years of legal protection, right whales remain on the brink of extinction in the eastern North Pacific." The main concentrations of right whales in the Southern Hemisphere are off Argentina and South Africa, off Campbell Island (Gaskin 1972), and around the Antarctic ice. There may be "a few hundred" in the North Atlantic (Scheffer 1976) and a similar number in the North Pacific (National Marine Fisheries Service 1974).

From the first, the right whales were doomed. Much has been written regarding the origin of the name "right": these animals were slow swimmers; the buoyant, thick blubber kept them afloat when they were killed; and they provided plentiful oil and bone. An additional factor rendered these whales even more susceptible to the whale hunters, their habit of coming into shallow bays, inlets, and even river mouths to breed and rear their young. The earliest whaling was conducted from shore, since the whales could be seen spouting and rolling in the shallows. As early as the tenth century, Basque whalers on the coasts of France and Spain hunted the whales in the Bay of Biscay. At first the Basques cut up whales that had stranded on the beaches, but then, realizing the great quantities of

---

*Mitchell (1974) suggested that the right whale has not recovered in the North Pacific and elsewhere because of its inability to compete with the faster-swimming sei whale for the same food resources. Mitchell, quoting a book by Omura, wrote that the sei whales, which eat copepods, and the pygmy blue and fin whales, which feed on euphausiids, may be keeping the less numerous right whales from recovering, even though they are no longer hunted.

meat and oil that could be obtained, they took to the sea in open boats. (In addition to their expertise in whale killing, the Basques made another important contribution to the whaling industry: the word "harpoon" comes from the Basque *arpoi,* which means "to take quickly" [Norman and Fraser 1938].) They watched for the whales from stone towers, and as soon as a whale was sighted, they lit fires of wet straw to attract the neighboring villagers (Markham 1881). This could hardly be considered high-intensity whaling, for Harmer calculated that 700–1,000 whales were taken by the Basques in the period from 1517 to 1617. But even so, the whales became scarce, and the whalers had to venture farther and farther afield. They went as far as Newfoundland to fish for cod and whales, but soon that stock of right whales was also exhausted, and the experienced Basque whalers signed aboard Dutch and English ships in the fishery for the Greenland right whale, *Balaena mysticetus.*

The first settlements in America seem to have depended heavily on the presence of whales. Starbuck observed that "Captain John Smith, in 1614, found whales so plentiful along the coast that he turned aside from the primary object of his voyage to pursue them," and the pilgrims on the *Mayflower* "intended to fish for whales here." Allen (1916) quoted the 1620 journal of Bradford and Winslow: "every day we saw whales playing hard by us; of which in that place if we had instruments and means to take them, we might have made a very rich return." The whale fishery prospered in the colonies, with its centers at Cape Cod, Connecticut, Long Island, Nantucket, Martha's Vineyard, and Salem. In 1690, Ichabod Paddock journeyed from Cape Cod to Nantucket to instruct the people there in the art of killing whales from shore (Allen 1908). As an indication of the abundance of right whales in Cape Cod Bay, Allen (1916) quoted a letter from Wait Winthrop of Boston to his brother Fitz-John, dated January 27, 1700: "the winter hath been so favourable that they have killed many whales in Cape Cod Bay; all the boates round the Bay killed twenty nine whales in one day." By the first quarter of the eighteenth century the shore whaling was over, and interest turned to deep-water whaling for the rights and the newly discovered sperm whales. (Tradition has it that in 1712 a Nantucket whaleship under Captain Christopher Hussey was blown offshore in a storm, sighted a pod of sperm whales, and killed one. Thus began the saga of American deep-water whaling.) While pursuing the sperm whale, which was "in general an inhabitant of tropical and temperate seas, ranging into cold waters only in very limited numbers" (Townsend 1935), the whalers chanced on the untouched stocks of southern right whales. The first whaling ship, *William and Anne,* arrived in New Zealand in 1792 (Gaskin 1972). Tasmania was settled in 1803 by colonists brought aboard a whaler, and "for the next forty years, this colony was mainly engaged in the pursuit of the southern right whale" (Chittleborough 1956). For about fifty years "bay whaling" was practiced in the coastal waters of Australia, New Zealand, Tasmania, and South Africa (especially Walfisch Bay and Delagoa Bay), and the right whales were slaughtered in unprecedented numbers. From 1804 to 1817, an incredible 193,522 right whales were captured, an average of 13,823 annually. Sir Sidney Harmer, who gave these figures in his "History of Whaling" (1928) remarked that "it is an amount comparable with the results of modern whaling."* Obviously, such an intensive fishery could not last, and by 1850 bay whaling had ceased altogether (Ommanney 1933).

The Japanese hunted black right whales in their coastal waters, as evidenced by numerous references to and drawings of this species (Fraser 1937). Theirs was a net fishery, in which the whales were driven into waiting nets, killed, and then hauled ashore for processing. From 1802 to 1850 about fifteen whales per year were killed in this manner, of which about 20 percent were right whales. The balance were fin, humpback, and gray whales (Omura 1958). When the American whalers invaded the whaling grounds of the North Pacific, which Rice (1974) characterized as "renowned in the nineteenth century as one of the best areas for hunting right whales in the summer," they virtually eliminated the population. Of all the right whale populations, the North Pacific was the most drastically depleted and, apparently, the least able to recover. In his presidential address to the Linnean Society of London in 1928, Sir Sidney Harmer made the following remarks. The lessons he speaks of went unheeded:

The history of the southern right whale is an object lesson of the past. The animal seems to have occurred in a profu-

*In his 1970 discussion of the exploitation and recovery of right whales off South Africa, Best wrote that "these figures seem to be given in error. . . . This estimate was based on the amount of whale oil landed at United States ports, so it included both southern and North Pacific catches." He did point out, however, that "by the time modern whaling started in the first few years of the twentieth century, less than 100 right whales were taken per year, so that a marked reduction in their numbers must have occurred." In 1652, when the first colonists arrived at Table Bay, South Africa, there were "many thousands" of whales in South African waters; by 1969, Best managed to locate 180.

sion as remarkable as that of the humpbacks and the rorquals of the Antarctic at the beginning of the twentieth century. It lived in seas practically illimitable in extent as its home was the great Southern Ocean. . . . The belief that it would be impossible to exterminate the right whales which occurred in immense numbers in so large an area may well have been present in the minds of the old whalers. If there are any of their modern successors who think that the stock of Antarctic rorquals is inexhaustible, the consideration of the history of the southern right whale, an animal which similarly inhabited the Southern Ocean, might perhaps induce them to feel some doubts on the subject.

BOWHEAD WHALE

Balaena mysticetus Linnaeus 1758

The bowhead is a thickset whale with a head that can account for one-third of its total length. It reaches a maximum length of 65 feet (19.8 meters) and a weight of approximately a ton per foot.* The whale is black overall, with a white area on the forward part of the lower jaw that often has a series of irregular black spots. These spots may each contain some of the hairs that grow sparsely on the upper and lower jaws (Nishiwaki and Kasuya 1970). In addition to the unpigmented lower jaw, there may be white on the belly and

*Scoresby (1820) recorded that of the 322 whales he actually observed after capture, none exceeded 58 feet, and the longest he ever heard of was a 67-foot specimen killed at Godhavn, Greenland, in 1813. Most of the information on this species comes from Captain William Scoresby, Jr., *An Account of the Arctic Regions with a History and Description of the Northern Whale-Fishery.* This work has been called "one of the most remarkable books in the English language" (Harmer 1928). It contains the most comprehensive account of the bowhead (or, as he called it, "the whale") and perhaps the most complete account of any species of whale in our literature. The son of a whaling captain, Scoresby was given his first command, the

lighter grayish coloration around the eyes and also at the junction of the tail with the body.

The origins of common names of some animals are hazy, but one assumes that the name "bowhead" comes from the bow of the huge, arched mouth. Other authors have assigned a different origin to the name: Winter and Schmitt (1975) wrote that its head "is simi-

Resolution, in 1810, when he was just 21 years old. He recorded virtually everything about his voyages and the animals he encountered in addition to his extensive review of the natural history of *B. mysticetus.* Since "the whale" was so heavily hunted in the nineteenth century, his description remains the best record we have and one that is not likely to be duplicated. Even though we now have more sophisticated methods of analysis and observation, Scoresby had more whales.

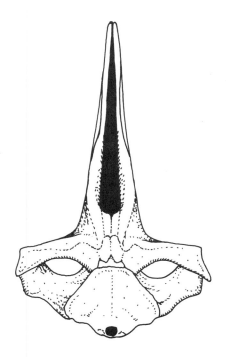

Dorsal view of the skull of the Greenland right whale, *Balaena mysticetus* (after Nishiwaki and Kasuya).

lar to a ship's bow, hence the name"; and others have even likened the bending of the baleen to an archer's bow. This is a whale of many names; it was called the bowhead only by American whalers. Among its other appellations are "great Polar whale," "common whale," "Arctic right whale," and "Greenland whale"; and because it was so important to various aspects of European economy, it was known simply as "the whale."

The bowhead's baleen is by far the longest of any whale's, reaching a recorded length of over 15 feet (4.5 meters), but 10–11 feet (3.0–3.3 meters) is average.* Durham (1972b) calculated that the "baleen plates from a large whale weigh a ton, and laid end-to-end stretch a mile." The plates are black, longer at the middle than at the front or rear, and number 250–300 per side. (It was these plates of baleen, along with the oil-rich blubber of this species, that very nearly brought about its extirpation.) The baleen, known in the eighteenth and nineteenth centuries as whalebone —although it is not bone at all, but a keratinous substance similar to that of nails and hair in other mammals—hangs from the arched upper jaw into the great, scooplike mouth. Scoresby wrote: "when the mouth is open it presents a cavity as large as a room, and capable of containing a merchant ship's jolly boat full of men, being 6 or 8 feet wide, 10 or 12 feet high (in front) and 15 or 16 feet long." The tongue of the bowhead can weigh as much as a ton; it is whitish in color and fairly immobile. Scammon (1874) said that it was "incapable of protrusion." The eyes and ears of the bowhead are small, but the flippers and the flukes are large. The deeply notched tail of a full-grown specimen may be 25 feet (7.6 meters) across, and the broad flippers can reach a length of 6 feet (1.8 me-

*Except where otherwise noted, specific references to size, shape, color, and other points of physical description, have been taken from Scoresby.

ters). The twin nostrils of this species are located on the "crown" of its head, a protrusion just anterior to the line of the eyes.

Swimming at the surface, the bowhead often exposes its blowhole and its back, but not the area between them that would correspond to its neck. Scammon referred to this characteristic when he wrote that "the spout holes terminate in sort of a cone," calling them "steeple-tops." The bowhead is a slow and ponderous swimmer, usually moving at a speed that has been estimated at 4 knots, but capable of bursts of speed of up to 9 knots. The "blow" of this whale is short and full, occurring six or eight times when the whale is at the surface; after this, the animal will dive for ten to twenty minutes. A peculiarity of the bowhead is the regularity of its dives: if it comes up twenty minutes after its first blow, it will surface again twenty minutes later (McVay 1973). As the animal surfaces to breathe, the "crown" is seen and then the broad, smooth expanse of back, which bears no dorsal fin. Finally, as the great black whale prepares to "retire from the surface," it slowly lifts its flukes out of the water and disappears.

The name *Balaena* is Latin for "whale"; *mysticetus* is composed of the Greek for "moustache" *(mystax)* and for "whale" *(ketos)*. The bowhead is one of the species known as the right whale, because it was the "right" whale to kill. It was slow and unaggressive, it was rich in oil and baleen, and because of its thick blubber (up to 28 inches) it floated when it was killed. (Faster-swimming species would be safe from the whalers until they could be caught and a method could be devised for keeping them afloat.)

Because of its unique appearance—large head, white chin, no dorsal fin—the bowhead is not easily confused with any other species. The only other large black whale that resembles the bowhead is the northern right, *Balaena glacialis,* which bears a characteristic

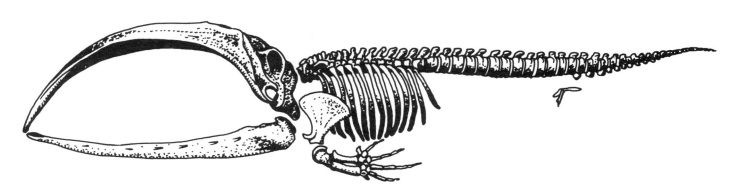

Skeleton of *Balaena mysticetus* (after Scammon).

horny "bonnet" on the upper jaw, has a less rotund form, and is not usually found in Arctic waters. These two forms of right whales have had a confusing history in regard to each other; for a long time they were not differentiated at all. Then they were placed into different genera, and currently they are placed in the same genus, being separated on the species level.

Scoresby, in discussing the distribution of the "common whale," said it "occurs most abundantly in the frozen seas of Greenland and Davis' Strait—in the bays of Baffin and Hudson—in the sea to the northward of Behring's Strait, and along some parts of the northern shores of Asia and probably America." This is an accurate description of the range of the bowhead, but Scoresby then went on to report the species "along the coasts of Africa and South America . . . periodically and in considerable numbers." This is obviously not the whale we now know as the bowhead or Arctic right whale, since it does not venture farther south than 50°N and has never been known off Africa, let alone South America. (He did notice a difference and pointed out that "the mysticetus found in southern regions is often covered with barnacles [Lepas Diadema &c.], while those of the arctic seas are free from these shell-fish.")

In his 1834 work, Dewhurst separated the two types of right whales: "This species [Balaena Icelandica, Nordcaper, the North Cape or Iceland Whale] differs from the preceding chiefly in having a more lengthened body and a proportionally smaller head," but he made no mention of the bonnet or the crustacean parasites so characteristic of the northern right whale.

When Melville wrote of the "right whale," he located the *Pequod* off the Crozets, in the southern Indian Ocean, "heading north-eastward towards the Island of Java." He wanted very much to demonstrate the superiority of the sperm whale to Scoresby's Greenland whale, but he was obviously discussing the southern black right whale.* Until Allen's 1908 "resurrection" of the name *Eubalaena* for the black right whale, the two species were considered congeneric (Eschricht and Reinhardt 1861), and it is now thought that they ought to be placed in the same genus *(Balaena)* again, since "the differences between the two species are no greater than those separating, e.g., the various species of Balaenoptera" (Rice 1977).

There appear to be enough variations in the Arctic whales themselves to further confuse observers. Although very little is known of their growth patterns, it is thought that bowheads become darker with age. Alaskan Eskimos have identified different forms of bowheads, usually differentiated by size and color, ranging from the *ingutuk,* a 1- or 2-year-old whale, to the *apsavak,* the biggest of all, which has tough meat and little oil (McVay 1973). The Eskimos are particularly interested in the *ingutuk,* because they make the best eating. Marquette (1978) pointed out that

*In *Moby-Dick,* Melville has rightly celebrated the sperm whale, but often to the detriment of other species, particularly the Greenland whale. He wrote that Scoresby "knew nothing and says nothing of the Great Sperm Whale, compared with which the Greenland Whale is almost unworthy mentioning. . . . the Greenland Whale is deposed,—the great Sperm Whale now reigneth!" From his description, it is obvious that Melville saw the black right whale, not the bowhead, since he had no firsthand knowledge of Arctic waters (Vincent 1949).

Dorsal view of bowhead whale, *Balaena mysticetus.* Notice narrow upper jaw, white chin, large head, and broad flukes.

"younger animals, particularly females, are often rotund and their profiles may lack the distinctive dip between the head and back that is characteristic of older animals."

Captain Thomas Roys in 1848 was the first whaler to penetrate the Bering Straits and enter the Chukchi Sea, where he took right whales, belugas, and bowheads. In discussions with Captain Scammon in San Francisco, Roys identified "bunchbacks," a form of bowhead with "a sort of hump on top of the 'small' which is situated about six feet forward of the flukes, extending along the top of the back two to three feet and in some individuals rises in the highest place about six inches." In W. H. Dall's "Catalogue of the Cetacea of the North Pacific Ocean," added as an appendix to Scammon's 1874 book, this form is called *Balaena mysticetus* var. *Roysii*. "Before this variety is confirmed," wrote Dall, "a more thorough knowledge of it is, of course, indispensable." Such knowledge was not forthcoming, and *Roysii* has vanished into the limbo reserved for invalid subspecies. Similarly, Bailey and Hendee (1926) described a small form that the Eskimos called *inito*, which was characterized by its "small size, flat head, and the thin, gray baleen which is 2 1/2 feet or less in length." In 1977, Marquette recorded the Eskimo designations of "whales that are especially fat as *Ingutuk* if small, and *Ingutuvak* if large." Although scientists recognize these distinctions, they do not accept the variations as defining subspecies. At present, there appears to be only one species of bowhead, with variations. (Scoresby reported a piebald specimen, and McVay [1973] was told by an Eskimo of an animal "that had no black pigment on its back or sides.")

For a huge animal that was the object of a concentrated fishery for over three centuries, surprisingly little is known of the biology of the bowhead whale. Scoresby's 1820 work is the primary source of information and has been quoted liberally in every subsequent attempt to describe the species, from Dewhurst in 1834 to Marquette's "biological summary of the species" in 1977. This account will take no exception to this tradition.

Breeding is thought to take place in April or May. (A spectacular aerial photograph taken on May 8, 1977, in the Beaufort Sea by NMFS biologist Bruce Krogman shows six or seven bowheads unequivocally engaged in reproductive activity.) Scoresby estimated the gestation period at nine to ten months. Thus, the young are born in January or February, but the location of these births is not known. Marquette (1978) revised Scoresby's estimate upward to "about twelve months" and added, "most calving probably occurs during April and May." Females with calves have been seen off Point Barrow on Alaska's northern shore from April to July, with some anomalous sightings being made in March and September. The size of a bowhead at birth is not known, but estimates are between 10 and 14 feet (3.0–4.2 meters). Scoresby recorded a "sucker" (baby whale) that was taken with the umbilical cord still attached, but he did not give the length, and Marquette (1977) documented a report of a 1954 calf that was 10–12 feet (3.0–3.6 meters). The calf probably nurses for a year or less, "until, by the evolution of the whalebone, it is enabled to procure its own nourishment" Females are said to be extremely protective of their calves, and Scoresby recorded numerous instances of cows standing by injured calves or charging boats when the young are threatened. In discussing the "maternal affection of the whale," he wrote:

There is something extremely painful in the destruction of a whale, when thus evincing a degree of affectionate regard for its offspring, that would do honour to the superior intelligence of human beings; yet the object of the adventure, the value of the prize, the joy of the capture, cannot be sacrificed to feelings of compassion.

The baleen in young whales is only a few inches long, reaching 6 feet when the whale is about 12 years old, and the whale is "full grown at the age of twenty or twenty five."

The bowhead feeds on copepods, amphipods, euphausiids, and pteropods of the northern seas (Braham and Krogman 1977). The whale's surface feeding has been described as "skimming," which entails swimming slowly with the mouth agape through masses of the invertebrates that make up its food. When the mouth is closed, the huge tongue is probably pressed upward, forcing the water out through the sieve of baleen, but this process has not been documented. (The alternative feeding method for baleen whales, called "swallowing," is a much more energetic activity, including rolling, splashing, and squirting water out through the plates. This is practiced by the rorquals, with the exception of the sei whale, which seems able to feed in both modes.) Durham (1972b) suggested that bowheads also feed on the bottom, from the presence in the stomachs of some specimens of "mud-dwelling tunicates, vegetation silt, and a few small pebbles" (quoted in Marquette 1977).

The bowhead whale favors close packs and patches of ice and is rarely seen in large open spaces. It dives under floating ice and can break ice up to three inches thick with its "crown." Harpooned bowheads can remain submerged for over an hour. (Scoresby recorded one instance in which a whale remained underwater for an hour and a half, but the longest time he personally observed was fifty-six minutes.) These whales are also capable of prodigious dives, up to "700 to 800 fathoms perpendicular," as well as great feats of strength and endurance, such as taking out 10,440 yards of line (spliced together from numerous boats); or resisting capture by towing the whaleboats all over the ocean off Spitsbergen. ("This disagreeable and unsuccessful adventure occupied between three and four days.") Scammon told of an action of this species that has been frequently repeated in the literature: "After the animal has been 'fastened to' it has darted to the depths beneath in such a state of trepidation as to unheedingly strike the rocks or sand with such force as to dislocate its head-bones, and cause instant death."

Although it is normally a placid, slow-swimming animal, the bowhead is occasionally given to great leaps out of the water for no apparent reason. Here is Scoresby on "breaching": "This feat they sometimes perform as an amusement apparently; to the high admiration of the distant spectator; but to the no small terror of the unexperienced fishers." When Scott McVay went to Alaska to record the sounds of bowheads (a venture in which he did not succeed, though he gained invaluable information on the species and filmed the first man to swim—intentionally—with a bowhead whale), his crew shot numerous spectacular leaps. Words cannot adequately describe the power and exuberance of a fifty-ton whale emerging from the water in a Niagara of foam. Most of us cannot expect to get to Alaska to see this scene live in the immediate future, so McVay's movie is an admirable substitute.*

We do not know what sounds bowhead whales make underwater, but some of their surface phonations have been heard. "Like the hoo-oo-oo of the hoot owl although longer and drawn out and more of a humming sound than a hoot," stated Aldrich (quoted in McVay 1973). "Wallowing and bellowing, sounding like a huge bathtub being drained," said Rau (1978). "A sound like a guitar playing," wrote McVay (1973). "The whale seems dull of hearing," wrote Scoresby,

"a noise in the air such as that produced by a person shouting, is not noticed by it. . . . but a very slight splash in the water, in calm weather, excites its attention, and alarms it." The whale's ears are usually underwater and the whaler's above, so they do not interact in each other's element. "Scoresby could not have known," wrote McVay, "that the air-water interface is nearly opaque to sound—less than one one-hundredth of a signal passes through." No wonder Scoresby claimed that "the whale has no voice"; the whale would probably write the same of us.

Although the Greenland whales were plentiful, they were never gregarious. They were (and are) usually seen as solitary individuals or in pairs. Krogman's 1977 photograph shows at least six whales together, but this group is associated with breeding and does not represent the more prevalent feeding or migratory behavior.

The bowhead is the only large whale that spends its entire life in polar waters. Although its movements are still not fully understood, it is known that two factors have substantially affected its distribution: ice and men. The ice was their sometime protector; it blocked off areas that would otherwise have been invaded by whaling ships; it gave them temporary sanctuary when the whalers found their long-unknown habitats; and toward the end of the whaling effort the ice destroyed a good proportion of the American whaling fleet. Before the exploitation began, the bowhead was common (although probably never numerous) throughout the northern Arctic. Basques in the sixteenth century were catching the whale in Greenland waters (Sanderson 1956), but their fishery, which concentrated on the more plentiful black right whale, was in decline by the seventeenth century. They were replaced by the Dutch and the English, who found the Greenland whale in the waters of Jan Mayen, Spitsbergen, and eastern Greenland. The fishery in these waters that began in the sixteenth century was over by the mid-eighteenth, the whales having been almost completely eliminated from this portion of their range. (The extent of the elimination can be seen in a 1964 article by Age Jonsgard, the Norwegian cetologist, wherein he recorded a sighting of what was "in all probability a Greenland right whale" in the Barents Sea. He then listed only two other references in the twentieth century in which this species has been observed east of Greenland.) It may be found in limited numbers in the Davis Strait, Baffin Bay, and the adjacent waters of the eastern Canadian Arctic and from the Bering, Chuk-

*Called *In Search of the Bowhead Whale,* it is distributed by the Canadian National Film Board and was originally issued in 1974.

chi, and Beaufort seas, along the northern shore of Alaska, to Banks and Victoria islands.

Information from the Soviet Arctic and the Sea of Okhotsk is sparse. Soviet Eskimos on the Chukchi Peninsula are reported to take an average of two whales per year (Marquette 1977). The species was assumed to be long extinct in the Sea of Japan, but in 1970 a young animal, about 21 feet (6.4 meters) long and estimated to be less than a year and a half old, was caught alive in Osaka Bay. It died the following morning and was hauled ashore, examined, and photographed by scientists from the Whales Research Institute in Tokyo. There is no question regarding the identification of the species, and it represents perhaps the most southerly record for the bowhead. Nishiwaki and Kasuya pointed out that "hitherto, this species has occurred no other place in the world on 33°28′ N around, San Diego and Casablanca, for example."

The migrations of bowhead whales have always mystified whalers and cetologists. The animals move seasonally, but their travels are also related to the unpredictable conditions of the Arctic ice, which may vary from one year to the next and may even close off certain areas that might be used for feeding or calving (Vibe 1967). By the time it occurred to the whalers that the bowheads east of Greenland were not a permanent resource, it was too late to investigate their migrations. Only the whalers of the western Arctic recorded the location of their catches. Townsend (1935) plotted the movements of various species of whales by examining the logbook records of American whaleships. From his maps it can be seen that the bowheads in the western Arctic have a protracted migration, from the western Bering Sea in May, through the Bering Straits in June and July, and to the north shore of Alaska in August and September.

More recent observations have confirmed Townsend's data, but since the current studies are conducted primarily from shore stations, they coincide with the Eskimos' whaling seasons, which, in turn, are governed by ice conditions. Whales are observed mostly from late April to June, as long as the leads (cracks in the ice) are open. In the spring these open leads are close to points of land such as Barrow and Point Hope, and it is from these villages that the Eskimo whalers set out. It now appears that there are three distinct "runs" of whales in the spring, the first two made up of small animals of both sexes and the third composed of large males and females with calves (Marquette 1977). These whales remain throughout the summer in the area of the MacKenzie River delta

and the Beaufort Sea (Braham and Krogman 1977). In the fall the whales move west and south to avoid the freezing up and closing of the leads. They again pass the Eskimo whaling villages and "retreat south of the Bering Sea" (Rice 1974). In the fall migration the whales seem to remain further offshore, and fewer animals are seen from the villages and shore stations. In the winter they are believed to favor the "loose, southern edge of the pack ice, which usually extends across the central Bering Sea from Kuskokwim Bay, Alaska, west-southwest to the northern shores of the Kamchatka Peninsula, USSR" (Rice 1974).

Although the Eskimos have been hunting the bowhead for centuries, the history of the whale and its hunters can be divided conveniently into two periods: the seventeenth- to nineteenth-century enterprise of the Europeans and the Americans and the more recent controversy over the Eskimos' taking the whales in Alaska. There are references to Eskimo whaling as early as 2000 B.C. (Rau 1978), but as long as the bowhead was plentiful, the subsistence hunting by the Eskimos was of little concern to anyone but anthropologists and the Eskimos themselves.

The bowhead whale is now officially listed as an endangered species (Red Data Book 1972), and it has not been hunted at all, except by Eskimos, since 1935. The whales are gone now from the waters of Spitsbergen and eastern Greenland, which they once inhabited; it is hard to believe that this species was once so plentiful that Scoresby could write "[the whale fishery] in a short time proved the most lucrative, and the most important branch of national commerce which had ever been offered to the industry of man."* What Scoresby refers to as Spitsbergen is a group of islands north of Scandinavia, only one of which is actually known as Spitsbergen. The entire group is known as Svalbard ("cold coast"). The islands were discovered in 1596 by Willem Barendz (or Barentz, or Barents, as the sea was named) and visited by the English explorers Steven Bennett in 1603 and Henry Hudson in 1607. The Russia or Muscovy Company, established by the English in 1555 to develop trade with Russia and the Baltic countries, sent out its first whaling ships in 1610, the *Mary Margaret* under the command of

*The reader is again referred to Scoresby's *Account of the Arctic Regions,* which contains a meticulously documented and authoritative history of the fishery from the Middle Ages up to his own voyages in 1818. Volume 2, *The Whale-Fishery,* from which my account is largely derived, includes a year-by-year chronology of the fishery, its politics, techniques, equipment, laws, commerce, and pertinent meteorological information. In short, it is the most complete history of a particular type of whaling ever published, and it is as important today, and as accurate, as it was when it originally appeared in 1820.

Thomas Edge and the *Elizabeth* under Jonas Poole. Their expedition was not an unqualified success—the *Mary Margaret* was wrecked on the ice—but they "observed a vast number of whales on the coast," according to Scoresby, and the whale fishery had officially commenced.

The Dutch and the Spanish outfitted vessels for the rich northern fishery, followed quickly by the Germans and the French. All these ships were originally accompanied by Basque harpooners, since the latter were the only people with the experience and the technology to take and process the whales. The ships would anchor in the various bays of the Spitsbergen group, sending out shallops to hunt the whales. The ships were not fitted out with tryworks for the rendering of the blubber into oil, even though a Basque captain named François Sopite is credited with this invention around the end of the sixteenth century, and therefore the whales were tried out (boiled down) on shore. The Dutch elaborated on the shore-based tryworks, and by 1622 they had built the town of Smeerenberg ("blubber-town") on Amsterdamøya, one of the islands of Svalbard. Of this period of Dutch whaling, Scoresby wrote:

The bold and unconscious manner in which the whales resorted to the bays and sea-coasts at this period, their easy and expeditious destruction, the consequent regularly productive state of the fishery, together with the immense herds in which the whales appeared, in comparison of the number which was killed,—encouraged the hope that the profitable nature of the fishery would continue unabated. This consideration induced the enterprising Dutch to incur very great expenses in making secure, ample and permanent erections, which they gradually extended in such a degree, that at length they assumed the form of a regular village, which, in reference to the use that it was designed for, they gave it the name of *Smeerenberg.*

Soon the "immense herds" of whales gave out, and the Dutch took to the sea again. By 1635 this "bay whaling" was in decline, and the ships had to cask the blubber for transport to shore, instead of simply towing the whale to the trypots.

In 1719 the enterprising Dutch sailed around Greenland's southernmost point, Kap Farvel (Cape Farewell), and discovered new stocks of whales in the Davis Straits, between the west coast of Greenland and Baffin Island, and beyond, in Baffin Bay. Scoresby explained that in 1721 there were 355 ships employed in the Greenland and Davis Straits whale fisheries: "251 of these ships were fitted out from different ports in Holland; 55 from Hamburgh; 24 from Bremen; 20 from the ports in the Bay of Biscay; and 5 from Bremen in Norway." The totals for this fishery are astonishing. For Greenland alone, from 1669 to 1778, the Dutch sent out 14,167 ships (of which 561 were lost) and took 54,100 whales. In the Davis Straits another 6,986 whales were killed from 1719 to 1778. If we calculate 1,500 pounds (675 kilograms) of baleen per whale—a conservative estimate, since some whales could produce twice that amount—the Dutch harvested over 45,000 tons of whalebone in a 110-year period. Let us assume a figure of 10 tons of oil per whale, again a conservative sum, since some whales had been known to yield 30 tons. Then, over 600,000 tons of oil were taken by the Dutch from the Greenland whales.

The inoffensive and placid Greenland right whale was slaughtered in these vast numbers because it provided materials that were in great demand in Europe, and the fishery represented an economic bonanza for the whaling nations. It has been said that the profits from a single whale were sometimes sufficient to cover the expenses of a year's whaling voyage (Harmer 1928). The baleen or whalebone was utilized in various ways, but primarily in women's fashions: it was made into stays for corsets and dresses. "The consumption of whalebone in the stiff stays used by the ladies was at this period very great," remarked Cap-

A baleen plate of a large bowhead whale.

tain Scoresby, "in consequence of which, notwithstanding the increasing importation from Greenland, Davis' Straits and the St. Lawrence, this article still maintained a high price." It was also employed in the making of ribs of umbrellas and parasols, fishing rods, ramrods, and buggy whips, and the fringes were used for stuffing chairs and sofas. The oil "was largely used in the lighting of the streets of towns, and the interior of places of worship, houses, shops, manufactories, &c.; it is extensively employed in the manufacture of soft soap, as well as in the preparing of leather and coarse woolen cloths." It was also used in the manufacture of paints and as a lubricant for machinery, as well as playing an important role in the manufacture of rope. In its contribution to industry, then, the Arctic right whale can be compared to the petroleum industry of today. The whale provided both the oil that served almost as many uses as petroleum and the strong, flexible raw material whose place is taken today by plastics. Is it any wonder that nearly all of Europe and America eventually came to depend on the whale? Since the species was treated as a natural resource, and since at this time very few people recognized that there was a limit to natural resources, it would have been more surprising if they had not hunted the whale as industriously and mercilessly as they did.

In 1818, John Ross in the *Isabella* and W. E. Parry in the *Alexander* sailed north, past Disko Bay, Greenland, to what was called the "north water," where they encountered whales in abundance, and two years later Captain John in the *Cumbrian* sailed into Lancaster Sound and found more whales in the "west water." By this time the Dutch had dropped out of the picture, and the competition was between the English and the Americans. Whales were being taken in the Bering Sea; and in 1848, Captain Thomas W. Roys of Long Island sailed through the Bering Straits to discover the last refuges of the bowhead whale, the Chukchi Sea, the north shore of Alaska, and the Beaufort Sea. The years 1840–60 were the best in the history of American whaling. During this period, the annual average gross value of the United States whale catch from around the world was $8 million (Bruemmer 1971). During the Civil War much of the New England whaling fleet was destroyed; in 1861 the Union sank sixteen whaleships in the harbors of Charleston and Savannah in an unsuccessful attempt to blockade these harbors with "the great stone fleet," and in 1865 the Confederate raider *Shenandoah* attacked and burned twenty-one whaleships near the Bering Strait.

New ships were built at New Bedford and other whaling ports and were sent around the horn to the bowhead grounds north of Alaska. The ice now took its toll of the fleet, for in 1871, of thirty-nine American vessels in the Arctic for the whaling season, all but seven were trapped in the closing ice and destroyed. (Over 1,200 men, women, and children took to open boats and were picked up by the remaining whalers. Not a single life was lost during this disaster.) Five years later, fifteen more ships were crushed by the inexorable power of the polar ice. It was now clear that conditions in northern Alaskan waters rendered the sailing ships helpless, and there seemed to be a possibility that the whales would be left to the pack ice, the Eskimos, and the killer whales. Of bowheads in the eastern Arctic, Mitchell and Reeves (1980) have written that "killer whales are known to prey on most species of large whales, and we believe bowhead whales and right whales *Eubalaena glacialis* are especially vulnerable." Bullen (1899) also wrote about a killer whale attack on a bowhead, but his accounts are now considered too exaggerated to be scientifically reliable.

It was not to be. Necessity mothered the requisite technology, and steam whaling arrived in the Arctic in 1879. There had been steam whaling before, of course; Svend Foyn was hunting whales in Varanger Fjord as early as 1868 in the steam-powered *Spes et Fides.* But as long as the whales were plentiful and the conditions amenable to sailing ships, there was no reason to incur the extra cost of fuel required for steamers. Steam whaling in the western Arctic was to be the last gasp of American whaling and the last assault on the bowhead's icy fortress. The demand for baleen had increased since the Civil War; hoopskirts were now the fashion, and only whalebone would do for the light, springy hoops that supported these skirts.

The *Mary and Helen,* first of the American steam whalers, was launched at Bath, Maine, in 1879 and sailed for the Arctic for the spring and summer of 1880. She returned to San Francisco in November of that year, carrying oil and baleen that brought its owners over $100,000, an amount considerably greater than the $65,000 it had cost to build and outfit the ship (Bockstoce 1977a). Other steam whalers followed, and in 1890 the first vessels "wintered over" in the Arctic. The harbor at Pauline Cove, Herschel Island, was found to be protected (and protective) enough for ships to spend the winter there, iced in and banked with snow for insulation, while the crew waited for the ice to open and the whales to come. The *Mary D. Hume* returned to San Francisco in September 1892, after a twenty-nine-month absence. She had taken 37 whales, and her cargo brought $400,000, "clearly among the most profitable in all of American whaling history" (Bockstoce 1977a). On hearing of the spectacular success of the *Mary D. Hume,* other whalers followed suit, and by the winter of 1894/95, there were fifteen steam whalers wintering over at Herschel. In 1894 over 400,000 pounds of baleen arrived in San Francisco, which had become the economic center of the whaling business in the United States. Inevitably, as the number of ships increased, the number of whales decreased proportionally, and by 1900 this fishery was following the Spitsbergen and eastern Arctic bowhead fisheries in the history of its decline. From 1848 until 1915, some 20,000 bowheads were killed in the western Arctic, an average of about 300 per year. Most of these whales were killed during the earlier years of the fishery; the numbers diminished dramatically toward the end of the nineteenth century, as the whale stocks declined (Bockstoce 1978c).

In 1907 the price of baleen fell from $5.00 to less than 50¢ per pound. A new product, spring steel, had been developed, and it quickly replaced the more exotic and expensive whalebone. Thus ended the last phase of commercial whaling for the bowhead, except for the Scots, who needed the oil for the manufacture of jute in Dundee. The whalers *Morning* and *Balaena* left Dundee for the eastern Arctic in 1913 and returned home "clean," that is, without any oil at all. The following year, the *Arctic* returned to Scotland without so much as seeing a whale. The bowhead had been eradicated or seriously depleted wherever whalers could find it. For perhaps half a century now, the whale has been left in peace, in hopes that it may rebuild its decimated numbers. The last of the bowhead whales inhabit the high northern Arctic, where only the Eskimos hunt them.

Eskimos have pursued the bowhead for at least 3,500 years. The whale has been a source of food in their subsistence economy and provided an unbroken continuation of their ancient traditions. When the species was legally protected in 1935 by the International Convention, the Eskimos were allowed to take those whales they needed for food. Paragraph 7 of the International Whaling Convention of 1946, revised in 1975, reads in part, "the taking of gray or right whales by aborigines . . . is permitted, but only when the meat and products of such whales are to be used exclusively for local consumption by the aborigines." The Marine Mammal Protection Act of 1972 (MMPA) has a similar clause (Section 101b), allowing "any Indian, Aleut or Eskimo who dwells on the coast of the North Pacific Ocean" to take bowhead whales, *if the taking is not accomplished in a wasteful manner.* It is hard to imagine Eskimos taking whales in a wasteful manner, since the hunting of the bowhead is a difficult, uncomfortable task, involving the dangers of small-boat whaling in icy waters and the task of towing of the huge carcass to shore so that it can be butchered before the meat spoils. The blubber, once the main object of the fishery, is hardly used at all. Some of it is eaten raw as *muktuk* by the Eskimos, but most of it is left at the butchering site (Marquette 1977).

From the decline of the commercial fishery in Alaska until 1960, the average annual bowhead catch of the Eskimos was about fifteen whales. The whales were hunted by traditional methods, supplanted by the adoption of innovations introduced by the whalers. The Eskimos were now using darting guns and bomb lances, explosive devices that made it possible to shoot the whale from the shore ice or from a boat without having to ride up on its back and stab it with a harpoon. Even with this advanced technology, the Eskimos did not kill very many whales.

By 1970, however, the picture began to change. This time it is not only the whales that are threatened; there have been arguments to the effect that the Eskimos' heritage is at stake or that the future of the world's remaining whales depends on the outcome of this situation. Money from the Alaska pipeline began to arrive on the North Slope and, with it, the ill winds of change. Whereas only the village elders could captain a whale boat in the past, now the younger men, flush with their earnings from Alaska's new industry, could take to whaling, the most prestigious activity for an Eskimo male. The number of whaling crews has increased dramatically. At Barrow, where twenty-five crews participated in spring hunting in 1971, thirty-six crews were operating in 1976. Other villages, such as Niuqsut and Kaktovik (Barter Island), began to hunt bowheads in the fall, adding to the totals.

Modern equipment notwithstanding, Eskimo whaling is remarkably inefficient, and the clause of the MMPA that refers to "taking whales in a wasteful manner" has become extremely important. There are various estimates on the number of whales "killed and recovered" versus those "struck and lost," but even the most conservative allow for 1 whale lost for every 1 brought to the ice. (There is a third category, "killed but lost," which is understandably difficult to incorporate into statistics, since these whales are almost never reported.) In 1976 a total of 48 whales were killed at various Alaskan villages during the spring and fall hunts. During this same period 43 whales were known to be killed but lost or they were struck and lost. (There is no way of knowing how many of the whales that are struck and lost will survive, but we are not talking about whales struck with old-fashioned harpoons. These whales are struck with bombs that explode inside their bodies, and they may take a long time to die.) The 1976 total, therefore, is possibly as high as 91 bowheads killed, far in excess of the food requirements of the Eskimos—for each whale may have ten to twenty tons of meat—and also in excess of the recovery abilities of a limited population of whales. In the spring hunt of 1977, the largest in Eskimo history, 26 whales were killed and recovered; another 78, struck and lost.

As a result there was a political battle at the International Whaling Commission in London in June 1977. At that time the IWC voted unanimously (with the United States abstaining) to reduce the aboriginal bowhead catch to zero. The ensuing furor brought the issue boiling before the American public, which quickly polarized on the basis of emotional oversimplifications of what were very complicated issues. The preservationists of whales claimed that the Eskimos were wantonly slaughtering whales and using snowmobiles, caterpillar tractors, outboard motors, C.B. radios, and hand grenades in an all-out war on the whales. The prowhaling arguments defended the traditional customs of the Eskimos and their need for food, all the while arguing that the animals were not as endangered as the conservationists said they were. The defenders of the whales also argued that allowing anyone to hunt them in American waters was in direct opposition to the U.S. position on whaling: the American delegation has supported the idea of a ten-year moratorium on all whaling, a position that has been defeated annually and perhaps been compromised by the bowhead situation. The most critical argument concerned the number of whales. If there are so few whales left that the Eskimo hunting will endanger the species, then there seems to be no question that the species ought to be saved, even if the Eskimos' traditions are sacrificed.

Since that London meeting, there was a special convention in December 1977, at which the IWC reinstated a limited bowhead hunt for 1978 with quotas of 12 whales killed and landed or 18 whales struck, whichever came first.

We do not know how many bowheads are left in Arctic waters. Estimates range from "low hundreds" (Sergeant and Hoek 1974), to 1,000 (Fay 1975), up to "4,000–5,000," which Rice (1974) figured to be the total bowhead population for the western Arctic between 1868 and 1884, when "an estimated average of 219 whales were killed each year (excluding 1871 and 1876 when most of the fleet was lost in the ice)." McVay (1979) calculated "approximately 18,000 whales, give or take 4,000 whales," as the size of the original Western Arctic bowhead population and stated that "the current estimate, approximately 2,264 . . . is only 12 percent of the unexploited population." In the most recent study, Bockstoce and Botkin (1980), using a study of logbook records from 1848 to 1914, suggested that the total number of bowheads in the year 1847—before Captain Roy's discovery of the whale stocks north of the Bering Straits—was "approximately 30,000, and was no less than 20,000 and no more than 40,000." Bockstoce and Botkin further conclude that the population remaining at the end of commercial bowhead whaling (in 1913, when the last of the Dundee whalers returned home "clean") was perhaps 4,000 bowheads. From that time until today, the only hunters of the bowhead in the western Arctic have been the Eskimos.

The controversy surrounding the past and present numbers of bowheads seems destined to continue. Braham and Krogman (1977) regard Rice's 1974 conclusion as "not a likely figure," and as soon as the exhaustive, computer-enhanced 1980 report of Bockstoce and Botkin was released, the validity of its methodology and conclusions was under attack. A measure of the difficulty inherent in this situation can be seen in this summary by Bockstoce and Botkin:

Estimating the changes in the relative abundance of the bowhead from 1848 to 1914 is the most difficult of all the tasks we have attempted. If the life-history characteristics of the bowhead whale were accurately known . . . then estimates of the changes in the size of the bowhead population would be a relatively straightforward problem. . . . Unfortunately, the bowhead is among the least studied of all large mammals, and we know little if anything about its primary life-history characteristics.

Whatever the number, the population cannot sustain any more major losses. The compromise solution of the IWC satisfies neither the Eskimos nor the conservationists. Further, these isolated leviathans need all the protection they can get, not only from the Eskimos with their darting guns, but from another, far more significant danger that now threatens them: there are oil lease sites in Norton, Hope, and Beaufort basins, areas that are now thought to be the breeding grounds of the bowhead whales (Braham and Krogman 1977).

A major oil spill, which would cover the seas with oil, could only be harmful to the whales and their food organisms. Although it seems to be happening far from civilization and therefore far from our awareness, the potential destruction of the whales' habitat is probably the most insidious of all threats to their future. If we can actually destroy a part of the ocean so that whales and other creatures cannot live there, then no place on earth is safe from man's destructive potential.

The conflict between the U.S. Government and the Alaskan Eskimos threatens to deteriorate further. At the 1979 IWC meeting (where the Eskimos were represented by their own organization, the Alaska Eskimo Whaling Commission), the bowhead quota was set at 48 animals. The hunting was so poor, however, that the Eskimos could not reach that number, and the problem was once again deferred. We cannot expect a resolution of this complex problem that will be satisfactory to both sides, and the further polarization of the participants appears inevitable. As Bockstoce (1980) points out:

Conventional law enforcement is, of course, based on general acceptance of laws and a disapproval of law-breaking. In the bowhead problem, however, the government confronts a society that has, on this issue, lost most of whatever confidence it once had in the government; to many Eskimos the issue is increasingly seen as racial. Some law enforcement officials concede that it would be exceedingly difficult to enforce any laws regarding whaling in northern Alaska.

Studies of the cultural and economic requirements of the Eskimos, such as Milan's 1980 report to the Department of the Interior, indicate that the bowhead is an important element in the culture of the Arctic Eskimo, not only providing food but also substantially contributing to "technical, cultural and spiritual activities." Because the gray whale has recovered to former population levels and also inhabits roughly the same habitat as the endangered bowhead, the suggestion has been made that the Eskimos substitute gray whales for bowheads. This idea has met with little enthusiasm. The Eskimos claim that the meat of the gray whale does not taste as good; that the skin, instead of being smooth and easily eaten (as *muktuk*), is covered with barnacles and other parasites; and that

the autumn arrival of the gray in the waters of the Chukchi Sea is inimical to their traditional spring whale festival.

The eastern bowhead was once so plentiful that Scoresby could write: "such a novel enterprise as the capture of whales which was rendered practical and even easy by the numbers in which they were found. . . . " There are still some bowheads left in the eastern Arctic (Mitchell and Reeves 1980), in the Sea of Okhotsk (Berzin and Doroshenko 1980), and even in the eastern North Atlantic (Jonsgard 1964, 1980). But the only population large enough to save the species from total extinction—and even now there are those who believe it is too late—is the Bering Sea population, and these are the whales that are involved in the Eskimo-conservationist–oil company controversy. The other populations are poorly known and infrequently observed, and the salvation of the "great Polar whale" now lies in the hands of man. As we witness the inexorable decline of the species (see Braham and Breiwick 1980), we must once again take note of our responsibilities to those creatures that cohabit with us this fragile planet.

PYGMY RIGHT WHALE

Caperea marginata Gray 1846

The pygmy right whale is the smallest whale with baleen and one of the world's most unfamiliar cetaceans. It is known to reach a maximum length of 21 feet (6.4 meters), but this figure may not represent the actual maximum length, since so few specimens have been examined. According to one survey, there have been seventy-one known individuals (Ross et al. 1975). *Caperea marginata* is dark above and light below. There are about 230 ivory-white baleen plates per side, but they have a dark outer margin (from which the name *marginata* is probably derived), which makes the baleen appear brown in the whale's mouth. Although this species has a small, falcate dorsal fin, which the other right whales do not, it is classified with the Balaenidae because of its long, flexible baleen, the absence of throat grooves, and the fusion of the seven neck vertebrae.

Based on the infrequent observations of the pygmy right whale at sea, it exhibits none of the behavior—lifting flukes, rolling, or "breaching"—of its large

Southern Hemisphere relative, the southern right whale. The small size, black coloring, and presence of a hooked dorsal fin make it quite probable that the species would often be mistaken for a minke whale. Davies and Guiler (1957) pointed out that the two species are similar in silhouette when seen from a distance of only 330 feet (100 meters). Minke whales in the Southern Hemisphere are often found without the white flipper stripe that characterizes the northern forms; this fact would increase the possibility of confusing the two smallest whalebone whales at sea. Beached specimens should be easy to distinguish; the minke has the throat grooves characteristic of the balaenopterids and exhibits short baleen plates that are usually whitish in color, but may be interspersed with some darker plates in the southern forms. In contrast, the pygmy right has no throat grooves, a dorsal fin, and long baleen plates.

This little whale is so rare that any observations of free-swimming individuals represent significant contributions to the knowledge of its habits. In South African waters a few pygmy right whales have been sighted, usually swimming slowly and not displaying a prominent spout, and one animal has been filmed un-

derwater. From this film, taken at Plettenberg Bay, South Africa, in December 1967, Ross and colleagues observed that the whale displayed an "extensive flexing . . . of the entire body" while swimming, as opposed to the usual cetacean locomotive action of moving only the posterior portion of the body and the flukes. This specimen, which eventually swam away, also showed a number of long parallel scars on the flanks, the origin of which was quite mysterious. Wrote the authors, "it is difficult to envisage an animate or inanimate object capable of causing such wounds."

Pygmy right whales are rarely seen at sea, and it has been suggested (Davies and Guiler 1957) that they remain submerged for long periods of time. Another factor contributing to the idea of the animal's long time between breaths is its curious osteology, in which the ribs, which number seventeen pairs (more than any other whalebone whale), extend very far back toward the tail, where "they must provide an almost continuous protection for the underlying viscera" (Norman and Fraser 1938). It has also been suggested that the number and shape of the ribs—those toward the rear are almost spatulate at the ends—"may be

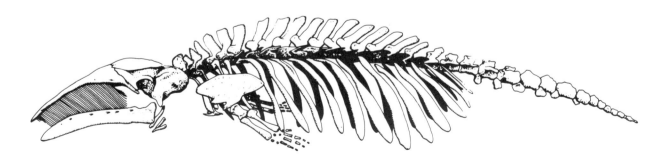

Skeleton of the pygmy right whale, *Caperea marginata,* showing the unusually wide and numerous ribs.

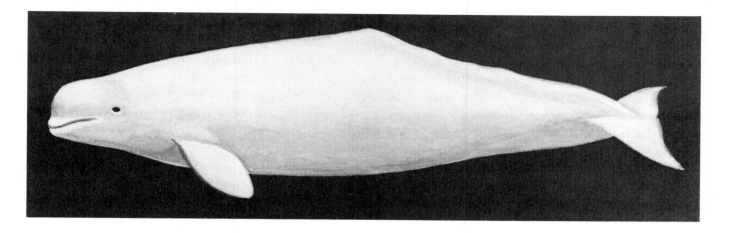

related to deep diving" (Kellogg 1940), because they might allow for greater lung expansion, but cetologists now believe that the pygmy right whale is not a deep-diving animal, nor does it spend inordinate amounts of time lying on the bottom. Most observations of the species have occurred in shallow water—the Plettenberg Bay film was made in water that was about 20 feet (6 meters) deep—and stranded animals, which make up most of the known records, are most often found "in bays with shoaling waters where extensive mud flats or sand spits are exposed at low tide" (Aitken 1971). If there is a reason for the numerous and strangely shaped ribs in this species, it has still not been discovered.

From the examination of a stranded, pregnant animal (Guiler 1961), it is believed that the species' movement into shallower waters may be associated with pregnancy or parturition. Otherwise, very little is known of its seasonal movements. Its diet consists of copepods, and "it might be expected that the distribution pattern would be similar to that of the plankton where it occurs in exploitable quantities" (Ross et al. 1975). The distribution pattern of this species has been deduced from strandings and infrequent sightings of live animals. The pygmy right whale is found only in the Southern Hemisphere, in a generally circumpolar distribution from 30°S to 50°S, and it has not been observed in waters south of the Antarctic Convergence. Specimens have been recorded from South Africa, southern Australia, New Zealand, Tasmania, and various locations in the South Atlantic, such as the Falkland and Crozet islands.

It is possible to list every known occurrence of this species, including beached animals and positive field identifications, and still to produce a list of less than a hundred records. In 1940, Remington Kellogg wrote, "Pygmy right whales are either few in numbers or their habits are such that they are rarely seen by whalers." This situation has not changed much, for in 1972, D. E. Gaskin concluded his brief description of the species with this plea: "Since this is such an unusual and little-known species, I would like in conclusion to entreat any reader who comes across a stranded specimen, to contact the nearest university or museum at once and to make every effort to preserve the body from damage until a biologist can examine it."

BELUGA

Delphinapterus leucas Pallas 1776

The beluga is a robust, medium-sized white whale with a rounded, prominent forehead and a ridge on the back in place of the dorsal fin. The name *Delphinapterus* means "dolphin without a fin" and is derived from the Greek *apteron* ("wingless"). *Leukos* is Greek for "white." Unlike its very close relative, the narwhal, the beluga has a normal complement of teeth, numbering eight to ten on each side of each jaw, or about forty in all. In juveniles the teeth are sharply pointed, but they become chiseled down or flattened with age. Full-grown males are larger than full-grown females, reaching a maximum length of 18 feet (5.5 meters) and a weight of 3,500 pounds (1,575 kilograms), but most animals are smaller. Females average between 13 and 14 feet (3.9–4.2 meters). The flippers of the beluga are broad and almost rhomboidal in shape. In 1943, V. D. Vladykov observed that as the animals mature, the flippers show a marked tendency to curve upward at the tips; and, in fact, this upturning, most apparent in old males, can be so pronounced "that hunters, after killing the old males, often used it as a handle to pull the Beluga out of the water."

There is a noticeable constriction behind the small head, giving the animal a feature that can be described only as a neck. The beluga and the narwhal are placed into a separate family because of the arrangement of the seven vertebrae of the neck, which are not fused together, as they are in many other species of cetaceans. Belugas have demonstrated a great flexibility of the neck, particularly with regard to lateral movements. (There have not been corresponding observations of narwhals, but narwhals are not common in captivity, and belugas are.) The name "beluga" is said to come from the Russian *belii* (or *byely*), which means "white." Some prefer to use the name "belukha," a minor variation, but one that differentiates the whale from the beluga that is responsible for caviar: the giant sturgeon of the Caspian and Black seas, *Huso huso.*

Its unique coloring and restricted boreal (northern) habitat make it almost impossible to confuse this species with any other. Both young narwhals and young belugas are dark gray, but the adult narwhal is heavily spotted, in contrast to the adult beluga, which is creamy white. Narwhals and belugas share three characteristics that may be interpreted as Arctic adaptations: they have no dorsal fin, which may be beneficial to animals that must swim around and under floating ice; they have thick skin; and they have thick blubber. (These last two make them particularly desirable prey

species to another Arctic inhabitant, the Eskimo. Leather and *muktuk* are made from the skin, and the blubber is rendered into oil.)

At birth a 5-foot (1.5-meter) beluga calf is a dark mouse-brown, soon changing to a bluish gray. As the animal matures, the color gradually lightens, until about the sixth year, when the animal attains the white adult coloration (Brodie 1971). In mature adults the only part that is not white is the trailing edge of the flukes, which may be grayish. The eyes of a beluga are brown. Males reach sexual maturity at about 8 years of age and females at 5. From analysis of growth layers on the teeth it has been estimated that the "maximal duration of life is about . . . 25 years in both sexes" (Sergeant 1973).

Its diet consists of large fish such as flounder and cod, but wherever smaller fish such as capelin or sand lance are plentiful, the beluga feeds on these (Vladykov 1947). Examination of stomach contents has disclosed nereid worms, as well as sand and stones, indicating a bottom-feeding propensity (Doan and Douglas 1953), The beluga has no beak, but it does have a pair of flexible lips that would be helpful in the consumption of bottom-dwelling species, and there is recent evidence that they use strong suction when feeding (Sergeant, personal communication). "When making prey of such bottom fish as the flounder and the halibut," wrote Scammon in 1874, "it often darts into shallows where it can hardly float; but . . . it

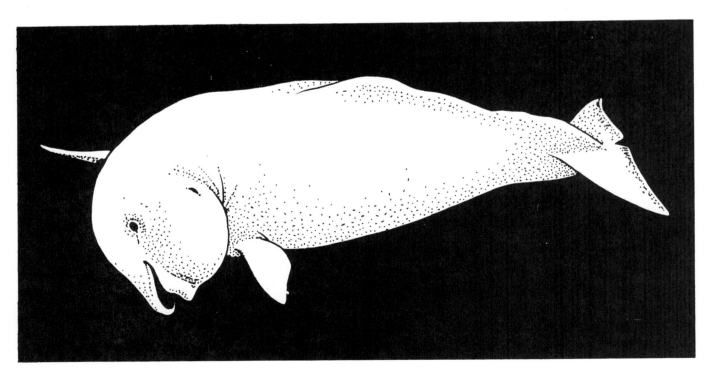

Flexibility of the neck of the beluga, *Delphinapterus leucas.*

92

evinces no alarm at its situation, and makes but little effort to reach a greater depth." In the area of the Kvichak River, Alaska, which supports "the greatest run of red salmon, *Oncorhynchus nerka,* in the world" (Fish and Vania 1971), the beluga swims upstream to feed on the plentiful smolts (young salmon at the stage when they migrate from fresh water to the sea).* Other food items include various species of fish, squid, shrimp, and crabs.

Insofar as variety of phonations is concerned (as opposed to volume), the beluga is probably the noisiest of all cetaceans. Early whalers actually called them "sea-canaries." Scammon, who could hear them only from the surface, claimed that they made a noise like "the faint lowing of an ox," and others referred to the various sounds of the beluga as bird calls, mooing, deep sighing and gnashing of teeth, grunting of pigs, badly played musical glasses, and the noise produced by vigorously shaking a large tin tray (Fish and Mowbray 1962). According to Tomilin (1957), the Russians "in the North" have a proverbial expression for one who is making too much noise: "screaming like a Beluga." With the advent of underwater listening devices, the full repertoire of this "canary" could be appreciated. In 1949, Schevill and Lawrence suspended a hydrophone overboard at Tadoussac, Quebec, where the Saguenay River flows into the Saint Lawrence. Although the belugas were never closer to their boat than two hundred yards, they recorded "high-pitched resonant whistles and squeals, varied with ticking and clucking sounds, slightly reminiscent of a string orchestra tuning up, as well as mewing and occasional chirps. Occasionally the calls would suggest a crowd of children shouting in the distance. At times there were sharp reports, somewhat like a blow with a split bat or a slap on the water." Describing this submarine chorus, Schevill and Lawrence wrote, "this loquaciousness contrasts markedly with most terrestrial herd mammals and compares with such chatterboxes as monkeys and men." In a study of the effects of sounds played back to wild and captive animals (in the Saguenay River and the New York Aquarium), Morgan (1979) identified the following sound types: "barks, squawks, jaw claps, whistles, squawls, buzzes, whinnys, and chirps." He also recorded a "long, loud whistle" and various combinations of all these sounds.

*A unique experiment was carried out there in an attempt to prevent the salmon population from being decimated by the predacious belugas. Underwater recordings of the sounds of killer whale phonations were broadcast as the belugas began to ascend the river. On hearing the recorded "screams" of the killers, the belugas immediately turned and headed back to the sea (Fish and Vania 1971).

When in the presence of killer whales, however, it was observed that the belugas became silent (Cummings and Thompson 1971). The shape of the prominent forehead of the beluga can be changed at will by muscular contractions. It is thought that this is an "acoustical lens" that enables the beluga (and some other species of odontocetes) to focus their echolocating clicks directionally. Belugas are not particularly fast swimmers, and they are not known to jump out of the water. The beluga is an extremely gregarious animal, sometimes seen in aggregations that may number in the thousands, but smaller groups of twenty to two hundred are more common. In small groups they sometimes "swim in parallel lines, a yet unexplained form of behaviour in these social whales" (Sergeant and Hoek 1973).

Like the narwhal, the beluga is restricted to Arctic waters, but its range is much greater. It is completely circumpolar in the high Arctic latitudes, found in the Arctic Ocean, in the Bering Sea, off the coast of Alaska south to the Aleutians, and in the Sea of Ohkotsk; in the eastern Canadian Arctic, particularly the Hudson Bay and Baffin Island regions; off Greenland; and in the White, Barents, and Kara seas of the Soviet Arctic. In the warmer months belugas move into protected waters of rivers and estuaries for calving as well as feeding. Their movements are also determined by the pack ice, since they will try to avoid being trapped when the leads close up. Where the water remains open year-round, as it does at James Bay, it seems reasonable to assume that the belugas do not migrate (Jonkel 1969). It is thought that there are separate stocks that live in various locations and do not integrate. Estimated numbers for the North American Arctic total some 30,000 animals: the largest herds (10,000-plus) in western Hudson Bay; at least as many in Lancaster Sound; and perhaps 5,000 in the Beaufort Sea (the Mackenzie River delta). The highly visible population of the Saint Lawrence River has been figured at about 500 individuals (Sergeant 1973).

Known populations in Alaskan waters are considerably smaller than those in the east and are segregated into smaller stocks of 500 to 1,500, usually seen on passage to or from the eastern Beaufort Sea, where there are few large rivers en route to attract them. Populations in the Soviet Arctic are known to be large, but the actual numbers are not available. Occasional specimens stray south of their Arctic range; isolated animals have been reported off Scotland, Ireland, France, and Buzzard's Bay, Massachusetts. In 1966 a single white whale swam 250 miles (400 kilometers) up the Rhine in Germany, and despite all efforts to capture it during a month in the river, it turned around and swam downstream to the North Sea and freedom (Slijper 1967). The southernmost record for the beluga was apparently set in July 1978 when two young animals, approximately 11 and 13 feet long, were sighted off Avalon, New Jersey. The two whales swam unconcernedly among boats and sport divers, and their identification was verified by various cetologists (Ulmer 1979). They soon left New Jersey waters, and were not seen there again. In the summer of 1979 another beluga was sighted in Fire Island Inlet, Long Island, New York, and it, too, ventured among the trappings of civilization. Possibly this whale was one of the previous year's visitors to New Jersey, and it might have overwintered somewhere offshore instead of making the long journey back to the eastern Canadian Arctic. The same whale, now recognizable by a scar on its back, was seen again in the spring of 1980, in Reynolds Channel, Great South Bay, Long Island.

In the Arctic the beluga is preyed on by the killer whale, and there have been numerous references and illustrations to document this threat. For example, the painting in the January 1975 issue of *Audubon* magazine shows killer whales attacking belugas, while the belugas unconcernedly feed on salmon—a highly unlikely occurrence, given the auditory sensitivity of the beluga and the known inclination of killer whales to "scream." (In a 1966 study, Schevill and Watkins recorded sounds they described as "strident screams" from killer whales.) Tomilin included a record of an attack by a pack of killer whales on belugas, "which were torn to pieces in such a manner that a large expanse of water was shiny with grease." Other observers have commented that the white whale becomes immobilized at the appearance of killers, but acoustic experiments indicate that flight is the typical reaction to the approach of killer whales. When the ice closes up, a situation known as a *savssat* in Greenland, belugas and other cetaceans are sometimes trapped. Besides the ice and the killer whales, we are the only other enemies of the belugas.

For thousands of years we have hunted the beluga. There is no record of the first Eskimo's realization that this animal represented a source of badly needed subsistence supplies, such as oil, meat, bone, skin, and *muktuk.* Although the Eskimos hunted the beluga extensively, it was not their basic resource. The ringed seal could be caught year-round, whereas the appearance of the beluga was seasonal.

European settlers in North America soon discovered the economic importance of this animal, which was predictable in its habits and occurrence and fairly easy to kill. As early as 1688, a resolution was passed by the Hudson's Bay Company "that the Churchill River be settled this yeare with a good shipp and a competent cargo for trade and materials for white whale fisheries" (Doan and Douglas 1953). In the centuries that followed, the white whale was harvested in Spitsbergen and Russia, as well as various Canadian locations. From 1870 to 1910, Scottish whalers hunted the beluga in the areas of Baffin Bay, East Greenland, and the Davis Straits, sometimes taking over 3,000 animals per year. In 1916, Roy Chapman Andrews wrote, "the white porpoise or white whale as it is more usually called, is not only the most beautiful, but also one of the most important members of the family, for it is this animal which furnishes most of the porpoise hide and porpoise oil of commerce." A drive fishery (to which belugas are particularly vulnerable) was operating at Cumberland Sound, Baffin Island, in the 1920s, and Eskimos are still hunting the white whales there, despite severe reduction in numbers (Sergeant and Brodie 1975). The plentiful white whales of Hudson Bay supported two distinct fisheries, one at Churchill, where the whales were chopped up, frozen, and shipped west to mink ranches in the Prairie Provinces, and another at Whale Cove, Northwest Territories, where *muktuk* was canned for human consumption.

By 1970 the discovery of high levels of mercury in the meat of the white whales signaled the end of their exploitation by the Canadians for commercial purposes. In the late 1960s a bizarre attempt was made by the Manitoba government to encourage sport hunting for whales at Churchill—"the latest thing for the sportsman who has done everything"—but this was banned in 1973 for humane reasons (Sergeant and Brodie 1975). White whales are now hunted in Soviet waters, where the annual catch has been estimated at 3,000–4,000 animals (Mitchell 1975b), and in the Canadian Arctic, where about 500 whales are killed each year. Recent studies have produced no evidence that the total population is threatened by these harvests (Mitchell 1975b; Sergeant and Brodie 1975).

Much of what we know about the biology and behavior of white whales has come from the observation of captive specimens. The first attempts to exhibit them were made in the late nineteenth century, when, in successive years, two specimens captured in Labrador were shipped to London in hopes that they might be exhibited at the Westminister Aquarium. The first specimen, brought over in 1877, died two days after its arrival, and in 1878 the second animal was shipped over "in a packing case filled with seaweed. *Five weeks* elapsed between the animal's capture and its return to its natural element in the Aquarium" (Norman and Fraser 1938; my italics). It is extraordinary that the animal could have survived for so long in transit, since we have only recently begun to learn about the requirements of cetaceans out of water, and the time thus spent is usually measured in hours, not weeks. Two specimens were brought from Rivière-du-loup, Quebec, again in seaweed-filled boxes, to the New York Aquarium in 1897, but they lasted only a few weeks (New York Zoological Society 1903). In 1961, Carleton Ray of the New York Aquarium led an expedition to the Kvichak River in southern Alaska, where three juvenile belugas were captured; and after being transported to the New York Aquarium, they became the first white whales successfully maintained in captivity (Ray 1961). (One of these whales, named Alex, is living at the Mystic Marinelife Aquarium in Connecticut, some nineteen years after his capture.)

There have been two belugas born in captivity, one at the New York Aquarium and the second at the Vancouver Public Aquarium. The New York specimen, which was conceived in the aquarium, lived only a few minutes before it smashed into the side of the tank and died of a cerebral hemorrhage. The baby in Vancouver, born to a beluga that was pregnant when captured, lived for sixteen weeks before it succumbed to a bacterial infection. Although there is hardly enough information to provide a statistical sample, it is interesting to note that both white whale births were headfirst, in contrast to the numerous observed births of the bottlenose dolphin, in which the baby is born tailfirst. From the bottlenose births (and one observed delivery of a common dolphin), it was assumed that "there is a fluke presentation prior to parturition. This is very important when giving birth under water; the infant's head is exposed to water at the very last moment, and this minimizes the danger of drowning with the first breath" (Yablakov 1974). However, Tomilin wrote that "the blowhole opens up normally only after the newborn animal has sensed a change of environment. Subsequently, the respiratory act (expiration) does not begin as a rule until the animal has broken the surface of the water." Even though there have been a far greater number of tailfirst births observed (as of 1976, over 100 bottlenose dolphins had been born in captivity), the births of the belugas should cause us to question the popular assumption that whales must be born tailfirst.

NARWHAL

Monodon monoceros Linnaeus 1758

The narwhal is a mottled cetacean that can measure up to 15 feet (4.6 meters) in length, not including the "horn" in males, which can add another 8–9 feet (2.5–2.7 meters) to the total. A full-grown male may weigh 3,000 pounds (1,350 kilograms). Adult females are smaller than males, attaining a length of about 13 feet (4.0 meters) and a weight of perhaps 2,000 pounds (900 kilograms). Whereas most other whales and dolphins have a dorsal fin, the narwhal has a low, bumpy ridge that begins at about the midpoint of the back and continues to the flukes.* The flukes have a unique convex curve to the rear margin, and in mature adults the flippers turn up at the ends.

The narwhal is heavily spotted, exhibiting what Melville called "a very picturesque leopard-like look, being of a milk-white ground color, dotted with round and oblong spots of black." Because the pattern comprises white spots on the dark areas and dark spots on the lighter regions, there is a confusion about the animals' actual coloration, especially in mature males. Newborn narwhals are dappled gray-brown in color, so it is natural to assume that the white spots appear as the animal matures, leading to "old males that are almost white" (Norman and Fraser 1938). In a 1975 study, however, it was stated that "at maturity the body becomes almost white ventrally and black dorsally. . . . the contrast in dorsal and ventral coloration is most pronounced in old males" (Mansfield et al. 1975). There is obviously a considerable amount of variation in the coloration of these animals, and it is probably related to age. Adult males and females are usually dark in the area of the head, especially the "melon" and the upper and lower jaws. The mouth of the narwhal is small, and it turns up, giving the animal a permanent smile.

The "horn," which is, in fact, an enormously elongated tooth, is almost always present in males, and there are infrequent records of a female with a tusk. In rare instances a narwhal with two protruding tusks has been taken (Clark 1871), but usually the males have a single spiral tooth on the left side of the skull.

*Randall Reeves, an authority on the narwhal, has pointed out (1976a) that three Arctic whales—the bowhead, the beluga, and the narwhal—do not have a dorsal fin, because such a fin might interfere with movement in icy areas. There are, of course, any number of cetaceans that inhabit polar waters that do have a dorsal fin, including the killer whale, which has the largest fin of any cetacean.

The tooth always spirals in a right-to-left (counter-clockwise) direction, as the whale would see it; and even when there are two tusks, they both spiral in the same direction. Narwhals have no other visible teeth in their jaws (females have no functional teeth at all), but vestigial teeth are often embedded in the upper jaws of males and females (Fraser 1938).

The scientific name, *Monodon monoceros,* can be translated to mean "one tooth, one horn." (*Keras* is Greek for "horn.") The name "narwhal" comes from the Norwegian *narhval* and means "corpse whale." It is usually assumed that this name is derived from the mottled coloration, which suggests a bloated corpse, but an alternative interpretation refers to the animals' habit of swimming belly up. The whiteness and swollen appearance of the narwhal in this attitude may also have contributed to the Norwegian name. Still another possible derivation can be found in a 1643 history from Iceland: Arnhald, the first bishop of that country, was shipwrecked there in 1126 and found himself in a marsh known as the Pool of Corpses, where the bodies of sailors had washed ashore. At the same location there were found many "teeth of whales," which had also come ashore. These *dentes balenarum* were the tusks of narwhals. The name of the animal may have come from the name of this location.

In the Arctic waters that make up the sole habitat of the narwhal, there is only one other animal of similar size with which it might be confused. The beluga also has no dorsal fin, and its young are dark gray or brown, but there the resemblance ends: Adult belugas are snow-white and bear no markings at all.

Narwhals are gregarious animals, usually seen in small groups of up to twenty, but they sometimes form much larger aggregations of up to two thousand. The smaller groups—perhaps some sort of family or breeding segregations—have been observed to have one tusked male per group (Ford and Fisher 1978). Individuals of all ages are seen in these groups; this has led to the erroneous assumption that narwhals have no particular breeding season (Vibe 1950). In fact, most births occur in the summer months, when the fjords and bays are free of ice and the females can take refuge in these protected areas (Best and Fisher 1974). After a fourteen-to-fifteen-month gestation period a 5-foot (1.5-meter) dark brown calf is born, and it remains close to its mother for as long as twenty months.

Narwhals usually loaf along, slowly breathing and rolling, but when pursued, they are remarkably fast swimmers. Scoresby (1820) wrote that they "are quick, active inoffensive animals. They swim with considerable velocity. When respiring at the surface, they frequently lay motionless for several minutes, with their backs and heads just appearing above the water." Narwhals seem to have no particular predisposition to swim with the dorsal surface uppermost; they are often seen swimming on their sides and sometimes upside down. There is even a record of narwhals swimming vertically: the only sighting of copulation described the animals as "vertically in the water, their bellies turned towards each other" (Vibe 1950).

The narwhal has been accused of making all sorts of noises, from shrill whistles to "a deep growl or groan, something like a bear or cow" (Burn Murdoch 1917). In 1975, J. B. MacInnis went to northern Baffin Island to search for and film narwhals. He wrote (1976), "Suddenly we heard a sound. It was a low whistling chorus as if the earth was breathing. . . . We heard a score of ocean voices, their easy inhalation and exhalation indicating related animals swimming in time." Because they are closely related to the very vocal beluga (together they comprise the family *Monodontidae*), narwhals were expected to be noisy animals. (In 1969, Norris wrote, "Although no definitive evidence exists for echolocation in the subfamily *Monodontidae* . . . it is reasonable to expect it.") After recording a group of narwhals off Baffin Island, Watkins and colleagues (1971) commented that "*Monodon* is much less noisy [than the beluga] and appears to have a smaller

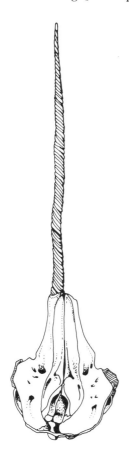

Dorsal view of the skull of a male narwhal, showing the single tooth and asymmetrical bone development.

variety of sounds." They recorded "clicks and squeals, with the clicks in a high-frequency range entirely out of the range of human hearing." Subsequent investigations (Ford and Fisher 1978) have identified the same vocabulary, but these researchers also heard whistles and remarked that "the animals were extremely loquacious under water."

The function of the male's long, twisted, hollow tusk has long been a subject for speculation. Among the suggestions for its use are the following: as an icebreaker or an instrument to poke breathing holes in the ice; as a rake to stir up the sea bottom in search of food; as a skewer to impale prey species; or as a weapon for fighting rival males or defending against predators. Some of these suggestions can be rejected out of hand: narwhals have been seen breaking the ice with the "thick and firm cushion on the upper side of the head" (Porsild 1918) and carefully avoiding getting the tusk in contact with the ice. They are not thought to be bottom feeders—although in some narwhal stomachs that were examined the contents have included skates and rays, certainly bottom-dwelling animals—so generally using the tusk to disturb the bottom would be unnecessary. And aside from the impossibility of removing a fish impaled on the end of an eight-foot tooth, this suggestion excludes females and juveniles, which seem to feed themselves without recourse to stabbing their food.

The thought of two male narwhals dueling is an intriguing one, as is the image of a narwhal joust, rivals charging each other from a distance, their tusks clashing underwater like medieval lances. Unfortunately for these romantic theories, narwhals are hardly ever found with the scars that would obviously result from such activities. There are, however, numerous records of broken tusks; Porsild (1922) examined 304 male narwhals; and of these, 107 tusks were broken. This might be attributable to fighting, although he reported that "fights have never been observed by Eskimos." His most unusual discovery was 4 broken tusks, in which the "*point of a smaller tusk is found thrust into the cavity and then broken off,*" as if one male approached another head-on, somehow inserted the point of his tusk into the broken tusk of his adversary, and then snapped the other's off. Porsild could offer no explanation for this curious phenomenon, but recent dental examinations of narwhal tusks has provided a much less dramatic explanation. "If the tusk breaks," wrote Newman (1978), "it is possible that infection is avoided because of dentine deposits which fill the broken end. This reparative function could explain descriptions by old whalers of narwhals with broken tusks exhibiting a 'plug' in the broken end." The high percentage of broken tusks would lend some credence to the idea of jousting males, and some cetologists believe this is the case. Nishiwaki (1972) stated, "to me the most acceptable hypothesis is that the long tooth is a weapon employed by males in fights to win females." Silverman and colleagues (1979) made numerous observations of male narwhals crossing tusks in what might be interpreted as "ritual fighting." In addition, one adult male had "the tip of a tusk, 9 cm long, embedded in its left upper jaw." These observations are unique, and their very rarity seems to support the idea of ritual—rather than aggressive—use of the tusk. Most scientists now believe that the tusk is "a secondary sex character which may play a part in aggressive male display" (Mansfield et al. 1975), although it may have an acoustic function as well.* When a captive male narwhal vocalized, "strong vibrations could be felt running down the tusk" (Ford and Fisher 1978).

The narwhal is a deep-water animal—Scoresby wrote that when harpooned, "it generally descends about 200 fathoms"—and its diet consists of various species of fish, especially the polar cod and the Greenland halibut, as well as various other fish, shrimps, and squid. Kellogg (1940) wrote that "fish are crushed between the jaws and swallowed without mastication, since there are no functional teeth." The narwhal has extremely thick blubber, as much as 4 inches thick in some places and perhaps 30–35 percent of the total body weight (Newman 1978). They are preyed upon by killer whales and perhaps by the Greenland shark. Tomilin (1957) has written that the tusk of the male "can be used to deliver frontal blows when the narwhal defends its young from Arctic sharks"; and Bigelow and Schroeder (1948) wrote, "their habit of gathering around whaling stations . . . or when there has been a big killing of narwhals in Greenland waters, is proverbial." The narwhal also has its own host-specific parasite, *Cyamus monodontis,* the narwhal louse.

In September 1969 a team of scientists flew to Ellesmere Island in Arctic Canada to examine and attempt to rescue an orphaned baby narwhal. The young male —named Umiak—was approximately 6 feet long and weighed about 250 pounds. It was being kept in a freshwater pond until preparations could be made to transport it to the New York Aquarium. Umiak was fed a formula of ground fish, milk, butterfat, and vitamins; and after traveling on numerous planes and trucks, he arrived at the New York Aquarium, where he was placed in a tank next to two adult belugas. (Intensive vocalizations were heard from the belugas, but no apparent sounds were made by the baby narwhal.) At one point the smaller of the two belugas was placed in the same tank with Umiak, but the white whale appeared to be frightened, so the "surrogate mother" approach was abandoned. After about six weeks in captivity, the baby died of malnutrition, complicated by pneumonia.*

In the spring of 1978 a young male narwhal with a 6-inch (15-centimeter) horn was trapped in the closing ice at Hall's Bay, Newfoundland, along with five humpback whales. For approximately a month the whales remained prisoners of the ice, and there was a strong suspicion that the whales were eating dead herring that were being fed to them by people in attendance. In April, following an unusually warm spell, the offshore winds opened an escape route, and the whales departed (Merdsoy et al. 1979: Beamish, personal communication).

The narwhal is considered the most northerly of all cetaceans. It is found throughout the Arctic Ocean, but it is most common in the North Atlantic region, especially northwestern Greenland and the eastern Canadian Arctic. The narwhal is also found in the waters of northern Alaska, but not in great numbers (Geist et al. 1960). It inhabits bays, fjords, and inlets in the warmer months, moving south into deeper water when the ice begins to form. "It seems as if the narwhal is always migrating in and out of fjords," wrote Vibe in 1950. In the area of northern Hudson Bay and Baffin Island the narwhal has been recorded from Jones and Lancaster sounds, Pond Inlet, Koluktoo and Frobisher bays, and Cape Dorset. It is particularly plentiful in western Greenland, where "all the

*Numerous horned animals use their horns not as weapons for actual fighting, but rather as symbols of rank; the animal with the longest (or widest) horns is the dominant male in the group. Writing of mountain sheep, Valerius Geist (1971) said, "Male dominance and breeding success run parallel with horn size, and rams use their horns not only as weapons or shields, but also as rank symbols." Perhaps the case that most closely parallels the narwhal's is that of the Irish elk. This animal did not use its twelve-foot antlers for fighting probably because it could not, since they were so awkward. Instead, it has been suggested that the huge deer merely displayed its antlers as "visual dominance-rank symbols" to rival bucks (Gould 1977). The Irish elk is comparable to the narwhal because neither species could effectively use the extreme overspecialization. Too, neither was ever observed in action—the Irish elk because it is extinct, and the narwhal because it is underwater.

*The details of this account have been provided by Dr. Jay Hyman, the marine mammal veterinarian who attended Umiak from Ellesmere Island to Coney Island.

meat and part of the blubber are still used for human consumption or for feeding the dogs" (Kapel 1977). In their southward migrations, narwhals have been recorded as far south as Labrador and Newfoundland. Although they have not been reported to strand frequently (probably because of their deep-water habitat and the occurrence of ice, which might melt and return stranded animals to the sea), there have been reports of beached animals off Labrador in the western North Atlantic and off England in the east. Two 13-foot females stranded in 1949 in southeastern England; one was thirty miles up the Thames estuary (Fraser 1974).

Since the earliest Norse traders made the tusk of the narwhal available in Europe, it has been most highly prized. At one time the tusks were said to be "worth ten times their weight in gold," according to Shepard (1967); and Bruemmer (1969) wrote, "A prince of Saxony paid 100,000 talers for a unicorn horn, and Charles V, Holy Roman Emperor, settled what would amount in present-day terms to a million-dollar debt to the Margrave of Beyreuth by presenting him with two unicorn horns." The long ivory shaft has been responsible to a great extent for the legend of the unicorn, although the dumpy little whale that actually grew the horn bears little resemblance to the wondrous beast of medieval heraldry and legend. When Martin Frobisher made his second voyage to the Canadian Arctic in the service of Queen Elizabeth I, he came upon

a great dead fish which, so it seemed, had been embalmed with ice. It was round like to a porpoise, being about twelve foot long and having a horn of two yards length growing out of the snout or nostrils. The horn is wreathed and straight, like in fashion to a taper made of wax, and may truly be thought to be the Sea Unicorn. This horn is to be reserved as a jewel by the Queen Majesty's Commandment, in her wardrobe of robes (Steffanson 1938).

The horn of the unicorn was supposed to have magical properties, including the quality of being able to detect and even counteract poison. It was also ground up and used as a potion "to overcome feminine modesty and resistance, to cure corns, heartburn and sore eyes, and for a variety of even more magical purposes" (Sanderson 1956). Numerous articles were made from the tapering shaft, including bishops' crosiers, walking sticks, drinking cups (if a pinch of ground alicorn could neutralize poison, a cup made entirely of this material would obviously render the user almost in-

vincible),* and even a throne. The anointment throne of the kings of Denmark at Rosenborg Castle, Copenhagen, has narwhal tusks as its numerous vertical elements.

The Eskimos have always hunted the narwhal, and in some areas, their entire existence depended on it. They use the oil, which is of a very high quality and burns without smoke; the meat mostly to feed sled dogs; the sinews for sewing; and the skin (*muktuk* or *matak*), an excellent source of vitamin C. (Vibe wrote that it is "very tasteful . . . almost like fresh hazelnuts"; and Newman said boiled *muktuk* "was soft, smelled quite good, and tasted like some other kind of seafood, perhaps lobster or steamed clams.") The horn was used to make tools or served as a trade item.

In recent times the advent of the snowmobile has eliminated much of the need for sled dogs—and, therefore, for dog food—and the Eskimos have found modern substitutes for sewing sinews and whale oil. The demand for the tusks, however, has risen as sharply as the demand for sinews has fallen, and more narwhals than ever are being killed. For the most part, the animals are shot from the shore or from boats as they surface to breathe, but they often sink when they are killed and cannot be retrieved in the deep, icy water. When the ice closes in and traps the animals, the killing becomes considerably easier. In Greenland when the animals are thus trapped in the ice, it is known as a *savssat* and becomes a cause for great celebration among the hunters. They wait by the hole until the animal surfaces and then shoot it and retrieve it with a harpoon. In the unusually cold winter of 1914–15, over 1,000 animals were killed at two *savssats* in Greenland; of these, more than 200 were tusk-bearing males (Porsild 1918).

In 1962, narwhal tusk ivory sold for $1.25 a pound; it was up to $25.00 in 1974 and to $35.00 in 1976 (Reeves 1976a). For entire tusks, collectors and decorators are willing to pay prices that seem to parallel the medieval craving to obtain an antipoison device. A horn was sold recently in New York for $4,500. The Marine Mammal Protection Act of 1972 has made it a federal offense to import whale products into the United States, so the market is for horns that are already in the country or for those that are smuggled in.

---

*At the base, the tusk is hollow and large enough to make a good-sized drinking cup. In the collection of Prince Takamatsu of Japan there are two "unicorn horns," one of which is 8 feet (247 centimeters) in length, and at the base its diameter is 8 inches (20.5 centimeters), about the size of an ordinary drinking glass (data from Nishiwaki 1969).

An eight-foot narwhal tusk is very difficult to hide in a suitcase.

A recent population study of narwhals has indicated that the mortality rate from hunting is higher than the estimated reproduction (Mansfield et al. 1975). In other words, the narwhal is being killed off faster than it can reproduce. The authors of this study recommended "a more efficient means of capturing the whales, such as netting," since an estimated 50 percent of the animals sink after they are shot. The Canadian government has imposed hunting restrictions on the Eskimos, but these laws, poorly enforced at best, may be inadequate to ensure the survival of the species. In addition, exploratory mining in the areas inhabited by the narwhals may pollute the waters and prove to be an even greater hazard to the species. Mansfield and associates estimated the total narwhal population for Canada and northwestern Greenland at about 10,000 animals; Newman quoted figures that are "up to two or three times" the earlier numbers. In the fragile and delicate Arctic environment, special care has to be taken to protect the endemic species. The real unicorn may, after all, join its mythical counterpart in extinction, and we will be left only with the magical horns.

SPERM WHALE

Physeter macrocephalus Linnaeus 1758

"The sperm whale," wrote Herman Melville (1851), "scientific or poetic, lives not complete in any literature. Far above all other hunted whales, his is an unwritten life." This is the most familiar of all whales; this is the image that comes to mind when the word "whale" is mentioned. But with the exception of the observation of some of its activities at the surface and the examination of the carcasses of dead animals, little is known of it. The sperm whale has been hunted longer than most of the whalebone whales—only the right whales and the humpback were hunted earlier—but we know almost nothing of its habits. We know what sperm whales look like, what they eat, and how much oil they can yield, but we don't know how they eat, why they move in such mysterious paths, or what purpose is served by the vast oil reservoir in the whale's head.*

It is this oil that gave the whale its common name. "Spermaceti"—later shortened to "sperm"—means "seed of the whale," because the mysterious clear oil in the head was presumed in earlier times to be the seminal fluid of the whale. *Physeter* means "blow" or "blowpipe" in Greek and refers, of course, to the spout. It is now believed that there is only one worldwide species of *Physeter,* but numerous other variations have been identified over the years, all given new and seemingly appropriate names. In an 1834 publication called *The Natural History of the Order Cetacea,* H. W. Dewhurst listed the following species: *P. macrocephalus, P. cetadon* [sic], *P. trumpo, P. cylindricus,* and *P. microps,* all of which are identifiable from the descriptions and illustrations as sperm whales, and *Physeter bidens sowerbyi,* which is the beaked whale now known as *Mesoplodon bidens.* The Dutch call the sperm whale *potvisch;* the Norwegians, *spermhval;* and the French, *cachalot,* from

*Although the portion of an animal's anatomy located at the anterior end is usually known as its head, the protrusion that characterizes this creature's external appearance is, in fact, its nose. All other cetaceans—except the curious little pygmy sperm whale—have the nostrils located on top of the head. The single breathing hole of the sperm whale is at the very tip of the protrusion, and there are distinct (though very unusual) nasal passages that run nearly the length of this organ. Raven and Gregory (1933) described it as "nothing more or less than a titanic nose, the greatest nose on record."

the Gascon *cachau* ("large tooth") (Norman and Fraser 1938). In Japanese the sperm whale is known as *Makko-kujira*, which means "like the color of *kô*, a powdered perfume which is burned at Buddhist funeral ceremonies" (Omura, personal communication).*

The sperm whale is black in color—or dark bluish gray, slate gray, or iron gray, depending on the description. When photographer William Curtsinger had the rare opportunity to see sperm whales underwater in the open ocean, he described the color this way: "The black was deep and rich next to the white pigments of their jaws, blacker than anything I'd ever seen or imagined" (Fadiman 1979). Most specimens, male and female, have some white on the body, usually on the underside in the genital and anal regions and on the lower jaw. These white or unpigmented areas are irregular and not necessarily symmetrical, consisting of spots, flecks, streaks, patches, and whorls. In many specimens the underside is lighter than the back or sides, but this trait is not consistent. Matthews (1938) illustrated a head-on view of an adult male

sperm whale with a lighter area on the flattened foremost portion of the head, calling it a "head-whorl." Some observers were of the opinion that lighter color on the head was an indication of age; Scammon (1874) referred to these animals as "vicious, gray-headed old Cachalots." Best and Gambell (1968) recorded head whorls in all sizes of animals killed off South Africa, but noted that "size seems to be an important factor in the development of the head whorl."

There have been all-white sperm whales recorded, although Moby-Dick was not one of them. In his description of the most famous of all sperm whales, Melville wrote, "he had a peculiar snow-white wrinkled forehead and a high pyramidal white hump. . . . the rest of his body was so streaked and spotted and marbled with the same shrouded hue, that, in the end, he had gained the distinctive appellation of the White Whale." (In other words, those portions of his anatomy that were visible as he swam at the surface were white.) Apparently, there was a white sperm whale, much given to counterattacks on whaleboats in the eastern North Pacific around the first half of the nineteenth century. This whale was called Mocha Dick, after the island off the coast of Chile at 38°28'S, known even today as Mocha Island. In an 1839 magazine article, which is held to be one of the primary sources for *Moby-Dick,* J. N. Reynolds described Mocha Dick as being "white as wool"; when the whale breached, he claimed, "the falling mass was white as a snow-drift!" In 1950, Japanese whalers caught a 50-foot (15-meter) male in the Antarctic with a white head, jaw, and ventral portion, and in 1957 a snow-white sperm whale was captured. It was a 35-foot (10.6-meter) male, "not so gigantic or grotesque as Moby Dick. If it had not been killed in young generation, it would have reigned

*The sperm whale is probably better known as *Physeter catodon,* but *P. macrocephalus* has recently been shown to be the correct name. The specific name *macrocephalus* means "big head," and its derivation is obvious. This name was originally employed by Linnaeus in 1758, and from that year to 1911 the species was known as *Physeter macrocephalus.* In a 1911 review of Linnaeus's nomenclature, Thomas "decided that *P. catodon* and *P. macrocephalus* were definitely synonymous and he accepted the name *P. catodon* for the species" (Husson and Holthuis 1974). The name *P. macrocephalus* had been uninterruptedly in use from 1758 to 1911, and Husson and Holthuis, in a comprehensive study of the synonymy of the species, concluded that "there seems to be no good reason not to apply the rules [of the International Code of Zoological Nomenclature] strictly here, and to adopt the name *P. macrocephalus.*" Rice, in the 1977 *List of the Marine Mammals of the World,* uses the name *macrocephalus,* citing Husson and Holthuis for authority. The junior synonym *P. catodon* comes from the Greek *kata* ("down") and *odous* ("tooth") and refers to the prominent teeth found in the lower jaw.

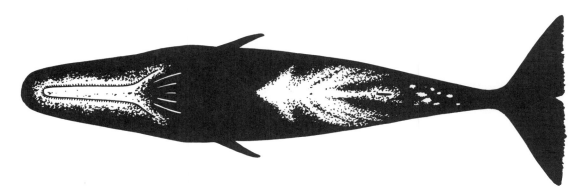

The highly variable ventral surface of the sperm whale, showing the white upper and lower jaws and the white "splashes" in the umbilical and genital areas. Notice throat grooves.

over the sea in [the] future like the ancestor Moby Dick" (Ohsumi 1958). In addition, there are Soviet records of "unusually light sperm whales with pinkish white eyes" (Berzin 1972).

Adult male sperm whales are much larger than females, reaching a maximum length of 62.32 feet (19 meters),* whereas the females do not get much beyond 40 feet (12.2 meters). Most contemporary writers do not extend their figures much beyond the 60-foot (18.24-meter) limit, but there were no such constraints on the earlier historians of the mighty sperm whale. Ashley (1926) mentioned a 90-foot specimen ("taken by the bark *Desdemona* in the late seventies"); Beale (1835) said that a full-grown male may be "about 80 feet"; and Bullen (1899) told of a whale "over seventy feet long." There is no question that the intensive hunting of sperm whales in recent years has resulted in a reduction of the average length of those whales taken (Jonsgard 1960), but it seems unlikely

that the largest bulls were much more than 62 feet long.

An old whaler's formula held that bull sperm whales weighed "a ton a foot," but this estimate seems to have been based on guesswork as much as anything else, since the whales were certainly not weighed at sea, where most of them were tried out (rendered) during the nineteenth-century period of deep-water whaling. Japanese scientists weighed sperm whales caught in the "adjacent waters of Japan" and produced the following figures (after Omura 1950):

Body Length in Feet	Metric Tons	Short Tons
30	6.82	7.55
35	11.14	12.28
40	17.03	18.77
45	24.77	27.30
50	34.36	37.86
55	46.89	51.67

These whales were weighed in parts, and a percentage was added for body fluids lost in the cutting process. In 1970 a 43.7-foot (13.32-meter) male was weighed in its entirety using a flatcar and a weighbridge at a Durban whaling station. It came to 69,300 pounds

*The figure is quoted in Nishiwaki (1972) along with "a 17 m [55.7-foot] female." This may be an error, since R. Clarke, an authority on sperm whales, examined a 40.3-foot (12.30-meter) female in the Azores and wrote (1956) "that there was no reliable record of a larger female." The extension of that record by almost 40 percent seems somewhat unlikely. Since the genital organs of sperm whales—like those of all other cetaceans—are contained within the body, it is possible to mistake a male for a female.

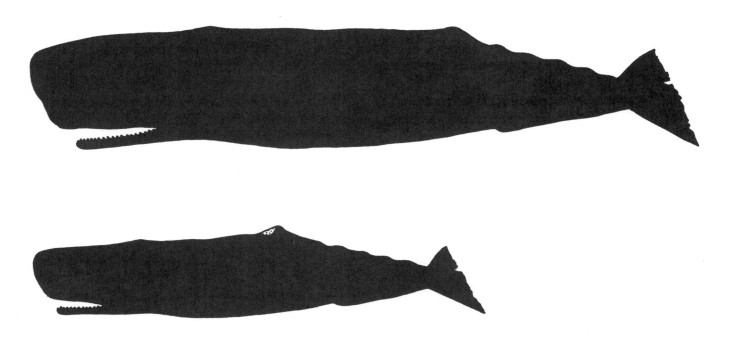

Bull sperm whales are considerably larger than cows. Though the bulls can reach a length of 60 feet or more, cows rarely reach 40 feet. Notice the callus on the dorsal hump of the female.

(31,450 kilograms), or nearly 31 long tons.* From the table above, it becomes apparent that the larger whales begin to approach the ton-per-foot figure of the whalers. Scheffer (1969) mentioned a 50.5-foot (15.4-meter) male that weighed 44 short tons, without blood and intestinal fluids. The figure given by Gambell (1970) for the percentage of the total weight accountable to these fluids was 12 percent. Therefore, adding 10,560 pounds to 88,000 pounds, we get 98,560 pounds, or 49.28 tons, almost exactly a ton per foot.

Females are also slimmer than males. In 1839, Beale wrote that they "are more slenderly formed which gives them that appearance of lightness and comparative weakness which the females of most species possess," and Scammon said that the female has "an effeminate appearance." This appearance is enhanced by the presence of a "callus" on the dorsal fin or hump of the cow, which has been referred to as a "secondary sexual characteristic" (Kasuya and Ohsumi 1966). Unlike the callosities on the right whale, this growth does not appear in the unborn calf, so it must be acquired. "[Because] it occurs in females at every sexual condition," wrote its discoverers, "it is presumed that [the] male sexual hormone inhibits the manifestation of the callus, and some female hormone, probably estrogen, stimulates it."

The head (or nose) of the sperm whale is its most unusual feature. In fact, it is one of the most unusual heads in the animal kingdom. Of the skull, Flower (1867) wrote, "In no known mammal does the cranium depart from the ordinary to such an extent as in the Cachalot. The expansion, elongation, flattening and dislocation of many of the cranial and facial bones, met with in a certain degree in all Cetaceans, is here carried so far as to render it by no means easy, at least in the adult animals, to recognize their homologies." The exterior of this head is no less unique. As described by Ommanney (1971), the head is "shaped like a boiler, the sides of which have been hammered in so as to make a longitudinal depression along each side below the middle line. The depression becomes shallower towards the rear and fuses with the rotundity of the boiler behind the angle of the mouth where the head becomes the body." The blowhole, a single S-shaped orifice, is located on the left side of the anterior end of the nose, and the spout that emanates from this single nostril is a bushy plume, angled

forward at an angle of approximately 45 degrees. (There is at least one documented record [Masaki 1969] of a sperm whale with two nostrils, but this is believed to a highly unusual specimen.) The eyes, located above and somewhat behind the gape (corner of the mouth), are relatively small and have movable lids. It has long been assumed that sperm whales cannot see to the front or rear, and whalers often tried to approach them from these "blind spots" (Ashley 1926). "The eyes were so far out on prominences," wrote Norris (1974), observing the carcass of a sperm whale, "that I wouldn't be surprised if the animal could simply roll them back and see dead astern, even though it couldn't see very well where it was going."

On the underside of the head is the narrow lower jaw with its complement of twenty to thirty teeth per side. The teeth have no enamel covering, which made it possible for the whalers to carve them with scrimshaw decorations, and they protrude from the gum for a third of their length. Ashley recorded a pair of teeth that weighed 8 pounds 7 ounces (3.8 kilograms) and were 11 inches long, but they were from a whale that was supposedly 90 feet long. When the mouth is closed, the teeth fit into sockets in the upper jaw, where there are also teeth, but these are rudimentary and usually unerupted. Since these upper teeth are not subject to wear, as are the lower teeth, they can be used in the determination of the age of the whales from the annual layers of dentine that are laid down (Nishiwaki et al. 1958). It might appear that the function of the sperm whale's teeth is obvious enough; they ought to be used in the procuring, holding, or

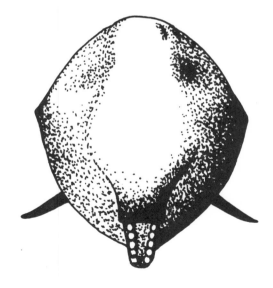

Head-on view of a sperm whale. The eyes are located on the prominences above the pectoral fins (after Matthews).

*A "long" or "metric" ton is 2,240 pounds, or 20 hundredweight. A hundredweight, abbreviated as "cwt," equals 50.8 kilograms.

perhaps even chewing of prey. But, like so many aspects of sperm whale biology, it is not nearly that simple. From the examination of many specimens it has been deduced that the lower teeth are not cut until the animal is between 28 and 31 feet long (8.54–9.45 meters), some time after weaning (R. Clarke 1956). This means that the whales have to feed themselves with no teeth, a situation similar to that of the female beaked whales, wherein the teeth do not erupt at all.

Occasionally, sperm whales of both sexes are found with a twisted or otherwise deformed lower jaw, but in most cases these animals were found to be well fed and otherwise healthy (Nasu 1958). (Moby-Dick was described as having a "sickle-shaped lower jaw," and this did not appear to affect his biting abilities, either the first time he encountered Ahab or the second.) It is apparent, therefore, that the teeth of the sperm whale play an insignificant role in feeding, since the animals seem capable of grasping and ingesting the cephalopods that make up the major part of their diet—without actually biting them. It has been noted that most of the squid from the examined stomachs of sperm whales lack tooth marks and are often whole (Okutani and Nemoto 1964).

The heads of male sperm whales are usually extensively scarred, indicating either scratch marks from squid—the sucking discs on the tentacles of some species are armed with sharp hooks—or from the teeth of other bull sperms. In an analysis of the parallel scars on the skin of large males, Best (1979) concluded that these scars could have been made only by the teeth of other large bulls and not by squid, females, or younger bulls. Adult males are also more heavily scarred about the head and mouth with sucker marks—some as large

as 7.8 inches (20 centimeters) in diameter—and since large males are the deepest divers (Lockyer 1976), it is therefore assumed that the larger males feed on the larger and deeper-ranging squid. (This assumption is partially confirmed by the examination of stomach contents, but it is far from conclusive because so little is known about the habits of pelagic squid.) Female sperm whales, identifiable even at a distance by their smaller size, do not dive as deeply (Beale 1835, Scammon 1874, and others); they do not hunt the larger squid; and they do not fight among themselves, so they are less heavily scarred than the males.

At the base of the lower jaw, sperm whales have a series of short, irregular grooves that can vary in size, shape, and number from whale to whale (R. Clarke 1956). The function of these grooves is not known, but R. Clarke suggested that "they may allow for the distention of the throat when swallowing prey." Berzin (1972), however, wrote that "the great difference in the number of folds in individual whales . . . and also the development of the folds as early as in uterine life . . . raise doubts as to whether this is their purpose."

Another variable is the dorsal fin, known to the Yankee whalers as the "hump." It is the largest of three to five such elevations that make an irregular, knobby ridge running back to the origin of the flukes. Both males and females have this ridge, but it is proportionally smaller in females (Gaskin 1972). Not a small protrusion, it can rise to 14 percent of the body length and have a base that may be as much as 68 inches (165–70 centimeters) long (Berzin 1972). On the undersurface of the tail stock is another ridge, which Matthews (1938) called the "post-anal ventral hump," a "constant occurrence" in both sexes. Its function is unknown, but it looks as if it might somehow be in-

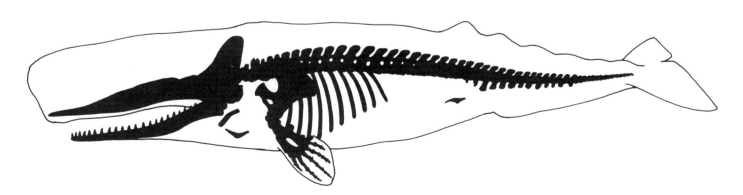

The skeleton of the sperm whale, *Physeter macrocephalus* (after Van Beneden and Gervais).

volved in the muscular flexion necessary for the species' deep diving.*

Unlike the smooth-skinned whalebone whales, the sperm whale is rather wrinkled, especially on the back and flanks. The wrinkles, which Matthews (1938) called "corrugations," are made up of longitudinal shallow ridges, running fore and aft, "which produce a very irregular surface to the body." The skin of the sperm whale is the thickest known in the animal kingdom, and on the back, where it reaches maximum thickness, it can be 14 inches (38 centimeters) thick (Berzin 1972).

Melville devoted an entire chapter of *Moby-Dick* to the tail of the sperm whale, writing, "In no living thing are the lines of beauty more exquisitely defined than in the crescentic borders of these flukes." The flukes are broad—up to 16 feet (4.8 meters) from tip to tip —and roughly triangular in shape. In some specimens the rear margin of one lobe overlaps the other. They are frequently seen with scalloped rear margins that would appear to be the result of bites by small fishes, rather than of abrasion. The ubiquitous semiovoid scars are probably the work of the little "cookie-cutter" shark. Beale (1835) wrote that the "swimming paws or fins are about 3 feet long and two broad," but in a full-grown male they are somewhat larger. (Scammon said that the pectoral limbs "rarely exceed six feet in length and three feet in width.") There have been infrequent records (Ogawa and Kamiya 1957, Nemoto 1963) of sperm whales that had rudimentary hind limbs. These specimens, supposedly throwbacks to the whales' terrestrial ancestors, had bones in the protrusions that would correspond to a femur and tibia.

Not only do male and female sperm whales differ in appearance, but they also differ noticeably in their habits. The species is polygamous—or, more accurately, it is polygynous, as males have more than one female mate—but the old theory that one bull services and protects a herd of females is not entirely accurate. In fact, the social structure of sperm whale society is extremely complicated; and rather than being a male-dominated system, it has been variously described as a "maternal family group" (Ohsumi 1971) or an "extended matricentric family" (Best 1979). When breeding bulls are not in evidence, the schools appear to be led by one or more females, but "there is no evidence

that females are dominant to all males (including adult bulls) when these are present in the school" (Best 1979).

Like many aspects of the natural history of this species, the social organization of sperm whales is not fully understood. Comparisons with other social animals, such as sea lions or deer, are not particularly useful, since the sperm whale seems to defy comparison, being *sui generis* and a creature of the open ocean besides. The basic unit, according to Ohsumi (1971), is the "mixed school," which includes juveniles, immature males and females, pregnant and lactating females. "Small bachelors" form separate schools that remain isolated from the mixed schools, and the adult bulls join these schools only during the breeding season. Not absolutely defined, the breeding season may last for eight months, including all but the summer months in each hemisphere, when the breeding bulls leave the schools and betake themselves to the high latitudes beyond 40°N and 40°S. It is only the adult males that frequent the polar waters; younger individuals and mature females remain all year in the temperate and tropical waters. Only a small number of bulls, known as "schoolmasters," join the mixed schools for breeding; but since there does not seem to be one dominant male per school, the term "harem" does not strictly apply. Bulls that have failed to obtain a place in a mixed school remain out of the breeding pool and are believed to associate loosely with one another, keeping a distance of a mile or more between themselves. At the conclusion of the breeding season the schoolmasters leave the tropical or temperate habitat of the females and return to the polar latitudes. These "lone bulls," therefore, are not outcasts that have been driven from the breeding aggregations, but they appear to leave for colder climates when their breeding duties have been accomplished.*

With the exception of the large and medium-sized bulls, the rest of the sperm whale population remains year-round in tropical and temperate waters. By no small coincidence, the area of the world ocean between 40°N and 40°S is believed to be the area of greatest abundance of the cephalopods on which sperm whales feed (Kondrakov in Berzin 1972). Food sources and breeding requirements affect the sperm

---

*A similar structure has recently been observed in males of the long-nosed spinner dolphin. Perrin (1972) suggested that it may be employed in interspecies recognition, but this would not seem applicable in sperm whales.

*That only the large bulls migrate to the higher latitudes is demonstrated by the presence of the Antarctic diatom *Cocconeis ceticola* only on males over 40 feet (12.2 meters) and by the marked differentiation of whale lice on large males and on all other classes. Only the bulls 40 feet or longer are infested with the cyamid species *Cyamis catodontis;* all others show only *Neocyamus physeteris.*

whale's social stratification, but other factors are also at work. We do not know what causes the expulsion of immature males from the mixed schools or why the large males should leave the food-rich tropics for the apparently less productive waters of the poles. There is no evidence to suggest that sperm whales undergo any prolonged period of fasting, such as that of the large baleen whales, which seem to feed only in certain locations and at certain times of the year.

The sperm whale is an extremely gregarious animal, and it is believed that schools—especially those composed of females—remain together for many years. From the recovery of tags it has been shown that the schools are stable units, experiencing little or no change in their composition. Best (1979) gave examples of whales that were marked together and were recaptured in the same school five or even ten years later.

After a gestation period of about sixteen months, a calf is born, approximately 13–14 feet long and weighing perhaps 1 ton. Opportunities to view the actual birth of a sperm whale are rare indeed, but Gambell and associates (1973) described their observations in South African waters, where they saw an individual "hanging vertically in the water with its head protruding above the surface." (Berzin [1972] quoted another account [Pervushin 1966] in which the same vertical attitude was observed on the part of the female, but in this case, a 13-foot calf was seen attached to the female by an umbilical cord.) An hour after their arrival on the scene—they had found the pod by locating a green dye marker that had been dropped from a spotter aircraft—they saw a newborn calf, "about 3.5m long, with strongly wrinkled skin and distinct light pigment streaks on the right flank posterior to the dorsal fin. The dorsal fin itself was folded over to the left, and the tail flukes were slightly curled, as in fetal whales." There were five whales in addition to the "vertical" female, and from the similarity in size it was assumed that all were females. On other occasions, groups of twenty-four to forty whales were seen in the company of a calving female (Gambell et al. 1973). One of the few instances in which a newborn sperm whale was examined (and illustrated) by a scientist occurred in Bermuda (Wheeler 1933), where a 13.2-foot female was captured by fishermen and exhibited alive for two days. After it died, it was presented to the Bermuda Biological Station. It was uniformly black in color, showing white markings around the lips and the umbilicus and, of course, it had no teeth. In September 1979 the first baby sperm whale—in fact, the first

sperm whale of any age—was held briefly in captivity. A newborn female, later estimated to be less than a week old, stranded on a beach in Rockaway, Oregon, and was transported 300 miles on a flatbed truck to the Seattle Aquarium. There, despite around-the-clock care and attempts at feeding her a mixture of goat's milk, krill, and vitamins, the animal died. She was 12 feet long and weighed 800 pounds.

Scammon described the nursing behavior in this way: "The new-born cub . . . obtains its nourishment from two teats, situated one on each side of the vaginal opening. In giving suck, it is said that the female reclines on her side, when the calf seizes the teat in the corner of its mouth, thereby giving the milk-food immediate passage to the throat." (The use of "it is said" in this description makes it likely that Scammon himself did not witness the actual nursing.) Typically, lactation lasts about two years, "but there is evidence that sperm whales continue to suckle to an apparent age of 13 years and 31 feet" (Best 1979). Young males usually leave the nursery school at an age of 4–5 years, when they are 25–26 feet long. After they are weaned, young whales segregate into juvenile schools composed of young males and young females. At sexual maturity, about 9 years of age for the females and 25 years of age for the males, the females join a "mixed" or "nursery" school—the same social unit at different times of the year—whereas the young males form "bachelor schools."*

A 25-year-old bull will be about 40 feet (12.2 meters) in length, and at this time the animal will engage in what Ohsumi (1971) called the "struggle for joining a nursery school in the breeding season." This struggle probably results in some of the scars, lacerations, missing teeth, and broken jaws found in older bulls. Many of the scars, especially the circular ones, are thought to result from the suckers of giant squid, and the broken jaws are here differentiated from the deformed jaws mentioned earlier, which are presumed to be birth defects. Although battles between sperm whales have been seen only infrequently, there are a few eyewitness descriptions of these titanic contests. Zenkovich (1962) observed "fights between two big male sperm whales on two occasions," and in another situation, described by Hopkins (1922), a bull tried to join an established herd and a battle between two bulls

---

*These designations were employed by Ohsumi (1971) on the basis of whale marking, whale sightings, and the unfortunate expedient of "catching all individuals which form the same school." Best's 1979 discussion owes much to Ohsumi, but he added a great deal to our attempts at understanding what is undoubtedly one of the most intricate social arrangements in nature.

ensued, wherein "great pieces of flesh were torn from the animal's heads" and the jaw of one of them (later captured) was badly broken and hanging by the flesh. In *The Year of the Whale,* Victor Scheffer (1969) gave the following fictionalized account of a battle between two bull sperm whales:

The young whale turns on his left side and charges, clapping his jaw violently, forcing each tooth with a smash into the firm white socket of the upper gum. The old bull turns deliberately on his back, belly up, responding in kind with a racket that carries through the sea for a league in all directions. His great jaw swings at right angles to his body, tip waving in the air. The first impact of the bodies with a total mass of a hundred tons throws a geyser of green water high in the sky. Within seconds the movements of the whales are lost in a smother of foam. Each infuriated beast is trying to engage the other's jaw, or to seize a flipper—the action is all confused.

When there are bulls attendant on a mixed school, it is known as a breeding school, and there may be more than one breeding bull present at a time. These schools vary in size, but Gambell (1972) has estimated one breeding bull per ten females.*

For all its romantic references to Ottomans, Sultans, Bashaws, and Lotharios, Melville's description of the social arrangement of sperm whales is remarkably accurate (*Moby-Dick,* chap. 88, "Schools and Schoolmasters"). He correctly identified the schools of "young and vigorous males" (the bachelor schools); the harem schools, made up of females only; as well as the dominant breeding bulls: "You meet them on the Line in time for the full flower of the Equatorial feeding season, having just returned perhaps from spending the summer in the Northern Seas, and so cheating summer of all unpleasant weariness and warmth." He observed that the "forty-barrel bulls" will leave a wounded comrade, "but strike a member of the harem school, and her companions swim around her with every token of concern, sometimes lingering so near her and so long, as themselves to fall a prey."†

The seasonal composition of schools is accom-

panied by migrations, although the movements are as poorly understood as the formation of the breeding units. Unlike the rorquals, which move toward the poles for feeding and then into more temperate waters for breeding and calving, the sperm whales make no such clearly defined movements. Only adult males are found in the higher latitudes, but adult females and juveniles of both sexes are found in the more temperate and tropical regions. Matthews (1938) suggested that males leave the herd while still sexually active and migrate to the high northern or southern latitudes. Later in the year they will again participate in a general movement toward the equator. The mass movements of sperm whales, known to the old whalers as "making a passage," often involve large numbers of animals, estimated at 200 to 1,000. Boyer (1946) observed "a school of gigantic proportions, maybe one thousand whales." These migratory herds can be differentiated from breeding herds by their numbers and their steady one-directional movement. On the Solander Grounds (south of New Zealand), "as far as the eye could reach," wrote Bullen, "extending all round one half of the horizon, the sea appeared to be alive with spouts—all sperm whales, all bulls of great size."* The maximum age of sperm whales has been estimated from 32 years (R. Clarke 1956), to 50 years (Gaskin 1972), and up to 70 years (Nishiwaki 1972). (In *Alaska's Animals and Fishes,* an otherwise responsible book, Dufresne [1946] wrote that the sperm whale "has one of the shortest life spans of any whale, usually not living more than 8 or 9 years.") In recent years, estimations of age have been made from the examination of a cross section of the teeth, particularly the upper teeth, which, being unerupted, are not worn down by normal usage (Nishiwaki et al. 1958). Age can also be estimated by examining a cross section of the lower mandible, where laminations are accumulated at the same rate as in the teeth (Laws 1961, Nishiwaki et al. 1961).

The teeth of sperm whales are probably not used for feeding, or if they are, they serve only a secondary function. Telling of a whale with a deformed lower jaw, Spaul (1964) wrote, "this condition would conform with the limited and possible non-essential function of the teeth in the sperm whale." The revelation also comes from the examination of the toothless jaws of animals that are no longer nursing. (The presence

*As mentioned earlier, there is no reason to assume that young bulls challenge older bulls for control or dominance of a harem. In all probability, bulls of approximately the same size and age engage in the struggle, unlike the battles that occur between bulls of the various pinnipeds—for instance, the fur seals—in which it is usually a younger male that challenges the beachmaster.
†Not surprisingly, much of the factual information contained in Melville's description comes directly from Beale (1839). But Beale was writing straight observational natural history, whereas Melville embellished his text with the curlicues and flourishes that make *Moby-Dick* the wonderful book that it is.

*Some are less inclined to accept Bullen's descriptions as factual. In many instances, such as the one in which he described a surface battle between a sperm whale and a giant squid, his report is unique in all the literature.

of milk in the stomach of a captured whale indicates that it has not yet been weaned.) Young animals seem to feed quite satisfactorily, and animals without teeth or with lower jaws so twisted that they could not possibly use their teeth to feed are usually found in good health as a result of normal feeding activity. It has been suggested (Caldwell et al. 1966) that the teeth of sperm whales are a secondary sexual characteristic more than a feeding mechanism and may be used by males primarily for fighting.

Teeth or no teeth—sperm whales feed on a variety of food organisms, predominantly squid, and very few of the latter show tooth marks. Although they do feed on the giant squid, this cephalopod is by no means the dominant food item in their diet. R. Clarke (1955) examined the stomach of a 47-foot bull sperm whale in the Azores that contained a squid measuring 34.5 feet (10.49 meters) from the tip of the mantle to the tip of the longest tentacle. The squid weighed over 400 pounds (181.4 kilograms). It has been suggested that sperm whales often regurgitate food items when they are harpooned, which may account for the absence of some of the larger squid. On the whaling brig *Daisy,* Robert Cushman Murphy (1933) saw a dying sperm whale "belching up squids . . . barrelful after barrelful of the tentacled creatures."

According to M. R. Clarke (1966), the giant squid can reach a maximum length of 60 feet (18.3 meters) and a weight of almost 1 ton. After examining the aforementioned 34-foot specimen, R. Clarke (1955) wrote, "I view with less reserve such a traveler's tale as Bullen's, telling of a struggle he watched at night between a sperm whale and a giant squid at the surface of the sea." (Not everyone found Bullen's story easy to accept. Ommanney wrote, "like a good deal of that fine book of travel and adventure, it should surely be taken with a grain of salt.") Bullen claimed:

A very large sperm whale was locked in deadly conflict with a cuttle-fish, or squid, almost as large as himself, whose interminable tentacles seemed to enlace the whole of his great body. The head of the whale especially seemed a perfect net-work of writhing arms—naturally, I suppose, for it appeared as if the whale had the tail part of the mollusc in his jaws, and, in a business-like, methodical way, was sawing through it. By the side of the black columnar head of the whale appeared the head of the great squid, as awful an object as one could well imagine even in a fevered dream. Judging as carefully as possible, I estimated it to be at least as large as one of our pipes, which contained three hundred and fifty gallons; but it may have been, and probably was, a good deal larger. The eyes were very remarkable from their size and blackness, which, contrasted with the livid whiteness of the head, made their appearance all the more striking. They were, at least, a foot in diameter, and, seen under such conditions, looked decidedly eerie and hobgoblin-like. All around the combatants were numerous sharks, like jackals round a lion, ready to share the feast, and apparently assisting in the destruction of the huge cephalopod. So the titanic struggle went on, in perfect silence as far as we were concerned, because, even if there had been any noise, our distance from the scene of conflict would have not permitted us to hear it.

Even though most of the squid consumed by sperm whales are smaller than the monster described above, the giant squid has been a part of the literature on sperm whales for so long that it is almost impossible to separate fact from fantasy. In 1856, Nordhoff wrote,

whalemen believe them ["a monster species of cuttle-fish"] to be much larger than the largest whale, even exceeding in size the hull of a large vessel, and those who pretend to have been favored with a sight of the body describe it as a huge, shapeless, jelly-like mass, of a dirty yellow, and having on all sides of it long arms . . . of the circumference of a flour barrel. If this be the size of the arms, of which they have probably hundreds, each furnished with air exhausters the size of a dinner plate, what must be the magnitude of the body which supports such an array?

Most of the squid consumed by sperm whales are less than three feet in total length. M. R. Clarke (1962) examined a bull sperm whale in Madeira that had over 4,000 squid mandibles in its stomach. Ninety-five percent of these came from squid that weighed less than 2.2 pounds (1 kilogram); 2.8 percent were from squid between 2.2 and 22.0 pounds (1 and 10 kilograms); and 2.2 percent came from squid that were estimated to weigh more than 22 pounds (10 kilograms). Compared with other animals that inhabit the oceans in substantial numbers, very little is known about squid. For example, all the existing data on the giant squid are derived from stranded specimens or from whole or partial specimens recovered from the stomachs of captured sperm whales. In a discussion of the systematics and ecology of oceanic squid, M. R. Clarke (1966) pointed out "that if it were not for the fact that large populations of Sperm whales feed mainly on such squids as *Architeuthis, Taningia, Lepidoteuthis, Histioteuthis,* etc., these would be considered extremely rare." Other species considered important food of sperm whales are *Dosidicus, Moroteuthis, Gonatus,* and *Calliteuthis.* (Only the generic names are listed here; M. R. Clarke commented [1966], "While a large number of species have been described, revisionists have been struggling to clarify the taxonomic tangle for over half a century.")

Voss (1959) did not believe that the giant squid *Architeuthis* is the powerful monster of mythology: "the funnel is flabby, the valve is weak and the locking cartilages are mere shallow grooves and ridges. Even the fins are but flimsy narrow bordering flaps, of little or no use as a means of propulsion. Most important of all, the great paired dorsal nerve axons, which control the movements of the body wall or mantle, are missing." He further speculated that *Architeuthis* is not even the largest of the squids, that there might be a giant squid that "could grow to a length of 50 to 60 feet, [and that] they in turn could prey upon and search out the sperm whale. They would be the most powerful fighting machines the marine world has ever produced, and there is no reason to believe they cannot exist." Until the marine world produces evidence of such a monster, however, we must allow *Architeuthis,* flabby or not, to retain its title.

The amount of squid eaten by sperm whales is enormous. Sperms have been taken with close to 30,000 squid beaks in their stomachs, indicating that at least 15,000 individual squid have been consumed in the near past. (Squid have upper and lower mandibles, so the total number of beaks must be halved.) M. R. Clarke (1979b) estimated that the 1.25 million sperm whales alive today (a conservative estimate) eat some 100 million tons of squid per year, "more than the 60–70 million tons for the total world annual catch of fish, and [the figure] probably approaches the total biomass of mankind."*

Sperm whales are also known to eat various fishes, including barracuda, albacore, sharks, skates, and rays. Spotters in airplanes for the Union Whaling Company of Durban, South Africa, reported a school that "appeared to have a large school of fish ahead, which they followed. Flock of forty to fifty birds diving constantly just ahead" (Gambell 1968). There is a record of a sperm whale with an 8.2-foot (2.5-meter) basking shark in its stomach (R. Clarke 1956), and Norman and Fraser mentioned "an authenticated report of a whale in whose stomach a 10-foot shark was found intact." Some of these prey species, such as

barracuda and albacore, are swift, mid-water inhabitants, whereas the rays and skates are bottom dwellers. Andrews (1916) found the remains of "several enormous spiny lobsters" in the stomach of a sperm whale. The habits of the larger squid are poorly known, but most squid are powerful swimmers, capable of quick, darting motions. (M. R. Clarke [1966] attributed our lack of knowledge of the giant squid "to our complete inability to catch these active animals in the open ocean.") We cannot catch the giant squid, but the sperm whale can, and it can also catch a variety of other food organisms. The sperm whale does not appear to be a particularly agile swimmer—certainly not in the class of an albacore.

Therefore, a question arises: how can the whale possibly catch this species and the fast-moving squid? And how does the sperm whale feed on skates, rays, and spiny lobsters? Beale (1835) quoted old whalers with the theory that the sperm whale

descends a certain depth below the surface of the ocean, and there remains in as quiet a state as possible, opening his enormous mouth until the lower jaw hangs perpendicularly, or at right angles, with the body. The roof of his mouth, the tongue, and especially his teeth, being of a bright glistening white colour, must of course present a remarkable appearance, and which seems to be the incitement by which his prey are attracted.

Commenting on this theory, Berzin (1972) wrote, "Strange though it may sound, this fantastic hypothesis found many supporters." Scammon was one, for he paraphrased and illustrated this description, attributing it to "several high authorities." Since he quoted at length from Beale's 1839 account, we may assume that at least one of these "high authorities" was Beale.* He also mentioned a whale that was "perfectly blind" and

---

*In addition to this startling figure, Clarke also suggested that the stomachs of sperm whales represent our only viable method of estimating squid populations; if samples are not collected in all regions where whaling is still going on, we will have no idea of the number of squid in the ocean. "If this is not done," he wrote, "we may, at some future date, find it impossible to make even the broadest estimate of some squid populations which have great importance in the sea but are inaccessible to us."

*Beale (1835, 1839) and Bennett (1840) are probably the dominant primary sources for information on sperm whaling in the nineteenth century. Obviously limited by the state of biological knowledge during their time, their works still stand as the foundation for much of what is known—or suspected—about the natural history of this animal. In *The Trying-Out of Moby-Dick,* a book about the writing of that great American novel, Howard Vincent (1949) points out "that the primary source book for Melville in composing the cetological section of *Moby-Dick* was Thomas Beale's *Natural History of the Sperm Whale.*" Melville himself referred to this book and to Bennett's *Narrative of a Whaling Voyage Around the Globe from the Year 1833 to 1836* as "exact and reliable," and he used them liberally in his preparation of *Moby-Dick.* Melville's other source, especially for those sections not directly concerned with the sperm whale, was Scoresby's *An Account of the Arctic Regions with a History and Description of the Northern Whale-Fishery* (1820). Those who have followed Beale and Bennett (that is, Scammon, Bullen, Ashley, Scheffer, and so on, including myself) have been more than willing to acknowledge their debt to these two intrepid British surgeons who, fortunately for science and literature, found themselves on whaling voyages in the heyday of the industry.

two specimens in which the lower jaw was so deformed "as to render it impossible for the animal to find the jaws useful in catching small fish . . . and yet these whales possessed as much blubber, and were as rich in oil as any of similar size I have seen before or since." It seems unlikely that sperm whales hang motionless in the water, waiting for food to swim into their mouths, but until someone actually observes a sperm whale feeding, this explanation is remotely possible.

Most of the species of squid mentioned above are deep-water inhabitants, and squid make up as much as 90 percent of the diet of sperm whales (M. R. Clarke 1966). Skates and rays are bottom dwellers; and since the sperm whale is known to be an inhabitant of deep waters, one must assume that the whale was somehow feeding on the bottom at significant depths. We have some idea of how deep this species can descend from an unusual source: transoceanic cable companies. Heezen (1957) has recorded fourteen instances of sperm whales entangled in deep-sea cables, six of which were in about 500 fathoms (3,000 feet), and one, among the deepest dives known for any mammal, was at 620 fathoms (3,720 feet or 1,135 meters). (Nishiwaki [1972] mentioned a "similar incident . . . on a cable between Lisbon and Malaga which had been set at a depth of 2,200 m" [7,216 feet], but gave no reference to corroborate this figure. The source may have been Heezen's remark about a one-pound lump of "amorphous fish tissue, highly odoriferous," that was hauled up from a depth of 1,200 fathoms. (There is no indication in Heezen's report that this material was from a whale, and the captain who hauled up the cable believed it was from an octopus.) In most cases in which the whale is identifiable, the cable had been wrapped around the lower jaw of the whale, indicating "that sperm whales often swim along the sea floor [and] become entangled while swimming with their lower jaw plowing through the sediment in search of food. It is possible that the whales attack tangled masses of slack cable, mistaking these for items of food" (Heezen 1957).

In 1969, M. R. Clarke was observing sperm whales from the spotter plane of the Union Whaling Company of Durban. Two whales were sighted; they dived; and when they surfaced, they were shot by the catcher boats. When one of these whales, which had been submerged for eighty-two minutes, was cut open, its stomach was found to contain two small sharks of the genus *Scymnodon,* known bottom dwellers. "It is difficult to avoid the conclusion that these whales probably dived to the bottom at a far greater depth than we have

hitherto thought likely," wrote Clarke (1976). The depth of the ocean at the location where they dived is in excess of 1,746 fathoms, or 10,476 feet. A dive of almost two miles surely represents one of the most spectacular accomplishments of an already amazing animal.

One might expect that an animal "plowing through the sediment" would collect odd and curious items in addition to edible ones, and this is exactly the case. In a 1963 discussion of "Stones and Other Aliens in the Stomachs of Sperm Whales in the Bering Sea," Nemoto and Nasu listed the following items: stones, rocks, sand, a glass buoy, crabs, a coconut, a deep-sea sponge, and the cut meat of a baleen whale. Rice (1963) mentioned a sperm whale taken from a California shore station that had a shoe in its stomach. Although they obviously prefer squid, sperm whales will eat various other objects, some intentionally and some accidentally. It is reasonable to assume that sperm whales also feed in what might be called a "normal" manner, chasing down and eating fish and squid at various depths. Although this explains neither the presence of stones and other aliens in the stomach nor the fact of a well-fed whale with a nonfunctioning lower jaw, it probably accounts for the greater proportion of the eating habits of most individuals.

However it is accomplished, sperm whales eat a lot of food. Sergeant (1969) estimated that they consume about 3 percent of their total body weight daily; for a whale of 30 tons this would amount to some 1,800 pounds (810 kilograms) of food per day.

On the question of Jonah, there seems to be no doubt that a sperm whale is capable of swallowing an object the size of a grown man. (There are reports of whales vomiting up pieces of squid "half the size of a whaleboat" after having been harpooned [Ashley 1927], so the whale ought to have no trouble with a puny *H. sapiens.*) There have been many tales of whalers swallowed up by whales, but perhaps the most persistent is the story recounted by Edgerton Y. Davis (1946), in which a young sealer fell into the sea off Saint John's, Newfoundland, and was swallowed up by "a huge sperm whale," which was then killed. When the whale was opened, the man was found, "badly crushed . . . and partially digested." Scheffer (1969) was skeptical of this story, claiming it strange that Davis waited half a century to tell his tale: the event was supposed to have happened in 1893 or 1894, but was not published until 1946. Budker (1959), however, reprinted Davis's story in full and found it an "accurate scientific account."

When moving at the surface, the sperm whale swims with an undulating motion: "a slow, shallow and dignified porpoising movement" (Gaskin 1964). The speed when "making a passage" has been estimated at 3–4 knots, and when alarmed, they can double this. The action of swimming has been described thus by Ashley: "At top speed his head lifts entirely from the water until the jaw is in view and the head rises and pitches with the rapid beat of his flukes, but he does not disappear beneath the waves." Beale commented (1835) that the "narrow inferior surface [of the head] bears some resemblance to the cutwater of a ship, and which would in fact answer the same purpose in the whale." Under extreme duress—that is, when harpooned—the sperm whale has been recorded to achieve speeds of 10–15 knots, often towing a whaleboat with a full crew—the "Nantucket sleigh ride."

Sperm whales have been observed "lob-tailing," which is slapping their flukes on the surface; creating great noise and commotion; "pitchpoling," a behavior that involves raising the upper portion of the head out of the water, presumably to enable the whale to see at the surface; and "settling," a peculiar action in which the whale will "sink bodily in the water with the apparent rapidity of a lump of lead . . . unaccompanied by any change in the horizontal position, or any movement of the tail or fins" (Starbuck 1878). Other unexplained behaviors include tail slapping, swimming in a circle, swimming in line, and swimming abreast (Gambell 1968). Gaskin (1964) also reported whales seen lying on their sides or submerging so that just the tip of the snout is visible as the whale hangs in a vertical position. Sperm whales breach frequently, energetically throwing themselves almost completely out of the water and then falling back with an enormous splash. Most accounts of this spectacular behavior indicate that the whale does not emerge completely from the water, but Ashley wrote, "I have seen an 85-barrel bull sperm leap clear out of the water so that the afternoon sun was framed for an instant under his hurtling form."

Breaching may occur when the whale surfaces from a deep dive, but this is not always the case. The largest whales, the mature bulls, dive the deepest (Lockyer 1976) and spend the most time at the surface recovering from their exertions. "Among the whole order of cetaceans," wrote Scammon, "there is no other which respires with the same regularity as the Cachalot." An old whaler's rule, quoted by Ashley, was that "a sperm whale will spout once for every minute he has been down." They will also stay down one minute for each foot of length. Combining these figures with the whaler's ton-per-foot estimate, we can therefore assume that a fifty-foot whale, weighing fifty tons, will stay down for fifty minutes and then breathe fifty times at the surface. As in the case of the length/weight ratio, the whalers were not far wrong. (The whales can stay below for more than an hour; Bennett recorded a ninety-minute dive; Beale, a dive of eighty minutes.) At the surface after a long dive, the whale pants, breathing short, rapid breaths approximately every ten seconds. If this pattern and the number of respirations are interrupted, the whale cannot remain submerged as long on the next dive (Caldwell et al. 1966).

In preparation for a deep dive, the sperm whale gives a strong spout, rounds its back into an arch with the hump prominently displayed, and descends steeply with the flukes raised almost vertically in the air. These deep dives are presumed to be hunting expeditions, with the whales searching for food at various depths. Females and juveniles do not dive as deeply as adult males and, therefore, do not remain submerged as long. By acoustic tracking, Watkins (1977) observed that the initial deep dive was converted immediately below the surface to a shallower dive angle; whales that had been together fanned out underwater, but returned to the surface close together again. Sperm whales have long been known to be able to maintain contact with one another even at considerable distances, but as Beale wrote in 1835, "the mode by which this is effected remains a curious secret."

The sounds of the sperm whale have been recognized at least since 1957, when Worthington and Schevill recorded a "muffled smashing noise" (first thought to be a hammering on board ship), a "grating sort of groan" (very low in pitch, reminding some of a rusty hinge creaking), and a series of clicks. A creaking noise was also heard by Hass (1959) while diving beneath a harpooned animal off the Azores: "A dying beast snapped open its lower jaw almost at right angles, and a most curious noise echoed through the water. It sounded like the creaking of a huge barn door turning on rusty hinges. It was quite a deep, harsh, vibrating tone, carried clear and powerful through the sea." The majority of sperm whale noises have been clicks, but whistles, chirps, pings, plinks, squawks, rasps, yelps, and wheezes have been reported by Perkins and associates 1966, and Norris (1974) described the sounds as " 'knocks,' (like someone tapping on an empty keg with a fist)."

After analyzing hundreds of hours of sperm whale sounds, Watkins and Schevill (1977) concluded that certain repeated sequences were probably an exchange between two whales and that these "repetitive temporal pulse patterns" (which they called "codas" because they came at the end of longer click sequences) were "signatures" of individual whales. Sperm whale sounds are very loud; they can be heard for miles by humans with good listening gear and, presumably, at even greater distances by whales, which have been shown to have an excellent sense of hearing (Yamada 1953). (Caldwell and colleagues [1966] wrote that "for exploration of the environment, this acoustic system may very well serve in the stead of primate hands and well-developed stereoscopic vision.") At first it was assumed that the clicks served the same echolocation function as those emitted by the bottlenose dolphin, but it is now believed that the clicks (and many of the other sounds) are also "intelligence-bearing communicative signals" (Perkins et al. 1966). Sperm whales can "talk" to each other, or, at least, they can locate and identify animals they cannot see.*

The means by which sperm whale sounds are produced is not clearly understood, but it is thought to be

related to the unique structure of the head. The spermaceti organ, nasal passages, and various air sacs are all assumed to be involved with deep-diving capability, buoyancy, and sound production, but the exact relationship and interaction of these organs are still a mystery. The spermaceti organ is a huge reservoir of straw-colored oil (known as spermaceti oil or sperm oil to the whalers), which hardens into a whitish wax when exposed to air. (In 1725, Paul Dudley wrote, "The *Sperma Ceti* Oil, so called, lies in a great Trunk about four or five Feet deep, and ten or twelve Feet long, near the whole Depth, Breadth, and Length of the Head, in the Place of the Brains, and seems to be the same.") The organ itself is encased in a tough membrane, known as the "case," which Beale described (1835) as a "beautiful glistening membrane . . . covered by a thick layer of muscular fibres." Immediately below the case is the "junk," a network of tough, spongy cells, also filled with oil. The sperm whale has two nasal passages, but only the left is connected directly to the blowhole. The right nasal passage is one-seventh the diameter of the left, and Norris (1969) believed it is involved in sound production by way of its connection with a pair of internal "lips" known as the *museau du singe* and with two air sacs, one at either end of the case.

Dissecting the head of a whale at Richmond, Cali-

*Bottlenose dolphins emit both whistles and clicks. The clicks are primarily used in echolocating, while the whistles are thought to be communication devices. By these "signature whistles," the dolphins identify each other and probably convey additional information as well (Caldwell and Caldwell 1965).

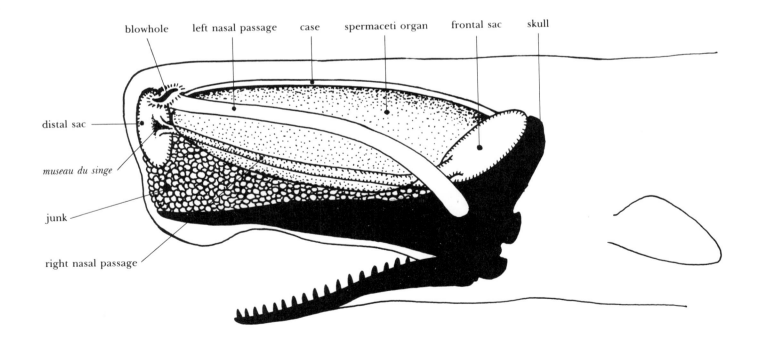

Diagrammatic cross section of the head of the sperm whale, from the left side (after Raven and Gregory).

fornia, Norris (1974) wrote, "I thought I could perceive from the almost unbelievably peculiar anatomy of the sperm whale's head that sperm whales produce sounds with a pair of huge lips located inside the soft tissue of the forehead (the lips were picturesquely called *museau du singe,* or monkey's muzzle, by French anatomists of the last century), and then rocket them back and forth between a pair of sacs also located inside the forehead, to produce the loud banging sounds we heard." Beale believed (1835) that the case, containing oil of a lighter specific gravity than water, "will always have a tendency to rise, at least, so far above the surface as to elevate the nostril or 'blow hole' sufficiently for all purposes of respiration." In a 1933 analysis of the spermaceti organ, Raven and Gregory wrote,

We infer that its main function is to act as a force pump for the bony narial passages, drawing a great quantity of air into the respiratory sacs and preventing the escape of air under pressures of great depth. It may possibly also act in part as a hydrostatic organ, since by severe contractions of part of its muscular sheath the contained oil might be squeezed toward one end or the other, while the air sacs were being inflated, thus lightening the specific gravity of that end and tending to alter the direction of motion of the animal.

Norris and Harvey (1972) suggested that "the spermaceti organ is an acoustic resonating and sound-focussing chamber used to form and process burst-pulsed clicks"; and, therefore, the physical evidence indicates that the organ is "especially useful for long-range echolocation in the deep sea." When spermaceti oil was tested for its sound-transmitting qualities, it was found to be far more effective than water and approximately twice as good a conductor as the oil of a known echolocator, the bottlenose dolphin. (Spermaceti transmitted sound at 8,857 feet [2,684 meters] per second, compared with 4,462 feet [1,352 meters] per second for the oil of the dolphin.) Norris and Harvey built an apparatus that approximated the nasal sacs of the spermaceti organ and were successful in duplicating the click pulses, demonstrating at least that the sounds could be produced by such an arrangement. They further postulated that the time between clicks was a function of the distance between the frontal and distal air sacs and could, therefore, be used as a measure of the animal's total length.*

Earlier, Backus and Schevill (1966) had remarked on the regularity of the clicks ("We are dealing here with a sensory system that is generally conceded to be elaborately developed, and a motor task that the whale can perform at a rapid rate"), but they were assuming that the clicks were generated physically rather than mechanically, as a function of the distance between the two air sacs. They pointed out that the clicks might be used "not only for echolocation, but for communication."

In a comprehensive survey of the literature, Malcolm R. Clarke (1978a) listed the suggestions that have been made for the function of this extraordinary organ: sound production, movement of air between the nostrils and the lungs when the whale is at depth, control of closure of the nasal passages, absorption of nitrogen under pressure, or even a means of attack and defense. His own theory is that the organ is used for buoyancy control. Briefly, he suggested that the organ regulates the whale's density, enabling it to maintain neutral buoyancy in dives deeper than 660 feet (200 meters). The whale accomplishes this by controlling the temperature of the spermaceti oil: "if the whale needs to achieve neutral buoyancy it must be able to increase its own density. . . . the necessary increase can be achieved if the whale can lower the temperature of the spermaceti oil of its head so that it freezes." Clarke hypothesized that the whale controls the temperature of the spermaceti oil by circulating sea water through the nasal passages (especially the right naris), although he admitted that "the mechanism by which the heat is lost is not irrefutably established." Since the sperm whale floats after death, it is neutrally buoyant at the surface, and some sort of buoyancy control is obviously necessary to enable the animal to dive as deeply as it does. In conclusion, Clarke wrote, "While the present work clearly shows the sperm whale *could* use the spermaceti organ for buoyancy control . . . final proof must await a measurement of temperature and density of the oil *in situ* in a diving sperm whale, a difficult but not impossible task."*

---

*Norris and Harvey's theory has been responsible for an interesting approach to estimating the age of whales. Møhl and colleagues (1976) wrote that current techniques involve killing a representative number of whales for purposes of aging. If we knew the time it took

for sound to bounce off the sacs, this could then be coordinated with known ratios of age/size and would eliminate the counterproductive killing of the whale to find out how old it was when it was killed.
*Although the paper by Norris and Harvey predated the one by Clarke that is quoted above, they commented on his 1970 paper in the British journal *Nature,* which presented a preliminary version of the same theory. Norris and Harvey wrote that the spermaceti organ could not possibly function as a heat exchanger: "It seems inconceivable to us that the gossamer webwork of connective tissue and blood vessels that invades the spermaceti could be an efficient heat exchanger capable of repeated heating and cooling of such massive

The skull that cradles the spermaceti and other organs is as curious as the organs themselves. It swoops down from a high posterior portion to a pointed rostrum, making a hollow basin, roughly the shape of "a wheel-less chariot—indeed, the whalers used to refer to it as the 'coach' or 'sleigh' " (Norman and Fraser). The nasal bones are asymmetrical—in fact, only the left one is visible at all—and the lower jaw is a Y-shaped rod of bone, the two halves being fused for most of their length. It is the largest skull of any whale and, *a fortiori,* larger than that of any mammal (Beddard 1900). The skull of a 43.7-foot (13.3-meter) bull weighed 4,760 pounds (Gambell 1970). The brain of the sperm whale is the largest brain known. The average weight in a study done by Kojima (1951) was 17.16 pounds (7.8 kilograms), and the heaviest brain he measured, from a 49-foot bull, weighed 20.24 pounds (9.2 kilograms). The world's largest brain does not necessarily mean the world's smartest animal. The body weight of a 40-ton whale is about 5,000 times greater than its 17-pound brain, as compared with a man's 180-pound body weight and 3-pound brain, a ratio of 1 to 60.

There seems to be no question that sperm whales echolocate, although the only evidence we have is circumstantial. The click sounds have been recorded (Worthington and Schevill 1957, Watkins and Schevill 1977, and others); sperm whales hunt at great depths

and, therefore, in total darkness; so a logical conclusion would be that they, like many other toothed whales, read the echoes of sounds bounced off potential prey organisms. However, we have seen that what seems obvious in the case of the sperm whale is often not so. In the matter of the spermaceti organ, for example, it has been suggested that the whale is able to focus sound into a shock wave that can be "an effective instrument for stunning and immobilizing prey far away" (Bel'kovich and Yablakov 1963). If the concept of projecting sonic booms to stun the prey is not bizarre enough, consider the theory of Kozak (1974): he hypothesized a "video-acoustic system" that enables the whale to transfer sound energy into images, using the surface of the rear wall of the spermaceti organ as an "acoustic retina." What actually transpires at the great depths at which the sperm whale feeds may never be known to us, but in his comprehensive review of the sperm whale's biology Berzin (1972) summarized the available information and produced this description of its feeding habits:

Having dived, the animal covers several hundred meters, investigating the surrounding waters by echo sounding with ultrasound of varying frequency (for dolphins it will be from 12 to 170 kHz) and intensity. Analyzing the returning signals, it receives the most detailed information on the objects around it. If the animal dives to the bottom, it swims with wide-open mouth (underwater cables damaged by sperm whales were usually coiled around the lower jaw). When mobile squid and fish are discovered, the ultrasonic beam narrows and focuses on them, its frequency sharply increases, and the prey is stunned and then seized.

Certainly, the idea of an animal immobilizing its prey with focused sound waves is incredible, but so is the image of a huge, slow-swimming creature foraging in total darkness and capturing thousands of pounds of fast-moving squid every day.

Sperm whales have few enemies other than the creature with the three-pound brain, but they are occasionally observed with whale lice, *Cyamus catodontis* and *Neocyamus physeteris;* Matthews (1938) reported that "some agent removes semi-ovoid pieces of blubber" (probably the eighteen-inch shark, *Isistius*); and stalked barnacles, *Conchoderma,* are sometimes found on the front lower teeth. These teeth are not always enclosed when the mouth is shut, and the barnacles also appear on the jaws and teeth of whales whose lower jaws are deformed (Nasu 1958, R. Clarke 1966). Mocha Dick, the white whale described by Reynolds in 1839, had barnacles on his head,

amounts of lipid tissue in short periods of time." They also contended that "a buoyancy organ on one end of the body seems a grotesque arrangement," since the animal would constantly be tipping up or down. The function of this organ is still unknown, although there is no shortage of hypotheses.

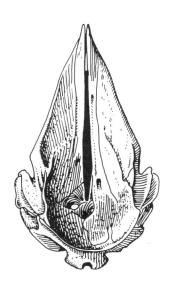

Dorsal view of the skull of the sperm whale (after Howell).

"clustered until it became absolutely rugged with the shells."

One of Bullen's more fascinating tales concerned a "bull cachalot and so powerful a combination of enemies that even one knowing the fighting qualities of the sperm whale would have hesitated to back him to win." The enemies were two killer whales and a swordfish, 16 feet long. The sperm whale took the torpedolike charge of the swordfish in "the impenetrable mass of the head, solid as a block of thirty tons of india-rubber"; the whale turned and caught the "momentarily motionless aggressor in the lethal sweep of those awful shears, crunching him in two halves, which writhing sections he swallowed *seriatim.*" The sperm whale then smashed one of the "allied forces" with his flukes, and the other killer whale fled "for an avalanche of living furious flesh was behind him, and coming with enormous leaps half out of the sea every time." It is wild and colorful descriptions like these that cast the balance of Bullen's work into an unfavorable light, for the exaggerations and unrealistic behavior of the combatants put the entire episode squarely in the realm of imaginative fiction.*

The first known sperm whales were probably beached; the early literature is replete with illustrations of bloated and badly drawn specimens, often surrounded by what appear to be Lilliputians. Because they are so demonstrably gregarious, sperm whales often strand in large numbers. (The only conclusion to be drawn from this is that whales remain together in death as well as in life; no assumptions can be made regarding parasite infestations, mass suicides, injured

---

*There are records of swordfish attacks on whales—or, rather, records of swordfish swords broken off in whales—but we cannot really assign a motive to the fish. Scheffer (1969) fictionalized an incident in which a sperm whale was thus pierced, and there are reports of swordfish swords or marlin bills in sei whales, minke whales, bales of rubber, and even a submarine. In 1967 the minisubmarine *Alvin* was "attacked" at 1,800 feet by a 200-pound swordfish, which was subsequently raised, cleaned, and eaten.

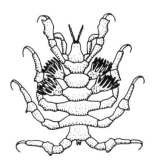

Neocyamus physeteris. Host: sperm whale (after Leung).

leaders, or any other possibilities.) Sperm whales are by far the largest of the socially organized whales, so a mass stranding is a momentous event. (Even though some of the balaenopterids are larger, they are not so gregarious and often associate in groups that may be no larger than a pair.) Some of the more noteworthy strandings, as recorded in Gilmore (1959), are these:

1723	Mouth of the Elbe, Germany–17 whales
1784	Coast of Brittany, France–31 whales
1888	Cape Canaveral, Florida–16 whales
1895	? New Zealand–27 whales
1911	Perkins Island, Tasmania–37 whales
1918	? New Zealand–25 whales
1954	La Paz, Gulf of California–22 whales

More recently, Bryant (1979) discussed a sperm whale stranding of 59 animals in 1970 and the largest known mass stranding, 72 animals in 1974, both in New Zealand. On New Year's Day, 1979, 56 sperm whales were discovered on the beach at Rancho San Bruno, on the Gulf Coast of Baja California. There were 38 males, 9 females, and 9 animals whose sex could not be determined, because by the time scientists arrived on the scene, Mexican fishermen had already begun to burn the carcasses. (The composition of this group raises numerous questions about the school structure and habits of sperm whales, since they are not supposed to aggregate in these peculiar proportions, nor are they normally found in the shallow waters of Baja California.*) In June 1979, 41 sperm whales beached themselves near Florence, Oregon. Much more information on the living habits of sperm whales will have to be accumulated before we can begin even to speculate on their dying habits.

At one time, ambergris was considered the most valuable product of the sperm whale, and in 1672 John Josselyn described it this way:

Now you must understand this *Whale* feeds upon *Ambergreece,* as is apparent, finding it in the *Whales* Maw in great quantity, but altered and excrementious: I conceive that *Ambergreece* is no other than a kind of Mushroom growing at the bottom of some Seas; I was once shewed (by a Mariner) a piece of *Ambergreece* having a root to it like that of the land Mushroom, which the *Whale* breaking up, some scape his devouring Paunch, and is afterwards cast upon shore.

---

*On a 1975 whale-marking cruise aboard the Soviet whaling ship *Vnushitelny,* Berzin (1978) recorded large concentrations of sperm whales in the tropical eastern Pacific, east of Central America: "One group of 30–40 whales was mixed; the animals in it were at various stages of maturity."

This material, pronounced "amber-gree" or "amber-griss" (Dewhurst and other nineteenth-century authors spelled it "ambergrease"), was used, according to Melville, "in perfumery, in pastilles, precious candles, hair powders, and pomatum." It is a marbled grayish (or black) waxy substance that is lighter than water and, therefore, floats. It has been known for centuries from lumps that had washed ashore, but it was only in the eighteenth century, claimed Beale (1835), that about twenty pounds were discovered "in a spermaceti bull-whale." Its primary use was—and still is—as a fixative for perfumes, since it has the property of holding scents. (As for its own smell, opinions vary. Ash [1962] wrote that it reminded him of "the scent you smell when you tear up the moss to uncover the dark soil beneath," but Gaskin [1972] said that "it has the smell of a good cigar.") It occurs only in sperm whales, and whalers would dream of making their fortunes by finding lumps of ambergris washed ashore or buried in the belly of a captured whale. In 1916, Andrews wrote that "as much as $60,000 worth has been taken from the intestines of a single whale." With the development of synthetic stabilizers, the price has dropped considerably, but Nishiwaki in 1972 wrote that "a recent reaffirmation of its quality has caused a rise in its value. In 1962, ambergris sold at an average of $100 per kilogram."* The largest lump ever recorded weighed 983 pounds (442 kilograms), and R. Clarke (1954b) found a "boulder" in the large intestine of a 49-foot bull in the Azores that weighed 926 pounds (416 kilograms). It is not known how this substance forms, but it is thought to be some sort of fecal impaction around a matrix of undigestible material, such as the mandible of a squid. Since the main object of the sperm whale's diet is squid, there are a great number of squid mandibles in the stomachs of a great number of whales, yet ambergris is only rarely encountered. Of course it may be voided or vomited up, but the percentage of whales found to contain this mysterious substance is very small, indeed. It is probably not the direct result of an intestinal irritation, for a whale, after all, is a mammal and not an oyster.

Very few of us will be fortunate enough to find ambergris washed up on the beach, but it would save scientists a lot of time and trouble (see Murphy 1933 for a description of his experiences with people bringing mysterious, smelly substances to him for identification) if we could identify ambergris if and when we find it. In *Marine Mammals of California*, Daugherty (1972) gave a detailed description of this mysterious substance:

Ambergris is waxy and moist when fresh, dry and brittle when old. The color varies from dull gray through brown to almost black, or may be mottled throughout in alternate layers of light and dark color. There is a characteristic somewhat pleasant earthy odor, intensified by warming in the hand. . . . It floats, even in fresh water. When slowly heated, it commences to soften at about 140°F, and melts between 145° and 150°F to a dark, oily liquid. Test it by inserting a heated wire into it; it will melt around the wire forming a dark, opaque liquid. Touched with the finger when partially melted, it is tacky; it adheres and strings. If the wire to which it adheres is re-heated over a flame, it soon emits a white fume with the characteristic odor, and then burns with a luminous flame. It is soluble in absolute alcohol, in ether, in fat, or in volatile oils. It may contain squid beaks.

In one peculiar and absolutely unique account, Murphy (1924) found the "characteristic, nodulated facial vibrissae [whiskers] of a seal" in a lump of ambergris taken from a sperm whale caught off Haiti in 1912. In the original description he did not venture to guess the species of seal, but later (1933) he wrote that "an animal which could engulf a West Indian monk seal would have no difficulty in taking in Jonah."

Although the distribution of this species is not clearly understood, it is assumed to be affected by two factors, food and reproductive needs. The food of the sperm whale consists mostly of deep-water cephalopods, so the whale is likely to be found in those areas where conditions for squid are propitious. These conditions include deep water, usually not less than 3,300 feet (1,000 meters) (Watkins 1977) and locations of cold-water upwellings, such as can be found off the northwestern coast of South America, off the coast of Japan, and in the vicinity of various island groups, including the Azores, Canaries, Cape Verdes, Madeira, and the Galapagos, Seychelles, Comoros, and New Zealand.

Townsend (1935) plotted the world distribution of sperm whale catches as recorded in the logbooks of New England whalers, but as Gilmore pointed out, he did not have access to the records of the west coast whalers from San Francisco and Seattle and "thus completely missed the extensive British Columbia and Kodiak grounds, both largely inhabited by summer males." Nevertheless, Townsend's charts represent a

*References to ambergris being "worth its weight in gold" are usually predicated on past—rather than contemporary—prices for gold. For instance, Murphy (1933) wrote that ambergris was worth more than the then current price of gold, which was $14–$20 per ounce. In early 1980 gold was selling in European markets at over $600 per ounce.

prodigious undertaking. When they are combined with Gilmore's additions of more recent statistics and records of the Pacific grounds that he claimed were lacking in Townsend, and with Holm and Jonsgard's 1959 review of sperm whale catches in the Antarctic, we can begin to see a picture of the cosmopolitan distribution of the sperm whale. Old whalemen knew certain grounds where the species was to be found in greatest numbers and, therefore, "where the masters of ships usually resort for the purpose of fishing" (Beale 1835). The best-known grounds are as follows: the west coast of South America (Callao, Coast of Chile, and Galapagos grounds); the east coast of the same continent (Platte Ground and Brazil Banks); the entire North Atlantic (Charleston, Southern, and Western grounds); the west coast of Africa (Carroll and Tristan grounds); the east coast of Africa (Delagoa Bay, Zanzibar Ground, Mahe Banks); the Arabian Sea (Coast of Arabia Ground); the western North Pacific (Coast of Japan, Japan, and Sulu Sea grounds); the west coast of Australia (Coast of New Holland Ground); the Tasman Sea area between eastern Australia and New Zealand (Middle Ground); and the New Zealand area (Vasquez and French Rock grounds). All along the equator in the Pacific, from the Celebes to Ecuador, was a particularly productive range known as "On the Line."

Townsend's records account for 36,908 sperm whales, taken from 1761 to 1920, but the North Pacific grounds, now considered to be the most productive of all (Nishiwaki 1967), are barren on his charts, as are the Antarctic waters. In the Southern Ocean, sperm whales, almost all of which are males, were not hunted as extensively as the whalebone whales, but when the stocks of blue, fin, sei, and humpback whales began to decline, the pelagic whalers turned toward the sperm. From 1910 to 1946 the annual world catch did not exceed 7,500 sperm whales per year, but postwar catches have increased to nearly 30,000 per year (Best 1974). The stocks of sperm whales are believed to be discontinuous—there are separate populations that do not integrate—but there is very little information on this subject. Sperm whales do not migrate with the predictable regularity of the baleen whales; and with the exception of the polar movements of the bulls, the populations may remain within the same general areas, occasionally moving en masse for unknown reasons.* We do not know for certain if the mature males

that exist in the high latitudes ever return to the breeding herds (Gaskin 1972).

Human involvement with the sperm whale goes back at least as far as biblical times, when Jonah was swallowed by a "great fish."* The species was recognized in the seventeenth century (an account and illustration appear in Clusius's 1605 *Exoticorum libri decem*), and by the early eighteenth century the first sperm whale had been killed by a Nantucket whaler, Christopher Hussey. This event did not set off an immediate and intensive quest for sperm whales, because right whales were still plentiful in New England waters and the hunters would not have the means or the incentive to pursue the sperm for another forty years. Around 1750, two innovations vastly broadened the opportunities available to American whalemen, the development of on-board tryworks and the invention of the spermaceti candle by a Newporter, Jacob Rodriguez Rivera (Kugler 1976). Earlier whaling efforts, such as the Dutch and English hunting of the Greenland right whale, involved killing the whales and then towing them to a shore station for processing. (The Spitsbergen village of Smeerenberg, established by the Dutch in the seventeenth century, was centered around the tryworks, where the blubber of the whales was rendered into oil.) With the development of tryworks on board the whaleships, the crew could now process the animals wherever they caught them and thus remain at sea until their holds were filled. At first the spermaceti oil was combined with the oil from the blubber and known collectively as "sperm oil," but when Rivera invented the smokeless spermaceti candle, the two types of oil were separated. (A large bull might have upward of a ton, or ten barrels, of spermaceti oil in the case, and the blubber, rendered down, might yield as much as one hundred barrels, but such large amounts were very rare.)

Except for enforced slowdowns during the Revolution and the War of 1812, the American sperm whale fishery flourished for about a century, from 1750 to 1850. It reached its zenith in the decade 1840–49, when over 126,000 barrels of sperm oil reached American ports† (Harmer 1928). The fishery was in

---

*In their study of the movements of sperm whales in the Antarctic, Holm and Jonsgard discovered that the whales form herds around the full moon and seem to disperse at other times. This might

coincide with the movements of squid, but their movements are even less well known than those of the whales.
*Of the larger whales, only the sperm has a gullet large enough to accommodate a person. Although they generally avoid landlocked waters, sperm whales are "known to occur in the Mediterranean," according to Norman and Fraser.
†One barrel equaled between 30 and 33 gallons. Scoresby (1820) reckoned 252 gallons to the ton, or almost 8 barrels. Estimates for the average sperm whale ran between 25 and 40 barrels per whale, although some whales exceeded this by three or even four times.

decline by 1850, when, for the first time, sperm oil imports fell below 100,000 barrels. The decline is attributable to the opening of the rich North Pacific and western Arctic whaling grounds for bowheads, as well as the increased expenses of outfitting whaling ships. It is often said that the sperm whale fishery dropped off because of the decrease in the number of whales. (Matthews [1938] wrote that "the decline could only have been due to over fishing.") Other historians, such as Harmer (1928), have attributed the demise of the fishery to the introduction of petroleum. Although the 1859 discovery of oil in Pennsylvania certainly contributed to the extinction of the American sperm whale industry, it occurred some twenty years after the fishery began its precipitous decline.

Unlike today's fishery, in which the whale is dispatched with an exploding harpoon and then dragged up the stern slipway of a factory ship to be rendered into oil and meat in an hour or so, open-boat whaling for sperm whales was a dangerous occupation, often because of the whale's belligerence and reluctance to be turned into candles. The literature of whaling is filled with authentic accounts of the destruction of boats by enraged or injured bull whales. There are also well-documented records of attacks on whale-ships, the best known of which is the destruction of the *Essex* in 1820. The account was written by Owen Chase, the mate of the *Essex;* and it is known that Melville met with Chase's son to discuss the incident, which obviously served as the basis for the destruction of the *Pequod* in *Moby-Dick.* From Chase's journal (1821), the narrative is picked up here after the whale has been struck and has stove a hole in one of the whaleboats:

I observed a very large spermaceti whale, as well as I could judge about eighty-five feet in length. He broke water about twenty rods off our weather bow and was lying quietly, with his head in the direction of the ship. He spouted two or three times and then disappeared. In less than two or three seconds, he came up again, about the length of the ship off, and made directly for us at about three knots. . . . he came down upon us with full speed and struck the ship with his head, just forward of the fore-chains. He gave us such an appalling and tremendous jar as nearly threw us all on our faces. The ship brought up as suddenly and violently as if she had struck a rock, and trembled for a few seconds like a leaf.

The whale remained still for a moment, "apparently stunned with the violence of the blow," then smashed his jaws together and came for the *Essex* again, this time completely stoving in the bow. Within ten minutes the 238-ton vessel had sunk. The remainder of this true story, as frightening as its inception, involves a three-month voyage in an open boat from the point of the accident at 0°40′S, 119°0′W—some 2,700 miles west of Ecuador—finally to the Juan Fernández Islands of Chile. Of the two boatloads that survived the charge of the whale, only one made it back.

In 1850 a whale stove and sank the *Ann Alexander* off Peru, but its crew was rescued within two days. More recently, Gaskin (1972) described the following encounter: "In May 1963 . . . one animal lifted its head and moved towards the boat at a speed of about 3 knots. Since the boat was only 38 feet in length and the whale about 50 feet, we did not follow his interesting behavior through to any conclusion, but departed rapidly for other waters."

Beale (1835) claimed that the larger whales are "sometimes known to turn upon their persecutors with unbounded fury, destroying everything that meets them in their course, sometimes by the powerful blows of their flukes, and sometimes attacking with jaw and head." Whales that are "fastened to" would sometimes thrash about wildly, biting at anything within range (Scammon 1874). There seems to be some question regarding the mobility of the sperm whale's lower jaw. Gaskin (1972) said that "the long narrow lower jaw has virtually no lateral movement, so that the sperm whale is capable of little more than a straight up and down biting movement," but Ashley warned that "his jaw is exceedingly mobile. . . . a boat fifteen feet away at either side is in imminent danger from a rolling sperm whale's jaw." Attacking whales often turned on their backs and swam upside down to bring the lower jaw into play above the surface, a behavior that Ashley referred to as "jawing back."* Even when the whale sounded, the whalers were in danger, for the sperm whale is capable of such deep dives that it might run out all the line; and if the line were not cut quickly, the whale might take the boat below.

Sperm whales are smaller than they used to be,† but

---

*Starbuck wrote "that if the right whale had the habit of 'jawing back' as the sperm whale has, it would be next to impossible to secure him. . . . on the tip of the upper jaw there is a spot . . . seemingly as sensitive in feeling as the antenna of an insect. However swiftly a right whale may be advancing, a slight prick on this point will arrest his forward motion at once."

†Jonsgard has shown that the average sperm whale is smaller today; from 1937 to 1959, the average length decreased from 53.2 feet to 47.2 feet. This may be a function of "gunner selection," by which the larger whales were taken in the earlier seasons, leaving the smaller ones for subsequent years, but this is unlikely, given the variability in whaling locations and the movement of the whales

not enough to account for the discrepancies between the old accounts and the more recent records. Numerous whales have been listed at "over 100 barrels"; for example, Starbuck mentioned a 79-foot whale that yielded 107 barrels and others that were good for 136 barrels and even 156 barrels. "In 1862 the *Ocmulgee*, of Edgartown, reported to have taken a 130-barrel sperm whale, with a jaw measuring 28 feet [8.5 meters] in length." (According to the calculations of Fujino [1956], the lower jaw of an adult male sperm whale is approximately 20 percent of its total length. A whale with a 28-foot lower jaw would therefore be about 140 feet long.)

Nineteenth-century sperm whaling was never the epitome of efficiency, since it took so long to complete a voyage. Trips of two or three years were not uncommon, and by the time the fishery began its decline, even longer voyages were necessary to fill the holds. Townsend wrote that "at its best period, the great fleet probably captured less than 10,000 whales [of all species] per year," and his records showed a total of 36,908 sperm whales for the period 1761–1920 from New England logbooks. (Obviously his figures are incomplete; the figures showed only whales captured by the ships whose logs Townsend examined. Not all logbooks survived, and not all whaleships were out of New England.) It would not do, however, to take Yankee whaling too lightly; Scammon estimated that between 1835 and 1872, "there were no less than 292,714 whales captured or destroyed by the American whaler's lance," an annual average of 7,703. Of this annual catch, Scammon figured some 4,253 ("or thereabouts") to be sperm whales; the rest were rights, bowheads, grays, and humpbacks.

The killing of sperm whales began to drop off during the first third of the twentieth century, as the hunters concentrated on the vast herds of whalebone whales in the Antarctic. Sperm whales were the specialty of some southern whaling stations, such as Durban, South Africa, where 10,136 sperms were taken between 1904 and 1939, or those of Chile and Peru (still the most productive of all sperm whale grounds), where, in the same period, 8,039 of the species were killed. The total number of sperm whales killed at southern whaling stations during that thirty-five-year period was 27,433. (As an indication of the intensity of the southern baleen whale fishery, during the same period, there were 261,945 blue whales, and 216,688

fin whales killed [Mackintosh 1942].) After World War II, the figure for sperm whales began to climb at an ever-increasing rate; as the stocks of baleen whales—obviously unable to withstand this mammoth slaughter—declined, the sperm whale again became the most heavily hunted of all the species. Although the peak years for blue and fin whale catches were 1931 and 1938, respectively, it was not until 1951 that the total kill of sperm whales reached 10,000 per year, and in 1963 the total climbed to over 20,000 per annum, holding at that level until 1971 (McHugh 1974).

Because of the discrepancy in size and in habitat, male and female sperm whales have been considered separately in the International Whaling Commission quotas. In 1937 the International Conference on Whaling (the precursor of the IWC) reached an agreement that was supposed to protect the stocks of sperm whales by restricting the catch to animals over 35 feet (10.6 meters) in length. Since most females are smaller than this, such a restriction was ostensibly more important to the breeding stock. It was assumed that the capture of bulls, "if not excessive, would in no way damage the stock" (Matthews 1938). Later, the figures were adjusted so that whales 38 feet in length could be taken from pelagic factory ships in the Antarctic and the North Pacific (the only areas in which these ships operate), and the limit remained 35 feet for shore-based sperm whaling.*

Probably because the general public regards the sperm whale as the quintessential whale—unlike baleen whales, its mouth is located where one might expect it to be: under the nose—there has always been an awareness of the plight of the sperm whale. The recent history of the fishery has been much in the news and marked by confusion, emotion, and massive public outcries to save the whale. Approximately a century after the New England fishery declined (about 1865), hunting for sperm whales resumed on a large scale. (Throughout the history of Antarctic whaling, sperm whales were taken in comparatively low numbers until the stocks of baleen whales fell to levels that made their hunting uneconomical.)

Shore fisheries existed in Albany, Western Australia, and Durban, South Africa. From 1970–72, a shore fishery was conducted at Dildo Bay, Nova Scotia, where a total of 105 sperm whales were killed. They

themselves. In any event, this information does not justify reports of 80- or 90-foot bull whales.

*As used here, "shore whaling" refers to those activities in which catcher boats set out from port to hunt whales and then return to the whaling station with the whales for processing. Matthiessen (1971) gave a good description of the operations of the Union Whaling Company of Durban, South Africa, which has recently gone out of business.

were all males, captured in water up to 1,000 fathoms deep, off the continental shelf (Mitchell 1975). In the Azores, the open-boat whalers continue their traditional fishery, initiated from shore observation posts. In recent years, however, the major part of the sperm whale fishery was conducted by the Japanese and the Soviets, using gigantic factory ships and flotillas of catcher boats in the North Pacific and the Southern Ocean. For the season 1972/73 and 1973/74, the IWC global quotas were 23,000 sperm whales per year.

In order to establish these quotas, the whaling nations had to have some idea of the number of sperm whales and their reproduction rates so that the scientific committees of the IWC could determine how many could be killed without damaging the population's ability to regenerate. It had always been assumed that females were critical to the breeding populations, and, therefore, the numbers of females included in the yearly quotas were always less than the males. In 1977, E. D. Mitchell questioned this concept and suggested that within the complex social structure of the sperm whale, the removal of the single bull (the "harem master") servicing a group of females "could reduce the pregnancy rate in this school drastically." This was indeed a remarkable observation, for the early fishery emphasized the taking of the largest bulls (they naturally had more oil), and for years the decline of the fishery was attributed to economics, the Civil War, the discovery of petroleum, and other factors. Until Mitchell's suggestion, it seems no one believed that the whales might not have been able to reproduce enough to maintain the species. "It is possible," Mitchell continues, "that the techniques of the early American fishery, coupled with the complex social behavior of the sperm whale, might have resulted in reduction of the population over decades far out of proportion to reduction judged from the landed catch or oil yield alone."

If determining the relative importance of males or females to the population seems difficult, estimating the population itself turns out to be almost impossible. At best it is difficult to count whales, but when the species is distributed over two-thirds of the surface of the earth and highly migratory as well, the problem becomes almost insurmountable. In 1965, N. A. Mackintosh, an authority on whale populations, wrote, "It is hard to see any way at present of making even a wild estimate on the magnitude of world populations of sperm whales." Despite his warning, experts in population dynamics have been hard at work, and by using

the marking of whales, the sighting of whales, and the application of various mathematical formulas, they have tried. Estimates vary widely, depending upon who is doing the estimating and what methods are employed. (There is also the variable of whether the estimater is in the whaling business; Japanese estimates of sperm whale populations always appear to be higher than those of, say, the British or the Americans.) Best (1975) reviewed the various estimates of world sperm whale stocks, and the following paragraph appeared in his report:

Division II. (East Atlantic). The least squares method gave estimates of 18,000 exploitable males (from Donkergat data) or 27,000 exploitable males (pelagic data) for the 1963 stock, and a rounded average of 22,000 was used to get an initial stock of 34,000 males. From this the original mature female stock was calculated to be 44,000 and the 1972 stock 42,000. An independent estimate of the mature female population size for the period 1957 to 1964 by Best (1970) gave values of 15,550 or 31,940, using fishing mortality rates and catches.

From this it would appear that Mackintosh was correct, and even the most sophisticated methods were not producing particularly accurate or helpful information. Using various sources Scheffer (1976) gave the following estimates for sperm whales remaining today: 212,000 males, 429,000 females, or 69 percent of the estimated virgin population of 922,000. As a further example of the difficulties inherent in estimating populations, M. R. Clarke (1979b) offered a figure of 1.25 million sperm whales alive today, a number considerably higher than Scheffer's estimate of the preexploitation population. Even if we accept these figures as the possible range of the population, there are probably more sperm whales than all other species of great whales combined.

Since 1968, the Scientific Committee of the International Whaling Commission has been unable to devise the best method for estimating sperm whale stocks, and in addition to the annual meetings of the IWC, a number of special meetings have been convened, at which the primary topic was the problem of sperm whale numbers. At one of these special meetings at La Jolla, California, in December 1976, in spite of the presentation of some twenty-nine papers on various aspects of sperm whale population biology, the scientists were forced to admit that they had very little real knowledge of the sheer numbers or the reproduction rate of the sperm whale. In short, the scientific committee was setting quotas for these whales with virtually no idea of how many there were or how to figure that out. In a report on the La Jolla meeting, Smith (1976) made the following comments: "We must assume that the harvesting of sperm whales is having an impact, even though we cannot determine the magnitude of that impact with certainty. . . . the one thing we do know is that harvesting of large whales can cause rapid and extensive reductions in abundance." Not a great revelation, to be sure, but it was the first time that the scientific community had publicly confessed to the possible adverse effects of "harvesting" whales without knowing their population figures.

In spite of their admitted ignorance, the Scientific Committee—under pressure from the sperm-whaling nations—recommended even higher quotas for the global catch of male and female sperm whales in the 1977/78 season: 13,037 as compared to 12,676 for the previous season.* At another special meeting convened at Cronulla, Australia, in June 1977, the IWC Scientific Committee recommended a quota of 763 sperm whales for the North Pacific (the area where the Japanese and the Soviets concentrated their efforts, and where, only four years previously, the quota had been 10,000 animals), but in a move that shocked the world and the whaling community as well, the IWC general meeting set the quota at 6,444 sperm whales, nearly *ten times* the number recommended by their own scientists. Reaction to this maneuver was a worldwide outcry, and directly and indirectly led to the application of tremendous pressure on the IWC. At the 1978 meeting in London, no quota at all was set for sperm whales; confusion and indecision seemed to be the order of the day. It took still another special meeting in Tokyo in December 1978 to establish the North Pacific quota of 3,800 animals, a reduction of almost 40 percent from the previous year's calamitous 6,444. It was now apparent that the IWC could no longer continue to function as a "gentlemen's club" for the whaling nations of the world, and attention had to be given to the pressures being administered from without, especially from the numerous conservation and environmental groups that had mounted such massive "save the whale" campaigns.

The year between the 1978 and 1979 meetings was marked by even greater pressure on the whaling industry, and by 1979 the stage was set for substantial changes. Not even the most hopeful of the observers, however, was prepared for the results. All factory-ship

whaling was banned—effectively putting the Soviets out of the whaling business* and relegating the Japanese to the Antarctic, where they can only hunt the minke whale—and the entire Indian Ocean was declared a whale sanctuary for ten years. (There is still an allowable quota of 2,203 sperm whales that can be taken from shore stations, but the figure is a two-thirds reduction of the quota for 1978/79.) Because the seasons are defined as "1978/79" and the meetings are held in single years—not to mention the special meetings for sperm whale quotas—the totals for worldwide sperm whale quotas are confusing and are presented here for the past six seasons:

Whaling Season	Quotas for male and female sperm whales, including North Pacific, North Atlantic, and Southern oceans
1974/75	23,000
1975/76	19,040
1976/77	12,676
1977/78	13,037
1978/79	9,921
1979/80	2,203

The sperm whale appears to have received another reprieve. Although this fascinating creature does not seem to be threatened—at least for now—it should be regarded as a worldwide natural treasure, to be studied for its extraordinary capabilities, preferably without being destroyed in the process. It should not be slaughtered for the oil in its head, which is used for the lubrication of machinery, or for its meat, which is used for hog and chicken feed. (The meat of the sperm whale is considered inedible by humans; it is greasy and purplish-black in color because of its high myoglobin content, and it is reported to taste terrible.)

The killing of sperm whales has slowed to its lowest level in over two hundred years. "Pirate whalers" still kill an occasional sperm, and the whalers of the Azores still hunt the mighty *cachalote* from open boats, exactly as the Yankee whalers did in the nineteenth century. The shore stations in Australia and South Africa have closed, as much victims of world indignation as of economics. In a report issued in 1978 by the government of Australia, it was strongly suggested that all

*All figures in this section were taken from the annually published schedules of the International Whaling Commission. These figures are then repeated in the year's *Annual Report* as an appendix.

*Those who hoped that the Soviets would immediately retire their whaling fleets were in for a disappointment. Only one month after the July 1979 IWC meeting, the USSR proposed—by postal vote—that they be allowed to take 1,508 male sperm whales. The proposal was soundly defeated, but the Soviets took 201 sperm whales anyway, claiming that they had misunderstood the IWC directive.

whaling cease in Australian waters (Frost 1978). Shortly thereafter, the last whaling station in that country closed forever. The Union Whaling Company of Durban, South Africa, shut down in 1976.

An insignificant little shrub may replace the oil for which so many sperm whales were killed. Known as the jojoba, or goatbush, this inhabitant of the arid southwestern deserts of North America is not related to any other known plant. It has waxy, grayish-brown leaves, and its fruit is a thumbnail-sized brown bean that may be converted into a waxy oil that is virtually indistinguishable from spermaceti oil. The oil of the jojoba can also be employed for the same purposes as sperm oil—that is, as a lubricant for fine machinery, in the manufacture of smokeless candles, and as an additive for transmission fluid. The jojoba oil has been used by the San Carlos Apache as fuel for lamps, ointment for sore joints, and lotion for skin problems. The plant grows slowly and has the added economic disadvantage of having to be planted and cultivated before it can be processed. Although it will take time to produce jojoba in sufficient quantities to replace sperm oil—the plant reaches maturity in five years—efforts are now being made to cultivate the plant and thus to make the killing of whales unnecessary.

Current energy problems, many of them related to the availability of oil, may once again threaten the world's whales. It would surprise few persons to hear the suggestion that a short-term solution to our energy problems be found in the killing and processing of whales, nature's floating oil factories. Assuming that this does not occur in the immediate future, we may now avail ourselves of the deeply moving realization that the sperm whales can swim unmolested—almost—in the seven seas, and we may once again recognize Melville's tribute to this absolute monarch of the sea, "the great Sperm Whale now reigneth!"

PYGMY SPERM WHALE

Kogia breviceps Blainville 1838

When it was first described, this animal was considered a member of the same genus as the great sperm whale (in 1838 Blainville named it *Physeter breviceps*), but it is now recognized as belonging to a separate genus. Some authors (for example, Nishiwaki 1972) would even put it into a separate family, the Kogiidae, but the latest classifications place this genus and the sperm whale into the same family, the Physeteridae. There are certainly enough anatomical similarities to warrant their association, including the undershot lower jaw, protruding forehead, left-of-center blowhole, and asymmetrical skull. Raven and Gregory (1933) have commented on the existence of the spermaceti organ in the pygmy sperm, a feature that is

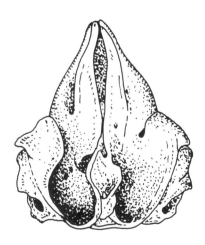

Dorsal view of the skull of a pygmy sperm whale, *Kogia breviceps.* The short snout from which this species takes its name is evident (After Raven and Gregory 1933).

122

unique to this genus and the sperm, and also on the structure of the nasal passages, only one of which is externally functional. In addition, the skull of the pygmy, in which the rostrum is proportionally the shortest of any cetacean, has the same hollowed-out configuration of the sperm whale's skull.

Other characteristics, not the least of which is size, would seem to differentiate the animals, rather than affiliate them. The pygmy sperm whale does not get much longer than 13 feet (4.0 meters), whereas the sperm whale reaches a length of 60 feet (18.3 meters). The pygmy has a dorsal fin where the sperm has a series of "dorsal humps." And the head-to-body proportions are substantially different: "the somewhat conical head of pygmy sperm whales is one of the smallest among the cetaceans" (Handley 1966), whereas the giant head of the sperm whale can be one-third of the animal's total length. The similarities seem to have prevailed, and the little whales with the undershot jaws are considered cousins of the enormous, deep-diving spermaceti whales.

The color of this animal is dark blue-gray or black above, with lighter undersides. The underslung lower jaw has often been compared to that of a shark (Harmer 1927), but there is no real possibility of confusing this horizontally tailed mammal with a fish. It does have a peculiar pigmentation pattern where the gills would be if whales had gills. This complicated and variable pattern behind the eye and the mouth has been called a "false gill" (Leatherwood et al. 1976), but it would be less confusing to call it a "bracket" or a "bracket-shaped mark," as Ross (1979) has done. In describing these marks, Carl Hubbs, an eminent ichthyologist, wrote (1951) that they "looked strangely like the gill opening of a teleost fish, but I see no significance in this relationship."

The dorsal fin in this species is quite small and is located posterior to the midpoint of the back. The teeth in the small mouth number between nine and sixteen on each side of the lower jaw, and they are thin and sharply curved, "strangely reminiscent of the teeth of pythons" (Handley 1966). Unlike the teeth of sperm whales, which have no enamel surface, the teeth of the pygmy have a thin layer of enamel (Tomilin 1957). In this species the upper jaw usually has no teeth at all, but occasional specimens are examined with one or two pairs of small teeth visible in the upper jaw.*

The name *breviceps* comes from the Latin for "short-head," but *Kogia* is more problematical. Norman and Fraser (1938) wrote that it is "said to be the Latinized form of 'codger,'" but they offer no explanation as to why a little whale would be called a "codger." (According to the *Oxford English Dictionary,* a "codger" is "a mean and miserly old man.") The Japanese call the animal *Komakko,* which means "lesser sperm whale," but Yamada recommended that a traditional name, *Uki-kujira,* be used, since it means "floating whale" and aptly describes the slow-moving, lethargic nature of this species.

There is an animal so similar to the pygmy sperm whale that cetologists have only recently concluded that two distinct species exist. *Kogia simus,* known as the dwarf sperm whale, was long considered to be conspecific with *K. breviceps,* as evidenced by this statement made by Hale in 1962: "The information so far recorded herein and elsewhere supports the view that only one species of *Kogia* exists." In a more recent analysis, Handley has established "beyond doubt the existence of two strongly differentiated species of pygmy sperm whales which are recognizable by many cranial, skeletal, and external characters." *K. breviceps* is the larger of the species and has a longer snout, as measured from the tip of the snout to the blowhole (Ross 1979). The dorsal fin of the larger species (*breviceps*) is proportionally smaller than that of *simus,* and it is located farther toward the tail. (Ross warned, however, that "the position of the dorsal fin varies considerably in both species" and that "this character should be used with caution in identification.") In shape, the dorsal fin of *breviceps* is "a small nubbin," whereas that of *simus* is "much taller and more 'dolphinlike' in appearance" (Leatherwood et al. 1976). An additional diagnostic is the number of teeth in the lower jaw: 12–16 pairs in *breviceps;* 8–11 pairs in *simus.*

Since the pygmy sperm whale has been rarely observed at sea, very little is known of its natural history. What little information there is can be summarized as follows: It is a timid, slow-moving creature, usually seen in pairs (possibly mother and calf) or in groups of three to five animals. Examination of the stomach contents of stranded animals has revealed an unremarkable menu of fish, crabs, shrimp, and squid. Some animals have been observed with parallel scars on the body, suggesting the possibility of fighting, and

---

*Handley wrote that the absence of upper teeth is diagnostic in this species, and distinguishes *K. breviceps* from *K. simus,* the dwarf sperm whale. *Simus* is supposed to have "up to 3 teeth in each upper jaw,"

but this figure also seems to vary. Of the six specimens of *breviceps* examined by Yamada (1954), all but one had upper teeth, and in that specimen the teeth "may possibly be lost."

"circular scars round the mouth," which seem to have been made by squid (Gaskin 1972). The records of full-term fetuses and newborn calves indicate that the length at birth is about 4 feet (1.2 meters), and Ross postulated a gestation period of about eleven months.

In commenting on the presentation of Handley's 1966 paper on the pygmy sperm whale F. G. Wood said, "As a matter of interest, and I don't think it has been published yet by anyone, the small right narial passage of *Kogia* contains a beautiful little noise-maker." When a specimen stranded alive at Playa del Rey, California, it was recorded as making "low intensity, low-frequency sounds" while it was out of the water (quoted in Caldwell et al. 1966). It is assumed that the highly differentiated nasal passages of the pygmy, like those of the sperm, are somehow involved in the regulation of deep diving and possibly in the production of sound. Schenkkan and Purves (1973), discussing the unique structure of the pygmy's nose, wrote, "The right naris is not used in external respiration, but forms an air reservoir subservient to phonation at extreme depths."

Probably because of their unique structure, the skull and head of the pygmy have been the subjects of numerous detailed observations. (The head of the sperm whale is equally fascinating, but at 18–20 feet long, it is considerably less manageable.) In 1933, Raven and Gregory examined the heads of a juvenile sperm whale and a pygmy and made the obvious comparisons of the nasal passages. They also referred to the "melon" of other odontocetes as a "spermaceti organ" (one illustration shows a narwhal's "spermaceti organ"), which Schenkkan and Purves disputed energetically: "the spermaceti organ is is no way homologous to the melon of other odontocetes." In the Physeteridae the spermaceti organ separates the right and left nasal passages and is located posterior to the blowhole. In all other toothed whales that have a melon, it is located forward of the blowhole. The function of this organ in the pygmy, like the massive spermaceti organ of the sperm whale, is not known, but it has been suggested that "it assists in the evacuation of the lungs prior to a deep dive" (Schenkkan and Purves 1973). Because this organ is so much smaller in the pygmy sperm whale, it probably cannot serve the same function as it does in the sperm whale, and the animal probably is not a particularly deep diver.

In the literature on this variety there are discussions of the head and musculature and summaries of the synonomy, but by far the most numerous references concern its arrival on various beaches around the world. Ross has written, "In the 140 years that have passed since Blainville (1838) described the first pygmy sperm whale *Kogia breviceps* from a skull collected at the Cape of Good Hope, approximately 150 specimens of this genus have been reported from strandings on shores bordering the temperate and tropical seas of the world." With its sharklike profile, sharp little teeth, and bracket marks, it has always been considered unusual. (Hale [1959] wrote that there were probably more strandings than were recorded, but in Australia, at least, people often thought they were simply "blackfish" and did not bother to report the strandings.) The numerous records demonstrate an almost worldwide distribution in warmer waters. In the western North Atlantic it has been recorded from Halifax Harbor, Nova Scotia (Allen 1941); down the entire eastern coast of the United States, including Massachusetts, New Jersey, Maryland, North Carolina, South Carolina, and Florida; and in the West Indies, from the island of Saint Vincent in the Lesser Antilles (Caldwell and Caldwell 1975). There have been only three records of the pygmy sperm whale from the coasts of Europe, but over twenty from eastern North America, suggesting that the gently shelving shores of the United States are somehow more conducive to its beaching itself. Handley cited records of the species from "the warmer seas of the world . . . only once in the South Pacific . . . once in the western Indian Ocean, and not at all in the South Atlantic. Most frequently stranded on the coasts of South Africa, southeastern Australia, New Zealand, and southeastern United States." Yamada examined more than twenty specimens from Japanese waters, but he did not clearly differentiate the species. Finally, one "probable record" comes from New Guinea (Gaskin 1966).

There is an interesting observation in Bullen's *Cruise of the Cachalot* (1899), in which the author, stationed in the crow's nest, sighted "something far away on the horizon." The boats were lowered and the chase begun, with Bullen hoping for sperm whales:

There was a little obliquity about the direction of the spout that made me hopeful, for the cachalot alone sends his spout diagonally upward, all others spout vertically. It was but a school of kogia, or "short-headed" cachalots; but as we secured five of them, averaging seven barrels apiece without any trouble, I felt quite pleased with myself. We had quite an exciting bit of sport with them, they were so lively; but as for danger—well, they only seemed like big "black-fish" to us now, and we enjoyed the fun. They were, in all respects, miniature sperm whales, except that the head was

much shorter and smaller in proportion to the body than their big relations.

Palmer (1948) discussed this account; and though he felt that it might be a rare account of the schooling behavior of pygmy sperm whales, he pointed out that the amount of oil is in error. So, it would seem, is the description of the animals as "lively"; and if anything, they would look like small—not big—"black-fish." It appears that this account, like many of the tales in his book, is a combination of observation, research, and imagination.

A rare category appears in Hubbs's 1951 paper: "gastronomic considerations." He reported that he and his co-workers, having found a pygmy sperm whale stranded at Imperial Beach, California, ate some of it, and "the responses ranged from disgust to enthusiasm."

DWARF SPERM WHALE

Kogia simus Owen 1866

The dwarf sperm whale is very similar to the pygmy sperm whale in general characteristics, but it is consid-

erably smaller, reaching only 8.5 feet (2.7 meters) in length. The color is dark gray or black above, shading to a lighter gray or white below. Like the pygmy, this species also has the distinctive "bracket marks" behind the eye and the mouth. The size and dorsal fin differentiate these species, since in the dwarf the fin is higher and more falcate than that of its close relative. The teeth in the lower jaw number eight to eleven pairs, and there are "one to three pairs (or none?) in the upper jaw" (Handley 1966). The name *simus* is from the Latin, meaning "snub-nosed."

Because of its dolphinlike fin, this animal might be confused with almost any other small cetacean at a distance. Under closer scrutiny, the overhanging snout and small lower jaw would be definitive, and the animal would be identifiable as *Kogia simus* (or *Kogia breviceps*). It might appear that the two species are indistinguishable and, therefore, conspecific, but there are enough differences, particularly in the comparative skull measurements, for an expert to tell them apart. Handley remarked that "the adults of *K. breviceps* are much larger in all cranial dimensions than any adult *K. simus*." Another character that seems to be constant is size: *K. breviceps* is much the larger species, for its calves, "still suckling, may be almost as big as an adult *K. simus*" (Handley 1966).

Dorsal view of *Kogia simus,* showing sinistral position of blowhole and the sharply pointed snout.

If the pygmy is poorly known in the wild, the dwarf is positively an enigma. We can assume only that its habits are similar to those of its larger relative and that it eats predominantly squid and also fish, crabs, and shrimp. It is probably found in small groups of not more than four to five animals, and there would be no reason to assume that it is any more energetic than the pygmy. Ross (1979) wrote that "the small blood volume and relatively small heart may indicate that *K. simus* is not a very active animal, though it appears to be capable of diving to at least 300 m (Fitch and Brownell 1968)." Ross also suggested that "calves of *K. simus* are born at about 1 m in length," but he felt that there were too few data to speculate on the length of the gestation period.

Since Handley recognized and clearly differentiated the two species in 1966, earlier records were undoubtedly confused. In recent years there have been records of the dwarf from Georgia south to Saint Vincent, where it is called the "rat porpoise" (Caldwell et al. 1973), and throughout the eastern and northern Gulf of Mexico. Other recent records are from Japan, where Yamada (1954) did not clearly differentiate the two whales, although most of the specimens he examined seemed to be *simus;* South Africa (Ross 1979); California (Roest 1970); and various other locations that probably coincide with records for *K. breviceps.* The distribution for the two species is similar, but Handley reported that "they have never been taken at the same time or from the same net. They have been found on the same coast, but whether in actual association is not known."

This species was first described by Sir Richard Owen in 1866 from material sent to him from India by Walter Elliot. Owen measured the skeletal material, examined the notes and drawings that Elliot had sent, and then published his conclusions. He pointed out the differences between this and the other specimens and believed (correctly, it seems) that this was a new species. He named it *Physeter (Euphysetes) simus,* because at that time all whales with an undershot lower jaw were thought to be *Physeter.* Owen also wrote that "it is known by the Teluga fishermen of the coast of Madras by the name of 'Wonga.'" After having surfaced briefly off the coast of India, the Wonga sank into taxonomic oblivion until it was resurrected by Handley in 1966.

Yamada hoped this would happen, for he wrote in 1954, "because no addition of a typical *K. simus* has been known after Owen . . . I wonder from time to time that the whole discussion might be utterly inappropriate and we should look forward to future specimens. . . . Who can deny the future possibility of Owen's *K. simus* to appear before us?" It took exactly one hundred years for the "future specimens" to appear and be recognized as different species.

THE BEAKED WHALES

In 1872, W. H. Flower made the following observations on the beaked whales:

Their very presence in the ocean seems to pass unnoticed and unsuspected by voyagers, and even by those whose special occupation is the pursuit and capture of various better known and more abundant cetaceans until one of the accidental occurrences just alluded to reveals the existence of animal life of considerable magnitude (for they range between fifteen and twenty feet in length) and at least sufficiently numerous to maintain the continuity of the race.

With the passage of time, the situation improved only slightly. In 1910, True wrote that "the beaked whales . . . are among the rarest of cetaceans," and he was able to locate only about one hundred specimens of all species known to him in the museum collections of the world. More than two centuries have passed since the description of the first beaked whale (*Hyperoodon ampullatus* in 1770), but the situation has not really changed very much. The beaked whales are still, by all criteria, the least known of all the large animals in the world, even though they live in all the oceans and are often large and imposing, the largest *(Berardius)* reaching a length of 42 feet (12.8 meters).

The typical beaked whale has a tapered, fusiform body, wide flukes that are not notched like those of most other cetaceans, small flippers, and some sort of an elongated snout that may account for the name "beaked whale." (Naturally, there are exceptions. Some of the species are known by much more descriptive common names, such as the "goosebeak whale," the "strap-toothed whale," or the "ginkgo-toothed whale," and one species is known in New Zealand as the "scamperdown whale.") There is a crescent-shaped blowhole with the horns pointing forward, and a small dorsal fin that is usually located much closer to the tail flukes than to the head. All members of the family have two throat grooves that converge toward the snout and relatively small eyes, located back and away from the gape of the mouth.

We do not know where most beaked whales live. Since most of our information comes from the examination of stranded specimens, it might be said that we are more knowledgeable about where they die. We are ignorant of where or when they breed, and we are not really sure of how many different species there are. At present there is one family, known variously as the Ziphiidae or Hyperoodontidae, composed of six genera and eighteen species.

Until the publication of "Relationships among the Living Genera of Beaked Whales . . ." by J. C. Moore in 1968, confusion was the order of the day. Since some of the species are known only from skeletal remains, many of the ordinary criteria employed in the differentiation of species—distribution, behavior, color, and so on—are not really applicable. With a few exceptions, the animals in this family have been shuffled around and argued over in scientific journals, as various taxonomists questioned the assignment of various species and discussed, in the reserved and courteous manner characteristic of scientific journals, whether there are more or fewer valid species than previously calculated. Even though the species in question are alive and swimming somewhere in the world's oceans, some of the discussions resemble paleontological problems, because all the cetologists have to study is some bones. Of the eighteen currently recognized species, one of them, *Indopacetus pacificus,* has never been seen in the flesh and another, *Mesoplodon bowdoini,* was described originally from skeletal remains (Andrews 1908); then some specimens referred to this species were identified in the flesh in California and Japan, but these were eventually reassigned to other species, so *bowdoini* has yet to be described from a fresh specimen.

Most evidence for the existence of these animals

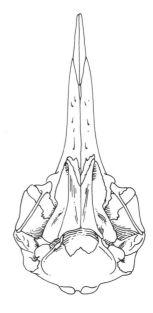

Ventral view of the skull of a beaked whale (*Mesoplodon europaeus*), showing the sharply pointed rostrum.

comes from bones picked up on the beach or from stranded or beached specimens. Occasionally a report of a live beaked whale is recorded, either at sea by someone who cannot make an identification or by whalers who soon dispatch it so that it becomes another study specimen or even mink food. Three of the larger species of beaked whales, *Berardius bairdii, Hyperoodon ampullatus,* and *Ziphius cavirostris,* have been fished by small whale fisheries out of Japan and Norway, so there exists a small body of observational and biological material on these species.

For the genus *Mesoplodon,* whose name means "with a tooth in the middle of the jaw," the scientific record is derived almost entirely from beached specimens. A small whale will come ashore; and if the local people do not dispose of it too quickly because of the smell, a government agency might be called and perhaps even a scientist will get to examine it. More often than not, however, the carcass will be vandalized, so the diagnostic characteristics that would otherwise enable scientists to identify the species are often disfigured or missing.

In *The Lady and the Sharks,* Eugenie Clark (1969) recounted the story of a beaked whale that washed ashore at Boca Grande, Florida, in 1959. She was called to examine the creature, and although she realized that it was a species of *Mesoplodon,* she was unable to determine which one it was, especially since the lower jaw and teeth were missing. After a careful search—much of it offshore and underwater—the lower jaw was found, and she sent a sketch of it to J. C. Moore, then at the American Museum of Natural History in New York. He identified it as *Mesoplodon gervaisi* (now known as *M. europaeus*), but he was dis-

tressed about the missing teeth, because this was only the second male ever found. (Only the males of this genus have visible teeth; the females have teeth, but they remain unerupted in the gums and are, therefore, invisible until a thorough examination of the skull is performed.) The son of the fisherman who had discovered the whale had taken the ivorylike teeth as souvenirs, but he voluntarily surrendered them to Clark, who sent them to Moore in New York so that he could properly record this rare occurrence of a *Mesoplodon* in Florida (Moore 1960).

The beaked whales can be differentiated by size, sometimes by color, by the shape of the beak, or by the comparative dimensions and characteristics of the skull. In fact, the cranial morphology is the primary determining factor in the identification and establishment of species, but only experts are trained to perform these highly technical and arcane examinations. That leaves the lower jaws and teeth, objects that can be examined and sometimes even identified by amateurs, provided that they have a proper key.

In the beaked whales the teeth are wondrous to behold. The males of some genera have perhaps the most unusual dental arrangements in the animal kingdom. Of the eighteen species, only one, *Tasmacetus,* has what might be considered a normal complement of teeth. Both the males and females of this species have about forty-eight pairs of small teeth in each jaw, and in addition, the males possess a pair of much larger teeth at the tip of the lower jaw. In the other species, however, there are all sorts of interesting arrangements. Both males and females of the genus *Berardius* own two pairs of teeth at the end of the lower

Mesoplodon europaeus, female and juvenile.

jaw and none in the upper. The *Mesoplodons* have only two teeth, one on each side of the lower jaw, and then visible only in adult males. *Mesoplodon bidens* has long, laterally flattened teeth that point backward; *Mesoplodon grayi* has two teeth that look like flat onions; and a species recently discovered in Japan is known as *Mesoplodon ginkgodens,* the "ginkgo-toothed whale," because the two teeth in males resemble the leaves of the ginkgo tree. The strangest teeth of all, however, belong to *Mesoplodon layardii,* the "strap-toothed whale." In mature males of this species, the teeth grow out, back, and over the upper jaw, so that the animal can hardly open its mouth. The "reason" for this strange modification remains totally obscure, but Baker (1972) has suggested that the teeth "act as guard rails to keep squid and fish on the right path towards the throat." (This, of course, presupposes an unnatural willingness on the part of the squid or fish to enter that throat in the first place.)

Many species of beaked whales are marked with single or parallel scars, which most authorities attribute to other males of the same species, fighting over females. Hubbs (1946) even suggested that the location of the scars (on the lower flanks) "indicates that the fighting male attacks from below and from the side." It is, indeed, possible that these scars are caused by rival males, and we certainly cannot prove otherwise, since there are almost no recorded observations of the behavior of beaked whales in the wild and none at all of two animals fighting. Most observers currently believe that the long scratches are caused by the teeth

of other males. McCann (1974), in fact, devoted an entire article to a discussion of the scars on toothed whales, concluding that most of them come from fighting, but some may have been the work of killer whales. Others are not so willing to recognize this intraspecies aggression, and Pike (1953) said that scratches from rival *Mesoplodon* males' teeth "seem unlikely, since they are either buried in the gum, or are blunt and protrude only slightly." In some of the species, particularly *M. densirostris, M. stejnegeri, M. bowdoini,* and *M. carlhubbsi,* the teeth are located at the middle, rather than at the tip, of the lower jaw. It would stretch the imagination—not to mention the lower jaws of these whales—for them to open their mouths far enough to inflict the double-line scars on other males.* In some cases it seems unlikely that the males could do this to each other, and in other cases it seems physically impossible, but we have only circumstantial and still inconclusive evidence: Whales have teeth; whales have scars; therefore, whales scar other whales.

The distribution of the beaked whales is another source of mystery. Some species are restricted to one ocean—or even one limited area of one ocean—

*When I wrote to Masaharu Nishiwaki at the Whales Research Institute in Tokyo to ask him about this, he replied, "Parallel scratches are thought to be made when males fight or play. A male might dash at another with his mouth shut; he turns himself on his back and bumps himself with his head on another's. His big teeth at the beak scratch the skin of his counterpart in this bump. . . . Females have lesser scars, and . . . scars are more apparent in the species which have bigger teeth."

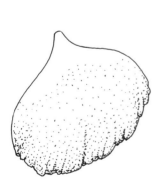 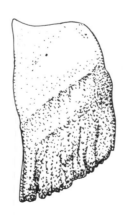 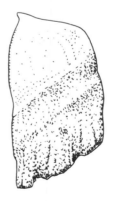 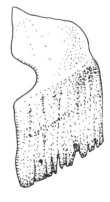

Mesoplodon ginkgodens;   *Mesoplodon carlhubbsi;*   *Mesoplodon stejnegeri;*   *Mesoplodon bowdoini.*

The teeth of some species of *Mesoplodon.* In all cases the teeth are positioned as if the animal faced to the reader's left. Note the high "shoulder" of the tooth of *M. carlhubbsi* and the characteristic worn area on the anterior edge of the tooth of *M. bowdoini.* All are teeth of adult males, and all are drawn to scale.

whereas others, such as the goosebeak whale are almost completely cosmopolitan, found in practically all the world's oceans. Others appear to have a neatly defined range, but then a specimen will show up thousands of miles from this range, thereby causing confusion, revision, and even admiration for these animals that can so thoroughly escape our scrutiny and our predations. *Mesoplodon grayi,* known previously to exist only in the Southern Hemisphere, suddenly appeared in the Netherlands. This specimen, like most of the other ziphioid whales, owes its existence in the literature to a stranding. Since all whales are creatures of the oceans and not of the shore, we must remember that stranded animals represent only the very borders of the animal's actual pelagic range, and we know absolutely nothing about their actual distribution patterns at sea.

Our limited evidence has shown us that there exists a family of fairly large whales that lives in the greatest and most protective of all the planet's biospheres. In *Wildlife in America* (1959), Peter Matthiessen wrote,

Some species of small beaked whales, an ancient group which may be passing slowly from existence, appear rarely in North American waters. There are only a few scattered records, on the Atlantic coast, of the Sowerby and the Gervais whales, and of the Stejneger's whale in the Pacific, and the habits of these mysterious creatures are virtually unknown.

The beaked whales may be "passing slowly from existence," or they may even be proliferating. We know that they are there and that they remain among nature's most closely guarded secrets. As I write this, another specimen may be stranding on some remote beach in Tasmania, Norway, or Jamaica, or it may be splashing helplessly in the waters of Rockaway Beach, New York. It might even be a new species.

SOUTHERN GIANT BOTTLENOSE WHALE

Berardius arnuxii Duvernoy 1851

The giant bottlenose is the only four-toothed whale found in the waters of the Southern Hemisphere. Unlike most of the other beaked whales, both males and females of this genus have teeth. There are two pairs, roughly triangular in shape and laterally compressed; the anterior pair is considerably larger than the posterior pair. The lower jaw extends beyond the upper, and often the forward pair of teeth is visible when the animal's mouth is closed. (Because there are no opposing teeth, barnacles sometimes adhere to these teeth.) Females are larger than males, "the usual ziphioid relationship between the sexes apparently being reversed" (Slipp and Wilke 1953). According to McCann (1975), the largest known specimen was 32 feet (9.6 meters) in length. It is dark above and lighter below, often conspicuously marked with white scars and patches. McCann's photographs (1975) of an old male stranded at Pukerua Bay, New Zealand, show an animal literally covered with spots, scars, scratches, and welts. He attributed these to the "battle-teeth" of rival adult males, but also said that they might have been inflicted by killer whales, lampreys, or whale-

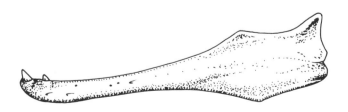

Berardius arnuxii

suckers, or perhaps they are the " 'jab' wounds caused by the tip of an opponent's rostrum."

The name of this species is derived directly from the names of the people involved in its discovery. Captain Berard commanded the French corvette *Rhin,* on which the type specimen was transported to France (described in detail by Duvernoy in 1851), and Arnoux was the surgeon on board who provided a brief description of the animal, which had been collected in New Zealand. For reasons long lost to history, the *o* in Arnoux's name was omitted in the original description, and despite the appearance of various spellings of the name (for example, *arnouxi* or *arnouxii*), the rules of zoological nomenclature require that the original spelling be retained, even though a spelling error was committed. (In taxonomy this kind of error is known as a *lapsus calami,* or a "slip of the pen.") According to Rice's 1977 *List of the Marine Mammals of the World,* the correct name of this animal is *Berardius arnuxii.* To complicate our limited knowledge of this rare whale further, practically everyone who discusses it uses a different common name. It has been variously referred to as the "southern four-toothed whale" (Moore 1968); the "southern beaked whale" (Nishiwaki 1972); "Arnoux's beaked whale" (Brownell 1974); the "southern porpoise whale" (McCann 1975); and the "southern giant bottlenose whale" (Rice 1977). A more convincing argument for the use of scientific nomenclature would be hard to find.

At sea this species can be confused with the southern bottlenose whale, and immature specimens could be mistaken for almost any species of beaked whale known to inhabit the Southern Ocean. The forehead of the male is not as bulbous as that of the southern bottlenose, and the former is usually a larger animal with a small dorsal fin.

Since this species is known from less than fifty specimens, almost all of them strandings or skeletal remains, there is hardly any information on the biology of the living animal.* One report of a stranded animal (Haast 1870) disclosed a large number of squid beaks in the stomach. In one of the few descriptions of a living specimen Taylor (1957) saw a single specimen trapped in the closing ice in Graham Land, Antarctica,

along with 60 killer whales and about 120 minke whales. "The author only saw the single specimen of *Berardius* on 14.8.55. It was jumping, and four jumps were recorded in 1.5 minutes. . . . The Argentines recorded *Berardius* in early September and after taking photographs, they fired repeatedly and presumably killed it."

The species is found only in the Southern Hemisphere, with strandings and sightings reported from scattered localities including South Australia, New Zealand, Argentina, the Falkland Islands, Tierra del Fuego, South Georgia, the South Shetlands, South Africa, and the Antarctic continent.

BAIRD'S BEAKED WHALE

Berardius bairdii Stejneger 1883

This is the largest of all the beaked whales, reaching a maximum length of 42 feet (12.8 meters) in a "specimen that stranded at Centerville, California (True 1910). On average, the females are larger; males reach a maximum length of about 39 feet (11.9 meters). Tomilin (1957) recorded a 35-foot specimen that weighed 7.5 tons. Like its southern relative *B. arnuxii,* the adults have four teeth in the lower jaw and none in the upper. The anterior pair is about twice the size of the posterior pair, and since the lower jaw extends beyond the upper, the teeth can often be seen even when the whale's mouth is closed. As the narrow beak widens somewhat at the end, Tomilin compared it "to a duck's beak." The head is small, accounting for only one-eighth of the total body length, and the forehead bulges, but not as much as it does in *Hyperoodon.* The flippers are small and rounded, but the flukes, which usually do not have a median notch, are large, equal to perhaps one-fourth of the body length of the animal. Their color has been described as black, dark gray, slate gray, or brownish-gray, and there are usually references to lighter undersides and some patches of lighter color, either on the forehead or on the dorsal fin. Another diagnostic feature is the presence of numerous scars and scratches covering the back and sides.

The species was named by Leonhard Stejneger in 1883 for Spencer F. Baird, an American naturalist and second secretary of the Smithsonian Institution (U. S. National Museum). In Japanese the species is known as *Tsuchi-kujira.* According to Omura and colleagues

*Recent discoveries by Japanese cetologists indicate that the gestation period for *Berardius bairdii,* the close northern relative of *arnuxii,* is perhaps as long as seventeen months (Kasuya 1977). Because they are so similar in other respects, the two species of this genus probably share this extraordinary distinction: they would appear to have the longest gestation period of any cetacean. Newborn calves of *B. bairdii* are about 15 feet (4.6 meters) in length, and the newborn *B. arnuxii* is probably about the same size.

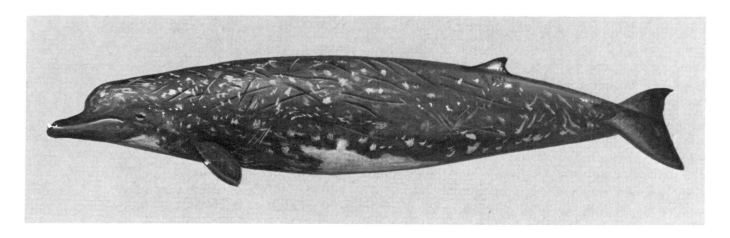

(1955), a *tsuchi* is a wooden hammer whose shape closely resembles a bottle, and *kujira* means "whale." It is this name, when translated into English as "bottlenose whale," that seems to have led to reports of *Hyperoodon* in the North Pacific. (In 1971, Nishiwaki and Oguro wrote that "the whales caught in Abashiri area [north of the island of Hokkaido] . . . should be *Hyperoodon ampullatus.*" They also noted that "further study is required.") Most cetologists now believe that Baird's is the only giant beaked whale in the North Pacific.

These whales congregate in offshore waters at least 3,300 feet (1,000 meters) deep and rarely enter shallower waters. They are seen in tightly organized groups of ten to thirty animals, comprising males, females, and juveniles. (A school of eighteen individuals was photographed off the coast of Japan [Nishiwaki and Oguro 1971], one of the few instances in which living beaked whales have been photographed and identified en masse.) Although they are deep-water inhabitants, they do occasionally strand, and beached animals have been found in the Aleutians, British Columbia, Washington, California, and Japan.

Like most beaked whales, this species is what Tomilin calls "teuthophagous," or squid-eating. Their main prey species are *Gonatus fabricii* and *Onchoteuthis* in California waters (Rice 1963), but elsewhere in its range there are records of its feeding on deep-sea fishes, mackerel, sardines, pollack, and sauries (Nishiwaki and Oguro 1971). Their behavior on the surface has been compared to that of the sperm whale: they take a number of short breaths before descending to hunt. It would appear that they are capable of deep dives, since they have been recorded to remain submerged for twenty minutes and even an hour (Tomilin 1957), and Rice (1978) quoted "Japanese whalers" who have reported a harpooned Baird's to "dive straight down—sometimes as deep as eight thousand feet" (2,439 meters). Pike (1953) observed a male struck by a harpoon that "dived straight down at amazing speed, taking with it 500 fathoms of line." When the animals surface again, they first show their foreheads and then breathe and roll, with the small dorsal fin rarely breaking the surface. Tomilin told of Soviet whalers who observed these whales "breaching" in the waters of Kamchatka, where they "jumped obliquely displaying three-fourths of the body in the air." Baird's is usually seen covered with myriad scratch marks, as are most of the beaked whales, but until someone actually observes the animals engaging in combat or wrestling with a squid that can scratch their skin in parallel lines, we can only speculate about the cause of these multiple surface wounds.

Full-term fetuses have been measured at 14.7 feet (4.5 meters), and it has been estimated that this animal is 15 feet (4.6 meters) long at birth. Earlier estimates of the gestation period (for example, Omura et al., Tomilin) gave a figure of 10 or 11 months, but in a 1977 study, Kasuya concluded that the actual gestation period is 519 days, or 17 months. (This is the longest known gestation period for any cetacean, and of all other mammals only the elephants, with gestation periods of over 600 days, surpass it.) Through the

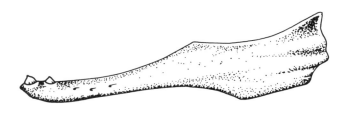

Berardius bairdii

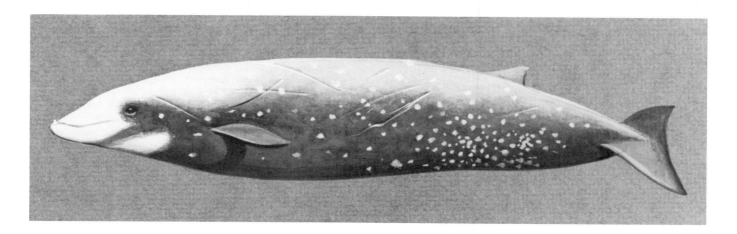

same examinations of the dentinal layers of the teeth, Kasuya also estimated that the life span is about 70 years.

In 1916, R. C. Andrews wrote, "When I was in Japan in 1910 I saw a photograph of a whale which was said to occur at certain times of the year only in Tokyo Bay, and when a skeleton was finally secured . . . the whale was found to represent an extremely rare species, *Berardius bairdii,* which had been taken only in Alaskan waters." In fact, the animal has been hunted for centuries by the Japanese, but catch figures have never been particularly high because of the rarity of the species. From 1969 to 1977 the Japanese fishery, mostly off the Boso Peninsula on the Pacific side of the main island of Honshu, has taken some 622 animals, or an average of 69 per year. (During this same period, the International Whaling Statistics reported no whales of this species taken by any other nations.) In the recent past the Soviets hunted them in the western North Pacific off Kamchatka and the Sea of Okhotsk, but Tomilin reported in 1957 that they found it uneconomical and "it is taken in the waters of the U.S.S.R. only by chance." He also claimed that the fat and flesh are inedible, but "boiled meat can be safely fed to fur animals." Tomilin quoted a 1755 author who wrote that the fat does not stay in the stomach, but "flows out imperceptibly through the inferior passage." The natives of Kamchatka do not eat it themselves, "but use it as a treat for offensive guests."

GOOSEBEAK WHALE

Ziphius cavirostris Cuvier 1823

The most frequently observed beaked whale, the goosebeak can be recognized by its sloping forehead, relatively short beak, and large size: mature individuals may be as long as 28 feet (8.5 meters). They are infrequently seen at sea, but they strand more often than other beaked whales (Daugherty [1972] counted 23 Californian records between 1945 and 1965), and they are known to "breach." Any large, "porpoise-like" animal may be this species.

The color is quite variable and may be a function of age or sex, but this is still unknown. Descriptions of the animals range from dark purplish-brown to slate gray and to fawn. Fraser (1946) reported that of the five specimens stranded on British coasts between 1933 and 1937, "four of them were described as being more or less white." In mature individuals the head and back are often white, and the whales are invariably marked with a profusion of oval spots and numerous linear scars. Many observers have commented on the reversal of the normal countershading, in which the animal typically is dark above and light below, to offset the dark appearance caused by shadows on the lower surface. The goosebeak is often light on the dorsal surface and dark gray on the undersides (Harmer

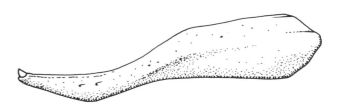

Ziphius cavirostris

1927), one of the few cetaceans—and one of the few mammals of any kind—to be colored this way. Most animals described have had dark flippers, and the underside of the tail flukes is light, sometimes even white. A living specimen was described by Aitken (1971) as "purple black on the dorsal half of the body and around the head, tail and pectoral fins, grading through dark gray-brown on the lower side to pale gray-brown on the belly."

The lower jaw extends well beyond the upper, and in males a pair of teeth can be seen in the lower jaw even when the animal's mouth is closed. The teeth of mature males are large and massive, but those of females, which are usually hidden below the gums, are slender and sharply pointed. Not surprisingly, this sexual dimorphism led to the separation of males and females into different species. True (1910) showed that the species previously known as *Hyperoodon gervaisi* was actually the female *Z. cavirostris,* and in the same study he also showed that the previously distinct *Ziphius semijunctus* and *Z. grebnitzki* constitute a single species. In younger specimens there are some thirty-three or thirty-four smaller teeth embedded in the gums, but these do not erupt and often remain undiscovered in mature adults. Tomilin (1957) wrote that the "single nonfunctional pair of teeth and the rostrum structure are a normal adaptive feature of the teuthophagi [squid-eaters]." McCann (1974) described the dietary adaptations in a somewhat more colorful manner: "The food consists largely of squids. The tongue and palate are sufficiently roughened with small papillate projections to secure the soft, slithery textures, such as cephalopod's." In one report (Hubbs 1946) a stranded specimen was described as having a "broad olive-gray tongue."

Goosebeak whales are usually seen in small groups of ten to twenty, and Tomilin reported that they submerge simultaneously when pursued. When they dive, they often raise their flukes straight out of the water and descend almost vertically, staying down for as long as thirty minutes (Kellogg 1940). Most species of beaked whales are characterized by the absence of a median notch in the tail flukes, but the goosebeak often has a small one. Except for the examination of stranded specimens and the observations by Japanese whalers, there is very little information on the natural history of this species. In 1961, Backus and Schevill wrote, "Japanese whalers and cetologists seem not yet to have recorded their observations of the living animal—a thing we may all look forward to." Omura in 1972 made an osteological study of the species in the northwest Pacific, but wrote, "On this problem [observations of the living animal] I am not able to contribute anything in this paper yet." During a 1976 whale-marking cruise, Miyazaki and Wada (1978) observed goosebeaks northeast of New Guinea, one of the few recent observations of living specimens:

Since Cuvier's beaked whale, *Ziphius cavirostris* is too nervous about the vessel and always dive into the sea for 30–40 minutes before approaching, it is difficult to identify the species by sighting. During their jumping above the sea, however, Cuvier's beaked whales were identified by body size, the position of the dorsal fin, and the shape of the head. Cuvier's beaked whales were observed four times. Two sightings were of single animal and three whales were found in each of the other two pods.

The French naturalist Baron Georges Cuvier described this species in 1823 from a skull found west of Marseilles in 1804. The generic name *Ziphius* means "sword" in Greek (although it is usually spelled *Xiphias,* as in *Xiphias gladias,* the broadbill swordfish) and refers to the sharply pointed rostrum. *Cavirostris,* from Latin *cavus* ("hollow") and *rostrum* ("beak"), describes the hollow above the rostrum in the skull. As in the case of most other beaked whales, the males of this species have exaggerated premaxillary crests, asymmetrically enlarged on the right side of the skull. According to Tomilin, "Cranial asymmetry [is] expressed very distinctly. . . . on the right side, the maxillary, premaxillary, nasal bone and occipital condyle are developed to a much greater degree than on the left. Right nasal and premaxillary bones [form] the greater part of the bony roof over the nostrils." In Japan the goosebeak whale is known as *Akabo-kujira,* or "baby-face whale," probably a reference to the small mouth and large, dark eyes.

The goosebeak is found in all oceans of the world, except the high Arctic and Antarctic. Records of strandings include Japan, the Aleutian Islands, Hawaii, Midway Island, the western coast of North America from Alaska to southern California, England, France, Spain, Italy, and the eastern coast of the United States from Cape Cod to Florida and the Caribbean. In the Southern Hemisphere the species has been recorded from the Cape of Good Hope, Australia, Tasmania, New Zealand, Brazil, Argentina, and Tierra del Fuego.

There is a fishery for small whales (predominantly minke whales, Baird's beaked whales, pilot whales, and killer whales) off the coast of Japan, and here a number of goosebeak whales are caught "inciden-

tally." They are usually found in waters deeper than 3,280 feet (1,000 meters) and examination of the specimens caught indicate that males mature at a length of 17.5 feet (5.33 meters) and females at 18 feet (5.5 meters).

Calves are believed to be born at a length of about 7.5 feet (2.3 meters), based on the examination of a 7-foot fetus that was nearly full term (Omura et al. 1955). Nishiwaki and Oguro (1972) reported a total of 85 whales of this species taken in Japanese waters from 1948–52 and 189 for the years 1965–70.

In 1956 a juvenile female was captured after stranding on Pebbly Beach, Santa Catalina Island, California. She was brought to Marineland of the Pacific and placed in a large tank. At first she swam slowly and seemed to be adjusting to captivity, but by the next morning "she began circling rapidly, rubbing her flukes against the tank walls. Soon she went into a frenzy, lashing the entire tank into a froth. Then she swam the length of the tank at high speed and crashed into the far wall with a thud that was felt throughout the building. A few moments later she was escorted from the tank into the connecting flume, where she died. Her charge against the wall had broken her lower jaw" (Norris and Prescott 1961). The postmortem revealed severe congestion of the lungs, which may have been a factor in the animal's stranding in the first place.

SHEPHERD'S BEAKED WHALE

Tasmacetus shepherdi Oliver 1937

This is the only beaked whale with a full set of teeth in addition to the large pair of teeth at the point, or apex, of the lower jaw. It is the presence of these apical teeth that affiliates this animal with the beaked whales, but the additional teeth cause it to be placed in a separate genus. Both males and females have teeth in the jaws: seventeen to twenty-one pairs in the upper jaw and eighteen to twenty-seven pairs in the lower jaw, including the apical teeth, which are erupted only in males. There is one record of an adult male at 30 feet (9.1 meters) in length (Sorenson 1940), but all the other specimens are considerably smaller. The forehead appears to be more pronounced and the rostrum more pointed than in the various species of *Mesoplodon* (Mead and Payne 1975). While sitting on a bluff overlooking the sea in Sumner, a suburb of Christchurch, New Zealand, W. A. Watkins (1976) made what is probably the only observation of this species by a cetologist. His field notes, quoted in his paper describing this sighting, read as follows: "wavy, light and dark streaks (2 each?) from shoulder down below fin along sides, beaked, light on top of head, dark back and triangular fin, short flippers, light belly."

Tasmacetus shepherdi

The one specimen that has been examined in the flesh had "the well-digested remains of a number of fish, a small crab, and one squid beak" in the stomach (Mead and Payne 1975).

Until a specimen was discovered washed ashore at Península Valdés, Chubut, Argentina, it had been assumed that this species was restricted to New Zealand waters. As of 1972, all five known specimens had been recorded from New Zealand: two stranded at Mason's Bay, Stewart Island, in February 1933, one (the type specimen) at Wanganui in October 1933; and two more from the Avon-Heathcote estuary and Birdling's Flat in March 1951 and in 1962, respectively (Gaskin 1972). The discovery of a female in Argentina by Mead and Payne "extended the range to another ocean," and in 1976, Brownell and colleagues published a report documenting the species in the eastern South Pacific, thousands of miles from its supposed restricted range. A cranium, mandible, and cervical vertebra were found on the beach at Loberia Vieja, in the Juan Fernández Islands, off the coast of Chile. This discovery "now suggests that *T. shepherdi* may have a circumpolar distribution in the southern temperate oceans, as do many other species of cetaceans."

Commenting on the increase in specimens in the last century of the false killer whale and on the more recent "rediscovery" of the very rare Fraser's dolphin, Mead and Payne wrote, "It is not known whether these have represented actual changes in population numbers or distribution, or merely an increased awareness on the part of scientists. It will be interesting to see if this sort of pattern develops for *Tasmacetus shepherdi.*"

INDO-PACIFIC BEAKED WHALE

Indopacetus pacificus Longman 1926

This may be the least-known large animal in the world today. (There may be others, including, perhaps, beaked whales that have not yet been discovered. But this is an animal whose existence is documented and about which we know nothing.) The second skull was found in 1955, "in a fertilizer factory not far from Mogadishu: it had been collected a few weeks before by local fishermen at Danane" (Azzaroli 1968). On the basis of the osteological differences between this and the known species of *Mesoplodon*, Moore (1968) erected the new genus. He wrote, "As *Indopacetus* is

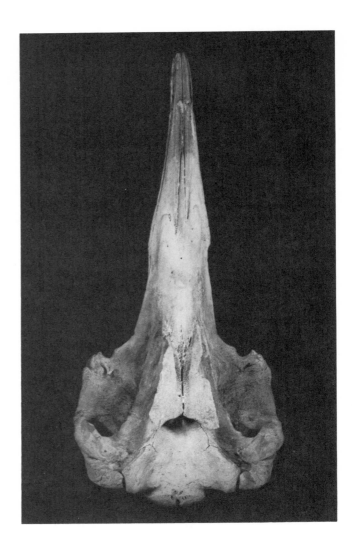

known from but two skulls, the character of its external appearance remains to be discovered."

Known from skulls only, this whale has never been seen in the flesh, so its description is based entirely on comparative measurements with skulls of similar species, particularly True's beaked whale, which it closely resembles. Both species have one pair of teeth at the apex of the lower jaw. The skull that Longman (1926) measured and described was nearly 4 feet (1.22 meters) in length, making this one of the largest of the beaked whales. It is thought that the skull is from a fully mature individual, 25 feet (7.6 meters) in length.

After it was described by Longman in 1926, various

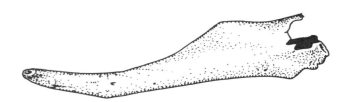

Indopacetus pacificus

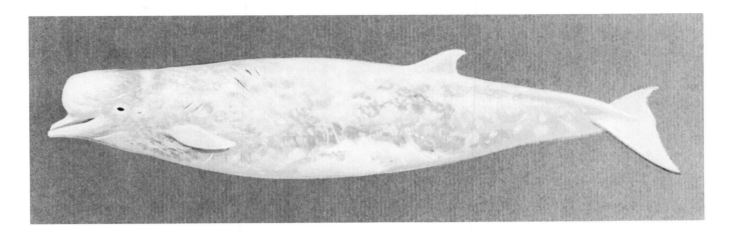

authors tried to place this species into other genera, either *Mesoplodon mirus* (Raven 1937) or *Hyperoodon planifrons* (McCann 1962a), but Moore (1968) regarded it as a good species. He believed it to be distinct enough from the other species of *Mesoplodon* that it required the erection of a new genus, *Indopacetus* (Moore 1968). Since Longman first described the animal, his name remains as the author of this species.

One skull was found on a Queensland beach and the second in Somalia, so one may say that this whale inhabits the waters of eastern Australia sometimes and the waters of eastern Africa sometimes.

NORTH ATLANTIC BOTTLENOSE WHALE

Hyperoodon ampullatus Forster 1770

Adult males have a bulging forehead, a small but conspicuous beak, and a mottled brownish or yellowish coloration, which becomes almost white in the oldest and largest of them. Females are usually smaller and darker in color and do not exhibit the overhanging forehead bulge. The maximum size is 30 feet (9.15 meters) for adult males and 24 feet (7.3 meters) for females. Males are also heavier in build; one nineteenth-century observer wrote that "the females, as is proper, have much more graceful outlines" (Southwell 1883). A 21-foot specimen was weighed at 4,480 pounds (Nishiwaki 1972). Although juveniles are dark in color (they have been described by Winn et al. [1970] as "dark chocolate brown"), they begin to lighten as they mature. Most cetaceans darken appreciably in color when they die, so many descriptions of this species from stranded specimens say that the animal is black. According to observations of live animals at sea (D. Gray 1882; Ohlin 1893; Winn et al. 1970), the animals are tan or brownish, often with lighter spots and scratches. Males are usually white or cream-colored on the forehead bulge, and occasionally an all-white animal is seen. Ohlin wrote, "I have seen but once such a 'whitefish.'" In some females there is a light ring around the neck, and Ohlin claimed that the Norwegian whalers call these specimens *ringfiskar,* or "fishes with a ring."

In the males the maxillary crests of the skull develop into an exaggerated pair of bony ridges, a development that does not occur in females. In some illustrations (for example, D. Gray 1882) the forehead is flattened on the forward surface of the males, whereas the females have a sloping profile more like that of the other beaked whales. This dimorphism is so pronounced that early anatomists believed that the variations represented two distinct species. In an article entitled "On the Genus *Hyperoodon:* The Two British Kinds and Their Food," J. E. Gray* (1860) wrote: "The structure and form of the two skulls is so different, that it is much more likely that they should be

*The literature on this species seems to be heavily populated by people named Gray. J. E. Gray (1800–1875) was Keeper of Zoology at the British Museum and a prodigious writer on cetacean subjects. David Gray of Peterhead, Scotland, was captain of the schooner *Eclipse,* the first ship to hunt bottlenose whales in the North Atlantic, and he presented his information to the Royal Zoological Society of London in 1882. His son, R. W. Gray, also wrote about bottlenoses and commented (probably accurately) that his father "taught the Norwegians to hunt the bottlenosed whale."

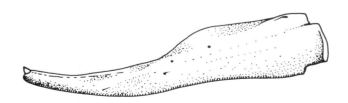

Hyperoodon ampullatus

referrable to two very distinct genera than to species of the same genus." It was later demonstrated that the two species, *H. latifrons* and *H. rostratus,* were actually the males and females of the same species (Flower 1882). The name *Hyperoodon* can be defined as "beyond teeth" or "over teeth," and it refers to the overhanging forehead in the males. *Ampullatus,* which means "flask-shaped," describes the animal's beak.

Males and females of this species have one pair of teeth located at the tip of the lower jaw. Elongated and conical in shape, these are set in the jaw pointing forward at an angle. The teeth are not a particularly reliable means of identification, because in some specimens the teeth do not erupt at all; and in other, older animals they might fall out or wear down completely. Some specimens have been described as having toothpick-sized teeth in addition to the apical pair, and some even have another pair of teeth embedded in the gums behind the first pair. In the X-ray examination of a small female that stranded at Waterford, Ireland, in 1938, investigators discovered a complete set of tiny, vestigial teeth buried in the upper and lower gums (Fraser 1953).

The northern bottlenose is a North Atlantic species. One report tells of the species being taken in the waters off the northern Japanese island of Hokkaido (Nishiwaki and Oguro 1971), but this seems to be a case of mistaken identity. (The even larger beaked whale, *Berardius bairdii,* is commonly fished in these North Pacific waters, and it would be quite possible to confuse them, especially when translating information from Japanese into English.) It is a cold-water, deepwater species, which spends the spring and summer around the edges of the pack ice and moves south in the fall and winter. The Norwegians have hunted this animal off East Greenland, usually in waters deeper than 3,300 feet (1,000 meters). The species does not usually occur in shallower waters, but it does strand

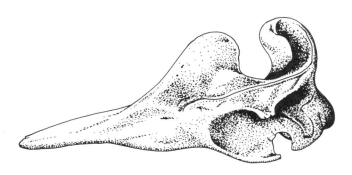

Lateral view of the skull of *Hyperoodon ampullatus,* showing the exaggerated development of the maxillary crests.

with some frequency on both sides of the North Atlantic. Fraser (1974) has recorded some sixty-six strandings of this species from 1913 to 1966, and Duguy (1977), writing of the coasts of France, said that "strandings occur regularly but without being frequent." There are numerous records of the northern bottlenose's stranding in North America, from various Canadian locations to New England, with the southernmost confirmed location being Rhode Island (Mitchell and Kozicki 1975).

The northern bottlenose congregates in small groups of five to fifteen, but much larger schools have been observed (Nansen, quoted in Benjaminsen and Christensen 1979). The deep-water habitat of this species is probably related to the habits of its predominant prey, the squid *Gonatus fabricii;* certain captured specimens have been found to have over 10,000 squid beaks in their multichambered stomachs (Ohlin 1893). Species members have also been known to feed on herring and other kinds of fish, and some bottom feeding is indicated by the existence in their stomachs of such bottom-dwelling creatures as starfish and holothurians (sea cucumbers) and even sand and stones. Ohlin observed "a thin covering of lime upon its beak from its rummagings in the muddy ground of the sea."

The northern bottlenose is reputed to be among the deepest diving of all cetaceans (Scholander 1940). When Ohlin observed them in the "Arctic Sea" in 1891, he saw them dive regularly for one to two hours and then "be seen to appear in the immediate vicinity whence they dived." Other firsthand observations corroborate this achievement, and Benjaminsen and Christensen recorded diving times (of unstressed animals) of fourteen to seventy minutes. Harpooned bottlenoses are said to "dive straight downward at tremendous speed, and have been known to take out five hundred fathoms of line in two minutes" (Andrews 1916). The ability to dive deeply and remain submerged for extended periods of time has been demonstrated by only a few other species of cetaceans, among them the sperm whale and perhaps the giant beaked whales of the genus *Berardius.* (Other species such as the bottlenose dolphin and the pilot whales have demonstrated deep-diving capabilities under training, but there is no evidence that they descend to extreme depths in the course of their normal feeding.)

The nose of the sperm whale—with its valves, sacs, tubes, and oil reservoir—is unique among cetaceans, but there are some similarities between *Physeter* and *Hyperoodon* that are probably related to their deep-diving propensities. Whereas the sperm whale has the spermaceti organ, most fully developed in the large bulls, northern bottlenose males develop a bulging forehead, exaggerated sagittal crests on the skull, and, between these crests, "a solid lump of fat similar in shape to, and twice the size of, a water-melon" (D. Gray 1882). Ohlin described this organ as being composed of "tissue resembling a bee-hive. The rooms between the bands are filled with a clear, thin-floating oil." Female bottlenoses, which lack the bony crests and the bulging forehead, have only a small amount of thin, yellow oil in their heads. The oil from the bottlenose appears to be "of fine quality and hardly distinguishable (if at all) from sperm" (Thompson 1919). The Soviet whalers sometimes obtained as much as 440 pounds (200 kilograms) of spermaceti and over two tons of oil from a large bottlenose (Tomilin 1957). The same author also noted that "the meat is unfit for human consumption. It must be boiled to eliminate its laxative properties, and can then be used as food for dogs and fur animals at state breeding farms." The spermaceti organ of the sperm whale is somehow involved with deep diving (see M. R. Clarke 1978, for elaboration), and it is probably so with the northern bottlenose as well.

Sound production in the sperm whale is an activity still shrouded in mystery, but most cetologists agree that the clicks, wheezes, and knocks are produced in the nose, wherein lies the massive spermaceti organ. In the bottlenose the maxillary crests of the skull almost certainly serve an acoustic function. Norris (1964) has written that "the scoop-shaped bones of the forehead . . . look for all the world like parabolic surfaces whose focal points lie in the general area of the soft anatomy of the forehead and hence might act as sound reflecting and focusing devices." Underwater sounds have indeed been recorded from this species by Winn and colleagues (1971)—the first recorded sounds ever described for a species of beaked whale—and they consist of "discrete frequency whistles, sweep frequency chirps, and possible burst-pulsed (modulated) tones." The surface sounds of this animal are also noteworthy. Tomilin claimed that "the bottlenose can be unmistakably distinguished from other cetaceans by the sharp noise of its breathing: this noise is brief [and] of a brassy pitch."

At birth the bottlenose whale is reported to be 10–11 feet (3.0–3.3 meters) in length; and although the gestation period is unknown, Benjaminsen (1972) estimated it at twelve months. The species is known for its strong schooling instinct, and females have been observed protecting their calves from boats or

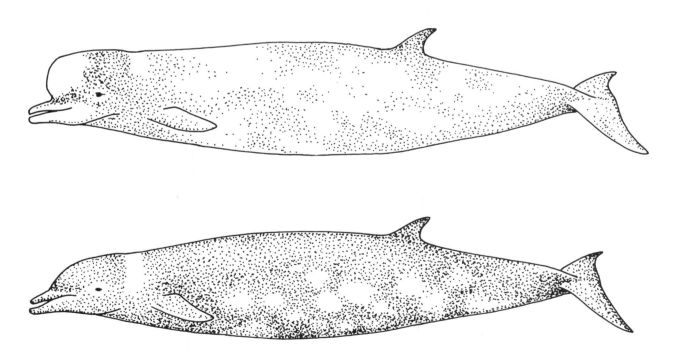

Males and females of the northern bottlenose whale look so different that for many years scientists believed that they were two different species. Males are lighter in color and have a bulbous forehead.

A Note on the Color Plates

Unlike the "field guide" illustrations that are used to introduce each species account, the color plates are reproductions of what N. C. Wyeth called "easel paintings" to distinguish them from specifically commissioned illustrations.

Rather than include the size of the painting, as might be expected in a catalog of this sort, I have indicated the size of the whale so the reader can appreciate the actual size of the animal depicted.

1

1   Sperm whale *(Physeter macrocephalus)*
         Maximum length: 60 feet (18.3 meters)

2   Gray whale *(Eschrichtius robustus)*
         Maximum length: 50 feet (15.2 meters)

3   Bryde's whale *(Balaenoptera edeni)*
         Maximum length: 50 feet (15.2 meters)

4   Sei whale *(Balaenoptera borealis)*
         Maximum length: 65 feet (19.8 meters)

5   Fin whale *(Balaenoptera physalus)*
         Maximum length: 80 feet (24.4 meters)

6   Blue whale *(Balaenoptera musculus)*
         Maximum length: 100 feet (30.5 meters)

7   Humpback whale *(Megaptera novaeangliae)*
         Maximum length: 50 feet (15.2 meters)

8   Right whale *(Balaena glacialis)*
         Maximum length: 60 feet (18.3 meters)

9   Bowhead whale *(Balaena mysticetus)*
         and Beluga *(Delphinapterus leucas)*
         Maximum lengths: 65 feet (19.8 meters) and
         20 feet (6.1 meters), respectively

10   Beluga *(Delphinapterus leucas)*
         Maximum length: 20 feet (6.1 meters)

11   Narwhal *(Monodon monoceros)*
         Maximum length, including tusk in males:
         25 feet (7.6 meters)

12   Sowerby's beaked whale *(Mesoplodon bidens)*
         Maximum length: 18 feet (5.5 meters)

13   Right whale *(Balaena glacialis)*
         Maximum length: 60 feet (18.3 meters)

2

7

3

8

4

9

5

10

6

11

12

13

RICHARD ELLIS · 1974

RICHARD ELLIS 1974

RICHARD ELLIS - 1974

RICHARD ELLIS

RICHARD E

"standing by" an injured or distressed adult. (The Norwegian whalers used this inclination to their advantage: since the school would not leave a wounded comrade, they often shot the whole school at once without having to chase them.) The northern bottlenose has also been described as playful and inquisitive, approaching boats from great distances, jumping, and tail-slapping within twenty-five feet of the vessel (Winn et al. 1971). Like most of the beaked whales, this species is often found with scratches and scars, and as usual, their specific origin is unknown. Benjaminsen and Christensen suggested that the forehead scars "may have been caused by the ice when the whales pushed through for breathing, although other explanations are possible." Because this species has what McCann (1974) called "battle-teeth"—that is, teeth located at the extremity of the jaws—he felt that the scars are caused by fighting males. Nishiwaki (1972) has suggested that "the large forehead is probably used in fighting for the females," and there is also the possibility that some of the scars are caused by the suckers of squid.

Ohlin believed this species to be the largest of the odontocetes next to the sperm whale, but it is not, for *Berardius* grows substantially larger. However, it has a long and productive history in the small-whale fishery. Captain David Gray of Peterhead, Scotland, was the first to seek these whales in the waters north of his homeland. In 1881 he brought in the first cargo of bottlenose oil to Dundee, and the following year he killed 200 bottlenoses. The Norwegians soon joined in this fishery, which was, after all, off their own coast; and by 1891, seventy Norwegian ships had taken 3,000 animals. Of this early period of bottlenose whaling, Mitchell (1977) has written:

In the period 1886–1911, catch efficiency undoubtedly increased as a rapidly evolving whale-catching technology saw the development of: whaling cannons, experimentation with chemical, explosive and other harpoon heads, bombs and grenades, lighter and stronger foregoers, spring systems to prevent breakage of lines when playing whales, motorised vessels, and many other innovations.

The bottlenose was hunted from small schooners of thirty to fifty tons and was shot directly with guns mounted on these vessels. (Unlike the catcher boats used for the larger species—which had a single harpoon cannon on the bow—these boats had guns all around, to take advantage of the bottlenose's habit of approaching boats from all points of the compass.) By 1920, when the first phase of the fishery began to decline, approximately 50,000 bottlenose whales had been killed (Jonsgard 1955). The modern Norwegian small-whale fishery is directed primarily toward minke whales, but other species, including killers, pilot whales, and bottlenoses, have been taken whenever they presented themselves. Mitchell and Kozicki reported a Canadian fishery out of Nova Scotia that took 87 bottlenoses from 1962 to 1967, and the species was also hunted by the Danes and the Icelanders.

The northern bottlenose whale is considerably less plentiful now than it was in the past. Christensen (1975) estimated the original stock size at 40,000–50,000 animals; and although "the present state of the stock of bottlenose is not known" (Mitchell 1977), it is considered depleted. The International Whaling Statistics show that the Norwegian fishery was taking some 2,000 animals per year at the turn of the century, but by the 1960s the annual catch was down to 300–700 animals. According to these records, Norway took 485 bottlenose whales in 1969, 535 in 1970, 213 in 1971, and only 17 in 1972. None have been killed since 1973. Mitchell (1977) attributed this decline in the fishery directly to the greatly reduced number of whales, and, in addition, the market for the meat of the bottlenose dried up. Most of it had been sold in England for pet food, but on "16 March 1973 an official British veto was put on the import of whale products for pet food" (Jonsgard 1977). The Red Data Book of the International Union for the Conservation of Nature (IUCN) listed this species as "vulnerable" and suggested "complete protection for the species at least until additional information is available to allow scientific conclusions regarding present status of the species."

SOUTHERN BOTTLENOSE WHALE

Hyperoodon planifrons Flower 1882

This is the Southern Ocean version of the bottlenose whale, and it resembles its northern relative in most particulars. Mature males have a bulging forehead that overhangs the base of the beak, and there are two teeth at the tip of the lower jaw. Both males and females have teeth, but those of the females are usually buried in the gums. There does not seem to be the same sequence of color change from dark to light during the animals' maturation as there is in *H. ampullatus,* since most descriptions refer only to its dark

color. Gaskin (1972) described it as "generally dark brownish-black dorsally and greyish white ventrally. White markings may be present on the back and flanks." The southern bottlenose whale reaches a maximum length of 25 feet (7.6 meters), and this is somewhat smaller than the northern species. Unlike its northern relative, for which information has been gathered from a prospering fishery in the North Atlantic, the southern variety is known primarily from the examination of stranded specimens. The Latin name *planifrons* means "flattened brow," referring to the shape of the head in the living animal or, perhaps, the shape of the maxillary crests of the skull. In Spanish it is known as *ballena pico de botella,* or "bottle-beak whale."

This species is found only in the Southern Ocean, from the Antarctic pack ice to southern Brazil (Gianuca and Castello 1976) on the east coast of South America and to Valparaiso, Chile, on the west. It has been found off Tierra del Fuego (Goodall 1978), the southern coasts of Australia, New Zealand, the Falkland Islands, and South Africa.

Although very little has been published on the variety of food items eaten by the bottlenose whales, one report (Hale 1932) mentioned a South Australian specimen whose stomach contained the beak of a squid known to reach a length of 46 inches (1,180 millimeters). The consumption of such large squid

might well explain some of the otherwise questionable scars on the beaked whales.

In his revision of the beaked whales Moore (1968) noted that the maxillary prominences of the southern bottlenose are not as high as those of the northern bottlenose. He therefore created a new subgenus, *Frasercetus,* to replace the former. But Brownell (1974) wrote that "subgeneric usage within *Hyperoodon* spp. is of no taxonomic or phylogenetic value and the genus is known only from two closely related allopatric species, [so] the subgeneric status would seem to be too extreme."

In the waters of the southern latitudes and the Antarctic this species could be confused with the giant bottlenose, and there does not seem to be an accurate way to differentiate them at sea. A skull examination would show that the bottlenose has greatly exaggerated crests—particularly in mature animals—whereas in the giant bottlenose the crests are less developed and the skull is more symmetrical. Also diagnostic would be the number of teeth in the end of the jaw: The bottlenose has only 2 teeth; the giant bottlenose, 4. These teeth were described by McCann (1961) as "large, obovate, or oboconical bodies surmounted by mammilate enamelled apices"—in other words, egg-shaped with enameled tips. There appears to be some confusion regarding the actual appearance of the teeth in the bottlenose, as Norman and Fraser (1938) described them as "conical but expanding somewhat at about half their length then narrowing slightly to the lower end." The illustrations of the teeth of the northern bottlenose in Moore (1968) correspond to this description, but not at all to McCann's "oboconical bodies." Moore has written that the teeth of males and females are quite different, and "the evidence is strong that the southern hemisphere species of *Hyperoodon* has achieved striking sexual dimor-

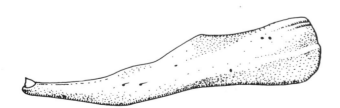

Hyperoodon planifrons

phism in the shape of the teeth." In addition, there is a marked change in the shape of the teeth as the animals mature.

Since we know so little about the habits of this animal, we can assume only that its habits are similar to those of the northern bottlenose. It is probably a squid eater; it is capable of deep dives; and its forehead, or "melon," contains a reservoir of waxy, solidified spermaceti. A full-term fetus measured 9 feet (2.7 meters), but nothing is known of its breeding or parturition behavior. Hale (1939) reported that a specimen stranded alive in Victoria, Australia, "made a grunting noise like a pig"; and Liouville, who observed the animals on the French Antarctic Expedition of 1908–1910, said it sounded like a trumpet when it breathed.

HECTOR'S BEAKED WHALE

Mesoplodon hectori Gray 1871

Until very recently, Hector's beaked whale was listed among the world's least-known cetaceans and as late as 1977 there was almost no information on the external appearance of the animal. Only six specimens were known, and of these, four were represented by only skulls, one was a complete skeleton, and another had been considered a different species. Although *Mesoplodon hectori* is still far from common, enough information has been obtained now to enable us to describe it fairly accurately and to speculate on its distribution.

In 1978 an account of a seventh specimen was published (Goodall 1978), and although an almost complete skeleton was discovered (only the scapulae and flippers were missing), the animal that had washed ashore at Bahia San Sebastian, Tierra del Fuego, was

"well decomposed," and thus the actual appearance of the animal still remained unknown. Many regarded this as one of the great mysteries of cetacean biology: an animal known from skeletal evidence to exist but never seen in the flesh (Ellis 1980).

There were, however, rumors of unknown beaked whales, particularly off the coast of southern California. In May 1975 a young calf and an adult female beaked whale of an undetermined species were discovered washed ashore at Camp Pendleton, the Marine base north of San Diego. The animals were collected by William F. Perrin of the National Marine Fisheries Service Southwest Laboratory at La Jolla and shipped to James G. Mead of the U.S. National Museum in Washington D.C. for identification. Mead (whose unpublished paper is the source of much of this information) wrote, "At that time I had determined that the species was close to *M. hectori* . . . but *M. hectori* was a Southern Hemisphere species and was known only from juveniles." In discussing the same two specimens in a book published in 1978, Dale Rice wrote, "On a beach in southern California, biologists found the carcasses of a *Mesoplodon* cow and calf that would not fit into the description of any known species," and in the same work a photograph was published of a free-swimming beaked whale, "possibly *M. carlhubbsi.*" The photograph was taken by Don Ljungblad off Catalina Island in July 1976. It now appears that the Pendleton specimens, Ljungblad's photographed animal, and

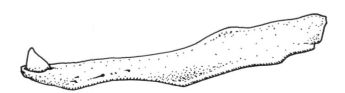

Mesoplodon hectori

two more specimens—one an adult male—were all *Mesoplodon hectori.* The animal that had been previously known only from skeletons from the Southern Hemisphere was beginning to appear in the waters and on the beaches of southern California.

In 1938 Norman and Fraser referred to this species as the "New Zealand Beaked Whale," since the only known specimens had been found in that area. The type specimen was from Titai Bay, New Zealand (Gray 1871), and a 9½-foot animal had been found at Plimmerton, in the same country (McCann 1962). There was the skull of an immature animal from the Falkland Islands (Fraser 1950), another skull from Adventure Bay, Tasmania (Guiler 1967), and two immature animals from the mouth of the Lottering River, South Africa (Ross 1970). The Tierra del Fuego specimen was discovered in 1975, but its description was not published until 1978 (Goodall 1978).

The taxonomic history of this species is no less convoluted than its geography. In 1871, J. E. Gray identified the type specimen as a new species of *Berardius* and named it *Berardius hectori* after Sir James Hector, who had originally described it as a juvenile *Berardius arnuxi.* It was subsequently assigned to the genus *Mesoplodon* (Turner 1872; Harmer 1924), where it has remained, in spite of the efforts of McCann (1962b) to reassign it to *Berardius arnuxi.* (He wrote that "*M. hectori* is known *only* from very young calves [near neonatals] although it was first discovered [1866] nearly a century ago. Conversely, *Berardius arnouxi,* although also known for over a century, is *only* known from adults!") In his 1968 classification of the beaked whales, Moore stated that "however sincere McCann may be in his concept of *hectori* representing in fact the young of *Berardius,* he has not succeeeded in being objective in his observations . . . and he musters no clear evidence that his concept is correct." Ross's 1970 discussion of the two South African specimens confirmed Moore's conclusion that *hectori* is "a distinct species in the genus *Mesoplodon.*"

Now that Mead has described the species in some detail and photographs of a living specimen have been published and examined (Rice 1978; Ellis 1980), it is possible to present some information on the external appearance of this previously unknown animal. It is a fairly small beaked whale, the 1975 female measuring 14.5 feet (4.43 meters). The third southern California specimen, an adult male beached at Carlsbad in September 1978, measured 12.79 feet (3.9 meters), and it was believed to be mature because of the complete eruption of the teeth. (The fourth California specimen

was stranded at Torrey Pines State Park, north of La Jolla, on December 27, 1979.) The calf discovered at Pendelton was 6.88 feet (2.10 meters) long, and although it was found some distance up the beach from the female, they were believed to be associated. Mead wrote that "the logical conclusion was that the female died first, and the calf hung around where it had last seen its mother until it died." *Mesoplodon hectori* is dark brownish-gray above and lighter below, with a relatively short beak. The teeth in adult males are flattened triangles and located at the tip of the lower jaw, very much like those of the males of *M. europaeus.*

With the appearance of this previously Southern Hemisphere species in the North Pacific, another *Mesoplodon* has been shown to exist in both hemispheres. The apparent anomaly of a southern species appearing in northern waters—Moore (1963) called the appearance of *Mesoplodon grayi* in Netherlands waters "fantastic," since it had been known previously only from high southern latitudes—now does not seem quite so unusual. There is also a precedent for a northern species being discovered in the south, as is the case of *Mesoplodon mirus.* Not only is the transhemispherical distribution of *M. hectori* noteworthy, but within the enormous coastline of western North America, *all* the recent specimens of this beaked whale have been found within a twenty-five mile stretch of coast.

TRUE'S BEAKED WHALE

Mesoplodon mirus True 1913

In his original description of this species in 1913, F. W. True gave this color pattern: "back slate black, lower side yellow purple flecked with black, median line of the belly somewhat darker; a grayish area in front of the vent; fins the color of the back." Subsequent authors have been less inclined toward "yellow purple," giving instead the ventral coloring as "light gray" or "slate-colored." Fraser (1946) quoted a description of a 15-foot 10-inch male that was "purplish white in color," lightest on the dorsal surface, and that unquestionably belonged to this species. When cetaceans are exposed to sunlight, the color often darkens quickly, so frequent reports of black-bodied animals may not be accurate descriptions of their color in life.

Mesoplodon mirus (the Latin name *mirus* means "wonderful" or "amazing") is not a particularly large spe-

cies, reaching a known maximum length of 17.5 feet (Fraser 1934). The two teeth of the male are located at the very tip of the mandible and angle slightly forward. They are heavier and thicker than those of the female, whose teeth are embedded in the gums. The position of these teeth in the male led McCann (1974) to suggest that "this species alone of the *Mesoplodon* would inflict parallel scars on its opponent." The other species, with their "defensive teeth" located in a less convenient position, would inflict "single linear scars at a time on their opponents." Even in males, however, the teeth are relatively small for the genus, rarely reaching a total length of 2 inches (50 millimeters). True's beaked whale has a proportionally small head with a pronounced forehead bulge and sharply defined throat grooves. In most specimens there is no notch in the tail fin, but Nishiwaki (1972) claimed that "the tail fluke is wide with a small notch at the posterior edge."

The only other beaked whale of the genus *Mesoplodon* with two teeth at or near the tip of the lower jaw is Hector's beaked whale, known from the Southern Hemisphere and the coast of southern California. There are, however, two species of *Mesoplodon* in the North Atlantic: *M. mirus* and *M. europaeus.* In analyzing their differences and similarities, Moore and Wood (1957) wrote that there is "evidence of some segregation between the species, although there is also considerable overlap." The distributional differences

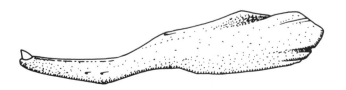

Mesoplodon mirus

seem to lie at the extremes of the range in the western North Atlantic. *M. mirus* has Cape Breton Island, Nova Scotia, as its northernmost limit, whereas *M. europaeus* has been found only as far north as Long Island, New York. Flagler Beach, Florida, is as far south as *M. mirus* seems to go, but *M. europeaus* is known from Trinidad (Fraser 1955) and Jamaica (Rankin 1953).

These scattered strandings would appear to suggest a solitary existence for the species, but the small number makes the sample less than useful. (In a summary of the strandings Moore [1966] listed a total of twelve; eight on the coast of North America and four in British waters.) A 17-foot female that beached on the North Carolina coast carried a 7-foot 2-inch fetus, apparently full-term (Brimley 1943). With this exception, we know hardly anything about the life history of the species. One must remember that strandings are unusual occurrences, and they do not represent the normal behavior of an animal, nor do they necessarily define its range. Those animals that do come ashore are probably sick or stressed, and we therefore must not interpret this behavior as representative or definitive of the species.

True's beaked whale has been recorded from the temperate waters of the North Atlantic, from Nova Scotia to Florida in the west, and from the Outer Hebrides to the west coast of Ireland in the eastern North Atlantic. In addition to this well-documented North Atlantic population, there also seems to be an isolated South African population, which has so far revealed a single adult male (Talbot 1960) and a 15-foot lactating mother accompanied by an 11-foot calf (Ross 1969). Since the two strandings occurred within two hundred miles of each other and none have been noted elsewhere in the Southern Hemisphere, a localized population has been suggested by Ross. In the light of some other geographical anomalies that occur with the

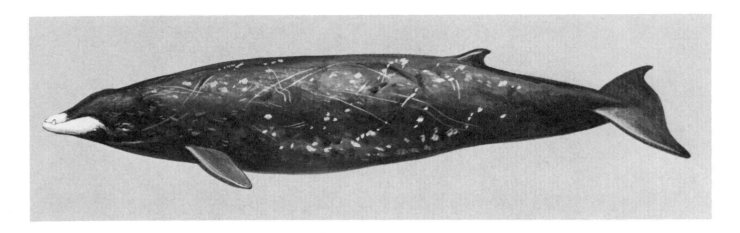

beaked whales, this separation of populations does not seem unusual. The scamperdown whale is recorded only from the Southern Hemisphere, except for a single specimen from the Netherlands; and all records for the Gulfstream beaked whale are from the western North Atlantic except one—the type specimen—which came from the English Channel. Nothing could better demonstrate the enigmatic nature of the beaked whales: only the opportunistic examination of a random beached specimen gives us what little information we have.

GULFSTREAM BEAKED WHALE

Mesoplodon europaeus Gervais 1855

This species, formerly known as *M. gervaisi,* is fairly large, reaching a maximum known length of 22 feet (6.7 meters) (True 1910). The head is small, the beak narrow, and the flukes wide, measuring as much as 33 percent of the total length of the whale. Normal coloration is black or dark gray above, sometimes with a white patch on the undersides. The dorsal fin, like that of many members of the genus *Mesoplodon,* is small, slightly falcate, and located far posterior to the midpoint of the back. Only adult males have teeth, which appear about one-third of the distance from the tip of the jaw to the corner of the mouth, not quite at the midpoint of the lower jaw. In his description of a specimen stranded in Cuba, Varona (1970) illustrated the teeth of an adult male and showed them to be roughly triangular in shape and flattened in what Moore (1968) referred to as the "antero-posterior plane"; in other words, they are flattened along the animal's long axis. In Varona's specimen a tooth was measured at

2.75 inches (68 millimeters) high, 1.75 inches (42 millimeters) long, and less than 0.5 inches (11 millimeters) thick. Moore (1968) described an adult male beached at Boca Grande, Florida; its teeth fit into grooves in the skin of the upper jaw when the whale's mouth was closed, a characteristic that has never before been observed in this—or any other—species of *Mesoplodon.* (Varona and other authors illustrated the teeth as protruding outside the upper jaw.)

In 1953, two specimens came ashore at Bull Bay, Jamaica: a 14-foot lactating female and a 7-foot calf. Rankin's article about the pair (1955) included "the first set of photographs ever to be published of the external appearance of this whale" and described the female as follows:

The shape of this whale is rather elegant, I think, with its tapering snout and dome-like crown of the head and streamlined body demarcated from the head by a distinct "neck" and ending posteriorly in horizontal and backswept tail flukes. Even the blow-hole is beautifully curved and is situated on top of the head as far back as the eyes. The latter features are somewhat small and beady and may be easily overlooked, especially if the lids are shut.

In October 1977 a 17-foot (5.2-meter) female stranded in Florida. She was accompanied by a 6.7-foot female calf that was kept alive for a few days at Sea World, Orlando, Florida. The female was black, with white on the tips of the upper and lower jaws, and the calf was

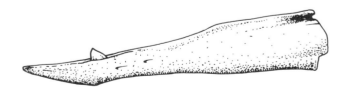

Mesoplodon europaeus

a soft gray, darker on the back and on the tip of the lower jaw. The calf was marked with vertical creases, sometimes referred to as "fetal folds," which indicate that it was curled up in the uterus shortly before it stranded with its mother.

Despite its name, *Mesoplodon europeaus* is known primarily from the coasts of North America and the islands of the Caribbean. It has been recorded from New Jersey, Long Island, North Carolina, Florida, Texas, Cuba, Jamaica, and Trinidad. There is one record from Europe.

The first known specimen was discovered floating in the English Channel in 1840. Because it was unique, "much doubt has been thrown on the validity of the species" (True 1910), but then two more specimens appeared on the shores of New Jersey, one in 1889 and another in 1905. All subsequent reports of this species have been from the western North Atlantic, leading to the assumption that the English Channel specimen might have been a stray. It is also possible that there is an eastern population that has not been discovered. There does not seem to be any doubt of the accuracy of the European specimen; it has been verified numerous times since its initial description by Gervais in 1855.

GINKGO-TOOTHED WHALE

Mesoplodon ginkgodens Nishiwaki and Kamiya 1958

In September 1957 a live beaked whale came close to shore at Oiso Beach, near Tokyo, where some boys were playing ball. The boys waded into the water and killed the whale with their baseball bats. When Nishiwaki and Kamiya (1958) examined the specimen, they realized that its measurements and proportions did not agree with those of any known species of *Mesoplodon,* and they therefore "ventured to settle a new species for this specimen and nominated it as *Mesoplodon ginkgodens.* This species name is chosen from the fact that the lateral view of the teeth of the present specimen resembles closely the shape of a leaf of the ginkgo tree (*Ginkgo biloba* Linneaus)." The teeth are wider than they are high, 4 inches by 2.5 inches (115 millimeters by 65 millimeters), compressed laterally, and located about one-third of the distance from the

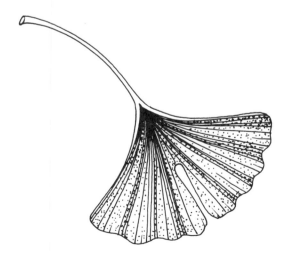

The leaf of the ginkgo tree, *Ginkgo biloba.*

tip of the lower jaw. As in other species of *Mesoplodon,* the teeth erupt over the gums only in the males.

The color of the whale is blackish gray, but it bears very few of the white scars that are so characteristic of all *Mesoplodon* species. In a 1972 paper Nishiwaki and associates commented on this phenomenon with regard to an old male that had stranded near Ito City, Shizuoka prefecture, in 1971. This animal had very few scars, "perhaps due to the inerupted teeth" of this species. Since so little of the tooth of this species is exposed, it would be difficult for these animals to inflict scratches on other individuals.

From the various Japanese specimens that have been so carefully measured, the maximum length has been estimated at 15.5 feet (4.7 meters). The flukes are very wide, as much as 25 percent of the body length, and they show a slight convexity, whereas other whales' flukes are notched. The dorsal fin is located approximately two-thirds of the way down the back and is markedly falcate (Nishiwaki et al.).

Of the eight ginkgo-toothed whales stranded on Japanese and Formosan beaches, six were discovered between 1962 and 1972. When this was established as a valid species, other previously unidentifiable specimens could be referred to it. The first specimen of *Mesoplodon* from Japan, reported in 1935, was variously identified as *M. densirostris* or *M. bidens.* From the shape of the teeth and other characters, Nishiwaki and Kamiya (1958) were "of the opinion that the first specimen might belong to the same species as the present specimen, viz. *Mesoplodon ginkgodens.*" In 1954 a 16-foot female drifted ashore at Delmar, California, fifteen miles north of San Diego. It was not identified until 1965, when J. C. Moore, revising the genus *Mesoplodon,* examined this specimen, using the data and photographs published by Nishiwaki and Kamiya in their 1958 description of the new species, and incorporated it into his 1968 revision of the relationships of the beaked whales. Deraniyagala (1963a) published a description of "a new beaked whale *Mesoplodon hotuala*" from Ceylon, but Moore examined this specimen, too, and recognized it as another *ginkgodens* (Moore and Gilmore 1965).

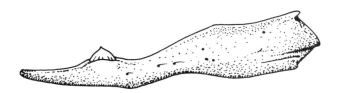

Mesoplodon ginkgodens

The known range of this species, therefore, is the waters of Japan (seven specimens); Taiwan (one specimen); Ceylon (one specimen); and southern California (one specimen). It is possible that more specimens will appear, and Moore and Gilmore "alert[ed] zoologists of the Pacific and Indian Oceans to the probability that more specimens will be found on other shores."

SCAMPERDOWN WHALE

Mesoplodon grayi von Haast 1876

Although this species is best known from stranding records in the Southern Hemisphere—particularly New Zealand—the best illustration and description are of an animal that beached in the totally unexpected location of Kijkduin, in the Netherlands:

[the] back is black to slate grey on the sides. Toward the ventral surface the colour gradually becomes lighter, the sides being of a brownish grey. The ventral surface is of a light grey with a brownish tinge with the exception of a broad darker median band gradually becoming mottled anteriorly and vanishing in the region of the flippers. The flippers and tail flukes on both sides are very dark grey to black, the edges of the flippers have a light border (Boschma 1950).

The scamperdown's head tapers to a pointed beak without much of a forehead bulge, and in adult animals the head and beak are often white. The flippers are small and the flukes broad without a median notch. Like most of the other beaked whales, the scamperdown is often marked with scars and scratches. The maximum known length for a male is 18 feet (5.5 meters); for a female it is 16 feet (4.9 meters).

The two onion-shaped teeth, flattened laterally, are located about midway in the lower jaw and erupt only in adult males. The species is further characterized by the presence of seventeen to nineteen pairs of upper teeth, in addition to the lower pair. Boschma (1951a) reported that these minute teeth (none of which are longer than 0.375 inches [10 millimeters]) are present in all examined specimens, and "they constantly form a so distinct regular row that they seem to perform a distinct function." The presence of these teeth would seem to suggest a phylogenetic connection—and pos-

sible confusion—with *Tasmacetus,* the only other beaked whale with teeth other than the large mandibular ones. In the latter, however, the lower teeth are located at the very tip of the jaw. *Tasmacetus* also has tooth rows in both the upper and lower jaws, unlike *M. grayi,* in which the minute teeth are embedded in the gums of the upper jaw only.

These animals are not often observed at sea, but Rice (1978) noted that "the scamperdown whale . . . has the peculiar habit of sticking its long, needlelike, white snout out of the water as it breaks the surface to breathe." There are many records of strandings, including a mass stranding of twenty-eight animals at New Zealand's Chatham Islands in 1874. From the mass strandings and field observations in New Zealand waters and elsewhere, it can be assumed that this species is more gregarious than other species of *Mesoplodon,* and the animals may travel in small groups. Nothing else is known about their habits.

The scamperdown has a circumpolar distribution in the Southern Hemisphere, south of 30°. It has been recorded in the Indian Ocean (South Africa); off South Australia and Victoria; and from New Zealand to the coast of Chile in the South Pacific. In the South Atlantic specimens have beached on the Argentine coast, the Falkland Islands, Tierra del Fuego, and South Africa.

The most recent accounts of this species include a single occurrence from the Netherlands. This whale, a 15-foot (4.6-meter) female, stranded in 1927, but apparently was not reported in the scientific literature until Boschma described it in 1950. (In 1938, Norman and Fraser wrote that "*M. grayi* is as yet only known from specimens in the southern hemisphere.") Because the location in Holland is over 7,000 miles from the nearest known specimen, Moore (1963) called the event "fantastic" and concluded that "Boschma's specimen . . . must be regarded as a straggler." Other beaked whales have been discovered far from their original ranges, and these discoveries may demonstrate nothing more than our own inabilities to find these elusive creatures at sea. The Gulfstream beaked whale has been observed exclusively from the coasts of North America, except for one animal that was found in the English Channel, and in recent years a population of True's beaked whale has been reported in South African waters, thousands of miles from its previous North Atlantic range.

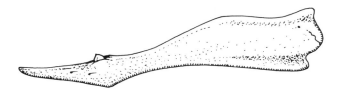

Mesoplodon grayi

HUBBS' BEAKED WHALE

Mesoplodon carlhubbsi Moore 1963

Hubbs' beaked whale reaches a length of 17 feet (5.2 meters) and is usually black with lighter undersides and a whitish beak (Nishiwaki and Kamiya 1959). The large teeth are located about one-fifth of the distance from the apex to the posterior edge of the lower jaw. The teeth in males are more or less straight-sided and have a point projecting forward. In this and the other "saber-toothed" whales, the large teeth are particularly thin and flat in cross section; one set of tooth dimensions was as follows: height, 6.3 inches (160 millimeters); width, 2.95 inches (75 millimeters); thickness, 0.55 inches (15 millimeters), according to Nishiwaki and Kamiya (1959). From photographs that they published, it is clear that the lower teeth of adult males are covered with skin, except for the protruding tips. Other species, such as the specimen of *M. stejnegeri* illustrated in Nishimura and Nishiwaki (1964), show the large teeth to be fully exposed.

To date, this species has been found only in the North Pacific. Records of stranded animals represent almost the entire body of knowledge about the life history of this species.

J. C. Moore described this species in 1963, making it the newest addition to the genus. He named the species after Carl L. Hubbs (1894–1979), one of the country's premier marine biologists. It was Hubbs (1946) who described a 17-foot male beaked whale that stranded at La Jolla, California, as *Mesoplodon bowdoini*. In 1953, R. T. Orr reviewed the species and concluded that *M. bowdoini* and *M. stejnegeri* "represent one species"; the purported differences between them being attributable to variations in the age and sex of the animals described. He believed that the specimens that had previously been assigned to *bowdoini* were old males of the genus *stejnegeri*. In his review of the North Pacific representatives of the genus *Mesoplodon*, Moore (1963) examined the skulls and teeth of the specimens that had been studied by Hubbs and by Orr. When he had separated the material by geographical location and cranial characteristics, he discovered that *bowdoini* and *stejnegeri* were, indeed, distinct species. Further, some of the skulls that had previously been assigned to these species were distinct enough from the others to warrant the establishment of yet a third species. Moore named it after Hubbs, "the discoverer of the first good specimen, who has made other contributions to cetology, and whose name is, we believe, not entirely unknown among ichthyologists."*

Moore differentiated Hubbs' beaked whale from other species of *Mesoplodon* on seventeen diagnostic characters, concerned mostly with skull proportions, but also with the actual shape of the teeth. He described the appearance of the teeth: "From [the] front view the beak is seen to lie between the teeth like a zero between parentheses."

The habitat of this whale is the North Pacific Ocean,

*One of Hubbs's little-known contributions to cetology concerns the edibility of certain cetaceans. In 1951 he reported that he and his fellow workers ate the meat of a recently stranded pygmy sperm whale, and since it was immediately after the war and red meat had been particularly scarce, they also ate about one hundred pounds of the meat of the La Jolla *Mesoplodon*. It was "much enjoyed."

Mesoplodon carlhubbsi

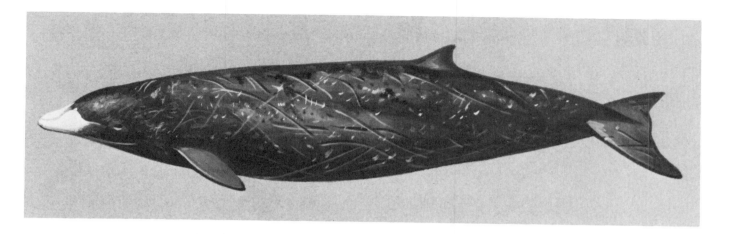

and the specimens identified as belonging to this species (Moore 1963) were found at La Jolla, California; Marin County, California; Gray's Harbor, Washington; San Simeon, California; Ayukawa, Japan; and Kinka-san, Japan.*

DEEP-CRESTED WHALE

Mesoplodon bowdoini Andrews 1908

Although there are very few specimens of this whale known to science, the largest skeleton is about 14 feet in length (4.2 meters). Thus, we assume that this species is one of the smaller of the beaked whales (Baker 1972). Because it is the southern version of a species that is known to be heavily scarred (Hubbs' beaked whale), it can be suggested that this species also is black with numerous white scratches and scars.

In the males the two large flattened teeth are set in partially raised sockets, just behind the point where the two pieces of the lower jaw are fused together. The lower teeth often have a peculiar "hollow" on the anterior margin, the cause of which is unknown. Moore (1963) has written that "the wear may have been accomplished by some kind of food that is long and slender and finely abrasive. . . . One could speculate that feeding on small, slender sharks with skin like fine sandpaper might abrade the teeth in this fashion." Not all specimens show this wear, indicating that it is an acquired characteristic, and it has also been shown that it is not restricted to this species. A Japanese specimen that Nishiwaki (1962a) identified as *bowdoini*

*Prior to the publication of Moore's 1963 discussion, many of these specimens had been recorded as belonging to different species; for example, the Ayukawa animal was identified as *M. stejnegeri* by Nishiwaki and Kamiya (1959), and the San Simeon specimen was identified as *stejnegeri* by Roest (1964).

—but cannot be, if we accept Moore's segregation of this species to the South Pacific—also had deep grooves in the teeth.* The type specimen (Andrews 1908), which came from New Zealand, has teeth that are unworn on the leading edge. Andrews named the species for George S. Bowdoin, one of his benefactors at the American Museum of Natural History in New York.

Nothing is known of the life cycle of this species, but one female was found to be carrying a 5-foot (1.5-meter) fetus in September, suggesting that the young are born in the spring (Gaskin 1972).

To the layman, *M. bowdoini*, *M. stejnegeri*, and *M. carlhubbsi* look very much alike, since they are all blackish, scarred animals with a white beak and (in the males) prominent, flattened teeth. Even cetologists have had a particularly difficult time with the large-toothed varieties of beaked whales, often putting them into the same species (Orr 1953) or moving them around in what appears to be a capricious fashion. This is attributable not so much to the contrary nature of the taxonomists as to the limited amount of study material for comparative purposes and to the extremely uncooperative nature of the beaked whales

*Many references to this species in the literature—for example, Hubbs 1946, Nishiwaki 1962a—are specimens that Moore (1963) has placed into different species. Thus the "Akita Beach specimen" of Nishiwaki, identified by him as *bowdoini*, must now be assigned to the North Pacific species, *M. stejnegeri* (Nishimura and Nishiwaki 1964).

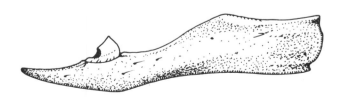

Mesoploden bowdoini

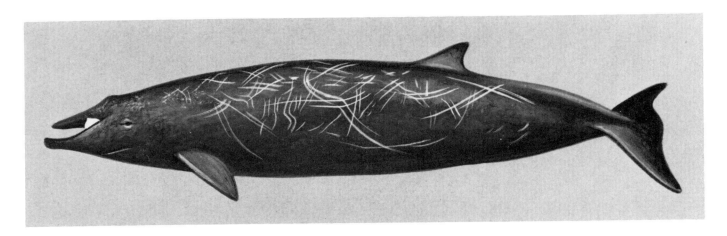

themselves. They do not strand very often, leading to the assumption that they are deep-water animals, and they are not frequently seen or recognized at sea. Rice (1978) wrote, "In the course of whale research cruises in the eastern North Pacific—totalling some five hundred days at sea during the past twenty years—I have never identified a *Mesoplodon.*"

In a 1963 paper entitled "Recognizing Certain Species of Beaked Whales of the Pacific Ocean," J. C. Moore addressed the thorny problem of differentiating *stejnegeri* from *bowdoini*—and, in the process, he identified the new species *Mesoplodon carlhubbsi.* He separated the "North Temperate Lot" into two distinct species, *stejnegeri* and *carlhubbsi,* and took the "South Temperate Lot" (all the known South Pacific specimens) to be *M. bowdoini.* He based his diagnosis on the obvious geographical separation, as well as on pronounced differences in the skull proportions and tooth shape.

This species is reported only from the South Pacific; the other two similar species, *stejnegeri* and *carlhubbsi,* are found only in the North Pacific. *M. bowdoini* has been recorded from New Zealand, Tasmania, Campbell Island (south of New Zealand in the subantarctic), and Western Australia.

STEJNEGER'S BEAKED WHALE

Mesoplodon stejnegeri True 1885

Stejneger's (pronounced "sty'-ne-gers") beaked whale is one of the little-known "saber-toothed" beaked whales from the North Pacific Ocean. In 1938 there were "but two specimens, both from the Pacific coast of North America" (Norman and Fraser). One of these was the type specimen, described from a skull found by Leonhard Stejneger on Bering Island in 1883, and the other was the first full specimen to be observed, a 17-foot male that washed ashore at Yaquina Bay, Oregon, in 1904 (True 1910). The Yaquina Bay specimen was described thus in a local newspaper (quoted in True):

On either side of the mouth are two villainous-looking tusks, several inches in length. They are at the back of the mouth, and extend up to a level with the top of the jaw. They are very wide and flat, squared on top. . . . The head is equipped with a blowhole, like that of a whale. The eyes are very low, almost underneath the lower jaw.

One of these tusks "measured 5 3/4 inches along its anterior border, 8 1/4 inches along its posterior border, 3 1/4 inches from anterior to posterior border,

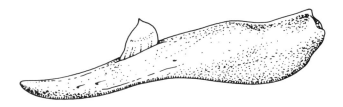

Mesoplodon stejnegeri

and just over 1/2 inch in traverse thickness" (Norman and Fraser 1938).

The species is usually black with scars and whitish patches, and the jaws forward of the teeth may be white. Two specimens were described and illustrated by Nishimura and Nishiwaki (1964). The 17-foot (5.2-meter) male was "dark gray all over" with white scars, and the 7.8-foot (2.4-meter) female was "grey on the dorsal surface as well as the areas around eyes and snout, and the upper surfaces of flippers and tail flukes, but whitish on the ventral side of the body including the under surface of flippers and tail flukes." From the illustrations it can be seen that the scars on the male's body are mostly paired parallel lines, and the authors made the "supposition that such streaks are nothing but scars formed by other full-grown males during plays or fightings. The female specimen, on the other hand, showed no traces of such streaks."

From the infrequent illustrations of the saber-toothed whales in the flesh, certain external differences become apparent. In True's (1910) discussion of *M. stejnegeri,* there is a photograph of the head of the Yaquina Bay specimen. The teeth are fully exposed, as they are in the male described and illustrated by Nishimura and Nishiwaki. Another photograph of a male appears in "Alaska Whales and Whaling" (1978), and again the teeth are fully exposed. Photographs of the head of *M. bowdoini* are virtually nonexistent, but there are at least two clear illustrations (one in color) of *carlhubbsi.* Nishiwaki and Kamiya (1959) illustrated in color the specimen from Ayukawa that they originally identified as *stejnegeri,* though Moore assigned this specimen to *carlhubbsi* in his 1963 review of the beaked whales of the Pacific. Hubbs's 1946 specimen from La Jolla, California, the type specimen of *M. carlhubbsi* (Moore 1963), is also well photographed. In both cases the large lower teeth are covered by flesh except for the small tip of the denticle. It is, therefore, possible to suggest that the fleshy tooth cover is characteristic of *M. carlhubbsi* of the North Pacific (and perhaps also of *M. bowdoini* in the South Pacific), whereas in *stejnegeri* the lower teeth of adult males are fully exposed. (In females of all three species the lower teeth do not erupt at all, so the shape of the tooth and the skull proportions must be the differentiating factors.)

Nothing is known of the biology of Stejneger's beaked whale. One report (Nishimura and Nishiwaki 1964) mentioned the possibility of this animal's "pursuing salmon as a rapacious predator," and the specimens that they examined were trapped in salmon gillnets, which would seem to support this observation.

Scheffer and Slipp (1948) quoted a Makah indian who observed whales that were thought to be of this species "offshore on the salmon trolling grounds."

Restricted to the North Pacific Ocean, this whale has been recorded from the Commander and Pribilof islands north to the northern Gulf of Alaska, south to the Sea of Japan in the west and to Oregon in the east. From the stranding records it appears that the range of Stejneger's beaked whale is more northerly than that of Hubbs' beaked whale, though they overlap in the areas of Washington state and northern Japan.

SOWERBY'S BEAKED WHALE

Mesoplodon bidens Sowerby 1804

Sowerby's beaked whale reaches a known length of 18 feet (5.6 meters) (Tomilin 1957). Like the other Atlantic species of *Mesoplodon,* it has a streamlined body, small head with a pointed beak, and flukes without a terminal notch. Its color is dark gray to black above, lighter below, and the skin is often marked with white spots or scars. The 2 teeth in the males (*bidens* means "two teeth") are typically flattened and are located at about the middle of the lower jaw. Unlike the symmetrical teeth of *M. mirus* or *M. europaeus,* the teeth of this species are unusually shaped, having a long root set obliquely into the jaw and a crown that points slightly toward the rear. In females they usually do not erupt, and Fraser (1953) showed X-rays of vestigial small teeth in the lower jaws of a 12-foot male that stranded at Glamorgan, Scotland. Without a careful examination of the skull and teeth, it would be possible to confuse this species with any of the other beaked whales. There are no distinguishing characteristics that could serve as field marks at sea.

Jonsgard and Høidal (1957) studied stranded specimens on the west coast of Norway and discovered that mating usually takes place in the late winter and spring. After a gestation period of about a year, a

Mesoplodon bidens

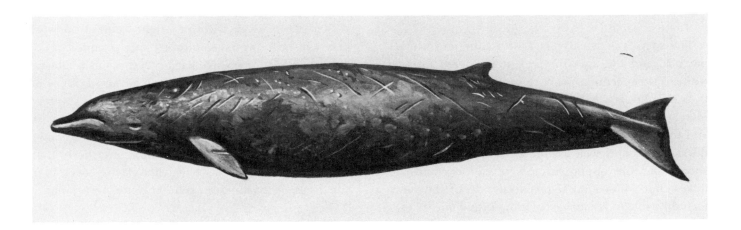

single 7-foot (2.13-meter) calf is born. During its first year the calf grows 3–4 feet, and it is weaned when it is about 10 feet (3 meters) long.

This is the most northerly of the Atlantic beaked whales, observed off Norway, in the Baltic Sea, in the Mediterranean, and off the British Isles. There are a few records from the western North Atlantic, including Nantucket, Massachusetts, and Notre Dame Bay, Newfoundland. From the concentration of strandings it appears that the population is centered in, but not restricted to, the North Sea.

This was the first beaked whale to be described for science. It was originally classified as *Physeter bidens* by Sowerby in 1804, and Dewhurst (1834) referred to it as the "two-toothed cachalot of Sowerby." The type specimen was a 16-foot male, found at Brodie-House, Scotland, in 1800. In addition to discovering what was to become the first *Mesoplodon,* Sowerby seems also to have initiated the idea of the "beaked" whale:

We might have called it *Physeter Rostratus,* with some propriety; but this might have created confusion. It is however a curious circumstance that such an appellation would suit better if it were described with the wrong side upwards; which will be easily observed, if the plate is reversed: and the jaws, in this case, very aptly resemble a bird's beak.

In 1828 a specimen was captured at Le Havre, France, and kept out of the water for two days before it died. It was fed on "soaked bread and other alimentary substances," and it was heard to emit "a low cavernous sound like the lowing of a cow" (Beddard 1900).

According to Fraser's 1974 summary, 21 have stranded on British coasts since 1913, and Duguy (1977) reports: "This species also appears among those which are found occasionally on the Atlantic and Channel coasts." A rare opportunity to observe a juve-

nile occurred in 1972, when a calf was captured off Ostend, Belgium, where its mother was beached and dying. The baby, 8.8 feet (2.7 meters), and later estimated to be less than a year old, was brought to the Delphinarium at Harderwijk, Holland, where it lived for three days before it died from a headlong crash into the tank wall. Postmortem examinations revealed a hydrodynamic shape designed for a species "built to go fast and straight, which seems logical for a pelagic animal. They are seriously hampered in narrow surroundings, let alone in a tank even when it is in a semi-circle with a radius of 15 m[eters] as at Harderwijk" (Dudok van Heel 1974).

STRAP-TOOTHED WHALE

Mesoplodon layardii Gray 1865

One of the largest members of the genus, this whale has been recorded to reach a length of over 19 feet (5.85 meters) (Waite 1922), but most of the other known specimens have been between 13 and 17 feet (Hale 1939). The color of a living animal has been described as follows: "bronze brown on the dorsum, pale gray ventro-laterally grading to off-white on the underside" (Hale 1947). Forty-eight hours after this stranded animal died, it became "black above, grading to purplish pink with isolated gray patches on the side of the head." The difference in these two descriptions demonstrates the postmortem changes that occur in the external appearance of whales and may very well account for the predominance of descriptions of stranded whales as "black," since in most species the skin color darkens appreciably with even short-term exposure to the sun.

Young animals are not easily distinguished from many other species of *Mesoplodon,* since they have the regular characteristics of the genus, including paired throat grooves converging toward the snout, a small dorsal fin and flippers, and flukes that are not notched. In the immature specimens the lower teeth, located toward the posterior border of the jaw, are triangular and flattened, much like those of any other *Mesoplodon.* With maturity, however, adult males of this species develop teeth that make them unique certainly among all whales and probably in the entire animal kingdom. The small triangular tooth begins to curve outward at first, "giving the appearance of the teeth having the concave surface outwards" (Oliver 1924). From this stage, where the denticles are pointing away from the lower jaw, they then curve up, back, and over the upper jaw, until they form an arch over the rostrum, finally preventing the animal from opening its mouth to any significant degree. These extraordinary teeth have been likened to "the tusks of a boar (Gaskin 1972), and Moore (1968) wrote that "the teeth of Mesoplodon attain great length in the second largest species of the genus, *M. layardi.* * The longest personally measured is 330 mm [12.9 inches]." (By comparison, the "tusks" of the species *M. densirostris, M. stejnegeri,* and *M. carlhubbsi,* known as the saber-toothed whales, rarely exceed 6 inches [150 millimeters] in height.) From the examination of the stomach contents of stranded specimens, it is known that strap-

*According to Rice's 1977 *List of the Marine Mammals of the World,* the correct spelling of the trivial name is *layardii.* Various authors have written it without the second "i", and wherever this spelling appears in the literature, I have retained it.

Mesoplodon layardii

The tooth of the strap-toothed whale, *Mesoplodon layardii.* In this position the whale would be facing to the reader's left (after Krefft and Gray 1871).

toothed whales eat squid, but how the males feed if they cannot open their mouths remains a mystery. Juveniles and adult females have no such problem, since their teeth do not develop in this amazing fashion.

Although McCann (1964) published a description of the female reproductive organs of this species, in which he wrote that "the calving of *M. layardi* takes place in the early spring of the Southern Hemisphere," almost nothing else is known of the life cycle of this species. (It might even be said that we know less than nothing, since the question of males feeding without being able to open their mouths adds a significant problem to the study of an animal that is already an enigma.)

There is one recorded observation of this species at sea: Gaskin (1972) wrote that "one male was recognized by the author. . . . the tooth on the left side of the head was clearly seen. This animal was one of a group of three, of which all were presumed to be of this species." Observers at Victor Harbor, Australia, saw two animals "sporting offshore" shortly before a male and female *layardii* beached themselves. The male was 15 feet long and the female 2 feet longer. Hale (1931a), who recorded the observations, indicated that the animals might have been mating.

The strap-toothed whale is known only from the Southern Hemisphere. Of the more than fifty specimens that have been examined to date, more than twenty have been found in New Zealand (Baker 1972). The species has also been recorded from the Cape of Good Hope (the type specimen), Australia, Tasmania, the Falkland Islands, and Tierra del Fuego, where Goodall (1978) discovered five crania, but no mandibles and, therefore, none of the teeth. In 1971, a 19-foot female was found near La Paloma, Uruguay, the northernmost record for this species (Praderi 1972).

DENSE-BEAKED WHALE

Mesoplodon densirostris de Blainville 1817

In adult males of this species, the modified lower jaw is a prominent and noteworthy characteristic. It is highly arched, and the teeth "protrude above the forehead somewhat like a pair of horns" (Rice 1978). The jaws are also unique in their configuration, and serve to accommodate the massive teeth. The beaked whales with exaggerated teeth are known collectively as the "deep socketed whales" (Moore 1968), since only a small portion of the teeth of the mature male protrudes beyond the jawbone. (Mörzer Bruyns [1971] referred to these species as the "saber-toothed whales.") Harmer (1927) described the jaw thus: "The lower jaw has a remarkable shape, due to its extraordinary depth in the region of the teeth, which are situated near the middle of the jaw. From this point the dorsal outline of the bone slopes down steeply to the low anterior region which corresponds with the beak above it." Out of the socket, one tooth was measured at 6 inches (152 millimeters) in height, 3.375 inches (85.9 millimeters) wide, and 1.75 inches (44.5 millimeters) thick (Norman and Fraser 1938). Adult

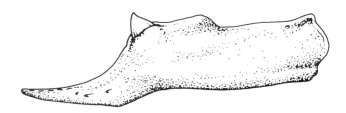

Mesoplodon densirostris

females and juveniles have the same jaw configuration, but the teeth, embedded in the gums, are not visible.

Like most of the other species of *Mesoplodon,* the dense-beaked whale is dark gray to black in color and bears some white scars and blotches. Also characteristically, there is no notch between the left and right lobes of the flukes, and the flippers and dorsal fin are proportionally small. The maximum recorded length for this species is 17 feet (5.2 meters).

Only *Mesoplodon stejnegeri, M. carlhubbsi,* and *M. bowdoini* have teeth that are as large as those of the dense-beaked whale (the straplike teeth of the male *M. layardii* are completely different), but no other species has the high, crested mandible. Moreover, the teeth of the other species are shaped differently, and the skulls have measurable proportional differences.

At sea it would be almost impossible to identify this species unless one could get a close look at an adult male. (This species is encountered in tropical waters more frequently than other *Mesoplodons,* but not enough specimens have been seen to make a convincing argument for the animal's distribution. As of 1971, Besharse listed all eighteen specimens known to date. Rice (1978) provided one of the few published observations of living dense-beaked whales seen at sea: "I once saw a group of ten or twelve in the Hawaiian Islands. They blew leisurely at the surface for several minutes, and then dived. We waited forty-five minutes for them to come up, but we never saw them again." On Midway Island, Galbreath (1963) discovered three beaked whales stranded at the same time. Two were dense-beaked whales, and the third was a goosebeak whale. No explanation was given for this peculiar association or the concurrent strandings. When Besharse described one of the dense-beaked whales from Midway, it was the only adult female then known to science.

This is the only species of *Mesoplodon* that occurs normally both north and south of the equator. It has been recorded from the tropical and warm temperate waters of the world's oceans, but it is nowhere common. (Rice 1977 offered "tropical beaked whale" as an alternative common name for the species.) Strandings include such diverse locations as New Jersey, Madeira, South Africa, Canada, Massachusetts, and the Bahamas in the Atlantic; Lord Howe Island and Queensland in Australia; Midway Island; Algoa Bay, South Africa; Tasmania; and the Seychelles, which was the source of the type specimen. In 1968, two females were harpooned off Formosa and brought to the fish markets (Kasuya and Nishiwaki 1971). For the North Atlantic population Moore (1966) has suggested a more offshore distribution than that of the other beaked whales of that region. There are no records of this species from the South Atlantic or from European shores.

One of the few records of a beaked whale maintained in captivity refers to a juvenile male of this species, kept for a short time at the New York Aquarium at Coney Island (Mead, personal communication). The sounds made by beaked whales of any species have rarely been heard. In 1971, Winn and associates taped the underwater sounds of *Hyperoodon ampullatus,* "the first time recorded sounds [were] described for a species of beaked whale." A dense-beaked whale, stranded in 1969 at Crescent Beach, Florida, was heard to emit "chirps or short whistles," which were later analyzed as pulsed sounds (Caldwell and Caldwell 1971).

REFERENCES

BIBLIOGRAPHY

INDEX

REFERENCES

Throughout the book the reader will encounter parenthetical references to authors—for example, (Beamish 1978). Even though this is intended to be a popular—that is, nontechnical—book, I have chosen to follow the style of scientific journals by incorporating the references into the text. In each case the date refers to the publication of the article or book and not to the date of the event discussed.

Because each chapter in this volume is devoted to a specific group of animals (usually a single species), each list of references represents a working bibliography for those particular animals. Many works are referred to frequently; these entries appear only in the bibliography and are not duplicated here in the individual lists of references.

INTRODUCTION

BEAMISH, P. 1978. Evidence that a captive humpback whale (*Megaptera novaeangliae*) does not use sonar. *Deep-Sea Research* 25(5): 469–72.

BESTON, H. 1928. *The Outermost House.* Viking Compass Edition. 1972.

CLARKE, R., L. A. AGUAYO, and S. B. DEL CAMPO. 1978. Whale observation and whale marking off the coast of Chile. *Sci. Rep. Whales Res. Inst.* 30: 117–77.

COLBERT, E. H. 1955. *Evolution of the Vertebrates.* John Wiley & Sons.

ERDMAN, D. S., J. HARMS, and M. M. FLORES. 1973. Cetacean records from the northeastern Caribbean region. *Cetology* 17: 1–14.

FANNING, J. 1979. The blow of whales and dolphins—a functional explanation. (Abstract.) *Third Biennial Conf. Biol. Marine Mammals.* Seattle.

GOODALL, R. N. P. 1978. Report on small cetaceans stranded on the coasts of Tierra del Fuego. *Sci. Rep. Whales Res. Inst.* 30: 197–230.

LOCKYER, C. 1976. Growth and energy budgets of large baleen whales from the Southern Hemisphere. *FAO Scientific Consultation on Marine Mammals.* ACMRR/SC/41.

MATTHIESSEN, P. 1971. *Blue Meridian.* Random House.

MOWAT, F. 1972. *A Whale for the Killing.* Little, Brown & Co.

NISHIWAKI, M. 1962. Aerial photographs show sperm whales' interesting habits. *Norsk Hvalfangst-tidende* 51(9): 395–98.

OSTROM, J. H. 1978. New ideas about dinosaurs. *National Geographic* 154(2): 152–85.

OWEN, R. 1866. On some Indian cetacea collected by Walter Elliot, Esq. *Trans. Zool. Soc. London.* 1866: 17–47.

PERRIN, W. F., E. D. MITCHELL, P. J. H. VAN BREE, and D. K. CALDWELL. 1977. Spinner dolphins, *Stenella* spp. in the Atlantic. Unpublished paper.

WATKINS, W. A., and W. E. SCHEVILL. 1977. Sperm whale codas. *Jour. Acoust. Soc. Amer.* 62(6): 1485–90 (+ phonograph record).

WILSON, E. A. 1905. On the whales, seals and birds of Ross Sea and South Victoria Land. In Captain R. F. Scott, *The Voyage of the 'Discovery,'* vol. 2, app. II, pp. 469–94. British Museum.

———. 1907. Mammalia (whales and seals). *Rep. Brit. Natl. Antarct. Expdn. 1901–1904,* Natural History, vol. 2, Zoology, 69 pp.

WOOD, F. G. 1978. The cetacean stranding phenomenon: An hypothesis. In J. R. Geraci and D. St. Aubin, eds., *Analysis of Marine Mammal Strandings and Recommendations for a Nationwide Stranding-Salvage Program.* Final Report to U.S. Marine Mammal Commission in Fulfillment of Contract MM7ACo20. National Technical Information Service, 48 pp.

GRAY WHALE

ANDREWS, R. C. 1914. Monographs of the Pacific Cetacea. I. The California Gray Whale (*Rhachianectes glaucus* Cope). *Mem. Amer. Mus. Nat. Hist.* n.s. 1: 227–87.

———. 1916. *Whale Hunting with Gun and Camera.* D. Appleton & Co.

ASA-DORIAN, P. V., and P. J. PERKINS. 1967. The controversial production of sound by the California gray whale, *Eschrichtius gibbosus. Norsk Hvalfangst-tidende* 56(4): 74–77.

BALDRIDGE, A. 1972. Killer whales attack and eat a gray whale. *Jour. Mammal.* 53(4): 898–900.

BARNARD, J. 1964. Marine amphipods of Bahia de San Quintin. *Pacific Naturalist* 20: 55–139.

BEEBE, W. 1908. *The Bird.* Henry Holt & Co.

BEIERLE, J. W., C. DENGEN, J. J. BEIERLE, D. R. PATTEN, and F. E. DURHAM. 1976. An analysis of the fluid contents in the postnatal sac of the gray whale, *Eschrichtius robustus. Bull. S. Calif. Acad. Sci.* 75(1): 5–10.

BOWEN, S. L. 1974. Probable extinction of the Korean stock of gray whales (*Eschrichtius robustus*). *Jour. Mammal.* 55(1): 208–9.

BREWINGTON, M. V., and D. BREWINGTON. 1969. *Kendall Whaling Museum Prints.* Kendall Whaling Museum, Sharon, Mass.

BROWNELL, R. L., JR., and C. L. CHUN. 1977. Probable existence of the Korean stock of the gray whale (*Eschrichtius robustus*). *Jour. Mammal.* 58(2): 237–39.

CALDWELL, D. K., and M. C. CALDWELL. 1963. Surf-riding by the California gray whale. *Bull. So. Calif. Acad. Sci.* 62(2): 99.

———. 1966. Epimeletic (care-giving) behavior in cetacea. In K. S. Norris, ed., *Whales, Dolphins and Porpoises,* pp. 755–89. University of California Press.

CARL, G. C. 1968. Diving rhythm of a gray whale. *Murrelet* 49(1): 10.

CEDERLUND, B. A. 1939. A subfossil gray whale discovered in Sweden in 1859. *Zool. Bidr. Uppsala* 18: 269–85.

COUSTEAU, J.-Y., and P. DIOLE. 1972. *The Whale.* Doubleday & Co.

CUMMINGS, W. C., and P. O. THOMPSON. 1971. Gray whales avoid the sounds of killer whales. *Fish. Bull.* 69(3): 525–36.

DRUCKER, P. 1951. The northern and central Nootkan tribes. *Bull. Bur. Amer. Ethnol.* 144: 1–460.

DUDLEY, P. 1725. An essay on the natural history of whales. *Phil. Trans. Roy. Soc. London* 7: 424–31.

DURHAM, F. E., and J. W. BEIERLE. 1976. Investigations on the postnatal sac of the gray whale *Eschrichtius robustus. Bull. S. Calif. Acad. Sci.* 75(1): 1–5.

EBERHARDT, R. L., and K. S. NORRIS. 1964. Observations of newborn Pacific gray whales on Mexican calving grounds. *Jour. Mammal.* 45(1): 88–95.

ELLIS, R. 1977. Of men, whales, and Captain Scammon. *National Parks and Conservation* 51(10): 8–13.

EVANS, W. E. 1974. Telemetering of temperature and depth data from a free ranging yearling California gray whale. *Mar. Fish. Rev.* 36(4): 52–58.

FISH, J. F., J. L. SUMICH, and G. L. LINGLE. 1974. Sounds produced by the gray whale, *Eschrichtius robustus. Mar. Fish. Rev.* 36(4): 38–45.

FRASER, F. C. 1937. Early Japanese whaling. *Proc. Linn. Soc. London* 150: 19–20.

———. 1970. An early 17th century record of the Californian grey whale in Icelandic waters. *Invest. on Cetacea* 2: 13–20.

GARD, R. 1974. Aerial census of gray whales in Baja California lagoons, 1970 and 1973, with notes on behavior, mortality, and conservation. *Calif. Fish and Game* 60(3): 132–43.

GARDNER, E. S. 1960. *Hunting the Desert Whale.* William Morrow & Company.

GILMORE, R. M. 1955. The return of the gray whale. *Scientific American* 192(1): 62–67.

———. 1959. On the mass strandings of sperm whales. *Pacific Naturalist* 1(9): 9–16.

———. 1960. Census and migration of the California gray whale. *Norsk Hvalfangst-tidende* 49(9): 409–31.

———. 1961. *The Story of the Gray Whale.* 2d ed. Privately published. 16 pp.

———. 1978. Some news and views of the gray whale, 1977. *Whalewatcher* 12(2): 9–13.

———, R. L. BROWNELL, J. G. MILLS, and A. HARRISON. 1967. Gray whales near Yavaros, southern Sonora, Golfo de California, Mexico. *Trans. San Diego Soc. Nat. Hist.* 14: 198–203.

GILMORE, R. M., and G. EWING. 1954. Calving of California grays. *Pacific Discovery* 7(3): 13–15.

GILMORE, R. M., and J. G. MILLS. 1962. Courting gray whales in the Gulf of California. *Pacific Discovery* 15(2): 26–27.

GOEBEL, C. A., and M. E. DALHEIM. 1979. A white California gray whale in the Bering Sea. *Murrelet* 60(3): 107.

HEIZER, R. F. 1943. Aconite poison whaling in Asia and America: An Aleutian transfer to the New World. *Bull. Bur. Amer. Ethnol.* 133: 415–68.

HENDERSON, D. A. 1972. *Men & Whales at Scammon's Lagoon.* Dawson's Book Shop, Los Angeles.

———, ed. 1970. *Journal Aboard the Bark Ocean Bird on a Whaling Voyage to Scammon's Lagoon, Winter of 1858–1859, by Charles Melville Scammon.* Dawson's Book Shop, Los Angeles.

HOUCK, W. J. 1962. Possible mating of gray whales on the northern California coast. *Murrelet* 43:54.

HOWELL, A. B., and L. M. HUEY. 1930. Food of the gray and other whales. *Jour. Mammal.* 11(4): 321–22.

HUBBS, C. L., and L. C. HUBBS. 1967. Gray whale censuses by airplane in Mexico. *Calif. Fish and Game* 53: 23–27.

HURLEY, D. E., and J. L. MOHR. 1957. On whale-lice (Amphipoda: Cyamidae) from the California gray whale, *Eschrichtius glaucus. Jour. Parasitol.* 43: 352–57.

ICHIHARA, T. 1958. Gray whale observed in the Bering Sea. *Sci. Rep. Whales Res. Inst.* 13: 201–5.

INTERNATIONAL WHALING COMMISSION. 1978. *Schedule* (As Amended by the Commission at the Special Meeting, Tokyo, December 1977). Cambridge.

KASUYA, T., and D. W. RICE. 1970. Note on the baleen plates and on arrangement of parasitic barnacles of gray whale. *Sci. Rep. Whales Res. Inst.* 22: 39–43.

KELLOGG, R. 1929. What is known of the migration of some of the whalebone whales. *Ann. Rept. Smithsonian Inst.* 1928: 467–94.

———. 1931. Whaling statistics for the Pacific coast of North America. *Jour. Mammal.* 12(1): 73–77.

KIMURA, S., and T. NEMOTO. 1956. Note on a minke whale kept alive in aquarium. *Sci. Rep. Whales Res. Inst.* 11: 181–89.

LARSON, K. 1978. Close encounters (of the whale kind). *Sea Frontiers* 24(4): 194–202.

LEATHERWOOD, S. 1974a. Aerial observations of migrating gray whales, *Eschrichtius robustus,* off southern California. *Mar. Fish. Rev.* 36(4): 45–49.

———. 1974b. A note on gray whale behavioral interactions with other marine mammals. *Mar. Fish. Rev.* 36(4): 50–51.

LEUNG, Y. M. 1965. A collection of whale-lice (Cyamidae: Amphipoda). *Bull. So. Calif. Acad. Sci.* 64: 132–43.

———. 1967. An illustrated key to the species of whale-lice (Amphipoda; Cyamidae), ectoparasites of Cetacea, with a guide to the literature. *Crustaceana* 12: 278–91.

———. 1976. Life-cycle of *Cyamus scammoni* (Amphipoda, Cyamidae), ectoparasite of gray whale, with a remark on the associated species. *Sci. Rep. Whales Res. Inst.* 28: 153–60.

LILLJEBORG, W. 1861. Hvalben funna i jorden pa Gräsön i Roslagen i Sverige. *Forhandl. Skand. Naturf.,* 8 de Møde, Kjöbenhavn. 1860: 599–616.

MAHER, W. J. 1960. Recent records of the California gray whale *(Eschrichtius glaucus)* along the north coast of Alaska. *Arctic* 13: 257–65.

MALLORY, G. K. 1977. Charles Melville Scammon. *Oceans* 10(4): 40–44.

MILLER, T. 1975. *The World of the California Gray Whale.* Baja Trail Publications.

MITCHELL, E. 1979. Magnitude of early catch of East Pacific gray whale *(Eschrichtius robustus). Rep. Int. Whal. Commn.* 29: 307–14.

MITCHELL, E. D., and J. G. MEAD. 1977. History of the gray whale in the Atlantic Ocean. (Abstract.) *Second Conf. Biol. Marine Mammals.* San Diego.

MIZUE, K. 1951. Grey whales in the East Sea area of Korea. *Sci. Rep. Whales Res. Inst.* 5: 71–79.

MOREJOHN, G. V. 1968. A killer whale–gray whale encounter. *Jour. Mammal.* 49(3): 327–28.

NASU, K. 1960. Oceanographic investigation in the Chukchi Sea during the summer of 1958. *Sci. Rep. Whales Res. Inst.* 15: 143–58.

NEW YORK TIMES. 1978. Hunting of gray whale could be revived. June 18, p. 10.

NICHOLS, G. 1975. *Eschrichtius robustus. Oceans* 8(3): 60–65.

NISHIWAKI, M. 1967. Distribution and migration of marine mammals in the North Pacific area. *Bull. Ocean Res. Inst. Univ. Tokyo* 1: 1–64.

———, and T. KASUYA. 1970. Recent record of gray whale in the adjacent waters of Japan and a consideration on its migration. *Sci. Rep. Whales Res. Inst.* 22: 29–37.

NORRIS, K. S., and R. L. GENTRY. 1974. Capturing and harnessing of young California gray whales. *Mar. Fish. Rev.* 36(4): 58–64.

NORRIS, K. S., R. M. GOODMAN, B. VILLA-RAMIREZ, and L. HUBBS. 1977. Behavior of California gray whale, *Eschrichtius robustus,* in southern Baja California, Mexico. *Fish. Bull.* 75(1): 159–72.

NORRIS, K. W., and B. WÜRSIG. 1979. Gray whale lagoon entrance aggregations. (Abstract). *Third Biennial Conf. Biol. Marine Mammals.* Seattle.

O'LEARY, B. 1977. Magic and poison: The whaling technologies of three northern cultures. Whaling Symposium, October 22, 1977, Kendall Whaling Museum, Sharon, Mass. 20 pp. mimeo.

OMURA, H. 1974. Possible migration route of the gray whale on the east coast of Japan. *Sci. Rep. Whales Res. Inst.* 26: 1–14.

PATTEN, D. R., and W. F. SAMARAS. 1977. Unseasonable occurences of gray whales. *Bull. S. Calif. Acad. Sci.* 76(3): 205–8.

PAYNE, R. 1976. At home with right whales. *National Geographic* 149(3): 322–39.

PIKE, G. C. 1962. Migration and feeding of the gray whale *(Eschrichtius gibbosus). Jour. Fish. Res. Bd. Canada* 19: 815–38.

POULTER, T. C. 1968. Vocalization of the gray whales in Laguna Ojo de Liebre (Scammon's Lagoon) Baja California, Mexico. *Norsk Hvalfangst-tidende* 57(3): 53–62.

RAY, G. C., and W. E. SCHEVILL. 1974. Feeding of a captive gray whale. *Mar. Fish. Rev.* 36(4): 31–38.

RICE, D. W. 1961. Census of the California gray whale. *Norsk Hvalfangst-tidende* 50(6): 219–25.

———. 1965. Offshore southward migration of gray whales off southern California. *Jour. Mammal.* 46(4): 504–5.

———. 1975. Status of the eastern Pacific (California) stock of the gray whale. *FAO Marine Mammals Symposium.* ACMRR/MM/EC/14.

———. 1978. Gray whale. In D. Haley, ed., *Marine Mammals of Eastern North Pacific and Arctic Waters,* pp. 54–61. Pacific Search Press.

———, and A. A. WOLMAN. 1971. *The Life History and Ecology of the Gray Whale* (Eschrichtius robustus). American Society of Mammalogists, spec. pub. no. 3.

RUGH, D. J., and H. W. BRAHAM, 1979. California gray whale *(Eschrichtius robustus)* fall migration through Unimak Pass, Alaska, 1977: A preliminary report. *Rep. Int. Whal. Commn.* 29: 315–20.

SAMARAS, W. F. 1974. Reproductive behavior of the gray whale, *Eschrichtius robustus,* in Baja California. *Bull. S. Calif. Acad. Sci.* 73(2): 57–64.

SCAMMON, C. M. 1874. *The Marine Mammals of the Northwestern Coast of North America; Together with an Account of the American Whale-Fishery.* Carmany, San Francisco, and Putnam's, N.Y.

SCHEVILL, W. E. 1952. On the nomenclature of the Pacific gray whale. *Breviora* 7: 1–3.

SPRAGUE, J. G., N. B. MILLER, and J. L. SUMICH. 1978. Observations of gray whales in Laguna de San Quintin, northwestern Baja California, Mexico. *Jour. Mammal.* 59(2): 425–27.

STORRO-PATTERSON, R. 1977. Gray whale protection. *Oceans* 10(4): 45–49.

———, and J. KIPPING. 1977. Observations of the birth and subsequent behavior and development of a gray whale, *Eschrichtius robustus.* (Abstract.) *Second Conf. Biol. Marine Mammals.* San Diego.

SUND, P. 1975. Evidence of feeding during migration and of an early birth of the California gray whale. *Jour. Mammal.* 56(1): 265–66.

———, and J. L. O'CONNOR. 1974. Aerial observations of gray whales during 1973. *Mar. Fish. Rev.* 36(4): 51–52.

SWARTZ, S. L., and W. C. CUMMINGS. 1978. *Gray whales,* Eschrichtius robustus, *in Laguna San Ignacio, Baja California, Mexico.* U.S. Marine Mammal Commission, report no. MMC-77/04. 38 pp.

———, and M. L. JONES. 1978. *The evaluation of human activities on gray whales,* Eschrichtius robustus, *in Laguna San Ignacio, Baja California, Mexico.* U.S. Marine Mammal Commission, report no. MMC-78/03. 34 pp.

TERRY, W. 1951. *Japanese whaling industry prior to 1946.* U.S. Department of the Interior, Fish and Wildlife Serv., fishery leaflet 371. 47 pp.

TOWNSEND, C. H. 1887, Present condition of the California gray whale fishery. *Bull. U.S. Fish. Comm.* 6: 340–50.

VAN DEINSE, A. B., and G. C. A. JUNGE. 1937. Recent and older finds of the California gray whale in the Atlantic. *Temminckia* 2: 161–88.

WAHRENBROCK, E. A., G. F. MARUSCHAK, R. ELSNER, and D. W. KENNEY. 1974. Respiration and metabolism in two baleen whale calves. *Mar. Fish. Rev.* 36(4): 3–9.

WALKER, L. W. 1949. Nursery of the gray whales. *Natural History* 58(6): 248–56.

WALKER, T. J. 1971. The California gray whale comes back. *National Geographic* 139(3): 394–415.

WHITE, P. D., and S. W. MATTHEWS. 1956. Hunting the heartbeat of a whale. *National Geographic* 110(1): 49–64.

WHITE, S. B., and H. J. GRIESE. 1978. Notes on lengths, weights, and mortality of gray whale calves. *Jour. Mammal.* 59(2): 440–41.

WILKE, F., and FISCUS, C. H. 1961. Gray whale observations. *Jour. Mammal.* 42(1): 108–9.

WOLMAN, A. A., and D. W. RICE. 1978. Current status of the gray whale. National Marine Fisheries Service, NAFC. 17 pp. mimeo.

———. 1979. Current status of the gray whale. *Rep. Int. Whal. Commn.* 29: 275–79.

THE RORQUALS

BANNISTER, J. L., and A. DE C. BAKER. 1967. Observations on food and feeding of baleen whales at Durban. *Norsk Hvalfangst-tidende* 56(4): 78–82.

BEST, P. B. 1967. Distribution and feeding habits of baleen whales off the Cape Province. *Invest. Rep. Div. Sea Fish. S. Afr.* 57: 1–44.

INTERNATIONAL WHALING COMMISSION. 1950–79. *Annual Reports.* Cambridge.

———. 1978. *Schedule.* Cambridge.

JONSGARD, A. 1966. Biology of the North Atlantic fin whale *Balaenoptera physalus* (L). Taxonomy, distribution, migration and food. *Hvalradets Skrifter* 49: 1–62.

LOCKYER, C. 1976. Growth and energy budgets of large baleen whales from the Southern Hemisphere. *FAO Scientific Committee on Marine Mammals.* ACMRR/MM/SC/41.

MARR, J. W. S. 1956. *Euphausia superba* and the Antarctic surface currents. *Norsk Hvalfangst-tidende* 45(3): 127–34.

MATTHEWS, L. H. 1932. Lobster-krill: Anomuran crustacea that are the food of whales. *Discovery Reports* 5: 467–84.

MITCHELL, E. D. 1974. Trophic relationships and competition for food in northwest Atlantic whales. *Proc. Can. Zool. Soc.* 123–33.

NEMOTO, T. 1959. Food of baleen whales with reference to whale movements. *Sci. Rep. Whales Res. Inst.* 14: 149–290.

PIVORUNAS, A. 1979. The feeding mechanisms of baleen whales. *Amer. Scientist* 67(4): 432–40.

SCHOLANDER, P. F. 1940. Experimental investigations on the respiratory function in diving mammals and birds. *Hvalradets Skrifter* 22(1): 1–131.

TOWNSEND, C. H. 1935. The distribution of certain whales as shown by logbook records of American whaleships. *Zoologica* 19(1): 3–50.

WILLIAMSON, G. R. 1972. The true body shape of rorqual whales. *J. Zool.* 167: 277–86.

———. 1974. The riddle of the rorquals. *Sea Frontiers* 20(3): 152–57.

MINKE WHALE

ARSENYEV, V. K. 1960. Distribution of *Balaenoptera acutorostrata* in the Antarctic. *Norsk Hvalfangst-tidende* 49(8): 380–82.

BEAMISH, P., and E. MITCHELL. 1973. Short pulse length audio frequency sounds recorded in the presence of a Minke whale (*Balaenoptera acutorostrata*). *Deep-Sea Research* 20: 375–86.

BURMEISTER, H. 1867. Preliminary description of a new species of fin whale (*Balaenoptera bonaërensis*). *Proc. Zool. Soc. London* 1867: 707–13.

CARL, C. G. 1946. Sharp-nosed finner whale stranded at Sidney, British Columbia. *Murrelet* 27:47–49.

COWAN, I. M. 1939. The sharp-nosed finner whale of the eastern Pacific. *Jour. Mammal.* 20(2): 215–25.

DERANIYAGALA, P. E. P. 1963. Mass mortality of the new subspecies of little piked whale *Balaenoptera acutorostrata thalmaha* and a new beaked whale *Mesoplodon hotaula* from Ceylon. *Spolia Zeylanica* 39(1): 79–84.

DOROSHENKO, N. V. 1979. Populations of minke whales in the Southern Hemisphere. *Rep. Int. Whal. Commn.* 29: 361–64.

FRASER, F. C. 1974. Report on cetacea stranded on the British coasts from 1948 to 1966. *Bull. Br. Mus. (Nat. Hist.)* 14: 1–65.

GAMBELL, R. 1975. A review of population assessments of southern minke whales. *FAO Marine Mammals Symposium.* ACMRR/MM/EC/11.

HANCOCK, D. 1965. Killer whales kill and eat a minke whale. *Jour. Mammal.* 46(2): 341–42.

HILL, D. O. 1975. Vanishing giants. *Audubon* 77(1): 56–107.

IVASHIN, M. V., and Y. A. MIKHALEV. 1978. To the problem of prenatal growth of minke whales *Balaenoptera acutorostrata* of the Southern Hemisphere and the biology of their reproduction. *Rep. Int. Whal. Commn.* 28: 201–6.

JONSGARD, A. 1951. Studies on the little piked whale or minke whale (*Balaenoptera acutorostrata* Lacepede). *Norsk Hvalfangsttidende* 40: 209–32.

———. 1966. The distribution of Balaenopteridae in the North Atlantic Ocean. In K. S. Norris, ed., *Whales, Dolphins and Porpoises,* pp. 114–24, University of California Press.

———. 1974. On whale exploitation in the eastern part of the North Atlantic Ocean. In W. E. Schevill, ed., *The Whale Problem,* pp. 97–107. Harvard University Press.

———, and E. J. LONG. 1959. Norway's small whales. *Sea Frontiers* 5(3): 168–74.

KAPEL, F. O. 1977. Catch statistics for minke whales, West Greenland, 1954–74. *Rep. Int. Whal. Commn.* 27: 456–59.

KASUYA, T., and T. ICHIHARA. 1965. Some informations on minke whales from the Antarctic. *Sci. Rep. Whales Res. Inst.* 19: 37–43.

KIMURA, S., and T. NEMOTO. 1956. Note on a minke whale kept alive in aquarium. *Sci. Rep. Whales Res. Inst.* 11: 181–89.

MITCHELL, E. D. 1974. Preliminary report on Newfoundland fishery for minke whales (*Balaenoptera acutorostrata*). *Rep. Int. Whal. Commn.* 24: 159–76.

———. 1978. Finner whales. In D. Haley, ed., *Marine Mammals of Eastern Pacific and Arctic Waters,* pp. 36–45. Pacific Search Press.

———, and V. M. KOZICKI. 1975. Supplementary information on minke whale (*Balaenoptera acutorostrata*) from Newfoundland fishery. *Jour. Fish. Res. Bd. Canada* 32(7): 985–94.

MOORE, J. C., and R. S. PALMER. 1955. More piked whales from the southern North Atlantic. *Jour. Mammal.* 36(3): 429–33.

OHSUMI, S. 1978. A note on minke whales in the coastal waters of Japan. *Rep. Int. Whal. Commn.* 28: 271–72.

———. 1978. Assessment of population sizes of the Southern Hemisphere minke whales adding the catch data of 1976/77. *Rep. Int. Whal. Commn.* 28: 273–76.

———, and Y. MASAKI. 1975. Biological parameters of the Antarctic minke whale at the virginal population level. *Jour. Fish. Res. Bd. Canada* 32(7): 995–1004.

———, and A. KAWAMURA. 1970. Stocks of the Antarctic minke whale. *Sci. Rep. Whales Res. Inst.* 22: 75–126.

OHSUMI, S., and S. WADA. 1978. Provisional report on the minke whale caught under special permit in the North Pacific. *Rep. Int. Whal. Commn.* 28: 289–91.

OMURA, H. 1975. Osteological study of the minke whale from the Antarctic. *Sci. Rep. Whales Res. Inst.* 27: 1–36.

———. 1976. A skull of the minke whale dug out from Osaka. *Sci. Rep. Whales Res. Inst.* 28: 69–72.

———, and T. KASUYA. 1976. Additional information on skeleton of the minke whale from the Antarctic. *Sci. Rep. Whales Res. Inst.* 28: 57–68.

OMURA, H., and H. SAKIURA. 1956. Studies on the little piked whale from the coast of Japan. *Sci. Rep. Whales Res. Inst.* 11: 1–39.

RØRVIK, C. J., and A. JONSGARD. 1975. Review of Balaenopterids in the North Atlantic Ocean. *FAO Marine Mammals Symposium.* ACMRR/MM/EC/13.

SCHEVILL, W. E., and W. A. WATKINS, 1972. Intense low-frequency sounds from an Antarctic minke whale, *Balaenoptera acutorostrata. Breviora* 388: 1–8.

SERGEANT, D. E. 1963. Minke whales, *Balaenoptera acutorostrata* Lacépède in the western North Atlantic. *Jour. Fish. Res. Bd. Canada* 20(6): 1489–1504.

———. 1975. An additional food supply for humpback (*Megaptera novaeangliae*) and minke whales (*Balaenoptera acutorostrata*). Int. Cons. Expl. Sea, Ann. Mtg. 1975, Marine Mammals Committee, C.M. 1975/N:13. 6 pp. mimeo.

SULLIVAN, R. M., and W. J. HOUCK. 1979. Sightings and strandings of cetaceans from northern California. *Jour. Mammal.* 60(4): 828–33.

TAYLOR, R. J. F. 1957. An unusual record of three species of whale being restricted to pools in Antarctic sea-ice. *Proc. Zool. Soc. London* 129: 325–31.

THOMPSON, T. J., H. E. WINN, and P. J. PERKINS. 1979. Mysticete sounds. In H. E. Winn and B. L. Olla, eds., *Behavior of Marine Animals.* Vol. 3: *Cetaceans,* pp. 403–31, Plenum Press.

VAN UTRECHT, W. L., and S. VAN DER SPOEL. 1962. Observation on a minke whale (Mammalia, Cetacea) from the Antarctic. *Zeitschrift fur Säugetierkunde* 27(4): 217–21.

WILLIAMSON, G. R. 1959. Three unusual rorqual whales from the Antarctic. *Proc. Zool. Soc. London* 133: 135–44.

———. 1961. Two kinds of minke whale in the Antarctic. *Norsk Hvalfangst-tidende* 50: 133–41.

———. 1975. Minke whales off Brazil. *Sci. Rep. Whales Res. Inst.* 27: 37–59.

WINN, H. E., and P. J. PERKINS. 1976. Distribution and sounds of the minke whale, with a review of mysticete sounds. *Cetology* 19: 1–12.

ZEMSKY, V. A., and D. D. TORMOSOV. 1964. Small rorqual (*Balaenoptera acutorostrata*) from the Antarctic. *Norsk Hvalfangst-tidende* 53(11): 302–5.

BRYDE'S WHALE

AGUAYO, L. 1965. Bryde's whale in the Southeast Pacific. *Norsk Hvalfangst-tidende* 54(7): 141–48.

ANDERSON, J. 1878. *Anatomical And Zoological Researches comprising an Account of the Zoological Results of the Two Expeditions to Western Yunnan in 1868 and 1975, and a Monograph of the two Cetacean Genera Platanista and Orcella.* London.

ANDREWS, R. C. 1916. The sei whale. *Mem. Amer. Mus. Nat. Hist.* n.s. 1(14): 291–388.

BEST, P. B. 1974. Status of the whale populations off the west coast of South Africa, and current research. In W. E. Schevill, ed., *The Whale Problem,* pp. 53–81. Harvard University Press.

———. 1975. Status of Bryde's whale (*Balaenoptera edeni* or *B. brydei*). *FAO Marine Mammals Symposium.* ACMRR/MM/SC/12.

———. 1977. Two allopatric forms of Bryde's whale off South Africa. *Rep. Int. Whal. Commn.* (special issue 1): 10–38.

CHITTLEBOROUGH, R. G. 1959. *Balaenoptera brydei* on the west coast of Australia. *Norsk Hvalfangst-tidende* 48(2): 62–66.

JUNGE, G. C. A. 1950. On a specimen of the rare fin whale *Balaenoptera edeni* Anderson, stranded on Puli Sugi near Singapore. *Zoologische Verhandenlingen* 9: 1–26.

KAWAMURA, A. 1974. Food and feeding ecology in the southern sei whale. *Sci. Rep. Whales Res. Inst.* 26: 25–144.

———. 1977. On the food of Bryde's whale caught in the South Pacific and Indian Oceans. *Sci. Rep. Whales Res. Inst.* 29: 49–58.

———. 1978. On the baleen filter area in the South Pacific Bryde's whales. *Sci. Rep. Whales Res. Inst.* 30: 291–300.

———, and Y. SATAKE. 1976. Preliminary report on the geographical distribution of the Bryde's whale in the North Pacific with special reference to the structure of the filtering apparatus. *Sci. Rep. Whales. Res. Inst.* 28: 1–35.

KELLOGG, R. 1931. Whaling statistics for the Pacific coast of North America. *Jour. Mammal.* 12(1): 73–77.

NEMOTO, T. 1959. Food of baleen whales with reference to whale movements. *Sci. Rep. Whales Res. Inst.* 14: 149–290.

———, and A. KAWAMURA. 1977. Characteristics of food habits and distribution of baleen whales with special reference to the abundance of North Pacific sei and Bryde's whales. *Rep. Int. Whal. Commn.* (special issue 1): 80–87.

OHSUMI, S. 1977. Bryde's whales in the pelagic whaling ground of the North Pacific. *Rep. Int. Whal. Commn.* (special issue 1): 140–49.

———. 1978. Provisional report on the Bryde's whales caught under special permit in the Southern Hemisphere. *Rep. Int. Whal. Commn.* 28: 281–87.

OLSEN, Ø. 1913. On the external character and biology of Bryde's whale (*Balaenoptera brydei*), a new rorqual from the coast of South Africa. *Proc. Zool. Soc. London.* 1073–90.

OMURA, H. 1959. Bryde's whale from the coast of Japan. *Sci. Rep. Whales Res. Inst.* 14: 1–33.

———. 1962a. Bryde's whale occurs on the coast of Brazil. *Sci. Rep. Whales Res. Inst.* 16: 1–5.

———. 1962b. Further information on Bryde's whale from the coast of Japan. *Sci. Rep. Whales Res. Inst.* 16: 7–18.

———. 1966. Bryde's whale in the northwest Pacific. In K. S. Norris, ed., *Whales, Dolphins and Porpoises,* pp. 70–78. University of California Press.

———. 1977. Review of the occurrence of Bryde's whale in the Northwest Pacific. *Rep. Int. Whal. Commn.* (special issue 1): 88–91.

———, and K. FUJINO. 1954. Sei whales in the adjacent waters of Japan. II. Further studies on the external characters. *Sci. Rep. Whales Res. Inst.* 9: 89–103.

PRIVALIKHIN, V. I., and A. A. BERZIN. 1978. Abundance and distribution of Bryde's whale (*Balaenoptera edeni*) in the Pacific Ocean. *Rep. Int. Whal. Commn.* 28: 301–2.

RICE, D. W. 1974. Whales and whale research in the eastern North Pacific. In W. E. Schevill, ed., *The Whale Problem.* pp. 170–95. Harvard University Press.

——. 1977. Report of the special meeting of the scientific committee on sei and Bryde's whales. *Rep. Int. Whal. Commn.* (special issue 1): 92–97.

——. 1979. Bryde's whales in the equatorial eastern Pacific. *Rep. Int. Whal. Commn.* 29: 321–25.

SHIMADA, B. M. 1947. *Japanese whaling in the Bonin Island area. (A preliminary report.)* U.S. Department of the Interior, Fish and Wildlife Serv., Fishery Leaflet 248. 16 pp.

SOOT-RYEN, T. 1961. On a Bryde's whale stranded at Curaçao. *Norsk Hvalfangst-tidende* 50(7): 323–32.

SYMONS, H. W. 1955. Do Bryde's whales migrate to the Antarctic? *Norsk Hvalfangst-tidende* 44(2): 84–87.

TERRY, W. M. 1951. *Japanese whaling industry prior to 1946.* U.S. Department of the Interior, Fish and Wildlife Serv., Fishery Leaflet 371. 47 pp.

SEI WHALE

AGUAYO, L. 1974. Baleen whales off continental Chile. In W. E. Schevill, ed., *The Whale Problem,* pp. 209–17. Harvard University Press.

ANDREWS, R. C. 1916a. The sei whale. *Mem. Amer. Mus. Nat. Hist.* n.s. 1(4): 291–388.

BANNISTER, J. L., and R. GAMBELL. 1965. The succession and abundance of fin, sei, and other whales off Durban. *Norsk Hvalfangst-tidende* 54(2): 45–60.

BREIWICK, J. M. 1978. Southern Hemisphere sei whale stock sizes prior to 1960. *Rep. Int. Whal. Commn.* 28: 179–82.

BROWN, S. G. 1965. The colour of the baleen plates in Southern Hemisphere sei whales. *Norsk Hvalfangst-tidende* 54(6): 131–35.

——. 1968. Feeding of sei whales at South Georgia. *Norsk Hvalfangst-tidende* 57(6): 118–25.

BUDYLENKO, G. A. 1978a. Distribution and migration of sei whales in the Southern Hemisphere. *Rep. Int. Whal. Commn.* 28: 373–77.

——. 1978b. On sei whale feeding in the Southern Ocean. *Rep. Int. Whal. Commn.* 28: 379–85.

CHAPMAN, D. G. 1974. Status of Antarctic rorqual stocks. In W. E. Schevill, ed., *The Whale Problem,* pp. 218–238. Harvard University Press.

COLLETT, R. 1886. On the external character of Rudolphi's rorqual, *Balaenoptera borealis. Proc. Zool. Soc. London* 1886: 242–65.

CUVIER, G. 1836. *Récherches sur les ossements fossiles.* Delille. Paris.

DOI, T., S. OHSUMI, and T. NEMOTO. 1967. Population assessment of sei whales in the Antarctic. *Norsk Hvalfangst-tidende* 56(2): 25–41.

GAMBELL, R. 1968. Seasonal cycles and reproduction in sei whales of the Southern Hemisphere. *Discovery Reports* 35: 31–134.

——. 1974. The fin and sei whale stocks off Durban. In W. E. Schevill, ed., *The Whale Problem,* pp. 82–86. Harvard University Press.

——. 1975. A review of population assessments of Antarctic sei whales. *FAO Marine Mammals Symposium.* ACMRR/MM/EC/10.

——. 1976. A note on the changes observed in the pregnancy rate and age at sexual maturity of some baleen whales in the Antarctic. *FAO Scientific Consultation on Marine Mammals.* ACMRR/MM/SC/37.

GASKIN, D. E. 1977. Sei and Bryde's whales in waters around New Zealand. *Rep. Int. Whal. Commn.* (special issue 1): 50–52.

INTERNATIONAL WHALING COMMISSION. 1978. Report of the special meeting on Southern Hemisphere sei whales. *Rep. Int. Whal. Commn.* 28: 335–478.

IVASHIN, M. V., and Y. P. GOLUBOVSKY. 1978. On the cause of appearance of white scars on the body of whales. *Rep. Int. Whal. Commn.* 28: 199.

JONES, E. 1971. *Isistius brasiliensis,* a squaloid shark, the probable cause of crater wounds in fishes and cetaceans. *Fish. Bull.* 69(4): 791–98.

JONES, R. 1978. Estimating growth rates in sei whales. *Rep. Int. Whal. Commn.* 28: 405–10.

JONSGARD, A. 1966. The distribution of Balaenopteridae in the North Atlantic Ocean. In K. S. Norris, ed., *Whales, Dolphins and Porpoises,* pp. 114–24. University of California Press.

——. 1974. On whale exploitation in the eastern part of the North Atlantic Ocean. In W. E. Schevill, ed., *The Whale Problem,* pp. 97–107. Harvard University Press.

——, and K. DARLING. 1977. On the biology of the eastern North Atlantic sei whale, *Balaenoptera borealis* Lesson. *Rep. Int. Whal. Commn.* (special issue 1): 124–29.

KAWAMURA, A. 1970. Food of sei whale taken by Japanese whaling expeditions in the Antarctic season 1967/68. *Sci. Rep. Whales Res. Inst.* 22: 127–52.

——. 1973. Food and feeding of sei whale caught in the waters south of 40° N in the North Pacific. *Sci. Rep. Whales Res. Inst.* 25: 219–36.

_____. 1974. Food and feeding ecology in the southern sei whale. *Sci. Rep. Whales Res. Inst.* 26: 25–144.

_____. 1978. An interim consideration on a possible interspecific relation in southern baleen whales from the viewpoint of their food habits. *Rep. Int. Whal. Commn.* 28: 411–20.

LOCKYER, C. 1976. Growth and energy budgets of large baleen whales from the Southern Hemisphere. *FAO Scientific Consultation on Marine Mammals.* ACMRR/MM/SC/41.

_____. 1978. A preliminary investigation on age, growth and reproduction of the sei whale off Iceland. *Rep. Int. Whal. Commn.* 28: 237–41.

MACHIDA, S. 1970. A sword-fish sword found from a North Pacific sei whale. *Sci. Rep. Whales Res. Inst.* 22: 163–64.

MACKINTOSH, N. A. 1942. The southern stocks of whalebone whales. *Discovery Reports* 22: 197–300.

_____, and S. G. BROWN. 1956. Preliminary estimates of the southern populations of the larger baleen whales. *Norsk Hvalfangst-tidende* 45(9): 467–80.

MARR, J. W. S. 1956. *Euphausia superba* and the Antarctic surface currents. *Norsk Hvalfangst-tidende* 45(3): 127–34.

MATTHEWS, L. H. 1932. Lobster-krill: Anomuran crustacea that are the food of whales. *Discovery Reports* 5: 467–84.

_____. 1938. The sei whale, *Balaenoptera borealis. Discovery Reports* 17: 183–290.

MCHUGH, J. L. 1974. The role and history of the International Whaling Commission. In W. E. Schevill, ed., *The Whale Problem,* pp. 305–35. Harvard University Press.

MEAD, J. G. 1977. Records of sei and Bryde's whales from the Atlantic coast of the United States, the Gulf of Mexico, and the Caribbean. *Rep. Int. Whal. Commn.* (special issue 1): 113–16.

MILLER, G. S. 1924. A pollack whale from Florida presented to the National Museum by the Miami Aquarium Association. *Proc. U.S. Nat. Mus.* 66:1–15.

MITCHELL, E. D. 1974. Trophic relationships and competition for food in northwest Atlantic whales. *Proc. Can. Zool. Soc.* 123–33.

_____. 1975. Preliminary report on Nova Scotia fishery for sei whales *(Balaenoptera borealis). Rep. Int. Whal. Commn.* 25: 18–225.

_____. 1978. Finner whales. In D. Haley, ed., *Marine Mammals of Eastern North Pacific and Arctic Waters,* pp. 37–45. Pacific Search Press.

NASU, K. 1973. Results of whale sighting cruises by *Chiyoda Maru No. 5* in the Pacific sector of the Antarctic and the Tasman Sea in the 1966/67 season. *Sci. Rep. Whales Res. Inst.* 25: 205–17.

_____, and Y. MASAKI. 1970. Some biological parameters for stock assessment of Antarctic sei whale. *Sci. Rep. Whales Res. Inst.* 22: 63–74.

NEMOTO, T. 1957. Foods of baleen whales in the northern Pacific. *Sci. Rep. Whales Res. Inst.* 12: 33–89.

_____. 1959. Food of baleen whales with reference to whale movements. *Sci. Rep. Whales Res. Inst.* 14: 149–290.

NISHIWAKI, M. 1966. Distribution and migration of the larger cetaceans in the North Pacific as shown by Japanese whaling results. In K. S. Norris, ed., *Whales, Dolphins and Porpoises,* pp. 171–91. University of California Press.

NORRIS, K. S. 1978. Marine mammals and man. In H. P. Brokaw, ed., *Wildlife and America,* pp. 320–38. U.S. Fish and Wildlife Service and National Oceanic and Atmospheric Administration.

OHSUMI, S., and K. YAMAMURA. 1978. A review on catch of sei whales in the Southern Hemisphere. *Rep. Int. Whal. Commn.* 28: 449–67.

OMURA, H. 1950a. On the body weight of sperm and sei whales located in the adjacent waters of Japan. *Sci. Rep. Whales Res. Inst.* 4: 1–13.

_____. 1950b. Whales in the adjacent waters of Japan. *Sci. Rep. Whales Res. Inst.* 4: 27–113.

_____. 1966. Bryde's whale in the northwest Pacific. In K. S. Norris, ed., *Whales, Dolphins and Porpoises,* pp. 70–78. University of California Press.

_____, and K. FUJINO. 1954. Sei whales in the adjacent waters of Japan. II. Further studies on the external characters. *Sci. Rep. Whales Res. Inst.* 9: 89–103.

OMURA, H., and S. OHSUMI. 1974. Research on whale biology of Japan with special reference to the North Pacific stocks. In W. E. Schevill, ed., *The Whale Problem,* pp. 196–208. Harvard University Press.

RICE, D. W. 1961. Sei whales with rudimentary baleen. *Norsk Hvalfangst-tidende* 50(5): 189–93.

_____. 1974. Whales and whale research in the eastern North Pacific. In W. E. Schevill, ed., *The Whale Problem,* pp. 170–95. Harvard University Press.

RØRVIK, C. J., and A. JONSGARD. 1975. Review of Balaenopterids in the North Atlantic Ocean. *FAO Marine Mammals Symposium.* ACMRR/MM/EC/13.

SHEVCHENKO, V. I. 1977. Application of white scars to the study of the location and migrations of sei whale populations in Area III of the Antarctic. *Rep. Int. Whal. Commn.* (special issue 1): 130–34.

FIN WHALE

ANON. 1975. Mammals in the Seas. Ad Hoc Group I on Large Cetaceans. *FAO Scientific Consultation on Marine Mammals.* ACMRR/MM/SC/2.

BRINKMANN, A. 1967. The identification and names of our fin whale species. *Norsk Hvalfangst-tidende* 56(1): 1–8.

BROWN, S. G. 1962a. A note on migration in fin whales. *Norsk Hvalfangst-tidende* 51(1): 13–16.

————. 1962b. The movement of fin and blue whales within the Antarctic zone. *Discovery Reports* 33: 1–54.

BUDKER, P., and M.-H. DU BUIT. 1968. On the stranding of a calf fin whale at Le Pouldu (South Brittany—France). *Norsk Hvalfangst-tidende* 57(1): 11–16.

CHAPMAN, D. G. 1974. Status of Antarctic rorqual stocks. In W. E. Schevill, ed., *The Whale Problem,* pp. 239–56. Harvard University Press.

FRASER, F. C. 1974. Report on cetacea stranded on the British coasts from 1948 to 1966. *Bull. Br. Mus. (Nat. Hist.)* 14: 1–65.

FUJINO, K. 1964. Fin whale sub-populations in the Antarctic whaling areas II, III and IV. *Sci. Rep. Whales Res. Inst.* 18: 1–27.

GAMBELL, R. 1974. The fin and sei whale stocks off Durban. In W. E. Schevill, ed., *The Whale Problem,* pp. 82–86. Harvard University Press.

————. 1975. Population assessments of Antarctic fin whales. *FAO Scientific Consultation on Marine Mammals.* ACMMR/MM/SC/9.

————. 1976. A note on the changes observed in the pregnancy rate and age at sexual maturity of some baleen whales in the Antarctic. *FAO Scientific Consultation on Marine Mammals.* ACMMR/MM/SC/37.

HOLT, S. J. 1976. Statistics of catches of large whales, by weight. (Provisional.) *FAO Scientific Consultation on Marine Mammals.* ACMMR/MM/SC/7.

JONSGARD, A. 1953. Fin whale *(Balaenoptera physalus)* with six foetuses. *Norsk Hvalfangst-tidende* 42(12): 685–86.

————. 1966a. Biology of the North Atlantic fin whale *Balaenoptera physalus* L.: Taxonomy, distribution, migration and food. *Hvalradets Skrifter* 49: 1–62.

————. 1966b. The distribution of Balaenopteridae in the North Atlantic Ocean. In K. S. Norris, ed., *Whales, Dolphins and Porpoises,* pp. 114–24. University of California Press.

————. 1969. Age determination in marine mammals. In H. T. Andersen, ed., *The Biology of Marine Mammals,* pp. 1–30. Academic Press.

————. 1974. On whale exploitation in the eastern part of the North Atlantic Ocean. In W. E. Schevill, ed., *The Whale Problem,* pp. 97–107. Harvard University Press.

KELLOGG, R. 1931. Whaling statistics for the Pacific coast of North America. *Jour. Mammal.* 12(1): 73–77.

KOOYMAN, G. L., and H. T. ANDERSEN. 1969. Deep Diving. In H. T. Andersen, ed., *The Biology of Marine Mammals,* pp. 65–94. Academic Press.

LAWS, R. M., and P. E. PURVES. 1956. The ear plug of the Mysteceti as an indication of age with special reference to the North Atlantic fin whale. *Norsk Hvalfangst-tidende* 45(8): 413–25.

MACKINTOSH, N. A. 1942. The southern stocks of whalebone whales. *Discovery Reports* 22: 197–300.

————. 1966. The distribution of southern blue and fin whales. In K. S. Norris, ed., *Whales, Dolphins and Porpoises,* pp. 125–44. University of California Press.

————, and S. G. BROWN. 1956. Preliminary estimates of the southern populations of the larger baleen whales. *Norsk Hvalfangst-tidende* 45(9): 467–80.

MACKINTOSH, N. A., and J. F. G. WHEELER. 1929. Southern blue and fin whales. *Discovery Reports* 1: 257–540.

MARR, J. W. S. 1956. *Euphausia superba* and the Antarctic surface currents. *Norsk Hvalfangst-tidende* 45(3): 127–34.

MCHUGH, J. L. 1974. The role and history of the International Whaling Commission. In W. E. Schevill, ed., *The Whale Problem,* pp. 305–35. Harvard University Press.

MITCHELL, E. D. 1974a. Present status of northwest Atlantic fin and other whale stocks. In W. E. Schevill, ed., *The Whale Problem,* pp. 108–69. Harvard University Press.

————. 1974b. Trophic relationships and competition for food in northwest Atlantic whales. *Proc. Can. Soc. Zool.* 123–33.

————. 1978. Finner whales. In D. Haley, ed., *Marine Mammals of Eastern North Pacific and Arctic Waters,* pp. 36–45. Pacific Search Press.

————, and V. M. KOZICKI. 1974. Northwest Atlantic fin whales *(Balaenoptera physalus):* The ear plug sample. *Rep. Int. Whal. Commn.* 24: 150–58.

MOWAT, F. 1972. *A Whale for the Killing.* Little, Brown & Co.

NEMOTO, T. 1959. Food of baleen whales with reference to whale movements. *Sci. Rep. Whales Res. Inst.* 14: 149–290.

————. 1962. A secondary sexual character of fin whales. *Sci. Rep. Whales Res. Inst.* 16: 29–34.

————, and K. NASU. 1958. *Thysanoessa macrura* as a food of baleen whales in the Antarctic. *Sci. Rep. Whales Res. Inst.* 13: 193–99.

NISHIWAKI, M. 1966. Distribution and migration of the larger cetaceans in the North Pacific as shown by Japanese whaling results. In K. S. Norris, ed., *Whales, Dolphins and Porpoises,* pp. 171–91. University of California Press.

OHSUMI, S. 1964. Examination on age determination of the whale. *Sci. Rep. Whales Res. Inst.* 18: 49–88.

—————— (KIMURA), M. NISHIWAKI, and T. HIBIYA. 1958. Growth of fin whale in the northern Pacific. *Sci. Rep. Whales Res. Inst.* 13: 97–133.

OMURA, H., and S. OHSUMI. 1974. Research on whale biology of Japan with special reference to the North Pacific stocks. In W. E. Schevill, ed., *The Whale Problem,* pp. 196–208. Harvard University Press.

PERKINS, P. J. 1966. Communication sounds of finback whales. *Norsk Hvalfangst-tidende* 55(10): 199.

PURVES, P. E. 1955. The wax plug in the external auditory meatus of the Mysteceti. *Discovery Reports* 27: 293–302.

RED DATA BOOK. 1976. Fin whale, *Balaenoptera physalus.* Code 11.100.1.1.V. IUCN, Morges, Switzerland.

RICE, D. W. 1974. Whales and whale research in the eastern North Pacific. In W. E. Schevill, ed., *The Whale Problem,* pp. 170–95. Harvard University Press.

ROE, H. S. J. 1967. Seasonal formation of laminae in the ear plug of the fin whale. *Discovery Reports* 35: 1–30.

RØRVIK, C. J., and A. JONSGARD. 1975. Review of Balaenopterids in the North Atlantic Ocean. *FAO Marine Mammals Symposium.* ACMRR/MM/EC/13.

SCHEVILL, W. E., ed. 1974. *The Whale Problem.* Harvard University Press.

SERGEANT, D. E. 1963. Stocks of fin whales *Balaenoptera physalus* L. in the North Atlantic Ocean. *FAO Scientific Consultation on Marine Mammals.* ACMRR/MM/SC/64.

——————. 1966. *Populations of Large Whale Species in the Western North Atlantic with Special Reference to the Fin Whale.* Fisheries Research Board of Canada, circular no. 9, 12 pp. + tables.

——————. 1976. Stocks of fin whales *Balaenoptera physalus L.* in the North Atlantic Ocean. FAO Scientific Consultation on Marine Mammals, Bergen, Norway. ACMRR/MM/SC/64.

THOMPSON, T. J., H. E. WINN, and P. J. PERKINS. 1979. Mysticete sounds. In H. E. Winn and B. L. Bolla, eds., *Behavior of Marine Animals.* Vol. 3: *Cetaceans,* pp. 403–31. Plenum Press.

WATKINS, W. A., and W. E. SCHEVILL. 1979. Aerial observation of feeding behavior in four baleen whales: *Eubalaena glacialis, Balaenoptera borealis, Megaptera novaeangliae,* and *Balaenoptera physalus. Jour. Mammal.* 60(1): 155–63.

WINN, H. E., and P. J. PERKINS. 1976. Distribution and sounds of the minke whale, with a review of mysticete sounds. *Cetology* 19: 1–12.

BLUE WHALE

AGUAYO, L. 1974. Baleen whales off continental Chile. In W. E. Schevill, ed., *The Whale Problem,* pp. 209–17. Harvard University Press.

ALLEN, K. R. 1970. A note on baleen whale stocks of the North West Atlantic. *Rep. Int. Whal. Commn.* 20: 112–13.

BEAMISH, P. 1979. Behavior and significance of entrapped baleen whales. In H. E. Winn and B. L. Bolla, eds., *Behavior of Marine Animals.* Vol. 3: *Cetaceans,* pp. 291–309. Plenum Press.

——————, and E. MITCHELL. 1971. Ultrasonic sounds recorded in the presence of a blue whale *Balaenoptera musculus. Deep-Sea Research* 18: 803–9.

BERZIN, A. A. 1978. Whale distribution in tropical Eastern Pacific waters. *Rep. Int. Whal. Commn.* 28: 173–77.

BEST, P. B. 1974. Status of the whale populations off the west coast of South Africa, and current research. In W. E. Schevill, ed., *The Whale Problem,* pp. 53–81. Harvard University Press.

BROWN, S. G. 1954. Dispersal in blue and fin whales. *Discovery Reports* 26: 355–84.

——————. 1959. Whale marks recovered in the Antarctic seasons 1955/56, 1958/59, and in South Africa 1958 and 1959. *Norsk Hvalfangst-tidende* 42(12): 609–16.

——————. 1962. The movement of fin and blue whales within the Antarctic zone. *Discovery Reports* 33: 1–54.

CHAPMAN, D. G. 1974a. Status of Antarctic rorqual stocks. In W. E. Schevill, ed., *The Whale Problem,* pp. 239–56. Harvard University Press.

——————. 1974b. Estimation of population parameters of Antarctic baleen whales. In W. E. Schevill, ed., *The Whale Problem,* pp. 336–51. Harvard University Press.

——————, K. R. ALLEN, and S. G. HOLT. 1964. Reports of the committee of three scientists on the special scientific investigations of the Antarctic whale stocks. *Rep. Int. Whal. Commn.* 14: 32–106.

CUMMINGS, W. C., and P. O. THOMPSON. 1971. Underwater sounds from the blue whale, *Balaenoptera musculus. Jour. Acoust. Soc. Amer.* 50(4): 1193–98.

DEWHURST, H. W. 1834. *The Natural History of the Order Cetacea and the Oceanic Inhabitants of the Arctic Regions.* London.

GAMBELL, R. 1964. A pygmy blue whale at Durban. *Norsk Hvalfangst-tidende* 53(3): 66–68.

GULLAND, J. 1972. Future of the blue whale. *New Scientist* 54(793): 198–99.

——————. 1976. A note on the abundance of Antarctic blue whales. *FAO Marine Mammals Symposium.* ACMRR/MM/SC/76.

HARMER, S. F. 1923. Cervical vertebrae of a gigantic blue whale from Panama. *Proc. Zool. Soc. London* 1923: 1085–89.

HJORT, J. 1933. Whales and whaling. *Hvalradets Skrifter* 7: 7–29.

———, J. LIE, and J. RUUD. 1933–39. Norwegian pelagic whaling in the Antarctic. *Hvalradets Skrifter.* Vols. 1–7, Nos. 3,7,8,9,12,14,18.

HOLT, S. J. 1976. Statistics of catches of large whales, by weight. (Provisional.) *FAO Scientific Consultation on Marine Mammals.* ACMRR/MM/SC/7.

ICHIHARA, T. 1961. Blue whales in the waters around Kerguelen Island. *Norsk Hvalfangst-tidende* 50(1): 1–20.

———. 1963. Identification of the pygmy blue whale in the Antarctic. *Norsk Hvalfangst-tidende* 52(5): 128–30.

———. 1966. The pygmy blue whale, *Balaenoptera musculus brevicauda,* a new subspecies from the Antarctic. In K. S. Norris, ed., *Whales, Dolphins and Porpoises,* pp. 79–113. University of California Press.

———. 1975. Review of pygmy blue whale stock in the Antarctic. *FAO Marine Mammals Symposium.* ACMRR/MM/EC/28.

———, and T. DOI. 1964. Stock assessment of pygmy blue whales in the Antarctic. *Norsk Hvalfangst-tidende* 53(6): 145–61.

JONSGARD, A. 1955. The stocks of blue whales *(Balaenoptera musculus)* in the northern Atlantic Ocean and adjacent Arctic. *Norsk Hvalfangst-tidende* 44(9): 297–311.

———. 1966. The distribution of Balaenopteridae in the North Atlantic Ocean. In K. S. Norris, ed., *Whales, Dolphins and Porpoises,* pp. 114–24. University of California Press.

———. 1974. On whale exploitation in the eastern part of the North Atlantic Ocean. In W. E. Schevill, ed., *The Whale Problem,* pp. 97–107. Harvard University Press.

LAURIE, A. H. 1933. Some aspects of respiration in blue and fin whales. *Discovery Reports* 7: 363–406.

LOCKYER, C. 1976. Growth and energy budgets of large baleen whales from the Southern Hemisphere. *FAO Scientific Consultation on Marine Mammals.* ACMRR/MM/SC/41.

LUND, J. 1950. Charting of whale stocks in the Antarctic on the basis of iodine values. *Norsk Hvalfangst-tidende* 39(7): 53–60.

MACKINTOSH, N. A. 1942. The southern stocks of whalebone whales. *Discovery Reports* 22: 197–300.

———. 1966. The distribution of southern blue and fin whales. In K. S. Norris, ed., *Whales, Dolphins and Porpoises,* pp. 125–44. University of California Press.

———, and S. G. BROWN. 1956. Preliminary estimates of the southern populations of the larger baleen whales. *Norsk Hvalfangst-tidende* 45(9): 467–80.

———. 1974. Whales and whaling. In *Antarctic Mammals.* Antarctic Map Folio Series, American Geographical Society.

MACKINTOSH, N. A., and J. F. G. WHEELER. 1929. Southern blue and fin whales. *Discovery Reports* 1: 257–540.

MARR, J. W. S. 1956. *Euphausia superba* and the Antarctic surface currents. *Norsk Hvalfangst-tidende* 45(3): 127–34.

MCHUGH, J. L. 1974. The role and history of the International Whaling Commission. In W. E. Schevill, ed., *The Whale Problem,* pp. 305–35. Harvard University Press.

MCWHINNIE, M. A., and C. J. DENYS. 1980. The high importance of lowly krill. *Natural History.* 89(3): 66–73.

MITCHELL, E. D. 1974. Present status of northwest Atlantic fin and other whale stocks. In W. E. Schevill, ed., *The Whale Problem,* pp. 108–69. Harvard University Press.

MURPHY, R. C. 1962. The oceanic life of the Antarctic. *Scientific American.* 207 (3): 168–210.

NAKAI, J., and T. SHIDA. 1948. The sinus hairs of the sei whale *(Balaenoptera borealis). Sci. Rep. Whales Res. Inst.* 1: 41–47.

NATIONAL MARINE FISHERIES SERVICE. 1973. Administration of the Marine Mammal Protection Act of 1972. December 21, 1972 to June 21, 1973. *Report to the Secretary of Commerce.* NMFS/NOAA.

NISHIWAKI, M. 1950. Determination of the age of Antarctic blue and fin whales by the color changes in crystalline lens. *Sci. Rep. Whales Res. Inst.* 4: 115–161.

———. 1966. Distribution and migration of the larger cetaceans in the North Pacific as shown by Japanese whaling results. In K. S. Norris, ed., *Whales, Dolphins and Porpoises,* pp. 171–91. University of California Press.

———, and T. OYE. 1951. The biological investigations on blue and fin whales caught by Japanese Antarctic fleet. *Sci. Rep. Whales Res. Inst.* 5: 91–167.

OHNO, M., and K. FUJINO. 1952. Biological investigation on the whales caught by the Japanese Antarctic whaling fleets in the 1951–52 season. *Sci. Rep. Whales Res. Inst.* 7: 125–88.

OMURA, H. 1950. Diatom infection on blue and fin whales in the Antarctic whaling Area V (The Ross Sea Area). *Sci. Rep. Whales Res. Inst.* 4: 14–26.

———, and S. OHSUMI. 1974. Research on whale biology of Japan with special reference to the North Pacific stocks. In W. E. Schevill, ed., *The Whale Problem,* pp. 196–208. Harvard University Press.

———, T. ICHIHARA, and T. KASUYA. 1970. Osteology of pygmy blue whale with additional information on external and other characteristics. *Sci. Rep. Whales Res. Inst.* 22: 1–29.

OSTROM, J. H. 1978. New ideas about dinosaurs. *National Geographic* 154(2): 152–85.

PAYNE, R. 1977. *Deep Voices: The Second Whale Record.* Capitol Records, ST-11598.

RED DATA BOOK. 1972. Blue whale, *Balaenoptera musculus.* Code 11.100.1.2. E. IUCN, Morges, Switzerland.

RICE, D. W. 1972. Blue whale. In A. Seed, ed., *Baleen Whales in Eastern North Pacific and Arctic Waters,* pp. 31–37. Pacific Search Press.

———. 1974. Whales and whale research in the eastern North Pacific. In W. E. Schevill, ed., *The Whale Problem,* pp. 170–95. Harvard University Press.

———. 1978. Blue whale. In D. Haley, ed., *Marine Mammals of Eastern North Pacific and Arctic Waters,* pp. 30–35. Pacific Search Press.

ROMER, A. S. 1974. *Vertebrate Paleontology.* 3d ed. University of Chicago Press.

RØRVIK, C. J., and A. JONSGARD. 1975. Review of Balaenopterids in the North Atlantic Ocean. *FAO Marine Mammals Symposium.* ACMRR/MM/EC/13.

RUUD, J. 1956a. The blue whale. *Scientific American* 195(6): 46–50.

———. 1956b. International regulation of whaling: A critical survey. *Norsk Hvalfangst-tidende* 45(7): 374–87.

SCHEFFER, V. B. 1976. The status of whales. *Pacific Discovery* 29(1): 2–8.

SIBBALD, R. 1692. *Phalainologia nova: sive, Observationes de rarioribus quibusdam balaenis in Scotiae littus nuper ejectis.* Edinburgh.

SMALL, G. 1971. *The Blue Whale.* Columbia University Press.

STONEHOUSE, B. 1972. *Animals of the Antarctic: The ecology of the Far South.* Holt, Rinehart & Winston.

TARPY, C. 1979. Killer whale attack! *National Geographic* 155(4): 542–45.

THOMPSON, T. J., H. E. WINN, and P. J. PERKINS. 1979. Mysticete sounds. In H. E. Winn and B. L. Bolla, eds., *Behavior of Marine Animals.* Vol. 3: *Cetaceans,* pp. 403–31. Plenum Press.

TURNER, W. 1872. An account of the great finner whale (*Balaenoptera sibbaldii*) stranded at Longniddry. Part I. The Soft Parts. *Trans. Roy. Soc. Edin.* 26: 197–251.

WALSH, J. 1967. Whales: Decline continues despite limitations on catch. *Science* 157: 1024–25.

WINN, H. E., and P. J. PERKINS. 1976. Distribution and sounds of the minke whale, with a review of mysticete sounds. *Cetology* 19: 1–12.

ZEMSKY, V. A., and V. A. BORONIN. 1964. On the question of the pygmy blue whale taxonomic position. *Norsk Hvalfangst-tidende* 53(11): 306–11.

HUMPBACK WHALE

ALLEN, G. M. 1942. *Extinct and Vanishing Mammals of the Western Hemisphere with the Marine Species of all the Oceans.* American Committee for International Wildlife Protection, spec. pub. no. 11.

ALLEN, K. R. 1970. A note on the baleen whale stocks of the North West Atlantic. *Rep. Int. Whal. Commn.* 20:112–13.

ANDREWS, R. C. 1909. Observations on the habits of the finback and humpback whales of the eastern North Pacific. *Bull. Amer. Mus. Nat. Hist.* 26: 213–26, pls. 30–40.

———. 1921. A remarkable case of external hind limbs in a humpback whale. *Amer. Mus. Novitates* 9: 1–6.

ASH, C. E. 1953. Weight of Antarctic humpback whales. *Norsk Hvalfangst-tidende* 42(7): 387–91.

———. 1957. Weights and oil yields of Antarctic humpback whales. *Norsk Hvalfangst-tidende* 46(10): 569–73.

BAKER, A. N. 1972. New Zealand whales and dolphins. *Tuatara* 20 (1): 1–49.

BAKER, C. S., P. H. FORESTELL, R. C. ANTINOJA, and L. M. HERMAN. 1979. Interactions of the Hawaiian humpback whale (*Megaptera novaeangliae*) with the right whale (*Balaena glacialis*) and odontocete cetaceans. (Abstract.) *Third Biennial Conf. Biol. Marine Mammals.* Seattle.

BALCOMB, K. C., and G. NICHOLS. 1978. Western North Atlantic humpback whales. *Rep. Int. Whal. Commn.* 28: 159–64.

BANNISTER, J. L. 1974. Whale populations and current research off Western Australia. In W. E. Schevill, ed., *The Whale Problem,* pp. 239–54. Harvard University Press.

———, and A. DE C. BAKER. 1967. Observations on food and feeding of baleen whales at Durban. *Norsk Hvalfangst-tidende* 56(4): 78–81.

BEAMISH, P. 1978. Evidence that a captive humpback whale (*Megaptera novaeangliae*) does not use sonar. *Deep-Sea Research* 25(5): 469–72.

———. 1979. Behavior and significance of entrapped baleen whales. In H. E. Winn and B. L. Olla, eds., *Behavior of Marine Animals.* Vol. 3: *Cetaceans,* pp. 291–309. Plenum Press.

BUDKER, P. 1954. Whaling in French overseas territories. *Norsk Hvalfangst-tidende* 43(6): 320–26.

CALDWELL, D. K., M. K. CALDWELL, W. F. RATHJEN, and J. R. SULLIVAN. 1971. Cetaceans from the Lesser Antillean island of St. Vincent. *Fish. Bull.* 69(2): 303–12.

CHAPMAN, D. G. 1974. Status of Antarctic rorqual stocks. In W. E. Schevill, ed., *The Whale Problem*, pp. 218–38. Harvard University Press.

CHITTLEBOROUGH, R. G. 1954. Aerial observations on whales in Australian waters. *Norsk Hvalfangst-tidende* 43(4): 198–200.

————. 1955. Aspects of reproduction in the male humpback whale, *Megaptera nodosa* (Bonnaterre). *Austral. Jour. Marine and Freshwater Res.* 6: 1–29.

————. 1959a. Australian marking of humpback whales. *Norsk Hvalfangst-tidende* 48(2): 47–55.

————. 1959b. Intermingling of two populations of humpback whales. *Norsk Hvalfangst-tidende* 48(10): 510–21.

————. 1960. Determination of age in the humpback whale, *Megaptera nodosa* (Bonnaterre). *Norsk Hvalfangst-tidende* 49(1): 12–37.

————. 1965. Dynamics of two populations of the humpback whale, *Megaptera novaeangliae* (Borowski). *Austral. Jour. Marine and Freshwater Res.* 16(1): 33–128.

DALL, W., and D. DUNSTAN. 1957. *Euphausia superba* Dana from a humpback whale *Megaptera nodosa* (Bonnaterre) caught off southern Queensland. *Norsk Hvalfangst-tidende* 46(1): 6–9.

DARLING, J. D., K. G. GIBSON, and G. K. SILBER. 1979. Observations on the abundance and behavior of humpback whales (*Megaptera novaeangliae*) off west Maui, Hawaii, 1977–1979. (Abstract.) *Third Biennial Conf. Biol. Marine Mammals.* Seattle.

DAWBIN, W. H. 1954. Maori whaling. *Norsk Hvalfangst-tidende* 43(8): 433–45.

————. 1956a. The migration of humpback whales which pass the New Zealand coast. *Trans. Roy. Soc. New Zealand* 84: 147–96.

————. 1956b. Whale marking in South Pacific waters. *Norsk Hvalfangst-tidende* 45(9): 485–508.

————. 1960. An analysis of New Zealand catches of humpback whales from 1947 to 1958. *Norsk Hvalfangst-tidende* 49(2): 61–75.

————. 1964. Movements of humpback whales marked in the South West Pacific Ocean, 1952 to 1962. *Norsk Hvalfangst-tidende* 53(3): 68–78.

————. 1966. The seasonal migratory cycle of humpback whales. In K. S. Norris, ed., *Whales, Dolphins and Porpoises*, pp. 145–70. University of California Press.

DUNSTAN, D. J. 1957. Caudal presentation of a humpback whale, *Megaptera nodosa* (Bonaterre). *Norsk Hvalfangst-tidende* 46(10): 553–55.

EARLE, S. A. 1979. Humpbacks: the gentle whales. *National Geographic* 155(1): 2:17.

ELLIS, R. 1978. The singing whale. *Ocean World* 1(2): 19–22.

FORESTELL, P. H., L. M. HERMAN, and R. S. WELLS. 1979. Behavior of "escort" accompanying mother-calf pairs of humpback whales. (Abstract.) *Third Biennial Conf. Biol. Marine Mammals.* Seattle.

GLOCKNER, D. A., and S. C. VENUS. 1979. Humpback whale (*Megaptera novaeangliae*) cows with calves identified off west Maui, Hawaii, 1977–1979. (Abstract.) *Third Biennial Conf. Biol. Marine Mammals.* Seattle.

HARMER, S. F. 1928. History of whaling. *Proc. Linn. Soc. London* 140: 51–95.

HERMAN, L. M. 1978. Humpback whales in Hawaiian waters: A study in historical ecology. Unpublished paper.

————, and R. C. ANTINOJA. 1977. Humpback whales in the Hawaiian breeding waters: Population and pod characteristics. *Sci. Rep. Whales Res. Inst.* 29: 59–85.

HERMAN, L. M., R. C. ANTINOJA, C. S. BAKER, and R. S. WELLS. 1979. Temporal and spatial distribution of humpback whales in Hawaii. (Abstract.) *Third Biennial Conf. Biol. Marine Mammals.* Seattle.

HERMAN, L. M., P. H. FORESTELL, and R. C. ANTINOJA. 1977. Study of the 1976/77 migration of humpback whales into Hawaiian waters: Composite description. Unpublished paper.

HERSEY, J. B. 1977. A chronicle of man's use of ocean acoustics. *Oceanus* 20(2): 8–21.

HUDNALL, J. 1977. In the company of great whales. *Audubon* 79(3): 62–73.

————. 1978. Whale park: Establishing a marine sanctuary in Hawaii. *Oceans* 11(2): 8–15.

JONES, E. C. 1971. *Isistius brasiliensis*, a squaloid shark, the probable cause of crater wounds in fishes and cetaceans. *Fish. Bull.* 69(4): 791–98.

JURASZ, C., and V. JURASZ. 1978. Humpback whales in southeastern Alaska. *Alaska Geographic* 5(4): 116–27.

KATONA, S. 1975. *A Field Guide to the Whales and Seals of the Gulf of Maine.* Maine Coast Printers.

————, B. BAXTER, O. BRAZIER, S. KRAUS, J. PERKINS, and H. WHITEHEAD. 1979. Identification of humpback whales by fluke photographs. In H. E. Winn and B. L. Bolla, eds., *Behavior of Marine Animals.* Vol. 3: *Cetaceans*, pp. 33–44. Plenum Press.

KELLOGG, R. 1929. What is known of the migration of some of the whalebone whales. *Ann. Rept. Smithsonian Inst.* 1928: 467–94.

————. 1931. Whaling statistics for the Pacific coast of North America. *Jour. Mammal.* 12(1): 73–77.

LIEN, J., and B. MERDSOY. 1979. The humpback is not over the hump. *Natural History* 88(6): 46–49.

LILLIE, D. G. 1915. Cetacea. British Antarctic ("Terra Nova") Expedition, 1910. *Nat. Hist. Rept. Zool.* 1: 85–124.

LOCKYER, C. 1976. Growth and energy budgets of large baleen whales from the Southern Hemisphere. *FAO Scientific Consultation on Marine Mammals.* ACMRR/MM/SC/41.

MACKINTOSH, N. A. 1942. The southern stocks of whalebone whales. *Discovery Reports* 22: 197–300.

———, and J. F. G. WHEELER. 1929. Southern blue and fin whales. *Discovery Reports* 1: 257–540.

MARR, J. W. S. 1957. Further comments on the occurrence of *Euphausia superba* in a humpback whale caught off Queensland. *Norsk Hvalfangst-tidende* 46(4): 181–82.

MATTHEWS, L. H. 1938. The humpback whale, *Megaptera nodosa. Discovery Reports* 17: 7–92.

MATTHIESSEN, P. 1971. *Blue Meridian.* Random House.

MITCHELL, E. D. 1974. Trophic relationships and competition for food in northwest Atlantic whales. *Proc. Can. Soc. Zool.* 123–33.

MÖRCH, J. A. 1911. On the natural history of whalebone whales. *Proc. Zool. Soc. London* 661–70.

MROZEK, C. 1978. Giant nightingales of the deep. *Oceans* 11(2): 2–7.

NATIONAL GEOGRAPHIC SOCIETY. 1976. *The Great Whales: Migration and Range.* Map supplement to vol. 150, no. 6.

———. 1978. *The Great Whales.* Television film. Los Angeles.

NEMOTO, T. 1978. Humpback whales observed within the continental shelf waters of the eastern Bering Sea. *Sci. Rep. Whales Res. Inst.* 30: 245–47.

NICKERSON, R. 1977. *Brother Whale: A Pacific Whalewatcher's Log.* Chronicle Books.

———. 1978. The Maui County whale reserve. *Whalewatcher* 12(2): 4–8.

NISHIWAKI, M. 1959. Humpback whales in Ryukyuan waters. *Sci. Rep. Whales Res. Inst.* 14: 49–87.

———. 1966. Distribution and migration of the larger cetaceans in the North Pacific as shown by Japanese whaling results. In K. S. Norris, ed., *Whales, Dolphins and Porpoises,* pp. 171–91. University of California Press.

NORRIS, K. S., and R. R. REEVES, eds., 1978. *Report on a Workshop on Problems Related to Humpback Whales (Megaptera novaeangliae) in Hawaii.* U.S. Marine Mammal Commission, Report No. MMC-77/03. 90 pp.

OMMANNEY, F. D. 1933. Whaling in the Dominion of New Zealand. *Discovery Reports* 7: 241–52.

OMURA, H. 1953. Biological studies on humpback whales in the Antarctic whaling areas IV and V. *Sci. Rep. Whales Res. Inst.* 8: 81–101.

PAYNE, K. 1979. Progressive changes in songs of humpback whales. (Abstract.) *Third Biennial Conf. Biol. Marine Mammals.* Seattle.

PAYNE, R. 1970. *Songs of the Humpback Whale.* Capitol Records, ST-620.

———. 1972. The song of the whale. In T. B. Allen, ed., *The Marvels of Animal Behavior,* pp. 144–67. National Geographic Society.

———. 1976. At home with right whales. *National Geographic* 149(3): 322–39.

———. 1977. *Deep Voices: The Second Whale Record.* Capitol Records, ST-11598.

———. 1979a. Humpback whale songs as an indicator of "stocks." (Abstract.) *Third Biennial Conf. Biol. Marine Mammals.* Seattle.

———. 1979b. Humpbacks: their mysterious songs. *National Geographic* 155(1): 18–25 (+ phonograph record).

———, and S. MCVAY. 1971. Songs of humpback whales. *Science* 173: 585–97.

PIKE, G. C. 1951. Lamprey marks on whales. *Jour. Fish. Res. Bd. Canada* 8: 275–80.

———. 1953. Color patterns of humpback whales from the coast of British Columbia. *Jour. Fish. Res. Bd. Canada.* 10: 320–25.

———. 1954. Whaling on the coast of British Columbia. *Norsk Hvalfangst-tidende* 43(3): 117–27.

RATHJEN, W. F., and J. R. SULLIVAN. 1970. West Indies whaling. *Sea Frontiers* 16(3): 130–37.

RAYNER, G. W. 1940. Whale marking: Progress and results to December 1939. *Discovery Reports* 19: 247–84.

RED DATA BOOK. 1972. Humpback whale, *Megaptera novaeangliae* Borowski 1781. Code: 11.100.2.1.E. IUCN, Morges, Switzerland.

RICE, D. W. 1963. Progress report on biological studies of the larger cetaceans in the waters off California. *Norsk Hvalfangst-tidende* 52(7): 181–87.

———. 1974. Whales and whale research in the eastern North Pacific. In W. E. Schevill, ed., *The Whale Problem,* pp. 170–95. Harvard University Press.

ROSS, A., and W. K. EMERSON, 1974. *Wonders of Barnacles.* Dodd, Mead & Co.

SCHEVILL, W. E., and R. H. BACKUS. 1960. Daily patrol of a *Megaptera. Jour. Mammal.* 41(2): 279–81.

SCHMITT, W. 1965. *Crustaceans.* University of Michigan Press.

SERGEANT, D. E. 1966. *Populations of Large Whale Species in the Western North Atlantic with Special Reference to the Fin Whale.* Fisheries Research Board of Canada, circular no. 9. 13 pp. + tables.

———. 1975. An additional food supply for humpback *(Megaptera novae-angliae)* and minke whales *(Balaenoptera acutorostrata).* Int. Cons. Expl. Sea, Ann. Mtg. 1975, Marine Mammals Committee, C.M. 1975/N:13. 6 pp. mimeo.

SLIJPER, E. J. 1949. On some phenomena concerning pregnancy and parturition of the cetacea. *Bijdr. Dierk.* 28: 418–48.

———. 1956. Some remarks on gestation and birth in cetacea and other aquatic mammals. *Hvalradets Skrifter.* 41: 62 pp.

STRASBURG, D. W. 1963. The diet and dentition of *Isistius brasiliensis,* with remarks on tooth replacement in other sharks. *Copeia* 1963: 33–40.

SYMONS, H. W., and R. D. WESTON, 1958. Studies of the humpback whale *Megaptera nodosa* in the Bellinghausen Sea. *Norsk Hvalfangst-tidende* 47(2): 53–81.

THOMPSON, T. J., H. E. WINN, and P. J. PERKINS. 1979. Mysticete sounds. In H. E. Winn and B. L. Bolla, eds., *Behavior of Marine Animals.* Vol. 3: *Cetaceans,* pp. 403–31. Plenum Press.

TOMICH, P. Q. 1969. *Mammals in Hawaii.* Bishop Museum Press.

TOWNSEND, C. H. 1935. The distribution of certain whales as shown by logbook records of American whaleships. *Zoologica* 19(1): 3–50.

TYACK, P. 1979. Interactions between singing humpback whales and nearby whales. (Abstract.) *Third Biennial Conf. Biol. Marine Mammals.* Seattle.

VAN BENEDEN, P. J., and P. GERVAIS. 1880. *Ostéologie des Cétacés Vivantes et Fossiles.* Paris.

WATKINS, W. A. 1967. Air-borne sounds of the humpback whale. *Megaptera novaeangliae. Jour. Mammal.* 48(4): 573–78.

———, and W. E. SCHEVILL. 1979. Aerial observation of feeding behavior in four baleen whales: *Eubalaena glacialis, Balaenoptera borealis, Megaptera novaeangliae,* and *Balaenoptera physalus. Jour. Mammal.* 60(1): 155–63.

WILLIAMSON, G. R. 1961. Winter sighting of a humpback suckling its calf on the Grand Bank of Newfoundland. *Norsk Hvalfangst-tidende* 50(8): 335–41.

WINN, H. E., R. K. EDEL, and A. G. TARUSKI. 1975. Population estimate of the humpback whale *Megaptera novaeangliae* in the West Indies by visual and acoustic techniques. *Jour. Fish. Res. Bd. Canada* 32: 499–506.

WINN, H. E., and P. J. PERKINS. 1976. Distribution and sounds of the minke whale, with a review of mysticete sounds. *Cetology* 19: 1–12.

———, and T. C. POULTER. 1971. Sounds of the humpback whale. *Proc. Seventh Ann. Conf. on Biol. Sonar and Diving Mamm., 1970,* pp. 39–52. Stanford Res. Inst.

WINN, H. E., and D. W. RICE. 1978. Humpback whales in the Sea of Cortez. *Currents* 2(4): 5–7.

WINN, H. E., and T. J. THOMPSON. 1979. Comparison of humpback whale sounds across the Northern Hemisphere. (Abstract.) *Third Biennial Conf. Biol. Marine Mammals.* Seattle.

WINN, H. E., and L. K. WINN. 1978. The song of the humpback whale *Megaptera novaeangliae* in the West Indies. *Marine Biol.* 47(2): 97–114.

WOLMAN, A. A. 1972. Humpback whale. In A. Seed, ed., *Baleen Whales in Eastern North Pacific and Arctic Waters,* pp. 38–42. Pacific Search Press.

———. 1978. Humpback whale. In D. Haley, ed., *Marine Mammals of Eastern North Pacific and Arctic Waters,* pp. 46–53. Pacific Search Press.

WÜRSIG, B. 1977. The photographic determination of group size, composition, and stability of coastal porpoises *(Tursiops truncatus). Science* 198: 755–56.

YABLAKOV, A. V., V. M. BEL'KOVICH, and V. I. BORISOV. 1974. *Whales and Dolphins.* Joint Publications Research Service, JPRS–62150–2.

ZEITLIN, H. 1977. Whale watch: A month in the life of a humpback. *Nature Canada* 6(4): 6–11.

RIGHT WHALE

AGUAYO, L. 1974. Baleen whales off continental Chile. In W. E. Schevill, ed., *The Whale Problem,* pp. 209–17. Harvard University Press.

ALLEN, J. A. 1908. The North Atlantic right whale and its near allies. *Bull. Amer. Mus. Nat. Hist.* 24: 277–329.

ANDREWS, R. C. 1908. Notes on external and internal anatomy of *Balaena glacialis. Bull. Amer. Mus. Nat. Hist.* 24: 171–82.

BAKER, C. S., P. H. FORESTELL, R. C. ANTINOJA, and L. M. HERMAN. 1979. Interactions of the Hawaiian humpback whale *(Megaptera novaeangliae)* with the right whale *(Balaena glacialis)* and odontocete cetaceans. (Abstract.) *Third Biennial Conf. Biol. Marine Mammals.* Seattle.

BEST, P. B. 1970. Exploitation and recovery of right whales *Eubalaena australis* off the Cape Province. *Invest. Rep. Div. Sea Fish. S. Afr.* 80: 1–20.

———. 1974. Status of the whale populations off the west coast of South Africa, and current research. In W. E. Schevill, ed., *The Whale Problem,* pp. 53–81. Harvard University Press.

————, and M. J. ROSCOE. 1974. Survey of right whales off South Africa, 1972, with observations from Tristan da Cunha, 1971/1972. *Rep. Int. Whal. Commn.* 24: 136–41.

BOCKSTOCE, J. R. 1978. History of commercial whaling in Arctic Alaska. *Alaska Geographic* 5(4): 135–43.

CASTELLO, H. P., and M. C. PINEDO. 1979. Southern right whales *(Eubalaena australis)* along the Brazilian coast. *Jour. Mammal.* 60(2): 429–30.

CHITTLEBOROUGH, R. 1956. Southern right whale in Australian waters. *Jour. Mammal.* 37(3): 456–57.

CLARK, E. 1958. Right whale *(Balaena glacialis)* enters Cape Cod Canal, Massachusetts, USA. *Norsk Hvalfangst-tidende* 47(3): 138–43.

CLARKE, R. 1962. Whale observation and whale marking off the coast of Chile in 1958 and from Ecuador towards and beyond the Galapagos Islands in 1959. *Norsk Hvalfangst-tidende* 51(7): 265–87.

————. 1965. Southern right whales on the coast of Chile. *Norsk Hvalfangst-tidende* 54(6): 121–28.

COLLETT, R. 1909. A few notes on the whale *Balaena glacialis* and its capture in recent years in the North Atlantic by Norwegian whalers. *Proc. Zool. Soc. London* 1909: 91–98.

CUMMINGS, W. C., and P. O. THOMPSON. 1971. Bioacoustics of marine mammals: R/V *Hero* cruise 70–3. *Antarctic Jour. U.S.* 6(5): 158–60.

CUMMINGS, W. C., J. F. FISH, and P. O. THOMPSON. 1972. Sound production and other behavior of southern right whales *Eubalaena glacialis. Trans. San Diego Soc. Nat. Hist.* 17(1): 1–14.

CUMMINGS, W. C., P. O. THOMPSON, and J. F. FISH. 1974. Behavior of southern right whales: R/V *Hero* cruise 72–3. *Antarctic Jour. U.S.* 9(2): 33–38.

CUMMINGS, W. C., J. F. FISH, P. O. THOMPSON, and J. R. JEHL. 1971. Bioacoustics of marine mammals off Argentina: R/V *Hero* cruise 71–3. *Antarctic Jour. U.S.* 6(6): 266–68.

DAKIN, W. J. 1938. *Whalemen Adventurers.* Angus & Robertson.

ELLIOT, H. F. I. 1953. The fauna of Tristan da Cunha. *Oryx* 2: 41–53.

FRASER, F. C. 1937. Early Japanese whaling. *Proc. Linn. Soc. London* 150: 19–20.

GASKIN, D. E. 1964. Return of the southern right whale *(Eubalaena australis* Desm.) to New Zealand waters. *Tuatara* 12(1): 115–18.

GILMORE, R. M. 1956. Rare right whale visits California. *Pacific Discovery* 9(4): 20–25.

————. 1978. Right whale. In D. Haley, ed., *Marine Mammals of Eastern Pacific and Arctic Waters,* pp. 62–69. Pacific Search Press.

HARMER, S. F. 1928. History of whaling. *Proc. Linn. Soc. London.* 140: 51–95.

KLUMOV, S. K. 1962. Right whale (Japanese) of the Pacific Ocean. *Trudy Inst. Okeanol.* 58: 202–97. (In Russian; English summary.)

LEUNG, Y. M. 1967. An illustrated key to the species of whale-lice (Amphipoda, Cyamidae), ectoparasites of Cetacea with a guide to the literature. *Crustaceana* 12: 278–91.

LIPTON, B. 1975. Whaling days in New Jersey. *Newark Mus. Quart.* 26(2–3): 1–72.

MARKHAM, C. 1881. On the whale fishery of the Basque province of Spain. *Proc. Zool. Soc. London* 1881: 969–76.

MARTIN, K. R. 1974. *Delaware Goes Whaling, 1833–1845.* Hagley Museum, Greenville, Del.

MATTHEWS, L. H. 1932. Lobster-krill: Anomuran crustacea that are the food of whales. *Discovery Reports* 5: 467–84.

————. 1938. Notes on the southern right whale, *Eubalaena australis. Discovery Reports* 17: 171–81.

MITCHELL, E. D. 1974. Trophic relationships and competition for food in northwest Atlantic whales. *Proc. Can. Zool. Soc.* 123–33.

MOORE, J. C., and E. CLARK. 1963. Discovery of right whales in the Gulf of Mexico. *Science* 141: 269.

MORGAN, L. 1978. Modern shore-based whaling. *Alaska Geographic* 5(4): 35–43.

NATIONAL MARINE FISHERIES SERVICE. 1974. Administration of the Marine Mammal Protection Act of 1972. June 22, 1973 to April 30, 1974. *Report to the Secretary of Commerce.* NMFS/NOAA.

OMMANNEY, F. D. 1933. Whaling in the Dominion of New Zealand. *Discovery Reports* 7: 239–52.

OMURA, H. 1957. Report on two right whales caught off Japan for scientific purposes under Article VII of the International Convention for Regulation of Whaling. *Norsk Hvalfangst-tidende* 46(7): 374–90.

————. 1958. North Pacific right whale. *Sci. Rep. Whales Res. Inst.* 13: 1–52.

————, S. OHSUMI, T. NEMOTO, K. NASU, and T. KASUYA. 1969. Black right whales in the North Pacific. *Sci. Rep. Whales Res. Inst.* 21: 1–78.

PAYNE, R. 1972a. Swimming with right whales. *National Geographic* 142(4): 576–87.

_____. 1972b. The song of the whale. In T. B. Allen, ed., *The Marvels of Animal Behavior,* pp. 140–67. National Geographic Society.

_____. 1974. A playground for whales—but for how long? *Animal Kingdom* 72(2): 7–12.

_____. 1976. At home with right whales. *National Geographic* 149(3): 322–39.

_____, and E. M. DORSEY. 1979. Sexual dimorphism in the callosities of southern right whales. (Abstract.) *Third Biennial Conf. Biol. Marine Mammals.* Seattle.

_____, and K. PAYNE. 1971. Underwater sounds of southern right whales. *Zoologica* 56(4): 159–65.

PRUNA, A. 1975. Secret life of the right whale. *Audubon* 77(1): 40–55.

RED DATA BOOK. 1972. Black right whale, *Eubalaena glacialis* Müller 1776. Code 11.101.2.1.E. IUCN, Morges, Switzerland.

REEVES, R. R. 1979. Right whale: Protected but still in trouble. *National Parks and Conservation* 53(2): 10–15.

_____, J. G. MEAD, and S. KATONA. 1978. The right whale, *Eubalaena glacialis,* in the western North Atlantic. *Rep. Int. Whal. Commn.* 28: 303–12.

RICE, D. W. 1974. Whales and whale research in the eastern North Pacific. In W. E. Schevill, ed., *The Whale Problem,* pp. 170–95. Harvard University Press.

_____, and C. H. FISCUS. 1968. Right whales in the southeastern North Pacific. *Norsk Hvalfangst-tidende* 57(5): 105–7.

RIDEWOOD, W. G. 1901. On the structure of the horny excrescence, known as the "bonnet" of the southern right whale (*Balaena australis*). *Proc. Zool. Soc. London* 1901(1): 44–47.

SAAYMAN, G. S., and C. K. TAYLER. 1973. Some behavior patterns of the southern right whale *Eubalaena australis. Zeitschrift fur Säugetierkunde* 38: 172–83.

STEWART, T. 1978. Day of the whale. *Skin Diving in Australia* 7(4): 40–41.

TERRY, W. M. 1951. *Japanese whaling industry prior to 1946.* U.S. Department of the Interior, Fish and Wildlife Serv., fishery leaflet 371. 47 pp.

TOWNSEND, C. H. 1935. The distribution of certain whales as shown by logbook records of American whaleships. *Zoologica* 19(1): 1–50.

ULMER, F. A. 1961. New Jersey's whales and dolphins. *New Jersey Nature News* 16(3): 80–93.

WATKINS, W. A., and W. E. SCHEVILL. 1976. Right whale feeding and baleen rattle. *Jour. Mammal.* 57(1): 58–66.

_____. 1979. Aerial observation of feeding behavior in four baleen whales: *Eubalaena glacialis, Balaenoptera borealis, Megaptera novaeangliae,* and *Balaenoptera physalus. Journ. Mammal.* 60(1): 155–63.

YAMAMOTO, Y., and H. HIRUTA. 1978. Stranding of a black right whale at Kumoni, southwestern coast of Izu Peninsula. *Sci. Rep. Whales Res. Inst.* 30: 249–51.

BOWHEAD

ADAMS, J. 1979. The IWC and bowhead whaling: An Eskimo perspective. *Orca* 1(1): 11–12.

ALLEN, E. S. 1973. *Children of the Light: The Rise and Fall of New Bedford Whaling and the Death of the Arctic Fleet.* Little, Brown & Co.

BAILEY, A. M., and R. W. HENDEE. 1926. Notes on mammals of northwestern Alaska. *Jour. Mammal.* 7(1): 9–28.

ALLEN, J. A. 1908. The North Atlantic right whale and its near allies. *Bull. Amer. Mus. Nat. Hist.* 24: 277–329.

BERZIN, A. A., and N. V. DOROSHENKO. 1980. Right whales of the Okhotsk Sea. *Scientific Committee Report, Int. Whal. Commn.* SC/32/PS2. 9 pp.

BOCKSTOCE, J. R. 1976. Nineteenth century commercial whaling: Its impact on the bowhead whale, *Balaena mysticetus,* of the western Arctic. *FAO Scientific Consultation on Marine Mammals.* ACMRR/MM/SC/71.

_____. 1977a. *Steam Whaling in the Western Arctic.* Old Dartmouth Historical Society, New Bedford, Mass.

_____. 1977b. Eskimo whaling in Alaska. *Alaska Magazine* 43(9): 4–6.

_____. 1977c. An issue of survival: Bowhead vs. tradition. *Audubon* 79(5): 142–45.

_____. 1978a. History of commercial whaling in Arctic Alaska. *Alaska Geographic* 5(4): 17–25.

_____. 1978b. The Arctic whaling disaster of 1897. *Alaska Geographic* 5(4): 27–34.

_____. 1978c. *A Preliminary Estimate of the Reduction of the Western Arctic Bowhead Whale* (Balaena mysticetus) *Population by the Pelagic Whaling Industry, 1848–1915.* U.S. Marine Mammal Commission report no. MMC-77/08. 32 pp.

_____. 1980. Battle of the bowheads. *Natural History* 89(5): 52–61.

_____, and D. B. BOTKIN. 1980. The historical status and reduction of the Western Arctic bowhead whale (*Balaena mysticetus*) population by the pelagic whaling industry, 1848–1914. *Final Report to the National Marine Fisheries Service by the Old Dartmouth Historical Society (New Bedford Whaling Museum) under Contract 03–78–M02–0212.* 120 pp.

BRAHAM, H., C. FISCUS, and D. RUGH. 1977. Marine Mammals of the Bering and Southern Chukchi Seas. In *Environmental Assessment of the Alaskan Continental Shelf.* Vol. 1: *Receptors:*

Mammals, pp. 1–99. U.S. Department of Commerce, National Oceanic and Atmospheric Administration.

BRAHAM, H. W., and B. D. KROGMAN. 1977. *Population Biology of the Bowhead* (Balaena mysticetus) *and Beluga* (Delphinapterus leucas) *Whale in the Bering, Chukchi and Beaufort Seas.* Northwest & Alaska Fisheries Center Processed Report, NOAA/NMFS.

BRAHAM, H. W., and J. M. BREIWICK. 1980. Projections of a decline in the Western Arctic population of bowhead whales. *Scientific Committee Report, Int. Whal. Commn.* SC/32/PS8. 15 pp.

BRUEMMER, F. 1971. Whalers of the North. *Beaver,* Winter 1971, pp. 44–55.

CARROLL, G. M. 1976. Utilization of the bowhead whale. *Mar. Fish. Rev.* 38(8): 18–21.

DALL, W. H. 1874. Catalogue of the Cetacea of the North Pacific Ocean. In C. M. Scammon, *The Marine Mammals of the Northwestern Coast of North America, Together with an Account of the American Whale-Fishery.* Carmany, San Francisco, and Putnam's, N.Y.

DEWHURST, H. W. 1834. *The Natural History of the Order Cetacea and the Oceanic Inhabitants of the Arctic Regions.* London.

DURHAM, F. E. 1972a. History of bowhead whaling. In A. Seed, ed., *Baleen Whales in Eastern North Pacific and Arctic Waters,* pp. 5–9. Pacific Search Press.

———. 1972b. Greenland or bowhead whale. In A. Seed, ed., *Baleen Whales in Eastern North Pacific and Arctic Waters,* pp. 10–14. Pacific Search Press.

———. 1979a. An historical perspective on eskimo whaling and the bowhead controversy. *Orca* 1(1): 5–6.

———. 1979b. *Recent trends in bowhead whaling by Eskimos in the western Arctic with emphasis on utilization.* Center for Environmental Education, Washington, D. C.

———. 1979c. The catch of bowhead whales (*Balaena mysticetus*) by Eskimos, with emphasis on the western Arctic. *Contrib. Sci. Natur. Hist. Mus. Los Angeles County.* 314: 1–14.

ESCHRICHT, D. F., and J. REINHARDT. 1861. Om Nordhvalen (*Balaena Mysticetus* L.). *Vidensk. Selsk. Skr. 5 Raekke, Naturvidensk. Mathem. Afd.* 5: 433–592.

EVERITT, R. D., and B. D. KROGMAN. 1979. Sexual behavior of bowhead whales observed off the north coast of Alaska. *Arctic* 32(3): 277–80.

FAY, F. H. 1975. Mammals and birds. In D. W. Hood and Y. Takenouti, eds., *Bering Sea Oceanography: An update, 1972–1974,* pp. 133–38. Inst. Mar. Sci. Univ. Alaska, no. 75-2.

———. 1977. Morbidity and mortality of marine mammals: Bering Sea. In *Environmental Assessment of the Alaskan Continental Shelf.* Vol. 1: *Receptors: Mammals,* pp. 161–88. U.S. Department of Commerce, National Oceanic and Atmospheric Administration.

HALL, J., and M. TILLMAN. 1977. A survey of cetaceans of Prince William Sound and adjacent vicinity: Their numbers and seasonal movement. In *Environmental Assessment of the Alaskan Continental Shelf.* Vol. 1: *Receptors: Mammals,* pp. 481–502. U.S. Department of Commerce, National Oceanic and Atmospheric Administration.

JACKSON, G. 1978. *The British Whaling Trade.* Adam & Charles Black.

JONSGARD, A. 1964. A right whale (*Balaena* sp.) in all probability a Greenland right whale (*Balaena mysticetus*) observed in the Barents Sea. *Norsk Hvalfangst-tidende* 53(11): 311–13.

———. 1980. Bowhead whales, *Balaena mysticetus,* observed in Arctic waters of the eastern North Atlantic after the Second World War. *Scientific Committee Report, Int. Whal. Commn.* SC/32/PS23. 2 pp.

MAHER, W. J., and N. J. WILIMOVSKY. 1963. Annual catch of bowhead whales by Eskimos at Point Barrow, Alaska. *Jour. Mammal.* 44(1): 16–20.

MANSFIELD, A. W. 1971. Occurrence of the bowhead or Greenland right whale (Balaena mysticetus) in Canadian Arctic waters. *Jour. Fish. Res. Bd. Canada* 28(12): 1873–75.

MARQUETTE, W. M. 1977. *The 1976 Annual Catch of Bowhead Whales* (Balaena mysticetus) *by Alaskan Eskimos, with a Review of the Fishery, 1973–1976, and a Biological Summary of the Species.* Northwest & Alaska Fisheries Center Processed Report, NOAA/NMFS.

———. 1978. Bowhead whale. In D. Haley, ed., *Marine Mammals of Eastern North Pacific and Arctic Waters,* pp. 70–81. Pacific Search Press.

———. 1979. The 1977 catch of bowhead whales (*Balaena mysticetus*) by Alaskan Eskimos. *Rep. Int. Whal. Commn.* 29: 281–89.

MCVAY, S. 1973. Stalking the Arctic whale. *American Scientist* 61(1): 23–37.

MERCER, R., H. BRAHAM, and C. FISCUS. 1977. Seasonal distribution and relative abundance of marine mammals in the Gulf of Alaska. In *Environmental Assessment of the Alaskan Continental Shelf.* Vol. 1: *Receptors: Mammals,* pp. 100–33. U.S. Department of Commerce, National Oceanic and Atmospheric Administration.

MILAN, F. A. 1980. On the need of Alaskan Eskimos to harvest bowhead whales. *U.S. Department of the Interior.* 94 pp. Mimeo.

MITCHELL, E. D., and R. R. REEVES. 1980. Factors affecting abundance of bowhead whales (*Balaena mysticetus*) in the eastern Arctic of North America, 1915–1980. *Scientific Committee Report, Int. Whal. Commn.* SC/32/PS1. 26 pp.

MORGAN, L. 1977. A new look at subsistence whaling. *Alaska Magazine* 43(9): 8–11.

———. 1978a. Early native whaling in Alaska. *Alaska Geographic* 5(4): 45–49.

_____. 1978b. Modern Eskimo whaling. *Alaska Geographic* 5(4): 135–43.

NAKASHIMA, L. 1977. Fall whaling in Barrow. *Alaska Magazine* 43(9): 97.

NEMOTO, T. 1959. Food of baleen whales with reference to whale movements. *Sci. Rep. Whales Res. Inst.* 14: 149–290.

NISHIWAKI, M., and T. KASUYA, 1970. A Greenland right whale caught in Osaka Bay. *Sci. Rep. Whales Res. Inst.* 22: 45–62.

RAINEY, F. 1940. Eskimo method of capturing bowhead whales. *Jour. Mammal.* 21(3): 362.

_____. 1947. The whale hunter of the Tigara. *Anthropology Papers Amer. Mus. Nat. Hist.* 41(2): 231–83.

RANDLEY, K. 1979. Barrow Inuit and the whale. *Orca* 1(1): 7–10.

RAU, R. 1978. The end of the hunt? *National Wildlife* 16(3): 4–11.

RED DATA BOOK. 1972. Bowhead or Greenland right whale, *Balaena mysticetus.* Code 11.101.1.1.E. IUCN, Morges, Switzerland.

RICE, D. W. 1974. Whales and whale research in the eastern North Pacific. In W. E. Schevill, ed., *The Whale Problem,* pp. 170–95. Harvard University Press.

SCORESBY, W. 1820. *An Account of the Arctic Regions with History and a Description of the Northern Whale-Fishery.* Archibald Constable, Edinburgh. (1969 edition.) David & Charles.

SERGEANT, D. E., and W. HOEK. 1974. Seasonal distribution of bowhead and white whales in the eastern Beaufort Sea. In J. C. Reed and J. E. Slater, eds., *The Coast and Shelf of the Beaufort Sea.* Arctic Inst. North America.

TOWNSEND, C. H. 1935. The distribution of certain whales as shown by logbook records of American whaleships. *Zoologica* 19(1): 3–50.

VIBE, C. 1967. Arctic animals in relation to climatic function. *Medd. om Grønland* 170(5): 66–227.

VINCENT, H. 1949. *The Trying-out of Moby-Dick.* Houghton Mifflin Company.

WILSON, M. S., and E. H. BUCK. 1979. Changes in Eskimo whaling methods. *Carnivore* 2(1): 35–42.

WINTER, F. H., and F. P. SCHMITT. 1975. Captain Thomas Welcome Roys. *Oceans* 8(3): 34–39.

PYGMY RIGHT WHALE

AITKEN, P. F. 1971. Whales from the coast of South Australia. *Trans. Roy. Soc. S. Aust.* 95(2): 95–103.

BAKER, A. N. 1972. New Zealand whales and dolphins. *Tuatara* 20(1): 1–49.

BEDDARD, F. E. 1903. Contribution towards a knowledge of the osteology of the pygmy right whale, *Neobalaena marginata. Trans. Zool. Soc. London* 16: 87–115.

DAVIES, J. L., and E. R. GUILER. 1957. A note on the pygmy right whale, *Caperea marginata* Gray. *Proc. Zool. Soc. London* 129: 579–89.

GUILER, E. R. 1961. A pregnant female pygmy right whale. *Aust. Jour. Sci.* 24:297.

HALE, H. M. 1931. The pygmy right whale in South Australian waters. *Rec. S. Aust. Mus.* 4: 314–19.

_____. 1964. Pygmy right whale (*Caperea marginata*) in South Australian waters, Part II. *Rec. S. Aust. Mus.* 14: 679–94.

ROSS, G. J. B., P. B. BEST, and B. G. DONNELLY. 1975. New records of the pygmy right whale (*Caperea marginata*) from South Africa, with comments on distribution, migration, appearance and behavior. *Jour. Fish. Res. Bd. Canada* 32(7): 1005–17.

WHITE WHALE (BELUGA)

BRAHAM, H. W., and B. D. KROGMAN. 1977. *Population Biology of the Bowhead* (Balaena mysticetus) *and Beluga* (Delphinapterus leucas) *Whale in the Bering, Chukchi and Beaufort Seas.* Northwest & Alaska Fisheries Center Processed Report, NOAA/NMFS.

BRODIE, P. F. 1971. A reconsideration of aspects of growth, reproduction, and behaviour of the white whale (*Delphinapterus leucas*) with reference to Cumberland Sound, Baffin Island, population. *Jour. Fish. Res. Bd. Canada* 28(9): 1309–18.

CUMMINGS, W. C., and P. O. THOMPSON. 1971. Gray whales avoid the underwater sounds of killer whales. *Fish. Bull.* 69(3): 525–30.

DOAN, K. H., and C. W. DOUGLAS. 1953. Beluga of the Churchill region of Hudson Bay. *Bull. Fish. Res. Bd. Canada* 98: 1–27.

DUGUY, R., and D. ROBINEAU. 1973. *Cétacés et Phoques des Côtes de France.* Ann. Soc. Sci. Nat. Charente-Maritime. Pp. 5–93.

FAY, F. H. 1978. Belukha whale. In D. Haley, ed., *Marine Mammals of Eastern North Pacific and Arctic Waters,* pp. 132–37. Pacific Search Press.

FISH, J. F., and J. S. VANIA. 1971. Killer whale (*Orcinus orca*) sounds repel white whales (*Delphinapterus leucas*). *Fish. Bull.* 69(3): 531–36.

FISH, M. P., and W. H. MOWBRAY. 1962. Production of underwater sound by the white whale or beluga. *Jour. Mar. Res.* 20: 149–62.

FRASER, F. C. 1934. Report on cetacea stranded on the British Coasts from 1927 to 1932. *Bull. Brit. Mus.* (Nat. Hist.) 11: 1–41.

HEWLETT, S. I. 1978. It's a boy! At the Vancouver Aquarium. *Animal Kingdom* 81(2): 15–27.

HOWELL, A. B. 1935. Observations on the white whale. *Jour. Mammal.* 16(2): 155–56.

JOHNSON, S. R. 1979. Fall observations of westward migrating white whales *(Delphinapterus leucas)* along the central Alaskan Beaufort Sea coast. *Arctic* 32(3): 275–76.

JONKEL, C. J. 1969. White whales wintering at James Bay. *Jour. Fish. Res. Bd. Canada* 26: 2205–7.

KAPEL, F. O. 1977. Catch of belugas, narwhals and harbour porpoises in Greenland, 1954–75, by year, month and region. *Rep. Int. Whal. Commn.* 27: 507–22.

MORGAN, D. W. 1979. The vocal and behavioral reactions of the beluga, *Delphinapterus leucas*, to playback of its sounds. In H. E. Winn and B. L. Olla, eds., *Behavior of Marine Animals.* Vol. 3: *Cetaceans*, pp. 311–43. Plenum Press.

NEWMAN, M. A. 1977. *A Beluga Is Born.* Vancouver Public Aquarium, special publication.

NEW YORK ZOOLOGICAL SOCIETY. 1903. *Bulletin* 9: 81.

RAY, C. 1961. White Whales for the Aquarium. *Animal Kingdom* 64(6): 162–70.

SCHEVILL, W. E., and B. LAWRENCE. 1949. Underwater listening to the white porpoise *(Delphinapterus leucas). Science* 109: 143–44.

SCHEVILL, W. E., and W. A. WATKINS. 1966. Sound structure and directionality in Orcinus (Killer whale). *Zoologica* 51(2): 71–76.

SERGEANT, D. E. 1973. Biology of white whales *(Delphinapterus leucas)* in western Hudson Bay. *Jour. Fish. Res. Bd. Canada* 30: 1065–90.

———, and BRODIE, P. F. 1969. Tagging white whales in the Canadian Arctic. *Jour. Fish Res. Bd. Canada* 25: 2201–5.

———. 1975. Identity, abundance, and present status of populations of white whales, *Delphinapterus leucas*, in North America. *Jour. Fish. Res. Bd. Canada* 32(7): 1047–54.

SERGEANT, D. E., and W. HOEK. 1973. Whale watching. *Nature Canada* 2(4): 27–30.

SERGEANT, D. E., A. W. MANSFIELD, and B. BECK. 1970. Inshore records of cetaceans for eastern Canada, 1949–68. *Jour. Fish. Res. Bd. Canada* 27(11): 1903–15.

SLIJPER, E. J. 1967. White whale in Netherlands waters. *Zeitschrift fur Säugetierkunde* 32(1): 86–89.

ULMER, F. J. 1979. Hans Toft's discovery. *New Jersey Audubon* 5(2): 12–13.

VIBE, C. 1950. The marine mammals and the marine fauna in the Thule district (northwest Greenland) with observations on ice-conditions in 1939–41. *Medd. om Grønland* 150(6): 1–115.

VLADYKOV, V. D. 1943. A modification on the pectoral fins in the beluga from the St. Lawrence River. *Studies in Aquatic Mammals* 2(11): 23–40.

———. 1944. Chasse, biologie et valeur économique de marsouin blanc ou beluga *(Delphinapterus leucas)* du fleuve et de golfe Saint-Laurent. *Studies in Aquatic Mammals* 3(15), 194 pp.

———. 1947. Nourriture du marsouin blanc ou beluga *(Delphinapterus leucas)* du fleuve Saint-Laurent. *Studies in Aquatic Mammals* 4(19), 131 pp.

YABLAKOV, A. V., V. M. BEL'KOVICH, and V. I. BORISOV. 1974. *Whales and Dolphins.* Joint Publications Research Service. JPRS–62150–2.

NARWHAL

ARVY, L. 1978a. Le narval *(Monodon monoceros L.). Acta Zool. Path. Antverp* 73: 43–118.

———. 1978b. Une erreur historique: La confusion entre foetus sirenien de Ruysch (1638–1731) et foetus narvalien. *Acta Zool. Path. Antverp* 73: 37–42.

BEST, R. C., and H. D. FISHER. 1974. Seasonal breeding of the narwhal *(Monodon monoceros). Canadian Jour. Zool.* 53: 429–31.

BIGELOW, H. B., and W. C. SCHROEDER. 1948. *Fishes of the Western North Atlantic.* Part 1: *Sharks.* Memoir of the Sears Foundation for Marine Research, Yale University.

BRUEMMER. F. 1969. The sea unicorn. *Audubon* 71(6): 58–63.

BURN MURDOCH, W. G. 1917. *Modern Whaling and Bear Hunting.* J. B. Lippincott & Co.

CLARK, J. W. 1871. On the skeleton of a narwhal, *Monodon monoceros*, with two fully developed tusks. *Proc. Zool. Soc. London* 1871: 42–53.

DART, J. O. 1969. The whale with the spiralled tooth. *L.A. County Mus. Nat. Hist. Quarterly* 7(4): 22–27.

DEWHURST, H. W. 1834. *The Natural History of the Order Cetacea and the Oceanic Inhabitants of the Arctic Regions.* London.

EALES, N. B. 1950. The skull of the foetal narwhal *Monodon monoceros. Phil. Trans. Roy. Soc.* 235: 1–33.

FORD, J. K. B., and H. D. FISHER. 1978. Underwater acoustic signals of the narwhal. *Canadian Jour. Zool.* 56(4): 552–60.

FRASER, F. C. 1938. Vestigial teeth in the narwhal. *Proc. Linn. Soc. London* 150: 155–62.

———. 1974. Report on cetacea stranded on the British coasts from 1948 to 1966. *Bull. Brit. Mus. (Nat. Hist.)* 14: 1–65.

GEIST, O. W., J. L. BUCKLEY, and R. H. MANVILLE. 1960. Alaskan records of the narwhal. *Jour. Mammal.* 41(2): 250–53.

GEIST, V. 1971. *Mountain Sheep: A Study in Behavior and Evolution.* University of Chicago Press.

GOULD, S. J. 1977. *Ever Since Darwin.* W. W. Norton & Co.

KAPEL, F. O. 1977. Catch of belugas, narwhals and harbour porpoises in Greenland, 1954–75, by year, month and region. *Rep. Int. Whal. Commn.* 27: 507–22.

MACINNIS, J. B. 1976. Whale song: In search of the narwhal. *Canadian Geog. Jour.* 92(3): 4–11.

MANSFIELD, A. W., T. G. SMITH, and B. BECK. 1975. The narwhal, *Monodon monoceros,* in eastern Canadian waters. *Jour. Fish. Res. Bd. Canada* 32(7): 1041–46.

MERDSOY, B., J. LIEN, and A. STOREY. 1979. Extralimital record of a narwhal *(Monodon monoceros)* in Hall's Bay, Newfoundland. *Canadian Field Naturalist* 93(3): 303–4.

NEWMAN, M. A. 1978. Narwhal. In D. Haley, ed., *Marine Mammals of Eastern North Pacific and Arctic Waters,* pp. 138–44. Pacific Search Press.

NISHIWAKI, M. 1969. Tusks of unicorn *(Monodon monoceros)* owned by Prince Takamatsu. *Jour. Mam. Soc. Japan* 4: 159–62.

NORRIS, K. S. 1969. The echolocation of marine mammals. In H. T. Andersen, ed., *The Biology of Marine Mammals,* pp. 391–423. Academic Press.

PORSILD, M. P. 1918. On "savssats": A crowding of arctic animals at holes in the sea ice. *Geog. Rev.* 6: 215–18.

———. 1922. Scattered observations on narwhals. *Jour. Mammal.* 3(1): 8–13.

RAVEN, H. C. 1927. Northward for narwhal. *Natural History* 27(1): 33–44.

REEVES, R. 1976a. Narwhals: Another endangered species. *Canadian Geog. Jour.* 92(3): 12–17.

———. 1976b. What fate for the narwhal? *North* 23(3): 17–21.

———. 1976c. Unicorns of the Arctic Sea. *Defenders* 51(4): 222–27.

———. 1977. Hunt for the narwhal. *Oceans* 10(4): 50–57.

SERGEANT, D. E. 1979. Seasonal movements and numbers of cetaceans summering in Lancaster Sound, Arctic Canada. (Abstract.) *Third Biennial Conf. Biol. Marine Mammals.* Seattle.

SHEPARD, O. 1967. *The Lore of the Unicorn.* Barnes & Noble.

SILVERMAN, H., M. DUNBAR, and J. HICKIE. 1979. Aggressive tusk use by the narwhal *(Monodon monoceros).* (Abstract.) *Third Biennial Conf. Biol. Marine Mammals.* Seattle.

STEFFANSON, V. 1938. *The Three Voyages of Martin Frobisher.* Argonaut Press.

VIBE, C. 1950. The marine mammals and the marine fauna in the Thule district (northwest Greenland) with observations on ice-conditions in 1939–41. *Medd. om Grønland* 150(6): 1–115.

WATKINS, W. A., W. E. SCHEVILL, and C. RAY. 1971. Underwater sounds of *Monodon* (Narwhal). *Jour. Acoust. Soc. Amer.* 49: 595–99.

SPERM WHALE

ASH, C. E. 1962. *Whaler's Eye.* Macmillan.

ASHLEY, C. W. 1926. *The Yankee Whaler.* Halcyon House.

BACKUS, R. H. 1966. A large shark in the stomach of a sperm whale. *Jour. Mammal.* 47(1): 142.

———, and W. E. SCHEVILL. 1966. *Physeter* clicks. In K. S. Norris, ed., *Whales, Dolphins and Porpoises,* pp. 510–28. University of California Press.

BANNISTER, J., and E. MITCHELL. 1978. North Pacific sperm whale stock identity: Distributional evidence from Maury and Townsend charts. Unpublished paper.

BEALE, T. 1835. *A Few Observations on the Natural History of the Sperm Whale.* Effingham Wilson.

———. 1839. *The Natural History of the Sperm Whale.* Voorst.

BEL'KOVICH, V. M., and A. V. YABLAKOV. 1963. The whale—an ultrasonic projector. *Yuchnyi Tekhnik* 3: 76–77.

BENNETT, F. D. 1840. *Narrative of a Whaling Voyage Around the Globe from the Year 1833 to 1836.* Richard Bentley.

BERZIN, A. A. 1972. *The Sperm Whale.* Israel Program for Scientific Translation, Jerusalem. Pp. 1–393.

———. 1978. Whale distribution in tropical eastern Pacific waters. *Rep. Int. Whal. Commn.* 28: 173–77.

———, and G. M. VEINGER. 1976. Investigations of the population morphology of sperm whales, *Physeter macrocephalus* L. 1758 of the Pacific Ocean. *FAO Symposium on Marine Mammals.* ACMRR/MM/SC/135.

BEST, P. B. 1967. The sperm whale *(Physeter catodon)* off the west coast of South Africa. I. Ovarian changes and their significance. *Invest. Rep. Div. Sea Fish. S. Afr.* 61: 1–27.

———. 1968. The sperm whale *(Physeter catodon)* off the west coast of South Africa. II. Reproduction in the female. *Invest. Rep. Div. Sea Fish. S. Afr.* 66: 1–32.

———. 1969a. The sperm whale. *(Physeter catodon)* off the west coast of South Africa. III. Reproduction in the male. *Invest. Rep. Div. Sea Fish. S. Afr.* 72: 1–20.

———. 1969b. The sperm whale *(Physeter catodon)* off the west coast of South Africa. IV. Distribution and movements. *Invest. Rep. Div. Sea Fish. S. Afr.* 78: 1–12.

_____. 1970. The sperm whale (*Physeter catodon*) off the west coast of South Africa. V. Age, growth and mortality. *Invest. Rep. Div. Sea Fish. S. Afr.* 79: 1–27.

_____. 1974. The biology of the sperm whale as it relates to stock management. In W. E. Schevill, ed., *The Whale Problem*, pp. 257–93. Harvard University Press.

_____. 1975. Review of world sperm whale stocks. *FAO Marine Mammals Symposium*. ACMRR/MM/EC/8.

_____. 1979. Social organization in sperm whales. In H. E. Winn and B. L. Olla, eds., *Behavior of Marine Animals*. Vol. 3: *Cetaceans*, pp. 227–89. Plenum Press.

_____, and R. GAMBELL. 1968. A comparison of the external characters of sperm whales off South Africa. *Norsk Hvalfangst-tidende* 57(6): 146–64.

BOSCHMA, H. 1938. On the teeth and some other particulars of the sperm whale (*Physeter macrocephalus* L.). *Temminckia* 3: 151–278.

BOW, J. M., and C. A. PURDAY. 1966. A method of preparing sperm whale teeth for age determination. *Nature* 210: 437–38.

BOYER, W. D. 1946. Letter to the editor. *Natural History* 55: 96.

BOYLSTEN, A. 1724. Ambergris found in whale. *Phil. Trans. Roy. Soc. London* 33.

BRYANT, P. 1979. The Baja sperm whale mass-stranding. *Whalewatcher* 13(2): p. 10.

BUIJS, D., and W. H. DUDOK VAN HEEL. 1979. Body-plan of a male sperm whale (*Physeter macrocephalus*) stranded near Breskens, Netherlands. *Aquatic Mammals* 7(1): 27–32.

BULLEN, F. 1899. *The Cruise of the Cachalot*. D. Appleton & Co. New York.

CALDWELL, D. K., M. C. CALDWELL, and D. W. RICE. 1966. Behavior of the sperm whale, *Physeter catodon* L. In K. S. Norris, ed., *Whales, Dolphins and Porpoises*, pp. 677–717. University of California Press.

CALDWELL, M. C., and D. K. CALDWELL. 1965. Individualized whistle contours in bottle-nosed dolphins (*Tursiops truncatus*). *Nature* 207(4995): 434–35.

_____. 1966. Epimeletic (Care-giving) behavior in Cetacea. In K. S. Norris, ed., *Whales, Dolphins and Porpoises*, pp. 755–89. University of California Press.

CHASE, O. 1821. *Narrative of the Most Extraordinary and Distressing Shipwreck of the Whale-ship Essex, of Nantucket; Which Was Attacked and Finally Destroyed by a Large Spermaceti-whale, in the Pacific Ocean*. New York.

CLARKE, M. R. 1962. Stomach contents of a sperm whale caught off Madeira in 1959. *Norsk Hvalfangst-tidende* 51(5): 173–91.

_____. 1966. A review of the systematics and ecology of oceanic squids. *Advances in Marine Biology* 4: 91–300.

_____. 1970. The function of the spermaceti organ of the sperm whale. *Nature* 228: 873–74.

_____. 1972. New technique for the study of sperm whale migrations. *Nature* 238: 405–6.

_____. 1976. Observation on sperm whale diving. *Jour. Mar. Biol. Assoc. U.K.* 56: 809–10.

_____. 1978a. Structure and proportions of the spermaceti organ in the sperm whale. *Jour. Mar. Biol. Assoc. U.K.* 58: 1–17.

_____. 1978b. Physical properties of spermaceti oil in the sperm whale. *Jour. Mar. Biol. Assoc. U.K.* 58: 19–26.

_____. 1978c. Buoyancy control as a function of the spermaceti organ in the sperm whale. *Jour. Mar. Biol. Assoc. U.K.* 58: 27–71.

_____. 1979a. The head of the sperm whale. *Scientific American* 240 (1): 128–41.

_____. 1979b. Whales and squid. *Jour. Mar. Biol. Assoc. U.K.* (in press).

_____, N. MACLEOD, and O. PALIZA. 1976. Cephalopod remains from the stomachs of sperm whales caught off Peru and Chile. *J. Zool. London* 180: 477–93.

CLARKE, R. 1953. Sperm whaling from open boats in the Azores. *Norsk Hvalfangst-tidende* 42(7): 373–86.

_____. 1954a. Open boat whaling in the Azores. *Discovery Reports* 26: 281–354.

_____. 1954b. A great haul of ambergris. *Norsk Hvalfangst-tidende* 43(8): 450–53.

_____. 1955. A giant squid swallowed by a sperm whale. *Norsk Hvalfangst-tidende* 44(10): 589–93.

_____. 1956. Sperm whales of the Azores. *Discovery Reports* 28: 237–98.

_____. 1966. The stalked barnacle *Conchoderma* ectoparasitic on whales. *Norsk Hvalfangst-tidende* 55(8): 154–68.

_____, A. AGUAYO, and G. PALIZA. 1964. Progress report on sperm whale research in the south east Pacific Ocean. *Norsk Hvalfangst-tidende* 53(11): 297–302.

_____. 1968. Sperm whales of the south east Pacific. *Hvalradets Skrifter* 51: 1–80.

COCKRILL, R. 1958. The great whales of the Antarctic. *Natural History* 67(10): 538–57.

COCKRUM, E. L. 1956. Sperm whales stranded on the beaches of the Gulf of California. *Jour. Mammal.* 37(2): 288.

DAUGHERTY, A. 1972. *Marine Mammals of California*. California Department of Fish and Game.

DAVIS, E. Y. 1946. "Man in Whale." *Natural History* 6: 241.

DEWHURST, H. W. 1834. *The Natural History of the Order Cetacea and the Oceanic Inhabitants of the Arctic Regions.* London.

DUDLEY, P. 1725. An essay upon the natural history of whales, with a particular account of the ambergris found in the sperma ceti whale. *Phil. Trans. Roy. Soc. London* 33 (387): 256–59.

DUFRESNE, F. 1946. *Alaska's Animals and Fishes.* A. S. Barnes and Company, New York.

ELLIS, R. 1979. The inscrutable hulk. *National Wildlife* 17(5): 12–16.

FADIMAN, A. 1979. Will we kill the last whale? *Life* 2(7) (July 1979): 18–26.

FLOWER, W. H. 1867. On the osteology of the cachalot or sperm whale. *Trans. Zool. Soc. London* 6(11): 309–78.

FROST, S. 1978. *Whales and Whaling.* Volumes I and II. Australian Government Printing Service. Canberra. Vol. I: pp. 1–342; Vol. II: pp. 1–220.

FUJINO, K. 1956. On the body proportions of the sperm whales *(Physeter catodon).* *Sci. Rep. Whales Res. Inst.* 11: 47–83.

GAMBELL, R. 1966. Foetal growth and the breeding season of sperm whales. *Norsk Hvalfangst-tidende* 55(6): 113–118.

———. 1968. Aerial observations of sperm whale behavior. *Norsk Hvalfangst-tidende* 57(6): 126–38.

———. 1970. Weight of a sperm whale, whole and in parts. *S. Afr. Jour. Sci.* 66: 225–27.

———. 1972. Sperm whales off Durban. *Discovery Reports* 35: 199–358.

———, and C. GRZEGORZEWSKA. 1967. The rate of lamina formation in sperm whale teeth. *Norsk Hvalfangst-tidende* 55(6): 117–21.

GAMBELL, R., C. LOCKYER, and G. J. B. ROSS. 1973. Observations on the birth of a sperm whale calf. *S. Afr. Jour. Sci.* 69: 147–48.

GASKIN, D. E. 1964. Recent observations in New Zealand waters on some aspects of behaviour of the sperm whale *(Physeter macrocephalus).* *Tuatara* 12(1): 106–14.

GILMORE, R. 1959. On the mass strandings of sperm whales. *Pacific Naturalist* 1(9): 9–16.

GRAY, R. W. 1927. The sleep of whales. *Nature* 121: 636–37.

———. 1928. The blubber of whales. *Nature* 121: 791–92.

———. 1935. Do whales descend to great depths? *Nature* 135: 656–57.

GUDKOV, V. M. 1963. On the peculiarities of the pigmentation of sperm whales in the Far East waters. *Trudy Inst. Okeanol.* 71: 207–22. (In Russian; English summary.)

HANNA, G. D. 1924. Sperm whales at St. George Island, Bering Sea. *Jour. Mammal.* 5(1): 64.

HARMER, S. F. 1928. History of whaling. *Proc. Linn. Soc. London* 140: 51–95.

———. 1933. Appendix to Wheeler's article, Notes on a young sperm whale from the Bermuda Islands. *Proc. Zool. Soc. London* 8: 409.

HARRISON, J. H. 1977. The whale and the wild jojoba. *Sea Frontiers* 23(5): 267–72.

HASS, H. 1959. *We Come from the Sea.* Doubleday & Co.

HEEZEN, B. C. 1957. Whales entangled in deep sea cables. *Norsk Hvalfangst-tidende* 46(12): 665–81.

HOLM, J. L., and A. JONSGARD. 1959. Occurrence of the sperm whale in the Antarctic and the possible influence of the moon. *Norsk Hvalfangst-tidende* 48(4): 161–82.

HOLT, S. J. 1977. Statement by observer representing FAO. Special meeting of IWC, Tokyo. 8 pp. mimeo.

HOPKINS, W. J. 1922. *She Blows! And Sperm at That!* Houghton Mifflin Company.

HOUSBY, T. 1971. *The Hand of God: Whaling in the Azores.* Abelard-Schuman.

HUSSON, A. M., and L. B. HOLTHUIS. 1974. *Physeter macrocephalus* Linnaeus, 1758, the valid name for the sperm whale. *Zoologische Mededelingen Leiden.* 48(19): 205–17.

INTERNATIONAL WHALING COMMISSION. 1978. *Schedule* (As Amended by the Commission at the Special Meeting, Tokyo, December 1977). Cambridge.

JONSGARD, A. 1960. On the stocks of sperm whales *(Physeter catodon)* in the Antarctic. *Norsk Hvalfangst-tidende* 49(7): 289–99.

JOSSELYN, J. 1672. *New England Rarities Discovered.* London. (Reissued 1972).

KASUYA, T., and S. OHSUMI. 1966. A secondary sexual character of the sperm whale. *Sci. Rep. Whales Res. Inst.* 20: 89–94.

KAWAKAMI, T. 1976. Squids found in the stomach of sperm whales in the northwestern Pacific. *Sci. Rep. Whales Res. Inst.* 28: 145–51.

KOJIMA, T. 1951. On the brain of the sperm whale. *Sci. Rep. Whales Res. Inst.* 6: 49–72.

KOZAK, V. A. 1974. Receptor zone of the video-acoustic system of the sperm whale (Physeter catadon L. 1758). *Fiziologichnyy Zhurnal Akademy Nauk Ukrayns'koy RSR* 120(3): 1–6. (National Technical Information Service, 1975.)

KUGLER, R. C. 1976. The historical records of American sperm whaling: What they tell us and what they don't. *FAO Scientific Consultation on Marine Mammals.* ACMRR/MM/SC/105.

LANE, F. W. 1957. *The Kingdom of the Octopus: The Life History of the Cephalopods.* Jarrolds.

LAWS, R. M. 1961. Laminated structure of bones in some marine mammals. *Norsk Hvalfangst-tidende* 50(12): 499–507.

LEUNG, Y. M. 1967. An illustrated key to the species of whale-lice (Amphipoda, Cyamidae), ectoparasites of Cetacea with a guide to the literature. *Crustaceana* 12: 278–91.

LILLY, J. C. 1961. *Man and Dolphin.* Doubleday & Co.

LOCKYER, C. 1976. Estimates of growth and energy budget for the sperm whale, *Physeter catodon. FAO Scientific Consultation on Marine Mammals.* ACMRR/MM/SC/38.

MACHIDA, S. 1970. A sword-fish sword found from a North Pacific sei whale. *Sci. Rep. Whales Res. Inst.* 22: 163–64.

————. 1975. Distribution of sperm whale catches in the southern Indian Ocean. *Sci. Rep. Whales Res. Inst.* 27: 141–57.

MACKINTOSH, N. A. 1942. The southern stocks of whalebone whales. *Discovery Reports* 22: 197–300.

MASAKI, Y. 1969. A malformed sperm whale with two nostrils. *Jour. Mam. Soc. Japan.* 4(4–6): 147–49.

MATTHEWS, L. H. 1938. The sperm whale, *Physeter catodon. Discovery Reports* 17: 95–164.

MATTHIESSEN, P. 1971. *Blue Meridian.* Random House.

MCHUGH, J. L. 1974. The role and history of the International Whaling Commission. In W. E. Schevill, ed., *The Whale Problem,* pp. 305–35. Harvard University Press.

MELVILLE, H. 1851. *Moby-Dick, or, The Whale.* Various editions.

MITCHELL, E. D. 1975. Preliminary report on Nova Scotia fishery for sperm whales *(Physeter catodon). Rep. Int. Whal. Commn.* 25: 226–35.

————. 1977. Sperm whale maximum length limit: proposed protection of "harem masters." *Rep. Int. Whal. Commn.* 27: 224–27.

————, and V. M. KOZICKI. 1978. Sperm whale regional closed seasons: Proposed protection during mating and calving. *Rep. Int. Whal. Commn.* 28: 195–98.

MIZUE, K., and H. JIMBO. 1950. Statistic study of foetuses of whales. *Sci. Rep. Whales Res. Inst.* 3: 119–31.

MØHL, B., E. LARSEN, and M. AMUNDIN. 1976. Sperm whales size determination: Outlines of an acoustic approach. *FAO Scientific Consultation on Marine Mammals.* ACMRR/MM/SC/84.

MURIE, J. 1865. On deformity of the lower jaw in the cachalot. *Proc. Zool. Soc. London.* 1865: 390–96.

MURPHY, R. C. 1924. Seals as sperm whale food. *Jour. Mammal.* 5(2): 132.

————. 1933. Floating gold: The romance of ambergris. *Natural History* 33(2): 117–130; 33(3): 303–10.

NASU, K. 1958. Deformed lower jaw of sperm whale. *Sci. Rep. Whales Res. Inst.* 13: 211–12.

NEMOTO, T. 1963. New records of sperm whales with protruded rudimentary hind limbs. *Sci. Rep. Whales Res. Inst.* 17: 79–81.

————, and K. NASU. 1963. Stones and other aliens in the stomachs of sperm whales in the Bering Sea. *Sci. Rep. Whales Res. Inst.* 17: 83–91.

NEWMAN, H. H. 1910. A large sperm whale captured in Texas waters. *Science,* n.s. 31: 631–32.

NISHIWAKI, M. 1955. On the sexual maturity of the Antarctic male sperm whale (*Physeter catodon* L.). *Sci. Rep. Whales Res. Inst.* 10: 143–49.

————, and T. HIBIYA. 1951. On the sexual maturity of the sperm whale *(Physeter catodon)* found in the adjacent waters of Japan. *Sci. Rep. Whales. Res. Inst.* 6: 153–65.

————. 1952. On the sexual maturity of the sperm whale *(Physeter catodon)* found in the adjacent waters of Japan. Part II. *Sci. Rep. Whales Res. Inst.* 7: 121–24.

NISHIWAKI, M., T. HIBIYA, and S. KIMURA. 1956. On the sexual maturity of the sperm whale *(Physeter catodon)* found in the North Pacific. *Sci. Rep. Whales Res. Inst.* 11: 39–46.

————. 1958. Age study of sperm whale based on reading of tooth laminations. *Sci. Rep. Whales Res. Inst.* 13: 135–53.

NISHIWAKI, M., S. OHSUMI, and T. KASUYA. 1961. Age characteristics of the sperm whale mandible. *Norsk Hvalfangst-tidende* 50(12): 499–507.

NISHIWAKI, M., S. OHSUMI, and T. MAEDA. 1963. Change of form in the sperm whale accompanied with growth. *Sci. Rep. Whales Res. Inst.* 17: 1–14.

NORDHOFF, C. 1856. *Whaling and Fishing.* Cincinnati.

NORRIS, K. S. 1969. The echolocation of marine mammals. In H. T. Andersen, ed., *The Biology of Marine Mammals,* pp. 391–423. Academic Press.

————. 1974. *The Porpoise Watcher.* W. W. Norton & Co.

————, and G. W. HARVEY. 1972. A theory for the function of the spermaceti organ of the sperm whale (*Physeter catodon* L.). In S. R. Galler, K. Schmidt-Koenig, G. J. Jacobs, and R. E. Belleville, eds., *Animal Orientation and Navigation,* pp. 397–419. NASA.

OGAWA, T., and T. KAMIYA. 1957. A case of the cachalot with protruded rudimentary hind limbs. *Sci. Rep. Whales Res. Inst.* 12: 197–208.

OHSUMI, S. 1958. A descendant of Moby Dick, or a white sperm whale. *Sci. Rep. Whales Res. Inst.* 13: 207–9.

_____. 1965. Reproduction of the sperm whale in the north-west Pacific. *Sci. Rep. Whales Res. Inst.* 19: 1–5.

_____. 1966. Sexual segregation of the sperm whale in the North Pacific. *Sci. Rep. Whales Res. Inst.* 20: 1–16.

_____. 1971. Some investigations on the school structure of sperm whale. *Sci. Rep. Whales Res. Inst.* 23: 1–25.

_____. 1973. Find of marlin spear from the Antarctic minke whales. *Sci. Rep. Whales Res. Inst.* 25: 237–39.

_____, T. KASUYA, and M. NISHIWAKI. 1963. The accumulation rate of dentinal growth layers in the maxillary tooth of the sperm whale. *Sci. Rep. Whales Res. Inst.* 17: 15–35.

OKUTANI, T., and T. NEMOTO. 1964. Squids as the food of sperm whales in the Bering Sea and Alaskan Gulf. *Sci. Rep. Whales Res. Inst.* 18: 111–22.

OMURA, H. 1950. On the body weight of sperm and sei whales located in the adjacent waters of Japan. *Sci. Rep. Whales Res. Inst.* 4: 1–13.

PERKINS, P. J., M. P. FISH, and W. H. MOWBRAY. 1966. Underwater communication sounds of the sperm whale, *Physeter catodon. Norsk Hvalfangst-tidende* 55(12): 225–28.

PERRIN, W. F. 1972. Color patterns of spinner porpoises *(Stenella* cf. *S. longirostris)* of the Eastern Pacific and Hawaii, with comments on delphinid pigmentation. *Fish. Bull.* 70(3): 983–1003.

PERVUSHIN, A. S. 1966. Nabliudeniia za rodami u kashlotov. *Zoologicheskiy Zhurnal* 45(12): 1892–93. (Not seen.)

PURRINGTON, P. A. 1955. A whale and her calf. *Natural History* 64(7): 363.

RAVEN, H. C., and W. K. GREGORY. 1933. The spermaceti organ and nasal passages of the sperm whale *(Physeter catodon)* and other odontocetes. *Amer. Mus. Novitates* 677: 1–17.

REYNOLDS, J. N. 1839. Mocha Dick, or The White Whale of the Pacific. *The Knickerbocker, New York Monthly Magazine* 13(5): 377–92.

RICE, D. W. 1963. Progress report on biological studies of the larger cetaceans in the waters off California. *Norsk Hvalfangst-tidende* 52(7): 181–87.

_____. 1978. Sperm whales. In D. Haley, ed., *Marine Mammals of Eastern North Pacific and Arctic Waters,* pp. 82–87. Pacific Search Press.

RIDGWAY, S. H. 1971. Buoyancy regulation in deep diving whales. *Nature* 232: 133–34.

ROSENBLUM, E. E. 1962. Distribution of sperm whales. *Jour. Mammal.* 43(1): 111–12.

ROTHFUS, J. A. 1976. Substitutes for sperm oil. *FAO Scientific Consultation on Marine Mammals.* ACMRR/MM/SC/62.

SCHEFFER, V. B. 1969. *The Year of the Whale.* Scribner's.

_____. 1976. The status of whales. *Pacific Discovery* 29(1): 2–8.

SCHENKKAN, E. J., and P. E. PURVES. 1973. The comparative anatomy of the nasal tract and the function of the spermaceti organ in the Physeteridae (Mammalia, Odontoceti). *Bijdr. Dierk.* 43(1): 93–112.

SCHMITT, F. P. 1979. Vessels vs. whales. *Sea Frontiers* 25(3): 140–44.

SCOGIN, R. 1977. Sperm whale oil and the jojoba shrub. *Oceans* 10(4): 65–66.

SERGEANT, D. E. 1969. Feeding rates of cetacea. *Fisk. Dir. Skr. Ser. Hav. Unders.* 15: 246–58.

SHERMAN, S. C. 1965. *The Voice of the Whaleman.* Providence Public Library, Providence, R.I.

SMITH, T. D. 1976. The adequacy of the scientific basis for the management of sperm whales. *Scientific Consultation on Marine Mammals, Bergen, Norway.* ACMRR/MM/SC/121. 1–15.

SPAUL, E. A. 1964. Deformity in the lower jaw of the sperm whale *(Physeter catodon). Proc. Zool. Soc. London* 142(3): 391–95.

STARBUCK, A. 1878. *History of the American Whale Fishery from its Earliest Inception to the Year 1876.* Part 4: *Report of the U.S. Commission on Fish and Fisheries.* Washington. (Reprinted 1964.)

TARASEVICH, M. N. 1968. The diet of sperm whales in the North Pacific Ocean. *Zoologicheskiy Zhurnal* 47(4): 595–601. (National Technical Information Service, 1974.)

TOWNSEND, C. H. 1935. The distribution of certain whales as shown by logbook records of American whaleships. *Zoologica* 19(1): 3–50.

VAN BENEDEN, P. J., and P. GERVAIS. 1880. *Ostéologie des Cétacés Vivantes et Fossiles.* Paris.

VINCENT, H. P. 1949. *The Trying-out of Moby-Dick.* Houghton Mifflin Company.

VOSS, G. L. 1959. Hunting sea monsters. *Sea Frontiers* 5(3): 134–46.

WATKINS, W. A. 1977. Acoustic behavior of sperm whales. *Oceanus* 20(2): 50–58.

_____, and W. E. SCHEVILL. 1975. Sperm whales *(Physeter catodon)* react to pingers. *Deep-Sea Res.* 22: 123–29.

_____. 1977. Sperm whale codas. *Jour. Acoust. Soc. Amer.* 62(6): 1485–90 (+ phonograph record).

WHEELER, J. F. G. 1933. Notes on a young sperm whale from the Bermuda Islands. *Proc. Zool. Soc. London* 1933: 407–10.

WORTHINGTON, L. V., and W. E. SCHEVILL. 1957. Underwater sounds heard from sperm whales. *Nature* 180: 191.

YAMADA, M. 1953. Contribution to the anatomy of the organ of hearing of whales. *Sci. Rep. Whales Res. Inst.* 8: 1–79.

ZENKOVICH, B. A. 1962. Sea mammals as observed by the round the world expedition of the Academy of Sciences of the USSR in 1957/1958. *Norsk Hvalfangst-tidende* 51(5): 198–

PYGMY SPERM WHALE
DWARF SPERM WHALE

AITKEN, P. F. 1971. Whales from the coast of South Australia. *Trans. Roy. Soc. S. Aust.* 95(2): 95–103.

ALLEN, G. M. 1941. Pygmy sperm whale in the Atlantic. *Zool. Ser. Field Mus. Nat. Hist.* 27: 17–36.

CALDWELL, D. K., and M. C. CALDWELL. 1975. Dolphin and small whale fisheries of the Caribbean and the West Indies: Occurrence, history, and catch statistics—with special reference to the Lesser Antillean island of St. Vincent. *Jour. Fish. Res. Bd. Canada* 32(7): 1105–10.

———, and G. ARRINDELL. 1973. Dwarf sperm whales, *Kogia simus,* from the Lesser Antillean island of St. Vincent. *Jour. Mammal.* 54(2): 515–17.

CALDWELL, D. K., and F. B. GOLLEY. 1965. Marine mammals from the coast of Georgia to Cape Hatteras. *Jour. Elisha Mitchell Sci. Soc.* 81(1): 24–32.

CALDWELL, D. K., A. INGLIS, and J. B. SIEBENALER. 1960. Sperm and pygmy sperm whales stranded in the Gulf of Mexico. *Jour. Mammal.* 41(1); 136–38.

CALDWELL, D. K., J. H. PRESCOTT, and M. C. CALDWELL. 1966. Production of pulsed sounds by the pigmy sperm whale *Kogia breviceps. Bull. So. Calif. Acad. Sci.* 65(4): 245–48.

DELL, R. K. 1960. The New Zealand occurrences of the pygmy sperm whale *Kogia breviceps. Rec. Dom. Mus. Wellington* 3(2): 229–35.

DUGUY, R. 1966. Quelques données nouvelles sur un cétacé rare sur les côtes d'Europe: Le cachalot à tête courte, *Kogia breviceps* (Blainville, 1838). *Mammalia* 30: 259–69.

———. 1972. Note sur trois odontocetes (Cetacea) échoués sur la côte de Charente-Maritime. *Mammalia* 36(1): 157–60.

———, and D. ROBINEAU. 1973. *Cétacés et Phoques des Côtes de France.* Ann. Soc. Sci. Nat. Charente-Maritime. Pp. 1–93.

EDMONSON, C. H. 1948. Records of *Kogia breviceps* from the Hawaiian Islands. *Jour. Mammal.* 29(1): 76–77.

GASKIN, D. E. 1966. New records of the pygmy sperm whale *Kogia breviceps* Blainville 1838, from New Zealand, and a probable record from New Guinea. *Norsk Hvalfangst-tidende* 55(2): 35–37.

GUNTER, G., C. L. HUBBS, and M. A. BEAL. 1955. Records of *Kogia breviceps* from Texas with remarks on movements and distribution. *Jour. Mammal.* 36(2): 263–70.

HALE, H. M. 1947. The pigmy sperm whale (*Kogia breviceps,* Blainville) on South Australian coasts. *Rec. S. Aust. Mus.* 8: 531–46.

———. 1959. The pigmy sperm whale on South Australian coasts—continued. *Rec. S. Aust. Mus.* 13: 333–38.

———. 1962. The pygmy sperm whale (*Kogia breviceps*) on southern Australian coasts. Part III. *Rec. S. Aust. Mus.* 14: 197–230.

———. 1963. Young female pigmy sperm whale (*Kogia breviceps*) from Western and South Australia. *Rec. S. Aust. Mus.* 14(3): 561–77.

HANDLEY, C. O. 1966. A synopsis of the genus *Kogia* (pygmy sperm whales). In K. S. Norris, ed., *Whales, Dolphins and Porpoises,* pp. 62–69. University of California Press.

HARMER, S. F. 1927. Report on cetacea stranded on the British Coasts from 1913 to 1926. *Bull. Brit. Mus. (Nat. Hist.)* 10: 1–91.

HARRISON, T., and G. JAMUH. 1958. Pygmy sperm whale in Borneo. *Nature* 182: 543.

HUBBS, C. L. 1951. Eastern Pacific records and general distribution of the pygmy sperm whale. *Jour. Mammal.* 32(4): 403–10.

MANVILLE, R. H., and R. P. SHANAHAN. 1961. *Kogia* stranded in Maryland. *Jour. Mammal.* 42(2): 169–270.

OWEN, R. 1866. On some Indian cetacea collected by Walter Elliot, Esq. *Trans. Zool. Soc. London* 1866: 17–47.

PALMER, R. S. 1948. A school of whales: *Kogia? Jour. Mammal.* 29(4): 421.

RAUN, G. G., H. D. HOESE, and F. MOSELEY. 1970. Pygmy sperm whales, genus *Kogia,* on the Texas coast. *Tex. Jour. Sci.* 21(3): 269–74.

RAVEN, H. C., and W. K. GREGORY. 1933. The spermaceti organ and nasal passages of the sperm whale (*Physeter catodon*) and other odontocetes. *Amer. Mus. Novitates* 677: 1–17.

ROEST, A. I. 1970. *Kogia simus* and other cetaceans from San Luis Obispo County, California. *Jour. Mammal.* 51(2): 410–17.

ROSS, G. J. B. 1979. Records of pygmy and dwarf sperm whales, genus *Kogia,* from southern Africa, with biological notes and some comparisons. *Ann. Cape Prov. Mus. (Nat. Hist.)* 11(14): 259–327.

SCHEFFER, V. B., and J. W. SLIPP. 1948. The whales and dolphins of Washington state with a key to the cetaceans of the west coast of North America. *Amer. Midl. Nat.* 39(2): 257–337.

SCHENKKAN, E. J., and P. E. PURVES. 1973. The comparative anatomy of the nasal tract and the function of the spermaceti organ in the Physeteridae (Mammalia, Odontoceti). *Bijdr. Dierk.* 43(1): 93–112.

SCHULTE, H. VON W. 1917. The skull of *Kogia breviceps* Blainv. *Bull. Amer. Mus. Nat. Hist.* 37: 361–404.

————, and DE F. SMITH. 1918. The external characters, skeletal muscles and peripheral nerves of *Kogia breviceps* (Blainville). *Bull. Am. Mus. Nat. Hist.* 38: 7–72.

SMALLEY, A. E. 1959. Pigmy sperm whale in Georgia. *Jour. Mammal.* 40(3): 452.

YAMADA, M. 1954. Some remarks on the pygmy sperm whale. *Sci. Rep. Whales Res. Inst.* 9: 37–58.

THE BEAKED WHALES

AITKEN, P. F. 1971. Whales from the coast of South Australia. *Trans. Roy. Soc. S. Aust.* 95(2): 95–103.

ALLEN, G. M. 1939. True's beaked whale in Nova Scotia. *Jour. Mammal.* 20(2): 259–60.

ANDREWS, R. C. 1908. Description of a new species of *Mesoplodon* from Canterbury Province, New Zealand. *Bull. Amer. Mus. Nat. Hist.* 24: 203–15.

————. 1914. Note of a rare ziphoid whale, *Mesoplodon densirostris* on the New Jersey Coast. *Proc. Acad. Nat. Sci. Phila.* 1914: 437–40.

ANON. 1978. Bering Sea beaked whale. In "Alaska Whales and Whaling." *Alaska Geographic* 5(4): 72–73.

AZZAROLI, M. L. 1968. Second specimen of *Mesoplodon pacificus,* the rarest living beaked whale. *Monitore Zool. Ital.* n.s. 2: 67–79.

BACKUS, R. H., and W. E. SCHEVILL. 1961. The stranding of a Cuvier's beaked whale *(Ziphius cavirostris)* in Rhode Island, U.S.A. *Norsk Hvalfangst-tidende* 50(5): 177–81.

BAKER, A. N. 1972. New Zealand whales and dolphins. *Tuatara* 20(1): 1–49

BALCOMB, K. C., and C. A. GOEBEL. 1977. Some information on a *Berardius bairdii* fishery in Japan. *Rep. Int. Whal. Commn.* 27: 485–86.

BENJAMINSEN, T. 1972. On the biology of the bottlenose whale *Hyperoodon ampullatus* (Foster). *Norw. Jour. Zool.* 20: 233–41.

————, and I. CHRISTENSEN. 1979. The natural history of the bottlenose whale, *Hyperoodon ampullatus* (Forster). In H. E. Winn and B. L. Olla, eds., *Behavior of Marine Animals.* Vol. 3: *Cetaceans,* pp. 143–64. Plenum Press.

BESHARSE, J. C. 1971. Maturity and sexual dimorphism in the skull, mandible and teeth of the beaked whale, *Mesoplodon densirostris. Jour. Mammal.* 52(2): 297–315.

BOSCHMA, H. 1950. Maxillary teeth in specimens of *Hyperoodon rostratus* (Muller) and *Mesoplodon grayi* von Haast stranded on the Dutch coasts. *Proc. Kon. Ned. Akad. Wetens.* 53(6): 775–86.

————. 1951a. Rows of small teeth in ziphoid whales. *Zoologische Mededelingen Leiden* 31: 139–48.

————. 1951b. Some smaller whales. *Endeavor* 10(39): 131–35.

BRAZENOR, C. W. 1933. First record of a beaked whale *(Mesoplodon grayi)* from Victoria. *Proc. Roy. Soc. Victoria* 45(1): 23–24.

BRIMLEY, H. H. 1943. A second specimen of True's beaked whale *Mesoplodon mirus* from North Carolina. *Jour. Mammal.* 24(2): 199–203.

BROWNELL, R. L. 1974. Small odontocetes of the Antarctic. In V. C. Bushnell, ed., *Antarctic Mammals,* folio 18, pp. 13–19. Antarctic Map Folio Series, American Geographic Society.

————, A. AGUAYO, and D. N. TORRES. 1976. A Shepherd's beaked whale, *Tasmacetus shepherdi,* from the eastern South Pacific. *Sci. Rep. Whales Res. Inst.* 28: 127–28.

CALDWELL, D. K., and M. C. CALDWELL. 1971. Sounds produced by two rare cetaceans stranded in Florida. *Cetology* 4: 1–6.

CHRISTENSEN, I. 1973. Age determination, age distribution and growth of bottlenose whale *Hyperoodon ampullatus* in the Labrador Sea. *Norw. Jour. Zool.* 21: 331–40.

————. 1975. Preliminary report on the Norwegian fishery for small whales: Expansion of Norwegian whaling to Arctic and northwest Atlantic waters, and Norwegian investigations of the biology of small whales. *Jour. Fish. Res. Bd. Canada* 32(7): 1083–94.

CLARK, E. 1969. *The Lady and the Sharks.* Harper & Row.

CLARKE, M. R. 1978. Bouyancy control as a function of the spermataceti organ in the sperm whale. *Jour. Mar. Biol. Ass. U. K.* 58: 27–71.

COFFEY, D. J. 1977. *Dolphins, Whales and Porpoises: An Encyclopedia of Sea Mammals.* Macmillan.

COWAN, I. M. 1945. A beaked whale stranded on the coast of British Columbia. *Jour. Mammal.* 26(1): 93–94.

DERANIYAGALA, P. E. P. 1963a. Mass mortality of the new subspecies of little piked whale *Balaenoptera acutorostrata thalmaha* and a new beaked whale *Mesoplodon hotaula* from Ceylon. *Spolia Zeylanica* 30(1): 79–84.

———. 1963b. Comparison of *Mesoplodon hotaula* Deraniyagala with *Ziphius cavirostris indicus* (van Beneden). *Spolia Zeylanica* 30(2): 248–56.

DEWHURST, W. H. 1834. *The Natural History of the Order Cetacea and the Oceanic Inhabitants of the Arctic Regions.* London.

DUDOK VAN HEEL, W. H. 1974. Remarks on a live ziphiid baby (*Mesoplodon bidens*). *Aquatic Mammals* 2(2): 3–7.

DUGUY, R. 1977. Notes on the small cetaceans off the coast of France. *Rep. Int. Whal. Commn.* 27: 500–1.

ELLIS, R. 1980. Beaked whales. *Sea Frontiers.* 26(1): 10–18.

ERDMAN, D. S. 1962. Stranding of a beaked whale *Ziphius cavirostris* Cuvier on the south coast of Puerto Rico. *Jour. Mammal.* 43(2): 276–77.

FLOWER, W. H. 1872. On the recent ziphoid whales, with a description of the skeleton of *Berardius arnouxi.* *Trans. Zool. Soc. London* 8(3): 203–33.

———. 1882. On the whales of the genus *Hyperoodon.* *Proc. Zool. Soc. London* 1882: 722–26.

FRASER, F. C. 1934. Report on cetacea stranded on the British coasts from 1927 to 1932. *Bull. Brit. Mus. (Nat. Hist.)* 11: 1–41.

———. 1945. On a specimen of the southern bottlenosed whale, *Hyperoodon planifrons.* *Discovery Reports* 23: 19–36.

———. 1946. Report on cetacea stranded on the British coasts from 1933 to 1937. *Bull. Brit. Mus. (Nat. Hist.)* 12: 1–56.

———. 1950. Notes on a skull of Hector's beaked whale *Mesoplodon hectori* (Gray) from the Falkland Islands. *Proc. Linn. Soc. London* 162: 50–52.

———. 1953. Report on cetacea stranded on the British coasts from 1938 to 1947. *Bull. Brit. Mus. (N. H.)* 13: 1–48.

———. 1955. A skull of *Mesoplodon gervaisi* (Deslongchamps) from Trinidad, West Indies. *Ann. Mag. Nat. Hist.* 8(92): 624–30.

———. 1974. Report on cetacea stranded on the British coasts from 1948 to 1966. *Bull. Brit. Mus. (Nat. Hist.)* 14: 1–65.

GALBREATH, E. C. 1963. Three beaked whales stranded in the Midway Islands, Central Pacific Ocean. *Jour. Mammal.* 44(3): 422–23.

GIANUCA, N. M., and H. P. CASTELLO. 1976. First record of the southern bottlenose whale, *Hyperoodon planifrons,* from Brazil. *Sci. Rep. Whales Res. Inst.* 28: 119–26.

GLAUERT, L. 1947. The genus *Mesoplodon* in western Australian seas. *Aust. Zool.* 11(2): 73–75.

GOODALL, R. N. P. 1978. Report on small cetaceans stranded on the coasts of Tierra del Fuego. *Sci. Rep. Whales Res. Inst.* 30: 197–230.

GRAY, D. 1882. Notes on the characters and habits of the bottle-nose whale (*Hyperoodon rostratus*). *Proc. Zool. Soc. London* 1882: 726–31.

GRAY, J. E. 1860. On the genus *Hyperoodon:* The two British kinds and their food. *Proc. Zool. Soc. London* 28: 422–26.

———. 1871. Notes on the *Berardius* of New Zealand. *Ann. Mag. Nat. Hist.* 48(8): 115–17.

GRAY, R. W. 1941. The bottlenose whale. *Naturalist* 791: 129–32.

GUILER, E. R. 1966. A stranding of *Mesoplodon densirostris* in Tasmania. *Jour. Mammal.* 47(2): 327.

———. 1967. Strandings of three species of *Mesoplodon* in Tasmania. *Jour. Mammal.* 48(4): 650–52.

GUNTER, G. 1955. Blainville's beaked whale, *Mesoplodon densirostris,* on the Texas coast. *Jour. Mammal.* 36(4): 573–74.

HAAST, J. VON. 1870. Preliminary notice of a ziphid whale, probably *Berardius arnuxi,* stranded on the 16th December, 1868, on the beach near New Brighton, Canterbury. *Trans. N.Z. Inst.* 2: 190–92.

HALE, H. M. 1931a. Beaked whales—*Hyperoodon planifrons* and *Mesoplodon layardi*—from South Australia. *Rec. S. Aust. Mus.* 4(3): 291–311.

———. 1931b. The goose-beaked whale (*Ziphius cavirostris*) in New Ireland. *Rec. S. Aust. Mus.* 4(3): 312–13.

———. 1932. The New Zealand scamperdown whale (*Mesoplodon grayi*) in South Australian waters. *Rec. S. Aust. Mus.* 4(4): 489–96.

———. 1939. Rare whales in South Australian waters. *S. Aust. Nat.* 19(4): 5–8.

———. 1947. The pigmy sperm whale (*Kogia breviceps* Blainville) on South Australian coasts. *Rec. S. Aust. Mus.* 8: 531–46.

———. 1962. Occurrence of the whale *Berardius arnouxi* in Southern Australia. *Rec. S. Aust. Mus.* 14(2): 231–43.

HARMER, S. F. 1924. On *Mesoplodon* and other beaked whales. *Proc. Zool. Soc. London* 1924: 541–87.

———. 1927. Report on cetaceans stranded on the British coasts from 1913 to 1926. *Bull. Brit. Mus. (Nat. Hist.)* 10: 1–91.

HOUCK, W. J. 1958. Cuvier's beaked whale from northern California. *Jour. Mammal.* 39(2): 308–9.

HUBBS, C. L. 1946. First records of two beaked whales *Mesoplodon bowdoini* and *Ziphius cavirostris* from the Pacific coast of the United States. *Jour. Mammal.* 27(3): 242–55.

———. 1951. Eastern Pacific records and general distribution of the pygmy sperm whale. *Jour. Mammal* 32(4): 403–10.

INTERNATIONAL WHALING STATISTICS. 1978. Sandefjord, Norway. Pp. 1–55.

JELLISON, W. M. 1953. A beaked whale, *Mesoplodon* sp., from the Pribilofs. *Jour. Mammal.* 34(2): 249–51.

JONSGARD, A. 1955. Development of the modern Norwegian small whale industry. *Norsk Hvalfangst-tidende* 57(3): 164–67.

————. 1977. A note on the value of bottlenose whales in relation to minke whales and the influence of the market situation and the prices on Norwegian whaling activity. *Rep. Int. Whal. Commn.* 27: 502–4.

————, and P. HØIDAL. 1957. Strandings of Sowerby's whale (*Mesoplodon bidens*) on the west coast of Norway. *Norsk Hvalfangst-tidende* 46(12): 507–12.

KASUYA, T. 1971. Consideration of distribution and migration of toothed whales off the Pacific coast of Japan based upon aerial sighting record. *Sci. Rep. Whales Res. Inst.* 32: 37–60.

————. 1977. Age determination and growth of the Baird's beaked whale with a comment on the fetal growth rate. *Sci. Rep. Whales Res. Inst.* 29: 1–20.

————, and M. NISHIWAKI. 1971. First record of *Mesoplodon densirostris* from Formosa. *Sci. Rep. Whales Res. Inst.* 23: 129–37.

KENYON, K. W. 1961. Cuvier beaked whales stranded in the Aleutian Islands. *Jour. Mammal.* 42(1): 71–76.

KERNAN, J. D. 1918. The skull of *Ziphius cavirostris. Bull. Amer. Mus. Nat. Hist.* 38: 349–94.

KREFFT, G., and J. E. GRAY. 1871. Notice of a new Australian ziphioid whale. *Ann. Mag. Nat. Hist.* 7: 368.

LIOUVILLE, J. 1913. *Cétacés de l'Antarctique (Baleinopteres, Ziphiides, Delphinides): Deuxième Expedition Antarctique Français, 1908–1918.* Masson, Paris.

LONGMAN, H. A. 1926. New records of Cetacea with a list of Queensland species. *Mem. Qld. Mus.* 8(3): 266–78.

MARLOW, B. J. 1963. Rare beaked whale washed up on Sydney beach. (*Mesoplodon layardi*). *Aust. Nat. Hist.* 14: 164.

MATTHIESSEN, P. 1959. *Wildlife in America.* Viking Press.

MCCANN, C. 1961. The occurrence of the southern bottlenosed whale, *Hyperoodon planifrons* Flower, in New Zealand waters. *Rec. Dom. Mus. Wellington* 4(3): 21–27.

————. 1962a. The taxonomic status of the beaked whale *Mesoplodon pacificus* Longman Cetacea. *Rec. Dom. Mus. Wellington* 4: 95–100.

————. 1962b. The taxonomic status of the beaked whale *Mesoplodon hectori* (Gray) Cetacea. *Rec. Dom. Mus. Wellington* 4: 83–94.

————. 1964. The female reproductive organs of Layard's beaked-whale, *Mesoplodon layardi* (Gray). *Rec. Dom. Mus. Wellington* 4: 311–16.

————. 1974. Body scarring on cetacea—odontocetes. *Sci. Rep. Whales Res. Inst.* 26: 145–55.

————. 1975. A study of the genus *Berardius* Duvernoy. *Sci. Rep. Whales Res. Inst.* 27: 111–37.

————, and F. H. TALBOT. 1963. The occurrence of True's beaked whale (*Mesoplodon mirus* True) in South African waters, with a key to South African species of the genus. *Proc. Linn. Soc. London* 175(2): 137–45.

MCLACHLAN, G. R., R. LIVERSIDGE, and R. M. TIETZ. 1966. A record of *Berardius arnouxi* from the south-east coast of South Africa. *Ann. Cape Prov. Mus. (Nat. Hist.)* 5: 91–100.

MEAD, J. G. *Mesoplodon hectori* from California (Cetacea, Ziphiidae). In press.

————, and R. PAYNE. 1975. A specimen of the Tasman beaked whale (*Tasmacetus shepherdi*) from Argentina. *Jour. Mammal.* 56(1): 213–18.

MITCHELL, E. 1968. Northeast Pacific stranding distribution and seasonality of Cuvier's beaked whale *Ziphius cavirostris. Canadian Jour. Zool.* 46: 265–79.

————. 1977. Evidence that the northern bottlenose whale is depleted. *Rep. Int. Whal. Commn.* 27: 195–205.

————, and W. J. HOUCK. 1967. Cuvier's beaked whale (*Ziphius cavirostris*) stranded in northern California. *Jour. Fish. Res. Bd. Canada* 24(12): 2503–13.

————, and V. M. KOZICKI. 1975. Autumn stranding of a northern bottlenose whale (*Hyperoodon ampullatus*) in the Bay of Fundy, Nova Scotia. *Jour. Fish. Res. Bd. Canada* 37(7): 1019–40.

MIYAZAKI, N., and S. WADA. 1978. Observation of cetacea during whale marking cruise in the western tropical Pacific, 1976. *Sci. Rep. Whales Res. Inst.* 30: 179–95.

MOORE, J. C. 1958. A beaked whale from the Bahama Islands and comments on the distribution of *Mesoplodon densirostris. Amer. Mus. Novitates* 1897: 1–12.

————. 1960. New records of the Gulf-Stream beaked whale, *Mesoplodon gervaisi,* and some taxonomic considerations. *Amer. Mus. Novitates* 1993: 1–35.

————. 1963. Recognizing certain species of beaked whales of the Pacific Ocean. *Amer. Midl. Nat.* 70(2): 396–428.

————. 1966. Diagnoses and distributions of beaked whales of the genus *Mesoplodon* known from North American waters. In K. S. Norris, ed., *Whales, Dolphins and Porpoises,* pp. 32–61. University of California Press.

————. 1968. Relationships among the living genera of beaked whales with classifications, diagnoses and keys. *Fieldiana: Zoology* 53(4): 209–98.

————, and R. M. GILMORE. 1965. A beaked whale new to the Western Hemisphere. *Nature* 205: 1239–40.

MOORE, J. C., and F. G. WOOD. 1957. Differences between the beaked whales *Mesoplodon mirus* and *Mesoplodon gervaisi*. *Amer. Mus. Novitates* 1831: 1–25.

NISHIMURA, S., and M. NISHIWAKI. 1964. Records of the beaked whale *Mesoplodon* from the Japan Sea. *Publ. Seto Mar. Biol. Lab.* 12(4): 323–34.

NISHIWAKI, M. 1962a. *Mesoplodon bowdoini* stranded at Akita Beach, Sea of Japan. *Sci. Rep. Whales Res. Inst.* 16: 61–77.

————. 1962b. Observations on two mandibles of *Mesoplodon*. *Sci. Rep. Whales Res. Inst.* 16: 79–82.

————, and T. KAMIYA, 1958. A beaked whale *Mesoplodon* stranded at Ōiso Beach, Japan. *Sci. Rep. Whales Res. Inst.* 13: 53–83.

————. 1959. *Mesoplodon stejnegeri* from the coast of Japan. *Sci. Rep. Whales Res. Inst.* 14: 35–48.

NISHIWAKI, M., and N. OGURO. 1971. Baird's beaked whales caught on the coast of Japan in recent 10 years. *Sci. Rep. Whales Res. Inst.* 23: 111–22.

————. 1972. Catch of the Cuvier's beaked whale off Japan in recent years. *Sci. Rep. Whales Res. Inst.* 24: 35–41.

NISHIWAKI, M., T. KASUYA, K. KUREHARA, and N. OGURO. 1972. Further comments on *Mesoplodon ginkgodens*. *Sci. Rep. Whales Res. Inst.* 24: 43–56.

NORRIS, K. S. 1964. Some problems of echolocation in cetaceans. In W. N. Tavolga, ed., *Marine Bioacoustics*, pp. 317–36. Pergamon Press.

————, and J. H. PRESCOTT. 1961. Observations on Pacific cetaceans of Californian and Mexican waters. *Univ. Calif. Publ. Zool.* 63(4): 291–402.

OHLIN, A. 1893. Some remarks on the bottlenose-whale, (*Hyperoodon*). *Lunds. Univ. Arskr.* 29: 1–14.

OHSUMI, S. 1975. Review of Japanese small-type whaling. *Jour. Fish. Res. Bd. Canada* 32(7): 1111–21.

OLIVER, W. R. B. 1922. The whales and dolphins of New Zealand. *N.Z. Jour. Sci. Tech.* 5(3): 129–41.

————. 1924. Strap-toothed whale at Kaitawa Point, entrance to Porirua Harbor. *N.Z. Jour. Sci. Tech.* 7: 187–88.

————. 1937. *Tasmacetus shepherdi:* A new genus and species of beaked whale from New Zealand. *Proc. Zool. Soc. London,* ser. B, 107: 371–81.

OMURA, H. 1972. An osteological study of the Cuvier's beaked whale, *Ziphius cavirostris,* in the northwest Pacific. *Sci. Rep. Whales Res. Inst.* 24: 1–34.

————, K. FUJINO, and S. KIMURA. 1955. Beaked whales *Berardius bairdii* off Japan, with notes on *Ziphius cavirostris*. *Sci. Rep. Whales Res. Inst.* 10: 89–132.

ORR, R. T. 1953. Beaked whale (*Mesoplodon*) from California with comments on taxonomy. *Jour. Mammal.* 34(2): 239–49.

PIKE, G. C. 1953. Two records of *Berardius bairdii* from the coast of British Columbia. *Jour. Mammal.* 34(1): 98–104.

PRADERI, R. 1972. Notas sobre un ejemplar de *Mesoplodon layardi* (Gray) (Cetacea, Hyperoodontidae), de la costa Atlantica de Uruguay. *Com. Zool. Mus. Hist. Nat. Montevideo* 10(137): 1–7.

RANKIN, J. J. 1953. First record of the rare beaked whale *Mesoplodon europaeus* Gervais from the West Indies. *Nature* 172: 873.

————. 1955. A rare whale in tropical seas (*Mesoplodon europaeus*). *Everglades Nat. Hist.* 3(1): 24–31.

————. 1956. The structure of the skull of the beaked whale *Mesoplodon gervaisi* Deslongchamps. *Jour. Morph.* 99(2): 329–58.

————. 1961. The bursa ovaries of the beaked whale *Mesoplodon gervaisi* Deslongchamps. *Anat. Rec.* 139(3): 379–86.

RAVEN, H. C. 1937. Notes on the taxonomy and osteology of two species of *Mesoplodon* (*M. europaeus* Gervais and *M. mirus* True). *Amer. Mus. Novitates* 905: 1–30.

RED DATA BOOK. 1976. Northern bottlenose whale, *Hyperoodon planifrons*. Code 11.93.5.1.V. IUCN, Morges, Switzerland.

RICE, D. W. 1963. Progress report on biological studies of the larger cetaceans in the waters off California. *Norsk Hvalfangst-tidende* 52(7): 181–87.

————. 1978. Beaked whales. In D. Haley, ed., *Marine Mammals of Eastern North Pacific and Arctic Waters*, pp. 88–95. Pacific Search Press.

RICHARDS, L. P. 1952. Cuvier's beaked whale from Hawaii. *Jour. Mammal.* 33(2): 355.

ROEST, A. I. 1964. *Physeter* and *Mesoplodon* strandings on the central California coast. *Jour. Mammal.* 45(1): 129–36.

————, R. M. STORM, and P. C. DUMAS. 1953. Cuvier's beaked whale (*Ziphius cavirostris*) from Oregon. *Jour. Mammal.* 34(2): 251–52.

ROSS, G. J. B. 1969. Evidence for a southern breeding population of True's beaked whale. *Nature* 222: 585.

————. 1970. The occurrence of Hector's beaked whale *Mesoplodon hectori* (Gray) in South African waters. *Ann. Cape Prov. Mus. (Nat. Hist.)* 8(13): 195–204.

SCHEFFER, V. B. 1949. Notes on three beaked whales from the Aleutian Islands. *Pacific Science* 3: 353.

———, and J. B. SLIPP. 1948. The whales and dolphins of Washington State. *Am. Midl. Nat.* 39(2): 257–337.

SCHOLANDER, P. F. 1940. Experimental investigations on the respiratory function in diving mammals and birds. *Hvalradets Skrifter* 22(1): 1–131.

SLIPP, J. W., and F. WILKE. 1953. The beaked whale *Berardius* on the Washington coast. *Jour. Mammal.* 34(1): 105–13.

SMITH, M. S. R. 1965. Fourth known individual of beaked whale genus *Tasmacetus. Mammalia* 29: 618–20.

SORENSEN, J. H. 1940. *Tasmacetus shepherdi:* History and description of specimens cast ashore at Mason's Bay, Stewart Island, in February, 1933. *Trans. Roy. Soc. New Zealand* 70: 200–4.

SOUTHWELL, T. 1883. On the beaked whale *(Hyperoodon rostratus). Trans. Norfolk Norwich Nat. Soc.* 3: 476–81.

SOWERBY, J. 1804. *The British Miscellany; or Coloured Figures of New, Rare or Little Known Animal Subjects, Many Not Before Ascertained to Be Inhabitants of the British Isles.* London.

STEJNEGER, L. 1883. Contributions to the history of the Commander Islands: Notes on the natural history, including descriptions of new cetaceans. *Proc. U.S. Nat. Mus.* 6: 58–89.

STEPHEN, A. C. 1931. True's beaked whale *(Mesoplodon mirus)* new to the Scottish fauna. *Scot. Nat.* 1931: 37–39.

TALBOT, F. H. 1960. True's beaked whale from the southeast coast of South Africa. *Nature* 186: 406.

TAYLOR, R. J. F. 1957. An unusual record of three species of whale being restricted to pools in Antarctic ice. *Proc. Zool. Soc. London* 129: 325–31.

THOMPSON, D. W. 1919. On whales landed at the Scottish whaling stations, especially during the years 1908–1914. *Scot. Nat.* 85: 1–16.

TIETZ, R. M. 1966. The southern bottlenose whale, *Hyperoodon planifrons,* from Humewood, Port Elizabeth. *Ann. Cape Prov. Mus.* 5: 101–7.

TRUE, F. W. 1885. Contributions to the history of the Commander Islands. No. 5. Description of a new species of *Mesoplodon, M. stejnegeri,* obtained by Dr. Leonard Stejneger in Bering Island. *Proc. U.S. Nat. Mus.* 8: 584–85.

———. 1910. An account of the beaked whales of the family Ziphiidae in the collection of the U.S. National Museum, with remarks on some specimens in other museums. *Bull. U.S. Nat. Mus.* 73: 1–89.

———. 1913. Description of *Mesoplodon mirus,* a beaked whale recently discovered on the coast of North Carolina. *Proc. U.S. Nat. Mus.* 45: 651–57.

TURNER, W. 1872. On the occurrence of *Ziphius cavirostris* in the Shetland Seas, and a comparison of its skull with that of Sowerby's whale *(Mesoplodon sowerbyi). Trans. Roy. Soc. Edin.* 26: 769–80.

———. 1879. The form and structure of the teeth of *Mesoplodon layardii* and *Mesoplodon sowerbyii. J. Anat. Physiol.* 13: 465–80.

———. 1882. A specimen of Sowerby's whale *(Mesoplodon bidens)* captured in Shetland. *J. Anat. Physiol.* 16: 458–70.

———. 1886. On the occurrence of the bottle-nosed whale, *(Hyperoodon rostratus)* in the Scottish seas, with observations on its external characters. *Proc. Royal Phys. Soc. Edinb.* 9: 25–47.

ULMER, F. A. 1941. *Mesoplodon mirus* in New Jersey with additional notes on the New Jersey *M. densirostris* and a list and key to the ziphioid whales of the Atlantic coast of North America. *Proc. Acad. Nat. Sci. Phila.* 93: 107–22.

———. 1947. A second Florida record of *Mesoplodon europaeus. Jour. Mammal.* 28(2): 184–85.

———. 1961. New Jersey's whales and dolphins. *New Jersey Nature News.* 16(3): 80–93.

VARONA, L. S. 1964. Un craneo de *Ziphius cavirostris* del sur de Isla de Pinos. *Poeyana,* ser. A(4): 1–3.

———. 1970. Morfologia externa y caracteres craneales de un macho adulto de *Mesoplodon europaeus* (Cetacea: Ziphiidae). *Poeyana,* ser. A(69): 1–17.

WAITE, E. R. 1922. Two ziphioid whales not previously recorded from South Australia. *Rec. S. Aust. Mus.* 2(2): 209–14.

WALKER, E. P. 1964. *Mammals of the World.* Johns Hopkins University Press.

WATKINS, W. A. 1976. A probable sighting of a live *Tasmacetus shepherdi* in New Zealand waters. *Jour. Mammal.* 57(2): 415.

WINN, H. E., P. J. PERKINS, and L. WINN. 1971. Sounds and behavior of the northern bottle-nosed whale. *Proc. Seventh Ann. Conf. on Biol. Sonar and Diving Mammals, 1970,* pp. 53–59. Stanford Res. Inst.

BIBLIOGRAPHY

In the area of general works—as contrasted with monographs or technical papers—there are a number of books and articles to which I have referred extensively. Whenever possible, I have included the citation in the text in an attempt to identify another author's words or thoughts. But I read most of the books listed here long before I began to write my own, and so I absorbed much of the information into my own store of knowledge. It is therefore transmitted to the reader without acknowledgment.

A library of the following works would contain the foundation blocks of a basic cetological collection. The books range from the technical to the popular, covering all the ground in between. Some scientists write engagingly and well, whereas others cannot seem to escape the tedious and labored prose of the technical journal. For the student who would pursue what Melville referred to as "the uncertain, unsettled condition of the science of Cetology," most of these works would be considered necessary. Those marked with an asterisk are currently in print; most of the others should be available in any good municipal or university library.

ALLEN, G. M. 1916. The whalebone whales of New England. *Mem. Boston Soc. Nat. Hist.* 8(2): 107–322.

ANDERSEN, H. T., ed. 1969. *The Biology of Marine Mammals.* Academic Press.

ANDREWS, R. C. 1916. *Whale Hunting with Gun and Camera.* D. Appleton & Co.

BEDDARD, F. 1900. *A Book of Whales.* John Murray.

BUDKER, P. 1959. *Whales and Whaling.* Macmillan.

BULLEN, F. T. 1899. *The Cruise of the Cachalot.* D. Appleton & Co.

DAUGHERTY, A. 1972. *Marine Mammals of California.* * State of California Department of Fish and Game.

GASKIN, D. E. 1972. *Whales, Dolphins and Seals, with Special Reference to the New Zealand Region.* Heinemann Educational Books.

HALEY, D., ed. 1978. *Marine Mammals of Eastern North Pacific and Arctic Waters.* * Pacific Search Press.

HARDY, A. 1967. *Great Waters.* Harper & Row.

HERSHKOVITZ, P. 1966. *Catalog of Living Whales.* U.S. National Museum, bulletin 246.

HILL, D. O. 1975. Vanishing giants. *Audubon* 77(1): 56–107.

KATONA, S. 1975. *A Field Guide to the Whales and Seals of the Gulf of Maine.* * Maine Coast Printers.

KELLOGG, R. 1940. Whales, giants of the sea. *National Geographic* 77(1): 35–90.

LEATHERWOOD, S., D. K. CALDWELL, and H. WINN. 1976. *Whales, Dolphins and Porpoises of the Western North Atlantic: A Guide to Their Identification.* * NOAA Technical Report NMFS CIRC-396.

LEATHERWOOD, S., W. E. EVANS, and D. W. RICE. 1972. *The Whales, Dolphins, and Porpoises of the Eastern North Pacific: A Guide to Their Identification in the Water.* Naval Undersea Center, San Diego.

MACKINTOSH, N. A. 1965. *The Stocks of Whales.* Fishing News (Books) Ltd.

MATTHEWS, L. H. 1978. *The Natural History of the Whale.* * Columbia University Press.

———, ed. 1968. *The Whale.* * Simon and Schuster.

MCINTYRE, J. 1974. *Mind in the Waters.* * Sierra Club/Scribner's.

MELVILLE, H. 1851. *Moby-Dick or, The Whale.* * Various editions.

MITCHELL, E. D. 1975. *Porpoise, Dolphin, and Small Whale Fisheries of the World: Status and Problems.* IUCN monograph no. 3. Morges, Switzerland. 129 pp.

———, ed. 1975. Review of biology and fisheries for smaller cetaceans. *Jour. Fish. Res. Bd. Canada* 32(7): 889–1240.

MÖRZER BRUYNS, W. F. J. 1971. *Field Guide of Whales and Dolphins.* Amsterdam.

NISHIWAKI, M. 1972. General biology. In S. H. Ridgway, ed., *Mammals of the Sea: Biology and Medicine,* pp. 3–204. Charles C Thomas.

NORMAN, J. R., and F. C. FRASER. 1938. *Giant Fishes, Whales and Dolphins.* W. W. Norton & Co.

NORRIS, K. S., ED. 1966. *Whales, Dolphins and Porpoises.* University of California Press.

OMMANNEY, F. D. 1971. *Lost Leviathan.* Dodd, Mead & Co.

RICE, D. W. 1977. *A List of the Marine Mammals of the World.* * NOAA Technical Report NMFS SSRF-711.

RIDGWAY, S. H., ed. 1972. *Mammals of the Sea: Biology and Medicine.* Charles C Thomas.

SANDERSON, I. 1956. *Follow the Whale.* Little, Brown & Co.

SCAMMON, C. M. 1874. *The Marine Mammals of the Northwestern Coast of North America; Together with an Account of the Whale-Fishery.* * Putnam's.

SCHEFFER, V. B. 1976. Exploring the lives of whales. *National Geographic* 150(6): 752–67.

SCHEVILL, W. E., ed. 1974. *The Whale Problem.* Harvard University Press.

SCORESBY, W. 1820. *An Account of the Arctic Regions with a History and Description of the Northern Whale-Fishery.* Archibald Constable, Edinburgh.

SLIJPER, E. J. 1962. *Whales.* * Trans. A. J. Pomerans. Basic Books. (Reissued 1979.)

———. 1977. *Whales and Dolphins.* * University of Michigan Press. (Paperback)

STARBUCK, A. 1878. *History of the American Whale Fishery from Its Earliest Inception to the Year 1876.* Part 4: *Report of the U.S. Commission on Fish and Fisheries.* Washington. (Reprinted 1964.)

TOMILIN, A. G. 1957. *Mammals of the U.S.S.R. and Adjacent Countries.* Vol. 9: *Cetacea.* Izdatel'stvo Akademi Nauk SSR, Moscow. (Israel Program for Scientific Translations, Jerusalem, 1967.)

TOWNSEND, C. H. 1935. The distribution of certain whales as shown by logbook records of American whaleships. *Zoologica* 19(1): 1–50.

TRUE, F. W. 1904. The whalebone whales of the western North Atlantic. *Smithsonian Contributions to Knowledge* 33: 1–332.

INDEX

Wood, F. G., 12, 124, 145
Worthington, L. V., 111, 114
Würsig, B., 20, 61

Yablakov, A. V., 62, 95, 114
Yamamada, M., 112, 123 n., 124, 126

Zemsky, V. A., 53, 56
Zenkovich, B. A., 106
Zeuglodon (basilosaurus), 3 (and illus.)

A NOTE ON THE TYPE

The text of this book was set, via computer-driven cathode-ray tube, in a film version of a typeface called Baskerville. The face itself is a facsimile reproduction of types cast from molds made for John Baskerville (1706–75) from his designs.

Baskerville's original face was one of the forerunners of the type style known as "modern face" to printers—a "modern" of the period A.D. 1800.

Type composition by Haddon Craftsmen, Scranton, Pennsylvania.

Book design by Albert Chiang

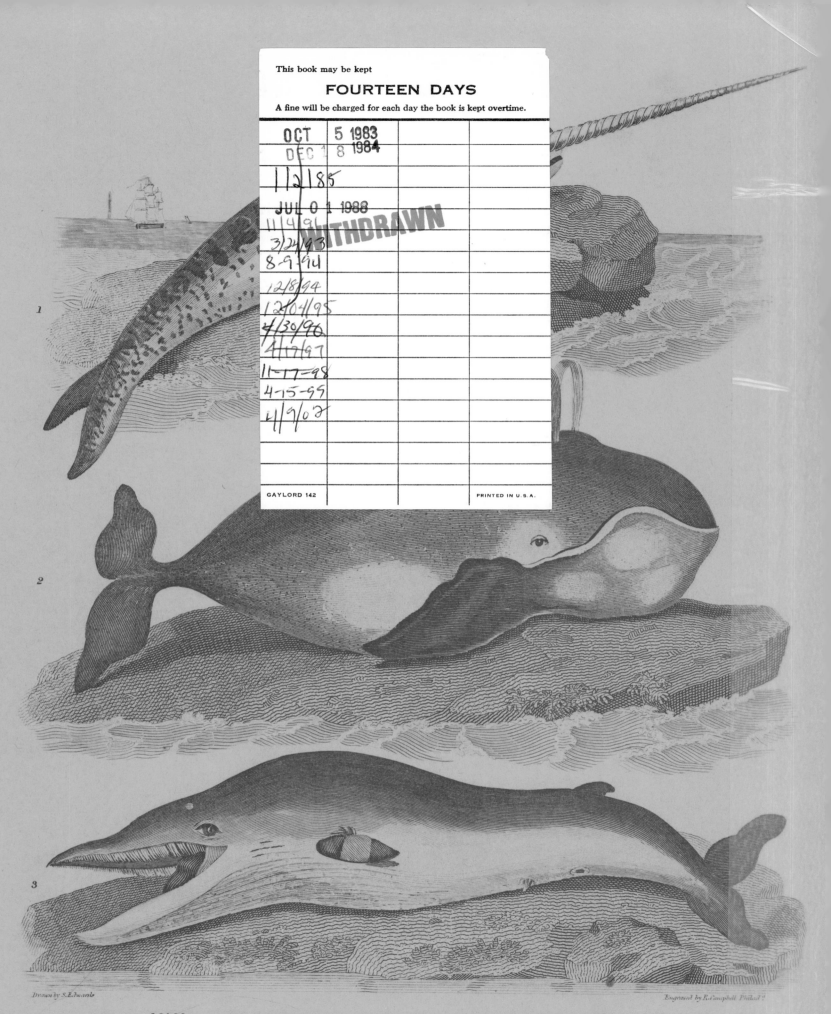

1. M. Monoceros. Unicorn N.— 2. B. Mysticetus Great M. or Common Whale.— 3. B. Boops Pike headed M.

Drawn by S. Edwards   Engraved by R. Campbell, Philad.